P9-CAN-039

Houghton Mifflin
Reading Series

Houghton Mifflin Reading Series

Book 1

HOUGHTON MIFFLIN COMPANY   Boston   New York

Senior Sponsoring Editor: Mary Jo Southern
Development Editor: Kellie Cardone
Editorial Assistant: Peter Mooney
Senior Project Editor: Fred Burns
Manufacturing Manager: Florence Cadran
Marketing Manager: Annamarie L. Rice

Copyright © 2003 by Houghton Mifflin Company. All rights reserved.

No part of this work may be reproduced or transmitted in any form or by any means, electronic or mechanical, including photocopying and recording, or by any information storage or retrieval system without the prior written permission of the copyright owner unless such copying is expressly permitted by federal copyright law. With the exception of non-profit transcription in Braille, Houghton Mifflin is not authorized to grant permission for further uses of copyrighted selections reprinted in this text without the permission of their owners. Permission must be obtained from the individual copyright owners as identified herein. Address requests for permission to make copies of Houghton Mifflin material to College Permissions, Houghton Mifflin Company, 222 Berkeley Street, Boston, MA 02116-3764.

Printed in the U.S.A.

Library of Congress Control Number: 2001135731

Student Edition ISBN: 0-618-11007-0
Instructor's Annotated Edition ISBN: 0-618-11010-0

1 2 3 4 5 6 7 8 9—QF—06 05 04 03 02

Contents

v

CHAPTER 6   **Patterns of Organization   237**

CHAPTER 7   **Reading Visual Aids   293**

Combined Skills Tests   443

Index   457

Preface

The Houghton Mifflin Reading Series is a three-level series designed to help students develop and refine their reading skills. Along with presenting the major reading skills—main idea, supporting details, implied main idea, transitions, patterns of organization, and more—the books will introduce students to the world of reading strategies to enable them to practice good habits while reading. Strategies such as SQ3R, REAP, annotating, and note taking will help students improve their comprehension of what they read and enable them to learn different strategies to help them comprehend and analyze what they read.

Book 1 is targeted at the beginning reader. Readings were chosen for their high interest, diversity of topic, and ease of reading. The Houghton Mifflin Reading Series is unique in that it includes the following features, all designed to make the development reader's experience a pleasant, fulfilling, and stimulating one.

▶ **Consistent Chapter Structure:** Each chapter covers skills and strategies in a consistent and clear manner.

▶ **Coverage of Visuals:** Chapter 7 is unique to this text in that it covers visuals students may encounter in their personal and professional reading: charts, graphs, tables, figures, and more.

▶ **Critical Thinking:** In addition to a multitude of skill exercises designed to help students build comprehension, questions at the end of the reading selections build on important critical thinking skills. Many practice exercises, too, require the application of critical thinking.

▶ **Vocabulary Building:** Every chapter covers a particular vocabulary concept and relates that concept to reading selections from the chapters.

▶ **Focus on Academic Achievement:** Tips and selected readings for studying and for succeeding in school are integrated throughout the text.

Each chapter in each level of the Houghton Mifflin Reading Series contains the following features, which are consistent throughout all three levels:

▶ **Pre-Test:** Pre-tests, which follow the reading strategy feature in Chapters 2–10, assess the students' knowledge of the skill to be introduced. This helps both instructors and students judge the amount of work they will need to do in order to master the learning objective of each individual chapter, whether it be finding main ideas, learning transitions, or identifying different patterns of organization.

▶ **Explanation:** Each chapter is broken up into sections of explanation regarding the main concept and followed by exercises. Every attempt has been made to break up material into manageable sections of information followed by practice of a specific skill.

▶ **Exercises:** An ample number and variety of exercises is included in every chapter. Most of the exercises include paragraphs from textbooks, magazines, newspapers, and journals, so that students can read different types of selections and learn new information about a variety of different subjects. Exercises are arranged using a step-by-step progression to build concepts and skills gradually.

▶ **Longer Reading Selections:** Longer reading selections follow the explanatory material in Chapters 1–9 and are included to give students practice in identifying different skills in context. Readings have been chosen for their high interest, diverse topics, and cultural relevance to today's students. The readings have been chosen with the level of student in mind, as well as their ethnic, cultural, and educational experience.

▶ **Vocabulary:** Words that may be unfamiliar to the student are taken from the longer reading selection that appears in Chapters 1–9 and used in a vocabulary exercise that follows the selection. Students are given the opportunity to glean the meanings of certain words from context and expand their overall vocabulary.

▶ **Questions for Discussion and Writing:** These questions ask students to think about their own experiences as well as what they have read in the longer reading selections. The main points, topics, and messages of the longer readings are used as springboards for student reflection on their past, their present goals, and their future. These questions give students the opportunity to develop their writing skills by responding to a professional piece of writing.

▶ Each chapter includes instruction in a specific vocabulary concept, such as context clues, that will help students improve their reading comprehension. The instruction is followed by one or more exercises that draw examples from readings in the text to give students practice with that particular concept.

▶ **Post-Tests:** Post-Tests follow each skill-based chapter. The post-tests are designed to assess students' progress from the beginning of the chapter when they took the pre-test (in Chapters 2–10). The post-tests cover individual skills from the chapter in a more detailed format than the exercises.

▶ **Combined Skills Tests:** A section following the final chapter contains combined skills tests that provide a thorough review of the book's contents.

In short, the Houghton Mifflin Reading Series provides clear, step-by-step instruction and thorough practice. The books also offer many opportunities for the improvement of thinking skills and expansion of cultural literacy. As a result, this series of texts will help students develop the skills they will need to become competent and confident readers and, ultimately, achieve academic success.

A special thanks to our Reading Series editorial board whose careful and thoughtful reviews of each book in the series proved incredibly helpful. Their talent and skill as longtime classroom teachers is clearly apparent. The insights of the following persons are gratefully appreciated:

Maureen Stradley, Community College of Allegheny County
Delia Duross, Long Beach City College
Diane Ruggerio, Broward Community College
Anita Van Ouwerkerk, Blinn College

We would also like to thank the following reviewers:

Jane Medver, Baton Rouge Community College
Carol Newman, Forsyth Technical Community College
Gwen Stiles, Santa Fe Community College
Maggie Hahn Wade, Triton College
Patricia L. Rottmund, Harrisburg Area Community College
Lois Brockelman, Grayson County College
Wanda Mayes, Trinity Valley Community College
Marlys Cordoba, College of Siskiyous
Beth Carlson, St. Petersburg Junior College
Helen Sabin, El Camino College
Gilda Feldman, Santa Monica College
Deborah Spradlin, Tyler Junior College
Rita McReynolds, Mississippi State University
Bill Morris, College of the Redwoods
Susan Messina, Solano Community College
Helen Carr, San Antonio College

Georgia Campbell, Gloucester County College
Carol Helton, Tennessee State University
Lori Chance, Chesapeake College
Loraine Phillips, Blinn College
Janet Rentsch, Saginaw Valley State University

Houghton Mifflin
Reading Series

CHAPTER **1**

Improving Reading and Thinking

GOALS FOR CHAPTER 1

▶ Explain and apply the steps of active reading.

▶ Explain why effective reading is critical to academic, professional, and personal success.

▶ Explain how reading improves thinking skills.

▶ Describe four techniques for improving reading skills.

▶ List the different goals of reading for information.

▶ Explain the four types of mental skills required for reading.

▶ Describe the organization and features of this book.

READING STRATEGY: Active Reading

Many people don't get everything they can out of reading simply because they are *passive* readers. Passive readers are people who try to read by just running their eyes over the words in a passage. They expect their brains to magically absorb the information after just one quick reading. If they don't, they blame the author and pronounce the work "dull" or "too difficult." They don't write anything down. If they come to a word they don't know, they just skip it and keep reading. If they get bored, they let their attention wander. They "read" long sections and then realize they have no memory or understanding of the information or ideas.

To read more effectively, you must become an **active reader.** Active readers know they have to do more than just sit with a book in front of them. They know they have to participate by interacting with the text and by thinking as they read. They read with a pen or pencil in their hand, marking key words or ideas or jotting notes in the margins. They reread the text if necessary. Also, they consciously try to connect the text's information to their own experiences and beliefs.

Continued

Copyright © Houghton Mifflin Company. All rights reserved.

1

Active reading is essential to understanding and remembering ideas and information, especially those in more difficult reading selections. It includes any or all of the following tasks:

- Identifying and writing down the point and purpose of the reading.

- Underlining, highlighting, or circling important words or phrases.

- Determining the meanings of unfamiliar words.

- Outlining a passage to understand the relationships in the information.

- Writing down questions when you're confused.

- Completing activities—such as reading comprehension questions—that follow a chapter or passage.

- Jotting down notes in the margins.

- Thinking about how you can use the information or how the information reinforces or contradicts your ideas or experiences.

- Predicting possible test questions on the material.

- Rereading and reviewing.

- Studying visual aids such as graphs, charts, and diagrams until you understand them.

Remember: The purpose of all these activities is to comprehend and retain more of what you read. So, for challenging reading, such as textbook chapters or journal articles, active reading is a must. Also, you should perform these tasks for any reading that you're expected to remember for a test.

However, even if you won't have to demonstrate your mastery of a reading selection, you should still get in the habit of reading actively when you read for information. Even if you're just reading for your own pleasure, you'll remember more by using active reading techniques.

To read actively, follow these steps:

1. When you sit down to read a book, get pens, pencils, and/or highlighter markers ready, too.

2. As you read each paragraph, mark points or terms that seem important. You may choose to underline them, highlight them, or enclose them in boxes or circles—this includes any words or key informa-

Continued

Copyright © Houghton Mifflin Company. All rights reserved.

tion phrases that are in bold print because the author wished to call attention to them. Consider jotting down an outline or notes in the margins as you read. If you're reading a textbook, write in the margins the questions you want to remember to ask your instructor.

3. As you read, continually ask yourself these questions: How can this information help me? How can I use this information? What will my instructor probably want me to remember? How does this reading support or contradict my own ideas or beliefs, and experiences?

4. After you have read the entire selection, complete any activities that follow it.

Now, try applying the active reading strategy. Complete steps 1 through 4 in the list above to actively read the following passage from a textbook.

Altering Your Body Image*

A growing number of people seem to be unhappy with how they look. Specifically, they are dissatisfied with the appearance of their body. *Psychology Today* uses the term "body image" to describe the perceptions people have of their physical appearance, attractiveness, and beauty. Body image is our mental representation of ourselves; it is what allows us to contemplate ourselves. The image we see in the mirror influences much of our behavior and self-esteem.

A negative body image can begin to take shape early in life. Teasing during childhood can have a crushing effect on body image. Memories of being teased haunt many people for years. Through adolescence, the pressure to achieve an attractive body image is intense, especially among women. Body weight has a major influence on overall satisfaction with appearance. In many cases, the ever-present media portray desirable women as thin.

Appearance is more important today than it was in the past, according to Mary Pipher, author of *Reviving Ophelia*. She notes that we have moved from communities of primary relationships in which people know each other to cities where secondary relationships are much more common:

In a community of primary relationships, appearance is only one of many dimensions that define people. Everyone knows everyone else in

Continued

* From Barry L. Reece and Rhonda Brandt, *Effective Human Relations in Organizations*, 7th ed., Boston: Houghton Mifflin, 1999, pp. 116–117. Copyright © 1999 by Houghton Mifflin Company. Reprinted by permission.

Copyright © Houghton Mifflin Company. All rights reserved.

1

different ways over time. In a city of strangers, appearance is the only dimension available for the rapid assessment of others. Thus it becomes incredibly important in defining value.

Preoccupation with body image follows many people throughout adulthood. Large numbers of people wish to conform to the body-size ideals projected in the media. The motivation to be thinner helps support a $50-billion-a-year diet industry. People have learned to judge themselves, in many cases, by the standards of physical attractiveness that appear in fashion magazines and television commercials.

Some people have found ways to remake their self-image and move away from a preoccupation with body image. One approach is to develop criteria for self-esteem that go beyond appearance. To make appearance less significant in your life, you develop other benchmarks for self-evaluation. These might include succeeding at work, forming new friendships, or achieving a greater feeling of self-worth through volunteer work. Another approach is to engage in exercise that makes you feel good about yourself. Exercise for strength, fitness, and health, not just for weight loss. You can also identify and change habitual and negative thoughts about your body. When you look in the mirror, try to say nice things about your body.

1. Professionals in the field of psychology say that people with low self-esteem rely too much on the views of others for a sense of self-worth. Is this a problem you currently face in your life? Explain.

   _____

2. Mary Pipher says that in large communities appearance is the only dimension available for rapid assessment of others. Do you find yourself placing a heavy emphasis on appearance when assessing the worth of others?

   _____

3. Joan Borysenko, director of the Mind/Body Clinic at Harvard Medical School, says you need to accept yourself as you are. Acceptance, she says, means actually honoring yourself as you are now. Is this good advice? Is it realistic advice? Explain.

   _____

4. If you currently have a negative body image, what other criteria could you use to help enhance your self-esteem?

   _____

Copyright © Houghton Mifflin Company. All rights reserved.

Copyright © Houghton Mifflin Company. All rights reserved.

Do you enjoy reading? If your answer is no, why not? Like many people, you may have several reasons for disliking the printed word. You might think reading is too passive, requiring you to sit still for too much time. You may not like it because it takes too long. You may say that most of the things you read just don't interest you or seem relevant to your life. You may object to reading because it seems too hard—you don't like having to struggle to understand information. These are the most common reasons people give to explain their dislike of reading.

What people don't realize is that most of these reasons arise from a lack of experience and effort. When you first decided you didn't like to read, you probably began to avoid it as much as possible. This avoidance led to a lack of practice, which set up a vicious cycle: lack of practice led to undeveloped skills. This lack of skills meant more difficult and unrewarding experiences when you did read. As a result, you probably read less and less, and you gave yourself few opportunities to practice your reading skills. So, the cycle began again.

You can break this cycle, though, and make your reading experiences more enjoyable. The first step is to realize how much you already know about the reading process.

The Importance of Good Reading Skills

As Figure 1.1 below shows, a college student spends a lot of his or her daily communication time reading. Obviously, then, good reading skills are an essential component of success in college.

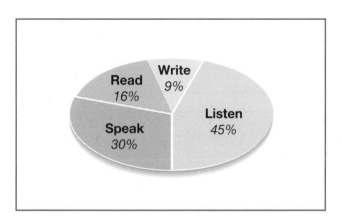

Figure 1.1   What You Do with Your Communication Time

Source: L. Barker et al., "An Investigation of Proportional Time Spent in Various Communication Activities of College Student," *Journal of Applied Communication Research* 8 [1981]: 101–109. Reprinted by permission.

1

Reading and Academic Success

Solid reading skills will be critical to your success in college. Most college courses require a great deal of reading. Your professors will ask you to read textbooks, articles, books, stories, and handouts. You'll be responsible for re-membering much of this information and revealing your knowledge of it on tests. You'll have to read the instructor's notes, and you'll have to read your own notes on lecture material to prepare for your tests. In addition, you'll be asked to conduct research, which requires reading all types of sources, includ-ing Web sites on the Internet. Various assignments will ask you to read not only your own writing but also that of your classmates.

Not only will you have to simply read and remember information, you also will be asked to evaluate it, judge it, agree or disagree with it, interpret it, compare it to something else, summarize it, and synthesize it with other things you've read. You can accomplish all of these tasks only if you can first attain a solid grasp of the ideas and information in the source.

Exercise 1.1

Answer the following questions about Figure 1.1 on page 5.

1. For a college student, what percentage of daily communication time is spent in reading? _____

2. How do you think your reading time compares to the average figure in the chart? _____

3. The information in the visual relates to a college student. How do you think the four percentages included in the chart change for someone who is not attending college? _____

_____

_____

Exercise 1.2

In the list below, place a checkmark beside every reading-related activity you've already done at least once. Then, answer the questions that follow.

_____ Read a textbook

Copyright © Houghton Mifflin Company. All rights reserved.

1

_____ Read a magazine or journal article assigned by a teacher

_____ Read information on a Web site for a class assignment

_____ Read a book or a novel assigned by a teacher

_____ Researched a topic in the library by reading several sources about it

_____ Read a memo at work

_____ Read a letter from a friend

_____ Read an e-mail message from a friend, teacher, or colleague

_____ Read subtitles while you watch a foreign film

_____ Read the newspaper

_____ Read a story to a child

_____ Read aloud in class

_____ Read a prepared speech to an audience

1. If you could choose anything to read, what would it be? Why?

   _____

   _____

   _____

2. What types of reading situations do you find the most difficult?

   _____

   _____

   _____

3. What do you think you need to do to become a better reader?

   _____

   _____

   _____

4. What would you like to learn in this textbook that you think would help
   you become a better reader? _____

   _____

Copyright © Houghton Mifflin Company. All rights reserved.

Reading and Professional Success

When you enter the work force, you might be surprised how much reading you'll need to do. Many jobs will require you to read e-mail messages, letters, memorandums, policy and procedure manuals, instructions, reports, logs and records, summaries of meetings, newsletters, and many other types of documents.

Often, a lot is at stake on your comprehension of these materials. Your personal safety may depend on your understanding of the information in manuals or other instructions. Your efficient and effective job performance may rest on your ability to comprehend written information sent to you by your supervisors and coworkers. Even your promotions and raises may depend, in part, on your ability to read and understand materials such as reports about trends, new research, or other innovations in your field.

Exercise 1.3

Read the following memo and answer the questions that follow.

To: All Employees of Ace Storage Facilities

From: Dan Denton, President

Date: January 2, 20xx

Re: New Bonus for Your Money-Saving Idea

To all employees:

On behalf of the executive team at Ace Storage Facilities, I'd like to thank each and every one of you for your hard work and commitment to this corporation. As you know, we value your input about making our company more efficient and effective. Therefore, we have created a new policy to encourage you to share more of your ideas with your management team.

Effective immediately, you may be able to earn a $500 bonus for an idea that saves our company money. To be eligible for this bonus, you must complete a new form that is now available in all break rooms. The information required on this form must be typed, and all sections of the form must be filled out. In the section about your suggestion, you must describe your idea and your estimate of its cost savings in 200 words or less. Completed forms

Copyright © Houghton Mifflin Company. All rights reserved.

1

should be placed in the box beside the time clock. You may submit as many ideas as you like, but each of them should be described on a separate form.

All ideas will be reviewed by the senior management team. If your idea is selected for implementation, you will receive a $500 bonus in your next month's paycheck. So please share with us your thoughts about making our company more cost-effective, and contact Betty in the Personnel Office if you have any questions about this new policy.

1. Are all ideas submitted rewarded with a $500 bonus? _____

2. Does President Dan Denton want you to call his office if you have questions about his new policy? _____

3. Can you hand-write the information on the form you fill out? _____

4. How long can the description of your idea be? _____

5. What should you do if you have more than one money-saving idea?

6. Where can you get one of the forms you need to fill out? _____

Reading and Personal Success

There are many occasions in your personal life when you will need to read well. For example, you may want to learn more about a hobby or subject area that interests you. So, you'll need to read books, articles, and Web site pages to increase your knowledge. You may want to find out how to improve your personal finances by learning how to save or invest your money. You may need to assemble something you purchased—such as a child's toy or a barbecue grill—by following the directions. You or one of your loved ones may become sick with a particular disease or disorder, causing you to want more information

Copyright © Houghton Mifflin Company. All rights reserved.

1

about treatment options. You may even want to read for entertainment, picking up a *People* magazine or a Stephen King novel just for the fun of it.

You'll also have to read personal correspondence such as letters and e-mail messages, legal documents such as contracts, and reports from your children's teachers, among other things. You'll read all of these documents more capably and confidently when you improve your reading skills.

Exercise 1.4

Read and answer the following questions about the reading selection below.

If you're like most homeowners, you think that laying tile is a job for the "pros." Boy, are you ever stupid! Because the truth is that anybody can do it! All it takes is a little planning, the right materials, and a Fire Rescue unit.

Consider the true story of a woman in Linthicum, Md., who decided to tile her kitchen floor, as reported in an excellent front-page newspaper article written by Eric Collins for the Sept. 26 issue of the Annapolis, Md., *Capital*, and sent in by many alert readers. According to this article, the woman, who wanted to be identified only as "Anne" for reasons that will become clear, decided to surprise her fiancé by tiling her kitchen floor herself, thus saving the $700 a so-called "expert" would have charged for the job.

Step One, of course, was for Anne to spread powerful glue on the floor, so the tiles would be bonded firmly in place. Anne then proceeded to Step Two, which—as you have probably already guessed—was to slip and fall face-first into the glue coat she created in Step One, thus bonding herself to the floor like a gum wad on a hot sidewalk.

Fortunately, Anne was not alone. Also in the house, thank goodness, was one of the most useful companions a person can ever hope to have: a small dog. Specifically, it was a Yorkshire Terrier, a breed originally developed in England to serve as makeup applicators. A full-grown "Yorkie" is about the size of a standard walnut, although it has more hair and a smaller brain.

Anne's dog—named Cleopatra—saw that her owner was in trouble, so she immediately ran outside and summoned a police officer.

Ha ha! No, seriously, Cleopatra did what all dogs do when their owners are in trouble: lick the owner's face. Dogs believe this is the correct response to every emergency. If Lassie had been a real dog, when little Timmy was sinking in the quicksand, Lassie, instead of racing back to the farmhouse to get help, would have helpfully licked Timmy on the face until he disappeared, at which point Lassie, having done all she could for him, would have resumed licking herself.

So anyway, when Cleopatra decided to help out, she naturally also became stuck in the glue. But again, luck was on Anne's side, because also at

Copyright © Houghton Mifflin Company. All rights reserved.

home were her two daughters, ages 9 and 10, who, realizing that the situation was no joking matter, immediately, in the words of the *Capital* article, "began laughing hysterically."

Eventually, with their help, Anne got unstuck from the floor and was able to lay the tile. But she still had glue all over herself. So, according to the *Capital* article, "she called a glue emergency hotline, but no one answered."

I don't know about you, but that sentence disturbs me. I think somebody should check on the glue-emergency-hotline staff. I picture an office reeking of glue fumes, with whacked-out workers permanently bonded to floors, walls, ceilings, each other, etc. Come to think of it, this is also how I picture Congress.

But getting back to Anne: Still trying to solve her personal glue problem, she called a tile contractor. During this conversation, the glue on her body hardened, such that (1) her right foot became stuck to the floor, (2) her legs became stuck together, (3) her body became stuck to a chair, and (4) her hand became stuck to the phone.

"I had to dial 911 with my nose," she is quoted as saying.

When the rescue personnel arrived, they found Anne still stuck. Perhaps this is a good time in our story to bring up the fact that she had been working in, and was still wearing, only her underwear. Fortunately, the rescue crews were serious, competent, highly trained professionals, and thus, to again quote the *Capital* article, they "laughed until they cried."

Once they recovered, the rescue crews were able to free Anne by following the standard procedure for this type of situation: licking her face.

No, seriously, they freed her with solvents, and everything was fine. Anne got her new floor and saved herself $700, which I am sure more than makes up for suffering enough humiliation to last four or five lifetimes. So the bottom line, homeowners, is this: Don't be afraid to tackle that tile job! Just be sure to have a dog handy, and always remember the No. 1 rule of tile-installation professionals: Wear clean underwear.*

1. What job did "Anne" decide to take on, even though she had never done it before? _____

2. When the author of the selection writes, "Fortunately, Anne was not alone," to whom is he referring as also being in her house? _____

_____

_____

* Adapted from "Laying Tile Requires Stick-to-itiveness," by Dave Barry, *The Miami Herald*, December 1, 2000. © Tribune Media Services, Inc. All rights reserved. Reprinted with permission.

Copyright © Houghton Mifflin Company. All rights reserved.

1

3. What happened when Cleopatra decided to help Anne? _____

_____

_____

4. How does the author describe the "glue-emergency-hotline staff"?

_____

_____

5. Is this story meant to entertain readers or teach them how to tile a floor?

How do you know? _____

_____

Reading and Better Thinking

Better reading skills help you improve your chances for academic, professional, and personal success. They will also help you improve your overall thinking skills. This is because reading requires you to follow and understand the thought processes of the writer. When you can do that effectively, you get opportunities to sharpen a variety of your own mental skills:

1. You evaluate information and decide what's important.

2. You learn to see relationships between things, events, and ideas.

3. You make new connections between things, events, and ideas.

4. You practice following the logic (or seeing the lack of logic) of someone else's thoughts.

5. You add more information to your memory.

These are the very skills that will strengthen your ability to make decisions, think creatively, and think logically in every area of your life.

Exercise 1.5

Read the following Letter to the Editor from a newspaper and respond to the questions that follow.

I think the best way to prevent most traffic accidents is to ban the use of cell phones while driving. In the past ten years, since cell phones were introduced to the American public and became part of everyone's life, traffic accidents

Copyright © Houghton Mifflin Company. All rights reserved.

and deaths in cars have increased significantly. In many of these accidents, it is a fact that someone talking on a cell phone has caused the accident.

It is a proven scientific fact that people cannot do two things at once, so why do people think that they can drive and talk on the phone at the same time?

However, I don't think that cell phones are the only cause of accidents or the only thing that should be banned. I think that in addition to banning the use of cell phones in cars, people should not be allowed to eat, chew gum, change the radio station they are listening to, sing along to the song on the radio, put on makeup while they drive, talk to anyone else in the car, or look out any window besides the windshield in front of them while driving. In my opinion, banning these activities will significantly cut down on the number of traffic accidents, injuries, and deaths that occur every day.

In the last three years, my car has been hit fourteen times, all by people either using cell phones, talking to someone else in their car, eating, or singing along to the radio. I have also witnessed a number of accidents and near-accidents involving drivers engaged in the activities mentioned above.

People should keep their eyes on the road at all times. Concentration is the key to being a good, safe driver, so by banning many activities that most of us associate with driving—talking on the phone, eating while driving, and singing—we will have safer roads in America.

1. What new piece of information did you learn by reading this excerpt?

   _____

   _____

2. Which sentence gave you your first clue that the author is not logical?

   _____

   _____

3. Can you think of another solution to decreasing the number of traffic accidents besides the ones the author suggests? _____

   _____

How to Improve Reading Skills

Now that you understand *why* it's so important to read well, you're probably wondering *how* you can be a better reader. The obvious answer is practice. The more you read, the more opportunities you'll have for improving your abilities. But simply reading everything in sight will not necessarily improve your skills. In general, you should commit yourself to doing four other things as well:

Copyright © Houghton Mifflin Company. All rights reserved.

1

1. Understand the different purposes for reading

2. Be aware of the mental skills required for reading

3. Develop individual reading skills

4. Learn and use different reading strategies

Understand the Different Purposes for Reading

When you set out to read something, you should know *why* you're reading it. The two basic purposes for reading are to gain information and to be entertained. Obviously, when you read for entertainment, your primary goal is your own pleasure. When you read for information, though, you may have one or more different goals:

1. **Gain a general understanding of the ideas or points.** For example, as you're reading this section of this textbook, you're trying to comprehend the ideas being presented.

2. **Discover the facts or answer questions about the material.** When you read the paragraphs in the exercises of this book, for example, you read them to find answers to the questions you must answer.

3. **Memorize the information.** You often read a textbook chapter so that you'll recall its information when you take a test.

4. **Find information or ideas that prove a point you want to make.** When you conduct research for a paper you need to write, you read to find statements or information that back up your opinions.

5. **Make a decision based on the information.** You read brochures from businesses, for example, to decide whether to buy their particular product or service.

When you read something, you may need to accomplish just one of the goals above or perhaps all five at the same time. In any case, getting the most of everything you read means clearly identifying your purpose before you begin.

Exercise 1.6

Read the following reading situations. Following each one, place checkmarks next to every MAJOR purpose for reading that applies to that situation. (More than one choice may apply.)

1. You read a newspaper article to find out about a fire that burned down a house in your neighborhood.

     _____ Gain a general understanding of the ideas or points.

Copyright © Houghton Mifflin Company. All rights reserved.

Copyright © Houghton Mifflin Company. All rights reserved.

_____ Discover the facts or answer questions.

_____ Memorize the information.

_____ Find information or ideas that prove a point you want to make.

_____ Make a decision based on the information.

2. You read the notes you wrote down during your professor's lecture as you prepare for your history exam.

_____ Gain a general understanding of the ideas or points.

_____ Discover the facts or answer questions.

_____ Memorize the information.

_____ Find information or ideas that prove a point you want to make.

_____ Make a decision based on the information.

3. You read the technical instructions that come with the bicycle you purchased and need to assemble.

_____ Gain a general understanding of the ideas or points.

_____ Discover the facts or answer questions.

_____ Memorize the information.

_____ Find information or ideas that prove a point you want to make.

_____ Make a decision based on the information.

4. You read a flyer sent to you by a candidate running for office in your town or city. This flyer states the opinions of the candidate.

_____ Gain a general understanding of the ideas or points.

_____ Discover the facts or answer questions.

_____ Memorize the information.

_____ Find information or ideas that prove a point you want to make.

_____ Make a decision based on the information.

5. You read a report to find out about the number of traffic accidents that occurred last year at an intersection in your neighborhood. You plan to argue that your city government needs to install a traffic light at that intersection.

_____ Gain a general understanding of the ideas or points.

_____ Discover the facts or answer questions.

1

_____ Memorize the information.

_____ Find information or ideas that prove a point you want to make.

_____ Make a decision based on the information.

Be Aware of the Mental Skills Required for Reading

"Reading" is actually a collection of different mental skills. They include attitude, concentration, memory, and logical thought. These skills are all interrelated and connected. Some of them depend upon others. When you become aware that these different skills are at work, you can learn to improve them.

Attitude. A positive attitude is the first essential mental component for successful reading. Your attitude includes your feelings about reading, about _what_ you read, and about your own abilities. If these feelings are negative, your reading experiences will be negative. If these feelings are positive, your experiences will be more enjoyable.

A positive attitude not only makes reading more pleasurable, it also creates the right mental environment for gaining new information. As a matter of fact, all of the other mental skills required for reading are useless unless you approach each reading task in the right frame of mind. If you are quick to pronounce a particular text "boring" or "worthless," you are likely to create a mental block that will prevent you from absorbing the information. Instead, approach each new reading task with intellectual curiosity. Expect to find something of value, something you'll be able to use in your life.

Also, don't let a poor attitude about your own reading abilities get in your way. If you expect to fail, if you tell yourself you just don't get it, then you virtually guarantee your failure. If you believe you can improve, however, then you'll create the necessary mental foundation for improving your skills and becoming a good reader.

Exercise 1.7

Read the following selection and answer the questions that follow.

Toward Right Livelihood

Visit Sena Plaza in downtown Santa Fe, and you will see a public garden that is a wonderland of color and texture. The person responsible for this beautiful garden is Barbara Fix, a graduate of Stanford Law School who chose gardening over a high-powered law career. She says, "I've been offered many jobs in

Copyright © Houghton Mifflin Company. All rights reserved.

my life. I could have been on Wall Street making six figures, but the only job I ever hustled for was this one—six dollars an hour as the gardener at Sena Plaza."

Barbara Fix is an example of someone who appears to have achieved "right livelihood." The original concept of right livelihood apparently came from the teachings of Buddha. In recent years, the concept has been described by Michael Phillips in his book *The Seven Laws of Money* and by Marsha Sinetar in her book *Do What You Love . . . The Money Will Follow*. Right livelihood is work consciously chosen, done with full awareness and care, and leading to enlightenment. When Jason Wilson gave up a challenging business career to become a carpenter, he embraced the concept of right livelihood. He later started his own home construction business. Ronald Sheade, once a vice president at a Fortune 1,000 company, now teaches eighth-grade science in a suburb of Chicago. He doesn't make big money anymore, but he loves teaching and now gets to spend more time with his family.*

1. When you read the title of the selection "Toward Right Livelihood," what did you think the selection would be about? Why? _____

   _____

2. Did you assume the passage would be boring or too difficult? If so, why?

   _____

   _____

3. As you read this passage, did you discover a fact or idea that interested you? Did you discover some information in this passage you could actually use in your life? If so, what was it? _____

   _____

4. If you followed the concept of right livelihood, what kind of work would you do? _____

   _____

Concentration.   Once your positive attitude has prepared your mind to absorb new information, you're ready to employ the second mental skill necessary for reading: concentration. Concentration is the ability to focus all of

* Adapted from Barry L. Reece and Rhonda Brandt, *Effective Human Relations in Organizations*, 7th ed., Boston: Houghton Mifflin, 1999, 458–459. Copyright © 1999 by Houghton Mifflin Company. Reprinted with permission.

Copyright © Houghton Mifflin Company. All rights reserved.

1

your attention on one thing while ignoring all distractions. You cannot understand or remember information unless you read with concentration.

Many people, however, find concentration difficult to achieve, especially when they read more challenging material. Too often, they allow distractions to pull their thoughts away from the sentences and paragraphs before them. But you can learn to concentrate better. How? By practicing effective techniques for combating the two types of distractions: external and internal.

External distractions are the sights, sounds, and other sensations that tempt you away from your reading. These distractions include ringing phones, people talking or walking nearby, the sound of a stereo, or a friend who stops by to chat. Though they are powerful, they are also the easier of the two types of distractions to eliminate.

To avoid having to deal with external distractions, you merely prevent them from happening by choosing or creating the right reading environment. Try to select a location for reading—such as an individual study area in your library or a quiet room in your house—where distractions will be minimal. Before a reading session, notify your friends and family that you'll be unavailable for conversation and socializing. If you must read in places with more activity, try wearing earplugs and/or sitting with your back to the action so you're not tempted to watch the comings and goings of others.

Internal distractions are often more challenging to overcome. They are the thoughts, worries, plans, daydreams, and other types of mental "noise" inside your own head. They will prevent you from concentrating on what you're reading and from absorbing the information you need to learn.

You can try to ignore these thoughts, but they will usually continue trying to intrude. So, how do you temporarily silence them so you can devote your full attention to your reading? Try the following suggestions:

1. Begin every reading task with a positive attitude. A negative attitude produces a lot of grumbling mental noise like complaints and objections to the task at hand. When you choose to keep a positive attitude, you'll eliminate an entire category of noisy thoughts that interfere with your concentration.

2. Instead of fighting internal distractions, try focusing completely on them for a short period of time. For five or ten minutes, allow yourself to sit and think about your job, your finances, your car problems, your boyfriend or girlfriend, the paper you need to write, or whatever is on your mind. Better yet, write these thoughts down. Do a free-writing exercise (a quick writing of your own thoughts on paper without censoring them or worrying about grammar and spelling) to empty your mind of the thoughts that clutter it. If you can't stop thinking about all of the other things you need to do, devote ten minutes to writing a detailed

Copyright © Houghton Mifflin Company. All rights reserved.

"To Do" list. Giving all of your attention to distracting thoughts will often clear them from your mind so you can focus on your reading.

3. Keep your purpose in mind as you read. As discussed earlier, having a clear goal when you read will help you concentrate on getting what you need to know from a text.

4. Use active reading techniques. These techniques were explained at the beginning of this chapter. They increase your level of interaction with the text, which will improve your concentration on the material.

5. Use visualization to increase your interest and improve your retention of the information. As you read, let the words create pictures and images in your mind. Try to "see" in your mind's eye the scenes, examples, people, and other information presented in the text.

Exercise 1.8

Free-write for 10 minutes about what's going on inside your mind at this moment. Attach a separate sheet of paper for this activity.

Exercise 1.9

Read the following passage and practice the visualization techniques you read about earlier.

It is not surprising that an intelligent and perceptive young woman in the nineteenth century sometimes approached marriage with anxiety, for her future depended on the man she chose. Lucy Breckinridge, a wealthy Virginia girl of twenty, sensed how much independence she would have to surrender on her wedding day. In her diary she recorded this forthright observation on marriage: "If [husbands] care for their wives at all it is only as a sort of servant, a being made to attend to their comforts and to keep the children out of the way. . . . A woman's life after she is married, unless there is an immense amount of love, is nothing but suffering and hard work."*

1. Picture Lucy Breckinridge in your mind. What does she look like? What is she wearing? _____

   _____

   _____

* Adapted from Mary Beth Norton et al., *A People and a Nation*, Vol. I. Boston: Houghton Mifflin, 1998, 297–298. Copyright © 1999 by Houghton Mifflin Company. Reprinted with permission.

Copyright © Houghton Mifflin Company. All rights reserved.

2. Picture Lucy writing in her diary. Where is she sitting as she writes? What does her diary look like? _____

_____

3. Picture a scene of a nineteenth-century wife enduring "suffering and hard work." What is she doing? _____

_____

Memory.   Memory, the ability to store and recall information, is also essential to the reading process. You use your memory constantly as you read. You must remember the meanings of words. You must remember what you know about people, places, and things when you encounter references to them. You must remember all of the ideas and information presented before that point in the text. You must remember the text's overall main point while you read the sub-points or details. You must remember your own experiences that either support or contradict the text's message. You may also need to remember other texts you've read that either agree or disagree with the new information you're reading.

There are many techniques you can use to improve your memory. A few of the most common are described below:

1. **Improve your concentration.** The more intensely you focus on something, the better the chance you'll remember it.

2. **Repeat and review.** Most of the time, the more you expose yourself to new information, the more easily you'll recall it.

3. **Recite.** Saying information aloud helps strengthen your memory of it.

4. **Associate new information with what you already know.** Making connections between your present knowledge and what you need to learn helps you to store new information in your mind more effectively.

Exercise 1.10

Read the following passage through once, then cover it so you can't see it and test your memory of the information by answering the questions that follow.

I was born in 1947 and we didn't get our first television until 1958. The first thing·I remember watching on it was *Robot Monster,* a film in which a guy dressed in an ape-suit with a goldfish bowl on his head—RO-Man, he was

Copyright © Houghton Mifflin Company. All rights reserved.

called—ran around trying to kill the last survivors of a nuclear war. I also watched *Highway Patrol* with Broderick Crawford as the fearless Dan Matthews, and *One Step Beyond,* hosted by John Newland, the man with the world's spookiest eyes.*

1. In what year was the author born? _____

2. What was the first thing he remembered watching on television? _____

   _____

3. What was the name of the character on *Robot Monster*? _____

4. Name one other show the author watched on television. _____

   _____

   _____

5. Who had the "world's spookiest eyes"? _____

Logical thought.   Another mental skill required for effective reading is logical thinking. Logical thought is composed of many different mental tasks, including those in the list below:

Sequencing and ordering: seeing the order of things and understanding cause/effect relationships.

Matching: noticing similarities.

Organizing: grouping things into categories.

Analysis: understanding how to examine the different parts of something.

Reasoning from the general to the particular and the particular to the general: drawing conclusions and making generalizations.

Abstract thought: understanding ideas and concepts.

Synthesis: putting things together in new combinations.

If you want to improve your ability to think logically, try one or more of the following suggestions:

1. **Practice active reading.** Using outlining, in particular, forces you to work harder to detect relationships in information.

*Adapted from *On Writing*, by Stephen King, © 2000 by Stephen King, 34.

Copyright © Houghton Mifflin Company. All rights reserved.

1

2. **Play with games and puzzles.** Card games, computer games, and board games such as chess, checkers, and backgammon will give you opportunities to sharpen your analytical skills.

3. **Solve problems.** Work math problems. Read mysteries (or watch them on television) and try to figure out who committed the crime before the detective does. Try to think of ways to solve everyday problems, both big and small. For example, come up with a solution for America's overflowing landfills. Or figure out how to alter backpacks so they don't strain your back.

4. **Practice your argument and debating skills.** Discuss controversial issues with people who hold the opposing viewpoint.

5. **Write more.** Writing requires a great deal of logical thought, so write letters to your newspaper editor or congressional representatives about issues that are important to you.

Exercise 1.11

Read this passage from a magazine and then answer the questions that follow.

The New American Family

One thing America has rediscovered in the wake of its terrorist attacks in September 2001 is that, in tough times, we can face adversity as a family might. That's because we are a *nation* of families, now more diverse in makeup than at any other time in our history. All of us know that more moms are working than ever before. We know that there's been a surge in single-parent homes. We know that women are marrying at a later age and that Hispanics have emerged as the country's fastest-growing minority. But the big news is that the most recent U.S. Census figures confirm the extent of these changes. For example, the country's Hispanic population, 35.3 million, now nearly equals that of African Americans. Where 23 percent of women with children under age 3 were in the labor force in the early 1970s, today that figure is 63 percent. Some 19 million households are now headed by one parent. While women married, on average, at age 20.8 in 1970, today they're more likely to exchange vows at 25. To be sure, many of the changes have presented families with new challenges. But parents are doing what they can to keep their households thriving.

The boom in the Hispanic population is but one factor changing the face of the American family. Interracial marriages have soared, from 315,000 in 1970 to 1.46 million today. And families are functioning much differently—

Copyright © Houghton Mifflin Company. All rights reserved.

somewhat. Although women still assume most of the housework, men are now devoting some ten hours a week to such chores, an increase of five hours since the late 1950s.

Median annual income for all families has grown from $27,334 in 1959, when single-earner families predominated, to $50,891 for all families and $69,467 for families with both partners working. Many are spending a lot of time earning that money. The Families and Work Institute says fathers with children under age 18 work an average of 50.9 hours weekly. Moms work an average of 41.4 hours weekly.

What lies ahead for the American family? Children could find themselves with less shuttling between Mom and Dad if the divorce rate remains stable, part of a trend that started in 1996. And experts predict continued growth in non-traditional families, such as same-sex couples and single women who have children either through adoption or with the help of medical technology. But the biggest shifts may come as belated responses to the transition we've made from single- to dual-paycheck families. Says sociologist Angela Hattery, Ph.D.: "I expect to see school systems redesign schedules to more closely conform to parents' work hours and more flextime and on-site child care." One thing is certain. America's families are committed to staying strong together, in good times and in bad.*

1. According to the author, what is one positive effect of stable divorce rates? Think of another positive effect not mentioned by the author.

_____

_____

2. Predict one positive effect and one negative effect for each of the following changes:

   a. On average, women are marrying at age 25. _____

   _____

   b. Men are now devoting about ten hours per week to housework.

   _____

   _____

   c. Fathers with children under age 18 work an average of 50.9 hours

      weekly. _____

   _____

* Adapted from Andrea Rock, "The New American Family," *Ladies' Home Journal*, December 2001, 102. Copyright © December 2001, Meredith Corporation. All rights reserved. Used with permission of *Ladies' Home Journal*.

Copyright © Houghton Mifflin Company. All rights reserved.

1

d. Do your own experiences support or refute the author's conclusion that "America's families are committed to staying strong together, in good times and in bad"? Explain your answer. _____

_____

_____

Develop Individual Reading Skills

Another way to improve your reading comprehension is to develop the isolated skills you must use to read well. For example, you can learn techniques for recognizing the main idea of a paragraph or for detecting patterns used to organize information. The rest of this book is designed to help you develop and practice these skills.

Exercise 1.12

Check off in the list below the skills you believe you need to improve. Next to each item that you check, write the number of the chapter in this book that focuses on helping you strengthen that skill.

_____ Recognizing the overall point (the main idea) of a reading selection

_____

_____ Understanding how details support the main idea of a reading selection _____

_____ Figuring out how a reading selection is organized _____

_____ Understanding visuals—maps, charts, graphs—in reading selections

_____

_____ Reading critically, or figuring out if a reading selection is accurate or trustworthy _____

_____ Understanding longer reading selections _____

_____ Figuring out implied main ideas, points that are not stated directly in a reading selection _____

_____ Recognizing transitions, words that link sentences and paragraphs together _____

Copyright © Houghton Mifflin Company. All rights reserved.

1

_____ "Reading between the lines" (making inferences) by drawing conclusions from the information in a reading selection _____

Learn and Use Different Reading Strategies

Reading strategies are techniques you use when you read. Some of them—such as active reading—are designed to improve your comprehension and retention of information. Others—such as skimming and scanning—provide you with tools you can use to find what you need in certain circumstances.

This book explains a different reading strategy in each chapter. Make sure you understand each of them so you can begin using them to read better right away.

How This Book Will Help You Improve

Goals of this Book

The Houghton Mifflin Reading Series is one of three books in a series designed to help you improve your reading skills. This text—the first in the sequence—focuses on the basic skills necessary to effective reading. Each chapter concentrates on one essential skill you can immediately use to strengthen your reading comprehension.

This book, along with the other two in the series, is based on the belief that you can indeed become a better reader. Even if you have struggled in the past, you can learn and practice the skills you need to get more out of anything you read.

Organization and Features

This book is organized into two sections. The first part includes ten chapters, one for each essential reading skill. The second includes a variety of tests designed to give you more practice with the skills covered in the first ten chapters.

Each of the ten chapters includes several helpful features.

Reading strategy. Each chapter opens with the explanation of a different reading strategy. Strategies are techniques you can use to get more out of what you read. Using these techniques, you can begin to improve your reading comprehension right away.

Pre-test. At the beginning of each chapter, a pre-test will help you identify what you already know about the skill covered in that chapter. It will also help you pinpoint specific areas you need to target for improvement.

Copyright © Houghton Mifflin Company. All rights reserved.

1

Practices. Throughout each chapter, you'll have numerous opportunities to check your understanding with practice activities. As you complete each practice and receive feedback on your answers, you will progress toward better reading comprehension.

Chapter review. Filling in the blanks in a brief summary of the major points and concepts in the chapter will help you reinforce them in your mind.

Interesting readings. The readings within practices, along with the longer reading selection in each chapter, are drawn from a variety of interesting sources. These readings have been carefully chosen to be enjoyable and/or useful. They have also been selected to clearly demonstrate a particular skill or concept. Furthermore, they'll give you practice reading different kinds of sources, including textbooks, magazine articles, newspaper articles, and essays.

The longer reading selection in each chapter is followed by questions designed to check your comprehension and increase your vocabulary. It also includes discussion questions that will encourage you to sharpen your thinking skills and find ways to apply the information to your own life.

Vocabulary. Each chapter presents a different vocabulary concept. In this section, you will learn techniques for discovering the meanings of unfamiliar words. You will also learn about different types of specialized vocabulary in order to improve your overall reading comprehension. A practice activity draws from the readings in the chapter to give you an opportunity to check your understanding.

Post-Tests. Each chapter concludes with a series of post-tests designed to help you measure your understanding of the concepts and skills you have learned. They will verify your mastery of the information and also identify areas for further study and review.

Exercise 1.13

Preview this textbook by answering the following questions about its features and organization.

1. How many chapters does this book contain? _____

2. In what chapter is the topic of "Main Ideas" covered? _____

3. In what chapter will you learn the different patterns of organization that

   writers use? _____

Copyright © Houghton Mifflin Company. All rights reserved.

1

4. In what chapter will you find the most "visual" material—that is, charts, graphs, maps, and photos—and find out how to read them? _____

5. In what chapter will you find information on how to read longer selections? _____

6. In what chapter will you learn how to use the dictionary? _____

7. Look at Chapter 8 and define the term "inference." _____

_____

8. How many additional readings appear in the combined skills test section?

_____

9. Look at the table of contents and count the number of reading selections contained in Part One of this text. _____

10. How many different reading strategies are presented in this text? _____

CHAPTER 1 REVIEW

Fill in the blanks in the following statements.

1. Good reading skills are important to _____, _____, and _____ success.

2. Reading helps strengthen _____ skills.

3. The two basic purposes for reading are to gain _____ and to be entertained.

4. When you read for information, you may have one or more of the following goals: gain a general _____ of the ideas or points; discover _____ or answer questions; memorize the information; find information or ideas that prove a _____ you want to make; make a _____ based on the information.

5. Reading is actually a collection of mental skills that include _____, concentration, _____, and _____ thought.

6. A positive _____ makes reading more pleasurable and more productive.

Copyright © Houghton Mifflin Company. All rights reserved.

7. _____ is the ability to focus all of your attention on one thing while ignoring distractions.

8. The two types of distractions are _____ and _____.

9. _____ is the ability to store and recall information.

10. Logical thought includes mental tasks such as sequencing and ordering, _____, _____, analysis, _____ from the general to the particular and the particular to the general, _____ thought, and synthesis.

11. Reading _____ are techniques you can use to get more out of what you read.

Reading Selections

Chapters 2–9 in this text contain a longer reading selection at the end, followed by vocabulary, comprehension, and discussion questions. To get you acquainted with the different types of selections you will be reading, this chapter contains one Web site, one literary, and one textbook selection. Read the following selections and answer the questions that follow, either independently or with your class.

WEB SITE SELECTION

If It's Going to Be, It's Up to Me: Taking Responsibility for Choices in Our Lives
By Jim Clemmer

1 A 38-year-old man was at his parents' home for Sunday dinner. He mournfully turned the discussion to his many problems. "I've just left my third failed marriage, I can't hold onto a job, I'm in debt up to my ears and will have to declare personal bankruptcy," he whimpered. "Where did you go wrong?"

2 When things go wrong, it's easy to blame others. Blaming others for our difficulties is the easy way out. That's why it's so popular. Turn on any daytime talk show and you'll find endless examples of people blaming everybody and everything for the way their lives have turned out.

3 But the happiest and most successful people—the leaders who get things done and get on with their lives—know that life is an endless series of choices, and take responsibility for these choices as well as the consequences of their actions. Leaders choose to control their destiny so fate and others don't. They believe that choice more

Copyright © Houghton Mifflin Company. All rights reserved.

than chance determines their circumstances. Even in circumstances for which they're not responsible, they still take responsibility for their actions.

4   Leaders recognize that they have control and choice over a number of key factors:

5   **Choose Not to Lose.** Whether we choose to focus on our problems or our possibilities is a key leadership issue. When we are faced with obstacles and failure, those who can overcome adversity and learn from their experiences, turning them into opportunities, are the ones who will be truly successful.

6   **Perceived Reality.** Most so-called "facts" are open to interpretation and are highly dependent upon what's being read into them. We don't see the world as it is, we see it as we are. Too often, we let our problems trap us deep inside our own "reality rut." As long as we're stuck there, we can't see out of the rut to the possibilities beyond.

7   **Choosing Our Outlook.** An optimist expects the best possible outcome and dwells on the most hopeful aspects of a situation. Pessimists stress the negative and take the gloomiest possible view. And while we may have been given a tendency toward optimism or pessimism at birth or from our upbringing, we decide what we want to be from today forward.

8   **Choosing to Let Go of Deadly Emotions.** Another milestone in our growth is when we accept responsibility for our emotions. It's less painful to believe that anger, jeal-ousy, or bitterness are somebody else's fault or beyond our control. But that makes us prisoners of our emotions. We stew in our deadly emotions. For our own health and happiness, we must exercise our choice to let go. No matter how long we nurse a grudge, it won't get better. We need to truly forgive and forget. Forgiveness is not for the other guy, it is for ourselves.

9   **Choosing Our Thoughts.** In his nineteenth-century journals, Ralph Waldo Emerson wrote, "Life consists of what a man is thinking of all day." If we continue to think like we've always thought, we'll continue to get what we've always got. Our daily thought choices translate into our daily actions. Our actions accumulate to form our habits. Our habits form our character. Our character attracts our circumstances. Our circumstances determine our future. . . . Taking responsibility for our choices starts with choosing our thoughts.

10   Leaders realize that life accumulates; the choices we make—good and bad—are like deposits in a bank account. Over the years we can build up a wealth of success and happiness or a deficit of despair and discouragement. It's up to us. As with any active bank account, few of these choice accumulations are permanent. However, the longer we allow poor choices to accumulate, the more time and effort will be needed to shift that balance. Now is the time for action. There's still time. If not now, when?

Excerpted from Jim Clemmer's latest bestseller *Growing the Distance: Timeless Principles for Personal, Career, and Family Success.* Jim Clemmer is an international keynote speaker, workshop leader, author, and president of The CLEMMER Group, a North American network of organization, team, and personal improvement consultants based in Kitchener, Ontario, Canada. His Web site is http://www.clemmer.net/.

Copyright © Houghton Mifflin Company. All rights reserved.

1

VOCABULARY

Read the following questions about some of the vocabulary words that appear in the previous selection. Circle the correct responses.

1. In paragraph 1, what does *mournfully* mean?
   a. happily
   b. gloriously
   c. sadly
   d. joyfully

2. In paragraph 1, what does *whimpered* mean?
   a. sang
   b. whined
   c. pained
   d. depressed

3. In paragraph 3, what does *consequences* mean?
   a. beginnings
   b. foundations
   c. ground works
   d. end results

4. In paragraph 5, what does *adversity* mean?
   a. hardship
   b. abundance
   c. simplicity
   d. complexity

5. In paragraph 6, what does *perceived* mean?
   a. heard
   b. spoken
   c. whispered
   d. understood

6. In paragraph 9, what does *accumulate* mean?
   a. throw
   b. collect
   c. disperse
   d. dispense

QUESTIONS FOR DISCUSSION AND WRITING

Answer the following questions based on your reading of the selection.

Copyright © Houghton Mifflin Company. All rights reserved.

1. Did you learn anything new from this article about setting goals? If so, what did you learn? Do you think this new information will help you? Why or why not? _____

   _____

2. What goals have you set for yourself in terms of your education? Will the information in this article help you achieve your educational goals? Why or why not? _____

   _____

3. Do you consider yourself to be an optimist or pessimist? Why? What events or experiences in your life have shaped your views—either optimistic or pessimistic? _____

   _____

LITERARY SELECTION

Being There
By Jerzy Kozinski

1 It was Sunday. Chance was in the garden. He moved slowly, dragging the green hose from one path to the next, carefully watching the flow of water. Very gently he let the stream touch every plant, every flower, every branch of the garden. Plants were like people; they needed care to live, to survive their diseases, and to die peacefully.

2 Yet plants were different from people. No plant is able to think about itself or able to know itself; there is no mirror in which the plant can recognize its face; no plant can do anything intentionally: it cannot help growing, and its growth has no meaning, since a plant cannot reason or dream.

3 It was safe and secure in the garden, which was separated from the street by a high, red brick wall covered with ivy, and not even the sounds of the passing cars disturbed the peace. Chance ignored the streets. Though he had never stepped outside the house and its garden, he was not curious about life on the other side of the wall.

4 The front part of the house where the Old Man lived might just as well have been another part of the wall or the street. He could not tell if anything in it was alive or not. In the rear of the ground floor facing the garden, the maid lived. Across the hall Chance had his room and his bathroom and his corridor leading to the garden.

5 What was particularly nice about the garden was that, at any moment, standing in the narrow paths or amidst the bushes and trees, Chance could start to wander, never knowing whether he was going forward or backward, unsure whether he was ahead of or behind his previous steps. All that mattered was moving in his own time, like the growing plants.

6 Once in a while Chance would turn off the water and sit on the grass and think.

Copyright © Houghton Mifflin Company. All rights reserved.

The wind, mindless of direction, intermittently swayed the bushes and trees. The city's dust settled evenly, darkening the flowers, which waited patiently to be rinsed by the rain and dried by the sunshine. And yet, with all its life, even at the peak of its bloom, the garden was its own graveyard. Under every tree and bush lay rotten trunks and disintegrated and decomposing roots. It was hard to know which was more important: the garden's surface or the graveyard from which it grew and into which it was constantly lapsing. For example, there were some hedges at the wall, which grew in complete disregard of the other plants; they grew faster, dwarfing the smaller flowers, and spreading onto the territory of weaker bushes.

7   Chance went inside and turned on the TV. The set created its own light, its own color, its own time. It did not follow the law of gravity that forever bent all plants downward. Everything on TV was tangled and mixed and yet smoothed out: night and day, big and small, tough and brittle, soft and rough, hot and cold, far and near. In this colored world of television, gardening was the white cane of a blind man.

From *Being There*, by Jerzy Kozinski, © 1970 by Jerzy Kozinski, Harcourt Brace Jovanovich, 3–5. Excerpt from Chapter 1 in *Being There*; copyright © 1970 by Jerzy Kozinski, reprinted by permission of Harcourt, Inc.

VOCABULARY

Read the following questions about some of the vocabulary words that appear in the previous selection. Circle the correct responses.

1. What is a *corridor* (Paragraph 4)? "Across the hall Chance had his room and his bathroom and his *corridor* leading to the garden."

    a. hallway
    b. room
    c. doorway
    d. arch

2. What does *amidst* mean? (Paragraph 5) ". . . standing in the narrow paths or *amidst* the bushes and trees. . . ."

    a. outdoors
    b. indoors
    c. surrounded by
    d. outside of

3. What does *intermittently* mean? (Paragraph 6) "The wind, mindless of direction, *intermittently* swayed the bushes and trees."

    a. often
    b. off and on
    c. eternally
    d. never

Copyright © Houghton Mifflin Company. All rights reserved.

1

4. What does *lapsing* mean in this context? (Paragraph 6) ". . . the garden's surface or the graveyard from which it grew and into which it was constantly *lapsing*."
   a. ending
   b. beginning
   c. swaying
   d. breaking

5. When something is *brittle*, what does that mean? (Paragraph 7) "Everything on TV was tangled and mixed and yet smoothed out: night and day, big and small, tough and *brittle*, soft and rough, hot and cold, far and near."
   a. hearty
   b. breakable
   c. funny
   d. happy

QUESTIONS FOR DISCUSSION AND WRITING

Answer the following questions based on your reading of the selection.

1. Did you enjoy this selection? Why or why not? _____

2. Based on your reading of the selection, particularly from the fact that you know that Chance never leaves the house and its grounds, what kind of person do you think Chance is, and why? _____

   _____

3. Does Chance's simple life sound appealing to you? Why or why not?

   _____

Copyright © Houghton Mifflin Company. All rights reserved.

TEXTBOOK SELECTION
Starbucks

1   It once seemed as if there might one day be a McDonald's restaurant on every street corner. But although there are certainly a large number of the venerable hamburger restaurants around today, Starbucks Corporation has, at least for the time being, replaced McDonald's as the highest-profile and fastest-growing food-and-beverage company in the United States. Starbucks was started in Seattle in 1971 by three coffee *aficionados* (fans). Their primary business at the time was buying premium coffee beans, roasting them, and then selling the coffee by the pound. The business performed modestly well and soon grew to nine stores, all in the Seattle area. The three partners sold Starbucks to a former employee, Howard Schultz, in 1987. Schultz promptly reoriented the business away from bulk coffee mail-order sales and emphasized retail coffee sales through the firm's coffee bars. Today, Starbucks is not only the largest coffee importer and roaster of specialty beans but also the largest specialty coffee bean retailer in the United States.

2   What is the key to the phenomenal growth and success of the Starbucks chain? One important ingredient is its well-conceived and well-implemented strategy. Starbucks is on an amazing growth pace, opening a new coffee shop somewhere almost every day. But this growth is planned and coordinated at each step through careful site selection. And through its astute promotional campaigns and commitment to quality, the firm has elevated the coffee-drinking taste of millions of Americans and fueled a significant increase in demand.

3   Starbucks also has created an organization that promotes growth and success. As long as they follow the firm's basic principles, managers at each store have considerable autonomy over how they run things. Starbucks also uses a state-of-the-art communication network to keep in contact with its employees.

4   Another ingredient of Starbucks' success is its relationship with its employees. The firm hires young people and starts them at hourly wages somewhat higher than those of most entry-level food-service jobs. The company also offers health insurance to all of its employees, including part-timers, and has a lucrative stock-option plan for everyone in the firm.

5   Yet another key to Starbucks' success is its emphasis on quality control. For example, milk must be warmed to a narrow range of 150 to 170 degrees, and espresso shots must be pulled within twenty-three seconds or else discarded. And no coffee is allowed to sit on a hot plate for more than twenty minutes. Schultz also refuses to franchise, fearing a loss of control and a potential deterioration of quality.

6   Starbucks remains on the alert for new business opportunities. In 1996, for example, the firm opened its first two coffee shops in Japan and another in Singapore, and most observers suggest that there is a world of opportunity awaiting Starbucks in foreign markets. Another way the company can grow is through brand extension with other companies. For instance, the firm has collaborated with Breyer's to distribute Starbucks coffee ice cream to grocery freez-

Copyright © Houghton Mifflin Company. All rights reserved.

ers across the country. Starbucks has also collaborated with Capitol Records on two Starbucks jazz CDs. And Redhook Brewery uses Starbucks coffee extract in its double black stout beer. All things considered, then, Starbucks' future looks so bright that its employees may need to wear sunshades the firm might soon begin to sell!

From R. Griffin *Management*, 6th ed. Boston: Houghton Mifflin, 1999, 5. Copyright © 1999 by Houghton Mifflin Company. Reprinted with permission.

VOCABULARY

Read the following questions about some of the vocabulary words that appear in the previous selection. Circle the correct response.

1. What does *venerable* mean? (Paragraph 1) "But although there are certainly a large number of the *venerable* hamburger restaurants around today. . . ."

   a. respected
   b. dirty
   c. fun
   d. happy

2. What does *reoriented* mean in this context? (Paragraph 1) "Schultz promptly *reoriented* the business away from bulk coffee mail-order sales. . . ."

   a. familiarize
   b. redirected
   c. clarify
   d. dignify

3. What does *phenomenal* mean? (Paragraph 2) "What is the key to the *phenomenal* growth and success of the Starbucks chain?"

   a. depressing
   b. amazing
   c. colorful
   d. dignified

4. What does *astute* mean? (Paragraph 2) "And through its *astute* promotional campaigns. . . ."

   a. artless
   b. innocent
   c. candid
   d. intelligent

5. When the author of the selection states that "Schultz also refuses to *franchise* . . ." what does he mean? What is a *franchise*? (Paragraph 5)

   a. a store that sells clothes, like Old Navy
   b. a store that is managed by a private businessperson but owned by a larger corporation, like McDonald's
   c. a store that only sells food
   d. a store that only sells coffee

Copyright © Houghton Mifflin Company. All rights reserved.

6. What does it mean to *collaborate*? (Paragraph 6) "Starbucks has also *collaborated* with Capitol Records on two Starbucks jazz CDs."

a. separate   c. work together

b. work apart   d. work alone

QUESTIONS FOR DISCUSSION AND WRITING

Answer the following questions based on your reading of the selection.

1. Did you enjoy this selection? Why or why not? _____

2. Summarize the keys to Starbucks' success. _____

_____

_____

3. Does Starbucks sound like a place you would like to work? Why or why not? _____

▶ Vocabulary: Using the Dictionary

To increase your vocabulary and to ensure your comprehension of what you read, you'll need to keep a dictionary close by. The best dictionaries for college level reading are those that include the word *college* or *collegiate* in their title. For example, *The American Heritage College Dictionary* would be a good reference to have at home.

Most dictionaries contain the following information:

- The spelling and pronunciation of the word, including its syllables and capital letters

- The word's part of speech (noun, verb, adjective, etc.)

- Words made from the main word, including plurals and verb forms

- The different meanings of the word, including special uses

- Synonyms (words that mean the same thing) for the word

- The history of the word

- Labels that identify the word's subject area or level of usage (for example, *slang* or *informal*)

The entry for a word may also contain a sentence that demonstrates the correct usage of the word. In addition, an entry may include antonyms, or words with the opposite meaning.

Copyright © Houghton Mifflin Company. All rights reserved.

1

To use the dictionary effectively, you must understand how to locate a word and how to read the entry for that word once you find it.

Guide Words

All dictionaries list words in alphabetical order, which helps you find a word quickly. Another feature that helps you locate a particular word is the two **guide words** at the top of the page. The first guide word identifies the first word listed on that page. The second guide word tells you the last word on the page. Refer to Figure 1.2 to see an example of a dictionary page with guide words. If you want to find the word *cobblestone*, for example, you'd know to look for it on the page labeled with the guide words *coarse* and *coca* because the first three letters of *cobblestone, cob*, come between *coa* and *coc*.

But what do you do if you're not sure how to spell a word you need to find? In that case, you'll have to try different possibilities based on the sound of the word. For example, let's say you were looking for the word *quay*, which means a wharf or dock. This is a tough one because the word sounds like *kay* and its letter *u* is silent. The beginning sound could be a *k*, a *c*, or a *q*. The long *a* sound could be spelled *a, ay, ey, uay,* or *eigh*. So you would try different combinations of these sounds until you found the right spelling. You could also try typing your best guess into a word processing program. Many of them include spell checkers that suggest other alternatives when you misspell a word.

Understanding a Dictionary Entry

Every dictionary includes a guide at the front of the book that explains how to read the entries. This guide explains the abbreviations, symbols, and organization of meanings, so you may need to consult it to know how to decipher the information. Various dictionaries differ in these details. However, they all usually contain certain types of standard information, as follows.

The main entry.   Each word in a dictionary appears in bold print with dots dividing its syllables. This word is correctly spelled, of course, and any alternative spellings for the word follow.

Pronunciation key.   Usually in parentheses following the main entry, the word's pronunciation is represented with symbols, letters, and other marks. The guide at the front of the dictionary will provide a list of the corresponding sounds for each letter or symbol. For example, the symbol ∂ is pronounced like "uh." The accent mark shows you what syllable to stress when you say the word. For example, the pronunciation key for the word *coaxial* on the sample dictionary page in Figure 1.2 tells you to emphasize the second syllable when you say the word.

Copyright © Houghton Mifflin Company. All rights reserved.

History of Word

Main Entries

Meaning

Pronunciation Key

Part of Speech

Guide Words

co-, co- + *artāre*, to compress (< *artus*, tight, confined; see ar-*).] — **co'arc•ta'tion** *n.*

coarse (kôrs, kōrs) *adj.* **coars•er, coars•est. 1.** Of low, common, or inferior quality. **2.a.** Lacking in delicacy or refinement. **b.** Vulgar or indecent. **3.** Consisting of large particles; not fine in texture. **4.** Rough, esp. to the touch: *a coarse tweed.* [ME *cors,* prob. < *course,* custom. See COURSE.] — **coarse'ly** *adv.* — **coars'en** *v.* — **coarse'ness** *n.*

coarse-grained (kôrs'grānd', kōrs'-) *adj.* **1.** Having a rough, coarse texture. **2.** Not refined; indelicate and crude.

coast (kōst) *n.* **1.a.** Land next to the sea; the seashore. **b. Coast.** The Pacific Coast of the United States. **2.** A hill or other slope down which one may coast. **3.** The act of sliding or coasting; slide. **4.** *Obsolete.* The frontier or border of a country. — *v.* **coast'ed, coast'ing, coasts.** — *intr.* **1.a.** To slide down an incline through the effect of gravity. **b.** To move effortlessly and smoothly. See Syns at **slide. 2.** To move without further use of propelling power. **3.** To act or move aimlessly or with little effort. **4.** *Naut.* To sail near or along a coast. — *tr. Naut.* To sail or move along the coast or border of. [ME *coste* < OFr. < Lat. *costa,* side. See kost-*.] — **coast'al** (kō'stəl) *adj.*

coast•er (kō'stər) *n.* **1.** One that coasts, as: **a.** One who acts in an aimless manner. **b.** A sled or toboggan. **c.** One who rides a sled or toboggan. **2.** *Naut.* A vessel engaged in coastal trade. **3.** A roller coaster. **4.a.** A disk, plate, or small mat placed under a bottle, pitcher, or drinking glass to protect the surface beneath. **b.** A small tray, often on wheels, for passing something around a table. **5.** A resident of a coastal region.

coaster brake *n.* A brake and clutch on the rear wheel and drive mechanism of a bicycle operated through reverse pressure on the pedals.

coast guard also **Coast Guard** *n.* **1.** The branch of a nation's armed forces responsible for coastal defense, protection of life and property at sea, and enforcement of customs, immigration, and navigation laws. **2.** A coast guard member.

coast•guards•man (kōst'gärdz'mən) *n.* A member of a coast guard.

coast•land (kōst'lānd') *n.* The land along a coast.

coast•line (kōst'līn') *n.* The shape or boundary of a coast.

Coast Mountains. A range of W British Columbia, Canada, and SE AK extending c. 1,609 km (1,000 mi) parallel to the Pacific coast and rising to 3,996.7 m (13,104 ft).

Coast Ranges. A series of mountain ranges of extreme W North America extending from SE AK to Baja California along the coastline of the Pacific Ocean.

Coast Salish *n.* The Salish-speaking Native American peoples inhabiting the northwest Pacific coast from the Strait of Georgia to southwest Washington.

coast-to-coast (kōst'tə-kōst') *adj.* Reaching, airing, or traveling from one coast to another.

coast•ward (kōst'wərd) *adv. & adj.* Toward or directed toward a coast. — **coast'wards** (-wərdz) *adv.*

coast•wise (kōst'wīz') *adv. & adj.* Along, by way of, or following a coast.

coat (kōt) *n.* **1.a.** A sleeved outer garment extending from the shoulders to the waist or below. **b.** A garment extending to just below the waist and usu. forming the top part of a suit. **2.** A natural outer covering; an integument. **3.** A layer of material covering something else; a coating. — *tr.v.* **coat'ed, coat'ing, coats. 1.** To provide or cover with a coat. **2.** To cover with a layer, as of paint. [ME *cote* < OFr., of Gmc. orig.] — **coat'ed** *adj.*

coat•dress (kōt'drĕs') *n.* A dress that buttons up the front and is tailored somewhat like a coat.

co•a•ti (kō-ä'tē) *n.* Any of four species of mammals of the genera *Nasua* or *Nasuella* of South and Central America and the southwest United States, related to the raccoon but having a longer snout and tail. [Sp. and Port. *coati* < Tupi : *cua,* belt + *tim,* nose.]

co•a•ti•mun•di also **co•a•ti•mon•di** (kō-ä'tē-mŭn'dē) *n.* A coati. [Poss. Tupi *coati* + *mundé,* animal trap.]

coat•ing (kō'tĭng) *n.* **1.** A layer of a substance spread over a surface for protection or decoration; a covering layer. **2.** Cloth for making coats.

coat of arms *n., pl.* **coats of arms.** *Her.* **1.** A tabard or surcoat blazoned with bearings. **2.a.** An arrangement of bearings, usu. depicted on and around a shield, that indicates ancestry and distinctions. **b.** A representation of bearings.

coat of mail *n., pl.* **coats of mail.** An armored coat made of chain mail, interlinked rings, or overlapping metal plates; a hauberk.

coat•room (kōt'rōōm', -rŏōm') *n.* See **cloakroom** 1.

coat•tail (kōt'tāl') *n.* **1.** The loose back part of a coat that hangs below the waist. **2.** coattails. The skirts of a formal or dress coat. — *idioms.* **on (someone's) coattails.** With the assistance of another. **on the coattails of. 1.** As a result of the success of another. **2.** Immediately following or as a direct result of.

coat tree *n.* See **clothes tree.**

co•au•thor or **co-au•thor** (kō-ô'thər) *n.* A collaborating or joint author. — **co•au'thor** *v.*

---

coax¹ (kōks) *v.* **coaxed, coax•ing, coax•es.** — *tr.* **1.** To persuade or try to persuade by pleading or flattery; cajole. **2.** To obtain by persistent persuasion. **3.** *Obsolete.* To caress; fondle. — *intr.* To use persuasion or inducement. [Obsolete *cokes,* to fool < *cokes,* fool.] — **coax'er** *n.*

co•ax² (kō'ăks, kō-ăks') *n. Informal.* A coaxial cable.

co•ax•i•al (kō-ăk'sē-əl) *adj.* Having or mounted on a common axis.

coaxial cable *n.* A cable consisting of a conducting metal tube enclosing and insulated from a central conducting core, used for transmitting high-frequency signals.

cob (kŏb) *n.* **1.** A corncob. **2.** A male swan. **3.** A thickset, stocky, short-legged horse. **4.** A small lump or mass, as of coal. **5.** A mixture of clay and straw used as a building material. [Prob. < obsolete *cob,* round object, head, testicle.]

co•bai•a•min (kō-băl'ə-mĭn) also **co•bai•a•mine** (-mēn') *n.* See **vitamin B₁₂.** [COBAL(T) + (VIT)AMIN.]

co•balt (kō'bôlt') *n. Symbol* **Co** A metallic element, used chiefly for magnetic alloys and high-temperature alloys and in the form of its salts for blue glass and ceramic pigments. Atomic number 27; atomic weight 58.9332; melting point 1,495°C; boiling point 2,900°C; specific gravity 8.9; valence 2, 3. See table at **element.** [Ger. *Kobalt* < MHGer. *kobolt,* goblin (from the trouble it gave silver miners).]

cobalt 60 *n.* A radioactive isotope of cobalt with mass number 60, used in radiotherapy, metallurgy, and materials testing.

cobalt blue *n.* **1.** A blue to green pigment consisting of a variable mixture of cobalt oxide and alumina. **2.** *Color.* A moderate to deep vivid blue or strong greenish blue.

co•balt•ic (kō-bôl'tĭk) *adj.* Of or containing cobalt, esp. with valence 3.

co•balt•ite (kō-bôl'tīt') also **co•balt•ine** (-tēn') *n.* A rare mineral, cobalt sulfarsenide, CoAsS, that is a cobalt ore.

co•balt•ous (kō-bôl'təs) *adj.* Of or containing cobalt, esp. with valence 2.

Cobb (kŏb), *Tyrus ("Ty") Raymond.* 1886–1961. Amer. baseball player and manager who was the first player elected to the National Baseball Hall of Fame (1936).

Cob•bett (kŏb'ĭt), *William.* 1763?–1835. British journalist noted for his essays on the deterioration of rural life brought about by the Industrial Revolution.

cob•ble¹ (kŏb'əl) *n.* **1.** A cobblestone. **2.** *Geol.* A rock fragment between 64 and 256 millimeters in diameter, esp. a naturally rounded one. **3.** cobbles. See **cob coal.** — *tr.v.* **-bled, -bling, -bles.** To pave with cobblestones.

cob•ble² (kŏb'əl) *tr.v.* **-bled, -bling, -bles. 1.** To make or mend (boots or shoes). **2.** To put together clumsily; bungle.

cob•bler¹ (kŏb'lər) *n.* **1.** One that mends or makes boots and shoes. **2.** *Archaic.* One who is clumsy at work; a bungler. [ME *cobeler.*]

cob•bler² (kŏb'lər) *n.* **1.** A deep-dish fruit pie with a thick top crust. **2.** An iced drink made of wine or liqueur, sugar, and citrus fruit. [?]

cob•ble•stone (kŏb'əl-stŏn') *n.* A naturally rounded paving stone. [ME *cobelston* : obsolete *cobel,* prob. dim. of *cob,* round object; see COB + ME *ston, stone,* stone; see STONE.]

cob coal *n.* Coal in rounded lumps of various sizes.

Cob•den (kŏb'dən), *Richard.* 1804–65. British politician who was a leading supporter of free trade.

co•bel•lig•er•ent (kō'bə-lĭj'ər-ənt) *n.* One, such as a nation, that assists another or others in waging war.

Cobh (kōv). An urban district of S Ireland on Cork Harbor; called Queenstown from 1849 to 1922. Pop. 6,587.

co•bi•a (kō'bē-ə) *n.* A large food and game fish (*Rachycentron canadum*) of tropical and subtropical seas. [Origin unknown.]

Co•blenz (kō'blĕnts'). See **Koblenz.**

cob•nut (kŏb'nŭt') *n.* **1.** The large edible nut of a cultivated variety of hazel. **2.** The plant bearing this fruit.

CO•BOL or **Co•bol** (kō'bôl') *n. Comp. Sci.* A programming language based on English words and phrases, used for business applications. [Co(mmon) B(usiness-)O(riented) L(anguage).]

co•bra (kō'brə) *n.* **1.** Any of several venomous snakes, esp. of the genus *Naja,* that are native to Asia and Africa and capable of expanding the skin of the neck to form a flattened hood. **2.** Leather made from the skin of one of these snakes. [Short for Port. *cobra (de capello),* snake (with a hood) < Lat. *colubra,* fem. of *coluber.*]

Co•burg (kō'bûrg'). A city of central Germany N of Nuremberg; first mentioned in the 11th cent. Pop. 44,239.

cob•web (kŏb'wĕb') *n.* **1.a.** The web spun by a spider to catch its prey. **b.** A single thread of a cobweb. **2.** Something resembling a cobweb. **3.** An intricate plot; a snare. **4.** cobwebs. Confusion; disorder. — *tr.v.* **-webbed, -web•bing, -webs.** To cover with or as if with cobwebs. [ME *coppeweb* : *coppe,* spider (short for *attercoppe* < OE *āttercoppe* : *ātor,* poison + *copp,* head) + *web,* web; see WEB.]

co•ca (kō'kə) *n.* **1.** Any of certain Andean evergreen shrubs or small trees of the genus *Erythroxylum,* esp. *E. coca,* whose leaves contain cocaine and other alkaloids. **2.** The dried leaves of such a plant, used for extraction of cocaine and other alkaloids. [Sp. < Quechua *kúka.*]

cobblestone
Acorn Street on Beacon Hill, Boston

cobra
Indian cobra
Naja naja

ă pat	oi boy
ā pay	ou out
âr care	ŏŏ took
ä father	ōŏ boot
ĕ pet	ŭ cut
ē be	ûr urge
ĭ pit	th thin
ī pie	th this
îr pier	hw which
ŏ pot	zh vision
ō toe	ə about,
ô paw	item

Stress marks:
' (primary);
' (secondary); as in
dictionary (dĭk'shə-nĕr'ē)

Figure 1.2   Dictionary Page

From *The American Heritage College Dictionary,* 3rd ed. Boston: Houghton Mifflin, 1993, 267. Copyright © 1993 by Houghton Mifflin Company. Reproduced by permission.

Copyright © Houghton Mifflin Company. All rights reserved.

Copyright © Houghton Mifflin Company. All rights reserved.

The part of speech. The next part of the entry is an abbreviation that identifies the word's part of speech. *N.* means noun, *v.* means verb, *adj.* stands for adjective, and so on. Refer to the list of abbreviations in the guide at the front of the dictionary to find out what other abbreviations mean.

The meanings of the word. The different meanings of a word are divided first according to their part of speech. All of the meanings related to a particular part of speech are grouped together. For example, the word *contact* can function as both a noun and a verb. All of its noun meanings appear first, followed by all of its verb meanings. Dictionaries order each set of meanings in different ways, usually from most common to least common or from oldest to newest. Different senses, or shades of meaning, are numbered. Following the list of meanings, the dictionary may provide synonyms and/or antonyms for the word.

The history of the word. Some dictionaries provide information about the origin of a word. This history usually includes the word's language of origin, along with its various evolutions.

Vocabulary Exercise 1

Put these words in alphabetical order.

oleander	_____
omelet	_____
once	_____
olive	_____
omen	_____
omnivore	_____
omega	_____
okra	_____

Vocabulary Exercise 2

Beneath each set of guide words, circle each word that would appear on the same page labeled with those guide words.

1. **playbook / pledge**

please	play	plaything
plead	pledger	plenary

2. **scamper / scarcely**

scar	scant	scarce
scarcity	scamp	scarecrow

3. **cellophane / census**

cello	cent	cement
cellular	censure	cell

4. **infantryman / infinitive**

infect	infinity	induction
infield	infer	infant

5. **photobiology / photophobia**

photocopy	photophobic	photon
photoactive	photograph	photolysis

Vocabulary Exercise 3

Write your answers to the following questions on the blanks provided.

1. What is the plural of *shelf*? _____

2. How many different parts of speech can the word *right* be? _____

   _____

3. What is a synonym for the word *ridicule*? _____

4. What language does the word *tattoo* come from? _____

5. How many different pronunciations does your dictionary provide for the word *harass*? _____

6. Does the verb *slough* rhyme with *tough* or *plow* or *flew*? _____

7. How many syllables does the word *schizophrenia* contain? _____

Vocabulary Exercise 4

On the blank following each sentence, write the correct meaning for the italicized word.

Copyright © Houghton Mifflin Company. All rights reserved.

1. The company president presented her with a *plaque* to recognize her twenty years of service.

   Definition: _____

2. A buildup of *plaque* within the arteries can cause a heart attack.

   Definition: _____

3. He won first prize for his science *project*, a study of bumblebees in a zero-gravity environment.

   Definition: _____

4. A ventriloquist *projects* his voice so the dummy appears to talk.

   Definition: _____

5. During her vacations at the beach, she was *content*.

   Definition: _____

6. The *content* of late night television shows is not appropriate for young children.

   Definition: _____

Copyright © Houghton Mifflin Company. All rights reserved.

1

Name _____ Date _____

POST-TEST 1

1. A dislike for reading often arises from undeveloped reading skills.

    a. true   b. false

2. Good reading skills are critical to success in college.

    a. true   b. false

3. Reading is actually a collection of different mental skills.

    a. true   b. false

4. A negative attitude about reading will not affect reading comprehension.

    a. true   b. false

5. You cannot understand or retain information unless you read with concentration.

    a. true   b. false

6. Thinking about your plans for the weekend while you're trying to read is an example of an external distraction.

    a. true   b. false

7. When you visualize, you pay extra attention to the visuals (such as graphs, charts, and photos) in a text.

    a. true   b. false

8. To improve memory, a reader can associate new information with what he or she already knows.

    a. true   b. false

9. Analysis is one type of logical thought.

    a. true   b. false

10. Reading strategies are techniques you use when you read.

    a. true   b. false

Copyright © Houghton Mifflin Company. All rights reserved.

For additional tests, see the Test Bank.

1

POST-TEST 2

Review the passage from a textbook below and answer the questions that follow.

1   In this period of extreme stress occurred an outbreak of witchcraft accusations in Salem Village (now Danvers), Massachusetts. Like their contemporaries elsewhere, seventeenth-century New Englanders believed in the existence of witches, whose evil powers came from the Devil. If people could not find other explanations for their troubles, they tended to suspect they were bewitched. Before 1689, 103 New Englanders, most of them middle-aged women, had been charged with practicing witchcraft, chiefly by neighbors who attributed their misfortunes to the suspected witch. Only a few of the accused were convicted, and fewer still were executed. Most such incidents were isolated; nothing else in New England's history came close to matching the Salem Village cataclysm.

2   The crisis began in early 1692 when a group of girls and young women accused some older female neighbors of having bewitched them. Before the hysteria spent itself ten months later, nineteen people (including several men, most of them related to convicted female witches) were hanged; one was pressed to death with heavy stones, and more than 100 persons were jailed. Historians have proposed various explanations for this puzzling episode, but to be understood it must be seen in the context of political and legal disorder, Indian war, and religious and economic crisis. Puritan* New Englanders must have felt as though their entire world was collapsing. At the very least they could have had no sense of security about their future.

3   Nowhere was that more true than in Salem Village, a farming town torn between old and new styles of life because of its position on the edge of the bustling port of Salem. And no residents of the village had more reason to feel insecure than those who issued the first accusations. Many of them had been orphaned in the recent Indian attacks on Maine; they were living in Salem Village as domestic servants. Their involvement with witchcraft began as an experiment with fortune-telling as a means of foreseeing their futures, in particular the identities of their eventual husbands. As the most powerless people in a town apparently powerless to direct its fate, they offered their fellow New Englanders a compelling explanation for the seemingly endless chain of troubles afflicting them: their province was under direct attack from the Devil and his legion of witches. Accordingly, it is not so much the number of witchcraft prosecutions that seems surprising but rather their abrupt cessation in the fall of 1692.

4   There were three reasons for the rapid end to the crisis. First, the accusers grew too bold. When they began to charge some of the colony's most distin-

*Protestant religious group

Copyright © Houghton Mifflin Company. All rights reserved.

1

guished and respected residents with being in league with the Devil, members of the ruling elite began to doubt their veracity. Second, the colony's ministers, led by Increase Mather, formally expressed strong reservations about the validity of the spectral evidence used against most of the accused. Third, the implementation of the new royal charter ended the worst period of political uncertainty, eliminating a major source of stress. King William's War continued, but, although the Puritans were not entirely pleased with the new charter, at least order had formally been restored.*

1. Seventeenth-century people blamed witches for

   a. the existence of the Devil   c. their misfortunes

   b. women's premature aging   d. King William's War

2. The people accused of witchcraft in Salem Village were witches.

   a. true   b. false

3. Which of the following is NOT true about those who accused others of practicing witchcraft?

   a. Many experimented with fortune-telling.

   b. Many were orphans.

   c. Many were the town's most powerful people.

   d. They offered an explanation for New Englanders' troubles.

4. Which of the following is a possible reason for the witchcraft hysteria in Salem Village?

   a. New Englanders felt like their world was collapsing.

   b. Elite New Englanders wanted to rid their village of troublemakers.

   c. Those accused of being witches were plotting to take over the town's government.

   d. The accusers were tired of working as farmers.

5. Which of the following is NOT a reason for the end of the Salem crisis?

   a. The accusers began targeting some of the village's most respected residents.

   b. A new royal charter ended the stress of political uncertainty.

   c. Ministers began to doubt the evidence offered by the accusers.

   d. Most of the male townspeople had to go fight in King William's War.

* Adapted from Mary Beth Norton et al., *A People and a Nation,* Vol. I, 5th ed., Boston: Houghton Mifflin, 1998, 86–87.

Copyright © Houghton Mifflin Company. All rights reserved.

1

Read the memo below and answer the questions that follow.

TO: All Employees

FROM: Dan Rogers

DATE: March 15, 20xx

SUBJECT: Proper Lifting Techniques

In the past three months, our company has seen a 60 percent increase in on-the-job back injuries. These accidents cost thousands of dollars in worker's compensation claims each year. Even worse, though, a back injury can cause long-term disability. Someone who hurts his or her back may never be able to return to work or handle simple, everyday tasks like combing hair or picking up a baby. So, please review the proper procedures for picking up heavy objects, both at work and at home. These techniques will significantly reduce your risk of experiencing back strain.

- Plan ahead what you want to do and don't be in a hurry. Position yourself close to the object you want to lift. Separate your feet shoulder-width apart to give yourself a solid base of support. Bend at the knees. Tighten your stomach muscles as you stand up. Don't try to lift by yourself an object that is too heavy or is an awkward shape. Get help.

- To lift a very light object from the floor, such as a piece of paper, lean over the object, slightly bend one knee and extend the other leg behind you. Hold on to a nearby chair or table for support as you reach down to the object.

- Whether you're lifting a heavy laundry basket or a heavy box on the job, remember to get close to the object, bend at the knees and lift with your leg muscles. Do not bend at your waist. When lifting luggage, stand alongside the luggage, bend at your knees, grasp the handle, and straighten up.

- While you are holding the object, keep your knees slightly bent to maintain your balance. If you have to move the object to one side, avoid twisting your body. Point your toes in the direction you want to move and pivot in that direction. Keep the object close to you when moving.

- If you must place an object on a shelf, move as close as possible to the shelf. Spread your feet in a wide stance, positioning one foot in front of the other, to give you a solid base of support. Do not lean forward and do not fully extend your arms while holding the object in your hands.

Copyright © Houghton Mifflin Company. All rights reserved.

Copyright © Houghton Mifflin Company. All rights reserved.

1

- If the shelf is chest high, move close to the shelf and place your feet apart and one foot forward. Lift the object chest high, keep your elbows at your side and position your hands so you can push the object up and onto the shelf. Remember to tighten your stomach muscles before lifting.

- When sitting, keep your back in a normal, slightly arched position. Make sure your chair supports your lower back. Keep your head and shoulders erect. Make sure your working surface is at the proper height so you don't have to lean forward.

- Once an hour, if possible, stand and stretch. Place your hands on your lower back and gently arch backward.

Following these procedures will help protect you from a costly and painful injury. Please call my office at extension 613 if you have any questions about this information.*

6. Which of the following is NOT a reason (according to this memo) to protect yourself from back injury?

   a. It costs your company money.

   b. It can prevent you from being able to work again.

   c. It can prevent you from being able to do simple, everyday activities.

   d. It can result in an addiction to painkilling drugs.

7. To lift a light object from the floor, you should lean over the object, bend one knee, and

   a. stretch one arm high into the air

   b. stretch your other leg out behind you

   c. lower the other knee to the floor

   d. bend at the waist

8. When lifting a heavy object, you should never

   a. bend your knees   c. bend at the waist

   b. lift with your leg muscles   d. get close to the object

9. If you sit all day, what should you try to do once every hour?

   a. lift something heavy   c. tighten your stomach muscles

   b. stand and stretch   d. pivot from side to side

* Adapted from "Preventing Back Pain at Work and at Home," American Academy of Orthopaedic Surgeons Web site, http://orthoinfo.aaos.org. Reprinted with permission.

Read the review of a film below and answer the questions that follow.

Scare the Heck Out of *Shrek*?

A "Monster"-size race for the first animated-feature Oscar

1 Shoulder to shoulder, they stride in heroic slow motion into the hangarlike factory, backlit like the space cowboys in *The Right Stuff*. Except these fierce, determined guys look weird. One of them is eight feet tall with turquoise and purple fur; another is an eight-legged reptile. These are the Scarers, the elite monsters who keep the city of Monstropolis running. Every night these astronauts of fear transport themselves through magical doors into the closets of human kids, reaching into their venerable bag of tricks to generate shrieks of terror. For, you see, the power source that keeps the lights burning in the land of the monsters is children's screams, captured in canisters. Trouble is, kids today don't scare so easily. Which has left Monstropolis facing an energy crisis, rolling blackouts predicted, run the headlines in the city's papers.

2 This is the fiendishly clever premise of *Monsters, Inc.*, the fourth computer-animated feature brought to life by Pixar, the wizards behind the two *Toy Story*s and *A Bug's Life*. These are tough acts to follow: three instant classics funny and sophisticated enough to equally charm adults and children. If *Monsters, Inc.* doesn't quite reach the same heights (it's the only one not directed by John Lasseter), it's still a terrific piece of work: smart, inventive, and executed with state-of-the-art finesse.

3 That turquoise and purple beast goes by the name of Sulley (voiced by John Goodman). He's the Michael Jordan of fearmongers, with the best stats in the business. This sticks in the reptilian craw of his rival Randall Boggs (Steve Buscemi), who'll do anything to steal his crown. Each of these working stiffs has a scare assistant, a combination of coach and corner man. Sulley's is his best friend, Mike Wazowski (Billy Crystal), a scrappy, fast-talking, green ovoid with a single giant eyeball. It's amazing how many expressions these animators can wrangle from one prize pupil.

4 The monsters' little secret is that they are actually terrified of kids: believing that children are toxic, they live in fear of being touched by one of the little devils. When one of the Scarers returns to the factory with a child's sock stuck on its fur, pandemonium sets in. Monsters protected by sterile uniforms rush in to "decontaminate" the area. *Monsters, Inc.* was conceived, of course, long before our newspapers were filled with images of guys in spacesuits searching for signs of anthrax, but these scenes now carry an unintended load of dread. When a monster-shrink, losing his cool, appears on the Monstropolis TV news and screams "It's time to panic!" at least some in the audience may be more inclined to squirm than laugh. But not to worry: the good-natured *Monsters, Inc.* is decidedly kid-friendly. With the exception of the slimy Randall, these odd-

Copyright © Houghton Mifflin Company. All rights reserved.

ball creatures are all softies, and none more so than the teddy-bearish Sulley, whose fearsome talents we have to take on faith.

5 The crisis that fuels the plot is Sulley's discovery of an enemy in their midst: Boo, a toddler from the human world, slips through a portal into Monstropolis, terrifying Sulley and Mike, who must figure out how to get her back home without anyone's discovering her. Boo has no fear of the gargoyles who surround her—she gurgles with preverbal delight at these funny-looking creatures. (Perhaps she's seen *Men in Black,* whose comic aliens were an obvious inspiration.) The three-year-old's voice is supplied by Mary Gibbs, and on the evidence of the hilarious noises director Pete Docter has coaxed out of her, she's got a bright comic future.

6 At first afraid to touch her, Sulley comes to realize she's not toxic at all, and falls in love with the human child. This is sweet, but it does raise questions. If kids really aren't dangerous, why all the fuss? Even the most fanciful of children's tales must have a rigorous inner logic, but there's something fuzzy at the core here. The story line depends on the ironic notion that monsters are afraid of children, but it seriously undercuts itself by revealing that they have nothing to be afraid of. And for a grown-up, Sulley is a rather bland hero: the great thing about Woody and the wonderfully fatuous Buzz Lightyear* was the double edge Pixar was able to work into its leading men. Sulley has little bark and no bite.

7 So Pixar isn't perfect. It's just darn good. *Monsters, Inc.* is first and foremost a pastel-hued treat for the eyes, a menagerie of benign grotesques punctuated by witty visual gags. (The street signs in Monstropolis flash "Stalk. Don't stalk.") In the spectacular chase near the end, we are transported into the factory's "door vault," where all the portals are stored: a dizzying vision that includes more than 5 million closet doors on hundreds of mile-long conveyer belts. These are sights only computer animation can bring to such eye-popping life. This is the first year the Academy will bestow an Oscar for best animated feature film. *Shrek* is the favorite, but the folks at Pixar have come up with a worthy competitor.†

10. According to the author of this review, *Monsters, Inc.* is a

   a. dull movie

   b. movie that's too frightening for children

   c. movie that's too difficult to follow

   d. great movie

* Characters in *Toy Story*
† Adapted from David Ansen, "Scare the Heck Out of *Shrek*?" *Newsweek,* November 5, 2001, 65.
© 2001 Newsweek, Inc. All rights reserved. Reprinted by permission.

Copyright © Houghton Mifflin Company. All rights reserved.

1

11. According to the author of this review, *Monsters, Inc.* is better than *Toy Story* and *A Bug's Life.*

    a. true   b. false

12. According to the author of this review, Sulley is not as interesting a character as Woody and Buzz Lightyear.

    a. true   b. false

13. Does the author of this review believe that *Monsters, Inc.* will win an Oscar?

    a. yes   c. He doesn't reveal his opinion

    b. no

14. The author of this review would advise you
    a. to go see *Monsters, Inc.*   b. not to waste your money on *Monsters, Inc.*

POST-TEST 3

For each of the following reading situations, choose the MAJOR purposes for reading that apply. Select as many as apply.

1. You visit a Web site on the Internet providing information about a company in which you are considering investing.

   a. Gain a general understanding of the ideas or points.

   b. Discover the facts or answer questions.

   c. Memorize the information.

   d. Find information or ideas that prove a point you want to make.

   e. Make a decision based on the information.

2. You read a letter that explains why your auto insurance rates have gone up and how to compare the rates of various insurance companies.

   a. Gain a general understanding of the ideas or points.

   b. Discover the facts or answer questions.

   c. Memorize the information.

   d. Find information or ideas that prove a point you want to make.

   e. Make a decision based on the information.

Copyright © Houghton Mifflin Company. All rights reserved.

1

3. You read the guidelines for selecting employees issued by a company for which you would like to work.

   a. Gain a general understanding of the ideas or points.

   b. Discover the facts or answer questions.

   c. Memorize the information.

   d. Find information or ideas that prove a point you want to make.

   e. Make a decision based on the information.

4. You read your state's driver's license handbook in preparation for taking your driving test.

   a. Gain a general understanding of the ideas or points.

   b. Discover the facts or answer questions.

   c. Memorize the information.

   d. Find information or ideas that prove a point you want to make.

   e. Make a decision based on the information.

5. You read a magazine article to see if it contains statistics that prove a statement you want to make in your research paper.

   a. Gain a general understanding of the ideas or points.

   b. Discover the facts or answer questions.

   c. Memorize the information.

   d. Find information or ideas that prove a point you want to make.

   e. Make a decision based on the information.

Copyright © Houghton Mifflin Company. All rights reserved.

Main Ideas

2

GOALS FOR CHAPTER 2

▶ Describe the characteristics of an effective reading environment.

▶ Define the terms *general* and *specific*.

▶ Order groups of sentences from most general to most specific.

▶ Identify the topic of a paragraph.

▶ Determine the main idea of a paragraph.

▶ Recognize the topic sentence of a paragraph.

▶ Recognize topic sentences in different locations in a paragraph.

READING STRATEGY: Creating an Effective Reading Environment

If you're like most students, you probably read both at home and outside your home: perhaps somewhere on your college campus and maybe even at work during your breaks. Your reading environment can greatly affect your comprehension. So, give some thought to how you can create or select the right reading environments. The right environment allows you to stay alert and to focus all of your concentration on the text, especially when it's a challenging one.

When you're at home, you can usually create effective conditions for reading. You might want to designate a particular place—a desk or table, for example—where you always read. Make sure the place you choose is well lit, and sit in a chair that requires you to sit upright. Reading in a chair that's too soft and comfortable tends to make you sleepy! Keep your active reading tools (pens, highlighter markers, notebook or paper) and a dictionary close at hand.

Before you sit down for a reading session, try to minimize all potential external distractions. Turn off your phone, the television, and the radio. Notify your family members or roommates that you'll be unavailable for a while. If necessary, put a "do not disturb" sign on your door!

Continued

Copyright © Houghton Mifflin Company. All rights reserved.

2

The more interruptions you must deal with while you read, the harder it will be to keep your attention on the task at hand.

Overcoming internal distractions, which are the thoughts, worries, plans, daydreams, and other types of mental "noise" inside your own head, is often even more challenging for readers. However, it's important to develop strategies for dealing with them, too. If you don't, they will inhibit you from concentrating on what you are reading. Internal distractions will also prevent you from absorbing the information you need to learn. You can try to ignore these thoughts, but they will usually continue trying to intrude. So, how do you temporarily silence them so you can devote your full attention to your reading? Instead of fighting them, try focusing completely on these thoughts for a short period of time. For five or ten minutes, allow yourself to sit and think about your job, your finances, your car problems, your boyfriend or girlfriend, the paper you need to write, or whatever is on your mind. Better yet, write these thoughts down. To empty your mind onto a piece of paper, try a free-writing exercise, which involves quickly writing your thoughts on paper without censoring them or worrying about grammar and spelling. If you can't stop thinking about all of the other things you need to do, devote ten minutes to writing a detailed "To Do" list. Giving all of your attention to distracting thoughts will often clear your mind so you can focus on your reading.

If you're reading somewhere other than at home (on your college campus, for instance), it will be more difficult to achieve ideal reading conditions. However, you can still search for places that have the right characteristics. First of all, find a location—such as the library—that is well lit and quiet. Try to sit at an individual study carrel so you can block out external distractions. If no carrels are available, choose a table that's out of the flow of traffic, and sit with your back to others so you're not tempted to watch their comings and goings. If you must read in a more distracting place like your college cafeteria or a bench on the grounds, you might want to get in the habit of carrying a pair of earplugs in your book bag so you can reduce external noise. Finally, don't forget to keep your active reading tools and dictionary with you so you'll have them on hand no matter where you end up reading.

Read and answer the following questions:

1. Where were you when you read this information about creating an effective reading environment? Describe your surroundings.

   <u>living room with my family</u>

Continued

Copyright © Houghton Mifflin Company. All rights reserved.

2

2. Is this the place where you do most of your reading? If not, where do you usually read?

bed room

3. What external distractions pulled your attention from the book as you read?

kids   TV.

4. Could you have done anything to prevent these external distractions from happening?

_____

5. Did you battle any internal distractions as you read? Briefly describe the thoughts that intruded upon your concentration.

_____

6. Based on the information in this section, where could you create the most ideal environment for reading? What objects and/or procedures will you need to create that environment?

_____

To read successfully, you must learn to determine the main idea of a paragraph or longer selection. The **main idea** is the overall point the author is trying to make. The rest of the paragraph or longer selection consists of information or examples that help the reader understand the main point.

What process do you go through to help you figure out the main idea of a selection? Take this pre-test to find out how much you already know about identifying and understanding main ideas.

PRE-TEST

Read the paragraph below and answer the questions that follow.

THE ABCs OF DAILY TO-DOs
(OR WORKING YOUR As OFF)

The advantage of keeping a daily list is that you don't have to remember what to do next. It's on the list. A typical day in the life of a student is full of

Copyright © Houghton Mifflin Company. All rights reserved.

2

separate, often unrelated tasks—reading, attending lectures, reviewing notes, working at a paid job, writing papers, doing special projects, research, errands. It's easy to forget an important job on a busy day. When that job is written down, you don't have to trust your memory.

1. What is the main idea of this paragraph? How do you know? _____
   daily list, because they are saying that
   if you have a list
   _____

2. To figure out the main idea, what part of the selection did you look at first? Why?
   first one because it give you the main idea

What is the main idea of each of the following passages? Write your answers in the spaces provided.

3. Martin Kimeldorf, author of *Portfolio Power*, notes that the word *portfolio* derives from two Latin terms: *port*, which means "to move," and *folio*, which means "papers" or "artifacts." True to these ancient meanings, portfolios are movable collections of papers and artifacts, or work products.

   Main Idea: _Portfolio_
   _____

4. Portfolios are different from résumés. A résumé lists facts, including your interests, skills, work history, and accomplishments. Although a portfolio might include these facts, it can also include tangible objects to verify the facts—anything from transcripts of your grades to a video you produced. Résumés offer facts; portfolios provide artifacts.

   Main Idea: _that Portfolio are different from resume_

5. Photographers, contractors, and designers regularly show portfolios filled with samples of their work. Today, employers and educators increasingly see the portfolio as a tool that's useful for everyone. Some schools require students to create them, and some employers expect to see a portfolio before they'll hire a job applicant.

   Main Idea: _____

6. A well-done portfolio benefits its intended audience. To an instructor, your portfolio gives a rich, detailed picture of what you did to create value from a class. To a potential employer, your portfolio gives observable evidence

Copyright © Houghton Mifflin Company. All rights reserved.

of your skills and achievements. In both cases, a portfolio also documents something more intangible—your levels of energy, passion, and creativity.

Main Idea: _____

7. Portfolios benefit you in specific ways. When you create a portfolio to document what you learned during a class, you review the content of the entire course. When you're creating a portfolio related to your career, you think about the skills you want to develop and ways to showcase those skills. And when you're applying for work, creating a portfolio prepares you for job interviews. Your portfolio can stand out from stacks of letters and résumés and distinguish you from other candidates.

Main idea: _____

General and Specific

Before you practice finding main ideas, it's helpful to learn to distinguish the difference between the terms **general** and **specific.** You must apply these concepts to figure out the relationships of sentences within a paragraph. Understanding these relationships is the first step in improving your comprehension of the author's meaning.

The word *general* means "broad" and "not limited." When we say a word or idea is general, we mean that it includes or refers to many different things in a large category. For example, *weather* is a general word that includes many different types of conditions, including wind, rain, snow, and hail. *Coins* is another general word that refers to a large group of items, including pennies, dimes, nickels, and quarters.

The word *specific* means "definite" or "particular." Specific things or ideas are limited or narrowed in scope, and they refer to one certain something within a larger group. In the previous paragraph, for instance, *wind, rain, snow,* and *hail* are all certain types of weather, so we say they are more specific. *Pepsi, Coca-Cola,* and *RC* are all specific colas. *Math, English,* and *science* are three specific subjects we study in school.

The terms *general* and *specific* are relative. In other words, they depend upon or are connected to the other things with which they are being compared. For example, you would say that *school subject* is a general term and that *math* is one specific subject. However, *math* becomes the more general term when you think of specific kinds of math, such as *algebra, trigonometry,* and *calculus.* Words and concepts, therefore, can change from being general or

Copyright © Houghton Mifflin Company. All rights reserved.

specific, depending on their relationships to other words and concepts. Look at this list:

weather   storm   hurricane

category 4 hurricanes   Hurricane Floyd

The words in this list are arranged from most general to most specific. In other words, each item on the list is more specific than the one above it. The last item, Hurricane Floyd, names one specific storm, so it is the most specific of all.

Exercise 2.1

Put these lists of words in order from most general to most specific.

1. Taurus   car   Ford   machine

_____

2. strawberry   fruit   food   plant

_____

3. subject   science   biology   microbiology

_____

4. hip-hop singer   performer   P. Diddy   singer

_____

5. Kobe Bryant   sports players   basketball players   L.A. Lakers team members

_____

To read well, you will need to be able to recognize the most general idea within a passage. Let's practice that skill by looking at groups of related items in different ways. Can you select the most general word in the list?

mixer   appliances   toaster   blender

Three of the words in the group are specific, and one of the words is the most general. If you chose *appliances* as most general, you are correct. The other three items are specific kinds of appliances.

    Now examine this list and decide how the items are related. Come up with a word that includes all three items in the list.

mouse   rat   hamster

Copyright © Houghton Mifflin Company. All rights reserved.

Did you say *rodent*? The three creatures above are all specific types of rodents. Finally, see if you can think of three specific examples of the phrase:

supernatural occurrences

Some possible answers include *ghosts, monsters,* and *UFOs.*

2

Exercise 2.2

The following groups of words include one general word and three specific words. Circle the most general word in each group.

1. Dance   Ballet   Tap   Modern
2. Hockey   Basketball   Sports   Baseball
3. Running   Jogging   Aerobics   Exercise
4. Roy Rogers McDonald's   Fast Food Restaurants Wendy's
5. Oak   Walnut   Maple   Trees

Exercise 2.3

On the blank following each group, write a general term that includes all of the items in the list.

1. Looking up words   Checking spelling   Reading definitions

   General Idea: _____

2. Hamburgers   Turkey   Ice cream

   General Idea: _____

3. Nurse   Doctor   X-Ray technician

   General idea: _____

4. Pine   Redwood   Weeping willow

   General Idea: _____

5. Attending class   Using a textbook   Taking notes

   General Idea: _____

Copyright © Houghton Mifflin Company. All rights reserved.

2

Exercise 2.4

Fill in the blanks provided with more specific ideas included by the general word.

1. General Idea: Doing laundry

   Specific Ideas: _____

2. General Idea: States in the United States

   Specific Ideas: _____

3. General Idea: Maintaining your car

   Specific Ideas: _____

4. General Idea: U.S. presidents

   Specific Ideas: _____

   _____

5. General Idea: Using e-mail

   Specific Ideas: _____

General and Specific Sentences

Now that you've reviewed how words can be general and specific, you'll be able to see how the sentences that express ideas are also general and specific in relation to each other. Paragraphs are composed of both general and specific sentences. A *general sentence* is one that states the broadest idea in the paragraph. This idea can often be explained or interpreted in a variety of different ways. The *specific sentences* in a paragraph are those that offer explanation or details that help us understand and accept the idea in the general sentence. Specific sentences are essential in helping readers correctly determine the meaning of the general statement.

We saw earlier how the terms *general* and *specific* are relative when applied to words. Sentences within a paragraph, too, are relatively general and specific. For example, read the following three statements:

Dessert is my favorite part of a meal.

I especially love to eat pie.

The after-dinner treat I like most to eat is a slice of warm cherry pie.

Copyright © Houghton Mifflin Company. All rights reserved.

The first sentence states the most general idea, then the second sentence clarifies a specific type of dessert—pie—that the writer enjoys. The third sentence is even more specific because it identifies the particular kind of pie the writer likes most. So, in this group of sentences, each statement is more specific than the one above it.

Exercise 2.5

Put these sentences in order from most general to most specific. Number them 1 to 3 from most general to most specific.

1. __2__ Paris is her favorite destination.

   __1__ Marcy has always loved to travel.

   __3__ She loves to visit Paris landmarks such as the Eiffel Tower and the Louvre.

2. __3__ Fresh, homegrown vegetables are a delicious addition to family meals.

   __2__ You can grow your own food in your back yard.

   __1__ Gardening is a rewarding hobby.

3. __1__ Many people suffer from foot pain.

   __3__ Firemen, nurses, and people in service jobs experience more foot pain than people in other professions.

   __2__ People whose jobs require that they stand for long periods of time have the most foot problems.

4. __3__ Courage, teamwork, and excellence are three of her father's values she celebrates in her book.

   __1__ Sharon Robinson, daughter of baseball great Jackie Robinson, wanted to honor her father and his values.

   __2__ Sharon Robinson published a collection of essays and stories about nine values embraced by her father.

5. __1__ If you're looking for news and information, you can get it on the World Wide Web.

   __3__ *U.S. News and World Report* posts its articles on its Web site.

   __2__ Twenty-three of the fifty largest U.S. magazines are available online.*

---

* Adapted from Joe Saltzman, "Too Much Information, Too Little Time," *USA Today,* September 1997, 67.

Copyright © Houghton Mifflin Company. All rights reserved.

2

Paragraphs are combinations of sentences that all work together to develop a main idea. So, sorting out the general and specific relationships among related sentences is the first step toward understanding what you read. Look at the three sentences below and try to identify the one that is the most general.

Surveys show that adults typically watch four hours of TV per day.

Americans watch too much television.

The average American school child watches about 28 hours of TV per week.

Did you choose the second sentence as most general? The other two sentences offer specific facts—the number of hours of TV adults and children watch—that help explain the idea of "too much television."

Now read these three specific sentences:

High school dropouts are 50 percent more likely than high school graduates to go on welfare.

Less than 50 percent of high school dropouts find jobs when they leave school.

When they do find jobs, high school dropouts earn 60 percent less income than high school graduates.

How could you state the general idea these three sentences explain or support? All three are examples of the negative effects of dropping out of high school, so the sentence "Dropping out of high school has several negative consequences" would be an accurate statement of the general idea they develop.

Finally, read this general sentence:

In many ways, college is tougher than high school.

What three specific sentences could you write to explain this sentence? Some possibilities include:

The course work is more difficult.

The instructors are more demanding.

The learning pace is much faster.

Exercise 2.6

The following groups of sentences include one general sentence and three specific sentences. Label each sentence with either a G for *general* or an S for *specific*.

1. __✓__ I enjoy eating fruit.

   _____ I put strawberries in my cereal.

Copyright © Houghton Mifflin Company. All rights reserved.

_____ I eat blueberry topping on my ice cream.

_____ I enjoy peach pancakes.

2. _____ In Florida, there has been much damage to homes and businesses as a result of hurricanes.

___✓__ Hurricanes can be very dangerous.

_____ Hurricane Floyd wiped out much of the beach area where I live.

_____ Many people died during Hurricane Andrew.

3. _____ She has a television show that millions of people watch.

_____ Her magazine, _O,_ is a great success.

___✓__ Oprah Winfrey is a very successful businesswoman and entertainer.

_____ She made a movie called _Beloved,_ in which she starred.

4. _____ Many town pools have rules requiring the use of "water wings" on children under five.

___✓__ There are safety standards at many public swimming areas to prevent drownings.

_____ The lake in my town requires that a lifeguard be on duty until dark.

_____ The local YMCA requires that swimmers wait 30 minutes after eating before getting back in the pool to avoid getting cramps.

5. ___✓__ For most college graduates working in an office from 9–5 is hard to get used to.

___✓__ Many college graduates find it difficult to conform to others' schedules.

_____ A lot of new graduates are used to sleeping very late and staying up past midnight.

_____ Many recent graduates do not like having to report to a boss after being on their own for four years.

6. _____ Most student drivers have a difficult time merging onto highways and into traffic.

_____ For a new driver changing lanes during rush hour is very hard to do.

___✓__ Learning to drive can be very difficult.

_____ Parking was the hardest part for me when I was a new driver.

Copyright © Houghton Mifflin Company. All rights reserved.

7. _____ My grandmother's apple pie won awards at county fairs.

   __✓__ My grandmother was a great cook.

   _____ Grandma Rose studied cooking at a very famous cooking school.

   _____ A soup manufacturer tried to buy her recipe for chicken soup.

8. _____ Running tones your muscles.

   _____ Running two times a week increases the number of calories burned by 10 percent.

   __✓__ Running is the best form of exercise.

   _____ When I run, I feel great.

9. _____ Janet meets a lot of new people when she walks her dog.

   __✓__ Janet enjoys walking her dog.

   _____ When Janet walks her dog, she gets to spend time outdoors.

   _____ Janet gets a lot of exercise when she walks her dog.

10. __✓__ My house needs to be painted.

    _____ The paint is chipping off the side of my house by the driveway.

    _____ Mold is growing underneath the shingles from dirt and rain.

    _____ I don't like the color of my house.

Exercise 2.7

Read the three specific sentences given. Then, in the list that follows them, circle the general sentence best supported by those three specific sentences.

1. Women and minorities make up the majority of people applying to colleges.

   Prior to 1980, the majority of college applications came from white men.

   Fewer men are applying to colleges because they are going directly into the work force.

   General Sentences:

   a. There is a change in the types of people who are applying to college.
   b. More women go to college than before.
   c. Prior to 1980, fewer women and minorities applied to college.

Copyright © Houghton Mifflin Company. All rights reserved.

2. Every American uses 80 to 100 gallons of water a day.

   U.S. citizens spend more than $5 million a year on bottled water.

   Many Americans frequently visit spas for relaxing and revitalizing water treatments.*

   General Sentences:
   a. Water can heal mental and physical ailments.
   b. Americans use too much water.
   c. Water is an important part of American life.

3. Flextime saves businesses money because they don't need as much office space.

   Flextime allows workers to more effectively balance their career schedules and personal lives.

   Flextime helps businesses recruit the best workers and keep them from leaving.†

   General Sentences:
   a. Flextime can work only with clear-cut guidelines for employees.
   b. Flextime, or flexible hours, offers several advantages.
   c. Flextime and telecommuting are becoming more widespread in American companies.

4. Composting involves making use of kitchen, lawn, and garden waste that would otherwise go to a landfill.

   Putting grass clippings in your compost heap cuts down on the use of plastic bags used for gardening.

   As the chemicals in the materials react and start to decompose, the compost heats up and yields rich, dark earth, perfect for fertilizing a garden.‡

   General Sentences:
   a. Composting is one of the best things you can do for your garden and for the environment.
   b. Composting is best done in the summer when it is hot.
   c. Composting is easy.

---

* Adapted from Marisa Fox, "Water Cures," *O* Magazine, June 2001, 171.

† Adapted from "Flextime Programs Gain Popularity," *USA Today Newsview,* April 1998, 5.

‡ Adapted from "Ask Martha," *New York Times,* June 2, 2001, 3e.

Copyright © Houghton Mifflin Company. All rights reserved.

2

5. *Riverdance,* a Broadway show that showcases Irish dance and music, is a big hit.

The Chieftains, an Irish group that has been playing together for many years, is suddenly selling more CDs than ever before.

Irish dancing is increasing in popularity with children enrolling in Irish step-dance classes.

General Sentences:

a. Irish culture is popular in other countries.
b. Irish culture, especially dance and music, is very popular now.
c. Many people take Irish dancing lessons.

Exercise 2.8

Read the general sentence given and then choose three of the sentences from the list that best explain or support that statement:

1. General Sentence: Stephen Huneck is fast becoming a folk artist of cult status in America, mostly because of his smile-provoking art involving dogs.*

Specific Sentences:

a. Stephen Huneck has many dogs.
b. One of his dogs is Sally, a black Labrador.
c. He has created woodcut prints involving dogs.
d. One of his sculptures shows dogs eating ice cream cones.
e. Huneck's dining room table is held up by four carved dogs.
f. Some of his sculptures show dogs with their heads sticking out of car windows.

2. General Sentence: A growing number of researchers say it is a good idea to let families have easier access to patients during emergency treatment in hospitals.†

Specific Sentences:

a. Family members can comfort patients in a way no health-care provider can.
b. When the patient is less scared and is surrounded by family members, procedures go more smoothly.
c. Health decisions are left to the physician in charge.
d. Few hospitals have formal rules on this issue.
e. This way of treating emergency room patients is most effective when the patient is a child and a parent can stay with him or her during treatment.
f. One physician thinks that this should be done on a case-by-case basis.

* Adapted from Craig Wilson, "Art and Religion, Gone to the Dogs," *USA Today,* June 5, 2001, Section D, Life.

† Adapted from Pat Wingert, "Family Notes," *Newsweek,* June 11, 2001, 60.

Copyright © Houghton Mifflin Company. All rights reserved.

3. General Sentence: Television host Regis Philbin is a very busy man.

   a. His talk show, *Live with Regis and Kelly*, is on five days a week from 9 A.M. to 10 A.M.

   b. Regis Philbin is a graduate of Notre Dame University and discusses his loyalty to the school and its sports teams on his television show.

   c. Regis also hosts the popular game show *Who Wants to Be a Millionaire?* several nights a week on the ABC network.

   d. Regis is married to Joy Philbin and is father of two adult daughters.

   e. Besides his hosting duties on *Live* and the *Millionaire* show, Regis is often seen on David Letterman's show as a guest.

   f. Regis has a house in Connecticut and an apartment in New York City.

4. General Sentence: Stephen King, sometimes called the "master of horror," is considered the most popular fiction writer ever and is loved by his fans.

   a. He has sold more than a billion books since his first one was published.

   b. He published a book after being hit by a car and suffering terrible injuries.

   c. He is a frequent guest on popular talk shows because he is very funny.

   d. His first manuscript was rejected.

   e. Fans line up in front of bookstores in anticipation of the book's publication and buy all copies available on the first day.

   f. He gets bags full of fan mail every day.

5. General Sentence: It is important that children, especially those who can't swim, be supervised by their parents or guardians around pools and bodies of water.

   a. Many children drown every summer because they have not been supervised properly.

   b. Even if children can swim, it is important that a parent be close by in case the children experience cramping in their legs or feet.

   c. Lifeguards should not be expected to supervise everyone's children, especially at a crowded swimming facility.

   d. Some children learn to swim at a very young age.

   e. The ocean is fun to swim in.

   f. Lakes are safer than oceans because there are no waves.

Determining the Topic

Now that you've reviewed the distinction between general and specific, let's look at the most general aspect of a paragraph: its topic. To understand what you read, you must be able to identify the topic, or subject, of a reading

Copyright © Houghton Mifflin Company. All rights reserved.

selection. The **topic** is the person, place, thing, event, or idea that the passage is about, and it is usually expressed in just a word or brief phrase. For example, read this paragraph:

> The Slinky has been a popular toy for over 50 years. The Slinky is available on every continent except Antarctica. Ninety percent of Americans know what this coiled wire toy is. Since 1946, 250 million Slinkys have been sold. Today, both boys and girls still enjoy this inexpensive plaything.

The topic of this paragraph is the Slinky. Every sentence in the paragraph refers to or mentions the Slinky.

To find the topic of a selection, look for the person, place, thing, event, or idea that is repeated again and again.

Exercise 2.9

Read each paragraph and write the correct topic in the space provided.

1. There wasn't a paved road on Cat Island. There wasn't a telephone on Cat Island. There were no stores except for a few petty shops, so my clothes were made out of the cloth of grain sacks. But Cat Island had plenty of paths.*

   Topic: _Cat Island_

2. Nelson Mandela refused to follow the script that said that blacks in South Africa were second-class citizens. For part of the 27 years he was imprisoned, he literally lived in a box—a seven-by-nine-foot cell—yet his spirit could not be contained there. He broke down all the old rules of apartheid and emerged as the man to lead a new South Africa.†

   Topic: _Nelson Mandala_

3. Success in school and in life is largely a matter of cultivating effective habits. The new habit that you choose does not have to make headlines. It can be one simple, small change in behavior. All of the researchers on studying and success in school agree that forming good habits regarding your school work is essential to your success.‡

   Topic: _Success_

---

* From Sidney Poitier, *The Measure of a Man: A Spiritual Autobiography.* San Francisco: Harper-Collins, 2000, 8.

† Adapted from Oprah Winfrey, *O Magazine,* "Set Yourself Free," April 2001, 37.

‡ Adapted from Dave Ellis, *Becoming a Master Student.* Boston: Houghton Mifflin, 2000, 120. Copyright © 2000 by Houghton Mifflin Company. Reprinted with permission.

Copyright © Houghton Mifflin Company. All rights reserved.

2

4. A writing center should have a table with chairs around it, containers of writing tools, and newsprint or unlined paper in various sizes and colors. Children like to experiment with colored felt-tipped pens, crayons, pencils, and chalk for individual chalkboards. Resource materials to encourage children to write include greeting cards, note pads, books and magazines, envelopes, special words related to a unit or holiday, magnetic letters, and the alphabet in upper- and lower-case letters. Writing centers may also contain notice or message boards for the children and teacher to use for exchanging information.*

   Topic: _A writing center_

5. It is said that women gossip more than men do. However, men gossip, too, though they tend to call it "networking." What really differs is the content of their gossip. Men are much more interested in who is up and who is down, an interest that <u>arises</u> from their enjoyment of competitive game playing. Women tend to gossip more about social inclusion and morality. They are more interested in who has merit.†

   Topic: _gossip_

When you are deciding on the topic of a paragraph or passage, make sure your choice is not too *broad* or too *narrow*. A topic that is too broad suggests much more than the paragraph actually offers. A topic that is too narrow does not include everything the paragraph covers. For example, look at the following paragraph:

> Many popular inventions were created by accident. In 1886, a pharmacist trying to create a nerve and brain tonic made a syrup that became Coca-Cola. In 1853, a chef accidentally created potato chips for a restaurant guest who complained that his French fries were too thick. In the 1920s, Yale University students who liked to toss and catch pie plates made by the Frisbie Pie Company accidentally came up with the popular toy known as the Frisbee.

Which of these is the correct topic of the paragraph?

_____ inventions

_____ the invention of Coca-Cola

__✓__ accidental inventions

---

* From Burns et al., *Teaching Reading in Today's Elementary Schools*, 7th ed. Boston: Houghton Mifflin, 1999, 69.

† Adapted from Nigel Nicholson, Ph.D., "The New Word on Gossip," *Psychology Today,* May/June 2001, 44.

Copyright © Houghton Mifflin Company. All rights reserved.

2

If you checked accidental inventions, you're correct. The first topic, inventions, is too broad because it includes all kinds of inventions, including those that were created intentionally. The second topic, the invention of Coca-Cola, is too narrow because the paragraph discusses potato chips and Frisbees, too. Accidental inventions is the right topic because the paragraph gives examples of three different products that were all discovered by accident.

Now read another example:

> Miss America Heather Whitestone overcame many obstacles on her path to the crown. When she was 18 months old, the H influenza virus almost killed her. Although she survived, the illness left her almost totally deaf. During her childhood she spent countless hours in speech therapy. It took her six years to learn to say her last name. She pushed herself to attend a regular high school instead of one for deaf students. She endured her parents' heartbreaking divorce. When she began entering pageants, she won only first runner-up in two Miss Alabama pageants. But she refused to give up and in 1995, she became the first person with a disability to win the Miss America pageant.

Which of the topics below is the correct one?

_____ Miss America pageant

__✓__ Heather Whitestone

__✓__ Heather Whitestone's speech therapy

The first choice, Miss America pageant, is too broad. This paragraph focuses on just one specific winner of that pageant. The last choice, Heather Whitestone's speech therapy, is too narrow because this paragraph also discusses other obstacles she overcame. Therefore, Heather Whitestone is the correct topic. This paragraph describes her difficulties and ultimate triumph over them.

Exercise 2.10

Following each paragraph are three topics. On each blank, label the topic B if it is too broad, N if it is too narrow, and T if it is the correct topic of the paragraph.

1. Route 66 may be the only road where travelers feel compelled to stop, dig up a chunk of cracked pavement, and take it home as a souvenir. The same goes for the road signs along Route 66. Such is the allure of Route 66—America's most famous highway.*

* Adapted from *U.S. News and World Report,* by Linda Kulman, 4/24/00.

Copyright © Houghton Mifflin Company. All rights reserved.

Route 66: _____

Traveling in America: _____

Stealing road signs along Route 66: _____

2. Reciting is saying each fact or idea in your notes out loud, in your own words, and from memory. Recitation is an extremely powerful aid to memory. Recitation makes you think, and thinking leaves a trace in your memory. Experiments show that students who recite retain 80 percent of the material; students who reread but do not recite retain only 20 percent when tested two weeks later. Without retention, there is no learning.*

Memory aids: _____

Reciting: _____

Memory experiments: _____

3. Speaking in public, whether it be standing on a platform facing a large audience, addressing a small committee, or making a classroom presentation, presents a special challenge. It arouses our anxiety more than any other communication situation. However, it also offers us a unique opportunity to share our ideas and to influence others.†

Speaking: _____

Public speaking: _____

Anxiety: _____

4. Goals are specific changes you'd like to make in yourself or in your environment. To help achieve your goals, state them as results you can measure. Think in detail about how things would be different if your goal were attained. List the specific changes in what you'd see, feel, touch, taste, hear, be, do, or have. Some goals that will aid you with your schoolwork include setting aside a specific time to study every day, taking good notes in class, and reviewing those notes from time to time to make sure you are retaining information.‡

Goals: _____

Changing yourself: _____

Taking notes in class: _____

---

* From Walter Pauk and John Fiore, *Succeed in College!* Boston: Houghton Mifflin, 2000, 47. Copyright © 2000 by Houghton Mifflin Company. Reprinted with permission.

† From Andrews et al., *Public Speaking.* Boston: Houghton Mifflin, 1999, 3.

‡ Adapted from Dave Ellis, *Becoming a Master Student.* Boston: Houghton Mifflin, 2000, 59.

Copyright © Houghton Mifflin Company. All rights reserved.

2

5. Being well prepared and confident is the first step in taking a test. Shorter, more regular study sessions are the best way to study for a test, and cramming (trying to learn everything in one study session) doesn't work in chemistry. You cannot open the book the night before the exam and learn a few weeks' worth of material in one sitting. Information must be studied gradually. If you have trouble understanding something, you may need to consult the instructor. That's difficult to do if you study all at once.*

Studying: ___

Learning in study sessions: ___

Cramming: ___

Determining the Main Idea

Once you've found the topic of a paragraph, you can determine its **main idea**, the general point the writer expressed about the topic. The main idea is what the writer wants to prove or explain. It's the point he or she wants you to know or to believe when you finish reading the paragraph. Therefore, being able to discern main ideas is a fundamental skill for successful reading.

To find the main idea, ask yourself what the writer is saying *about* the topic. For example, read this paragraph:

The Eagles' *Greatest Hits* album is the most successful album in history. It has sold 26 million copies, more than any other album. It was the first album ever to gain platinum status for sales of one million copies. *Greatest Hits* was the number one album on the Billboard Charts for five weeks, and it spent a total of 133 weeks on the charts altogether.

The topic of this paragraph is the Eagles' *Greatest Hits* album. It's the thing that is mentioned in every sentence of the paragraph. But what is the author's point about this topic? In the first sentence, she states that this album was more successful than any other. Then, all of the other sentences in the paragraph offer details to explain that idea.

As you read the next paragraph, try to identify the topic and main idea.

Single mothers face many challenges. Their greatest difficulties are usually financial. They are the primary family breadwinners, so their greatest struggles, especially for those who are younger and less edu-

* Adapted from Sherman and Sherman, *Essential Concepts of Chemistry*. Boston: Houghton Mifflin, 1999, xxxvi. Copyright © 1999 by Houghton Mifflin Company. Reprinted with permission.

Copyright © Houghton Mifflin Company. All rights reserved.

cated, often involve making ends meet. To make matters worse, single moms often do not receive regular child support from their children's fathers. They also must curtail their work hours due to childcare limitations, so many can't earn full-time wages.

Did you say that the topic is *single mothers' financial challenges*? That is correct. Every sentence of this paragraph mentions single mothers, single moms, or includes a pronoun (*they* or *their*) that refers to single moms. Also, each sentence refers to difficulties related to money. Now, what does the author want you to know or believe about that topic? The second sentence says that financial difficulties are their greatest hardship. Then, the remainder of the paragraph explains why the reader should accept that idea as true.

Exercise 2.11

Read each paragraph and then choose the correct topic.

1. In any subject, learning is enhanced when we ask questions. And there are no dumb questions. To master math and science, ask whatever questions will aid your understanding. Don't worry about what other students do or don't ask. What you need to ask may not be the same as for the other people in your class.*

   Topic:

   a. learning math and science
   b. asking questions to aid understanding
   c. students in higher education

2. Most college lecturers speak about 120 words per minute. In a fifty-minute lecture, you hear up to 6,000 words expressing ideas, facts, and details. To make sure that students understand the ideas, facts, and details they are presenting, lecturers use signal words and phrases. Signal words help lecturers convey important information. Some signal words and phrases include *to illustrate, before/after, furthermore, as a result*, and *more importantly*. Being able to recognize signal words and phrases will improve your reading, writing, speaking, and listening, as well as your note taking.†

   Topic:

   a. fifty-minute lectures
   b. signal words and phrases
   c. college lecturers

* Adapted from Dave Ellis, *Becoming a Master Student.* Boston: Houghton Mifflin, 2000, 181.
† Adapted from Walter Pauk and John Fiore, *Succeed in College!* Boston: Houghton Mifflin, 2000, 38.

Copyright © Houghton Mifflin Company. All rights reserved.

2

3. Developing the ability to concentrate is an important study skill. Keep your mind on what you're doing and try hard to ignore distractions. Remove the telephone and the television set, and try to eliminate any other interruptions. Find a quiet place where you'll be isolated from things that might disturb you. Sometimes low-level noise like instrumental music or a steady flow of traffic helps stimulate concentration. And don't try to study if you are hungry. That's a sure way to break your concentration.*

Topic:

a. developing the ability to concentrate
b. low-level noise
c. eliminating interruptions

4. The principal objective of science is to discover the fundamental patterns of the natural world. In trying to find the reasons underlying natural phenomena, scientists use a strategy called *the scientific method.* First, they gather all available information on their subject. Then, they develop a hypothesis, or a tentative explanation that fits all of the information collected.†

Topic:

a. the fundamental patterns of the natural world
b. natural phenomena
c. the scientific method

5. The recent tragedy involving 13-year-old Brittanie Cecil, who was hit and killed by a flying puck at a hockey game, could have been prevented. American hockey stadiums, like those in Europe, need to install protective netting. Even fans who are alertly watching the game cannot dodge a puck traveling 100 miles per hour, so nets would protect spectators from getting injured or killed. Some fans of the game argue that nets are difficult to see through or distracting. But in Europe, where nets are common, they are barely visible. So, protective netting should be mandatory in order to prevent any more deaths or injuries.

Topic:

a. Hockey
b. Protective nets for hockey stadiums
c. Hockey fans

---

* Adapted from Sherman and Sherman, *Essential Concepts of Chemistry*. Boston: Houghton Mifflin, 1999, xxxi.
† Adapted from Chernicoff/Fox, *Essentials of Geology,* 2nd ed. Boston: Houghton Mifflin, 2000, 5.

Copyright © Houghton Mifflin Company. All rights reserved.

Exercise 2.12

Now, read each paragraph again and choose the correct main idea from the list.

1. In any subject, learning is enhanced when we ask questions. And there are no dumb questions. To master math and science, ask whatever questions will aid your understanding. Students come to higher education with widely varying backgrounds in these subjects. What you need to ask may not be the same as for the other people in your class.*

Main Idea:

_____ Asking questions helps students learn.

_____ Students' questions are very different.

_____ Math and science are tough subjects to master.

2. Most college lecturers speak about 120 words per minute. In a fifty-minute lecture, you hear up to 6,000 words expressing ideas, facts, and details. To make sure that students understand the ideas, facts, and details they are presenting, lecturers use signal words and phrases. Signal words help lecturers convey important information. Some signal words and phrases include *to illustrate, before/after, furthermore, as a result,* and *more importantly.* Being able to recognize signal words and phrases will improve your reading, writing, speaking, and listening, as well as your note taking.†

Main Idea:

_____ Most college lectures last for fifty minutes.

_____ Signal words and phrases help students better understand lectures.

_____ Most college lecturers speak too quickly.

3. Developing the ability to concentrate is an important study skill. Keep your mind on what you're doing and try hard to ignore distractions. Remove the telephone and the television set, and try to eliminate any other interruptions. Find a quiet place where you'll be isolated from things that might disturb you. Sometimes low-level noise like instrumental music or

* Adapted from Dave Ellis, *Becoming a Master Student.* Boston: Houghton Mifflin, 2000, 181.

† Adapted from Walter Pauk and John Fiore, *Succeed in College!* Boston: Houghton Mifflin, 2000, 38.

Copyright © Houghton Mifflin Company. All rights reserved.

a steady flow of traffic helps stimulate concentration. And don't try to study if you are hungry. That's a sure way to break your concentration.*

Main Idea:

_____ The ability to concentrate can be developed.

_____ Interruptions are sure ways to break your concentration.

_____ Hunger inhibits effective studying.

4. The principal objective of science is to discover the fundamental patterns of the natural world. In trying to find the reasons underlying natural phenomena, scientists use a strategy called *the scientific method*. First, they gather all available information on their subject. Then, they develop a hypothesis, or a tentative explanation that fits all of the information collected.†

Main Idea:

_____ The scientific method is scientists' main strategy.

_____ A hypothesis is a possible explanation of some natural phenomenon.

_____ The principal objective of science is to study the natural world.

5. Die-hard fans may think the recent tragedy involving 13-year-old Brittanie Cecil, who died after being hit by a hockey puck, was a fluke. They claim that protective measures aren't necessary. However, as a safety professional and lover of the game, I feel, after one tragic death and the numerous puck-related injuries, that stadiums should be required to install protective netting, a practice common in Europe. The theory that fans are injured because they are not alert is weak. The puck that hit Cecil is believed to have been traveling 100 mph. Even if she were watching the game with her undivided attention, it is unlikely she would have had time to react quickly enough to dodge injury. I also disagree with the argument that the use of netting will negatively affect the way the game is played. In Europe the netting is barely visible. Once the fans get used to the net, they, too, will not be distracted by it. Protective netting is a small price to pay if it prevents even one more death or serious injury.‡

* Adapted from *Essential Concepts of Chemistry*, Sherman and Sherman, © 1999, Houghton Mifflin, p. xxxi.

† Adapted from Chernicoff/Fox, *Essentials of Geology*, 2nd ed. Boston: Houghton Mifflin, 2000, 5.

‡ Adapted from Linda Tapp, "Letters," *USA Today*, March 28, 2002, 12A.

Copyright © Houghton Mifflin Company. All rights reserved.

Main idea:

_____ Hockey is a very dangerous game.

_____ Hockey stadiums need to install nets to protect fans.

_____ Hockey fans are very safety-conscious.

2

The Topic Sentence

The **topic sentence** is the single statement that presents the main point or idea of the paragraph. Topic sentences have two parts: they state the topic, and they state what the author has to say about that topic. Writers do not have to include such a sentence. Chapter 4 of this book will discuss in more detail paragraphs that lack a topic sentence. However, writers often include a topic sentence to help readers quickly and easily see the main idea.

To find the topic sentence, look for the most general statement in the paragraph and then make sure the other sentences all offer information or details. See if you can locate the topic sentence in the following paragraph:

> Within hours of its collapse, the debate began over what—if anything—should be built to replace the World Trade Center in New York City. Some suggested rebuilding exact replicas of the original towers—a signal to terrorists that the city's spirit is intact. Others suggested creating a park as a memorial to the attack's victims. The World Trade Center's current manager, Larry Silverstein, has suggested erecting something new: a cluster of four 50-story buildings.*

If you chose the first sentence, you're right. That statement expresses the paragraph's main idea, and the rest of the paragraph explains that idea.

Exercise 2.13

For each of the following paragraphs, write in the correct topic on the space provided. Write on the blank provided the number of the sentence that expresses the main idea.

1. (1) Cheating in high school is very common. (2) Three out of every four high school students admit to breaking the rules by cheating on a test at least once. (3) Seventy-five percent of students have also confessed to handing in work that was completed by someone else. (4) A quarter of all

* Adapted from Michael Dolan, "Standing Tall," *Popular Science*, December 2001, 78.

Copyright © Houghton Mifflin Company. All rights reserved.

2

students say they've been dishonest by working with others when they were instructed to work by themselves.*

Topic: _Cheating_

Topic Sentence: _1_

2. (1) Teenagers are master rationalizers. (2) Some say that sports and other activities interfered with homework. (3) They also claim that they cheated if the assignment seemed meaningless or boring. (4) Many cited the pressure to get good grades. (5) Indeed, to many of these kids, high school seems like simply a tedious hurdle. (6) Once in college, though, many students appear to start taking school more seriously, at least when classes seem relevant to their goals. (7) They say, "I've never cheated in my major, but when it comes to general education requirements—those courses don't matter."

Topic: _reso reasons / excuses for cheating_

Topic Sentence: _1_

3. (1) Students also cite famous cheaters as examples of what it takes to succeed. (2) As one student wrote: "This world is full of cheaters because cheaters are the ones who most often get to the top. (3) News flash: Cheaters do prosper!" (4) In past surveys, names like Michael Milken and Donald Trump came up. (5) This year, a student put it this way: "If Clinton can do it and get away with it, why can't we?"

Topic: _Examples of (famos) cheaters_

Topic Sentence: _1_

Locations of Topic Sentences

Main ideas are often stated in the first sentence of the paragraph. However, they can appear in other places in a paragraph, too. Writers sometimes place the topic sentence in the middle of a paragraph or even at the end.

Topic Sentence as First Sentence

It's very common for writers to announce the main idea in the first sentence of the paragraph. Then, the remainder of the paragraph explains why the

* Adapted from Emily Sohn, "The Young and the Virtueless," *U.S. News and World Report*, www.usnews.com/usnews/issue/010521/education/cheating.b.htm.

Copyright © Houghton Mifflin Company. All rights reserved.

reader should accept that point. In the following paragraph, for example, the topic sentence, which is in boldface type, is at the beginning.

> **Newspapers have definite advantages over other sources of information.** The wonderful thing about the newspaper is that all the work is done for you. There is nothing to turn on, nothing to search for, nothing between you and the information. Somebody else has already categorized, organized, edited, and condensed the information for you in a form easily handled and assimilated. Another great thing about the newspaper is it brings the family together. Different sections of the paper can be parceled out to members of the family. There is something wonderful about the habit of a family reading and digesting the daily newspaper. Ideas are shared, opinions voiced, and lives and deaths verified.*

Topic Sentence as Second or Third Sentence

Sometimes, though, a writer needs to present a sentence or two of introductory information before stating the main point. This means that the topic sentence might occur in the second or third sentence of the paragraph. Take a look at this example:

> As much as 80 percent of Web sites on the Internet include inaccurate information. If you're doing research, how do you make sure the information you find is true? **You can examine certain parts of a Web site to evaluate its reliability.** Web sites with addresses that include .org, .gov, or .edu are usually accurate. Web sites that give the sources of their information, too, tend to be more trustworthy. Also, look for identification of the site's creators, as well as contact information for those people.

The main idea is "You can examine certain parts of a Web site to evaluate its reliability" because most of the paragraph is about what those parts are. However, the writer included some background information and a question at the beginning of the paragraph. Both of these sentences led up to the topic sentence in the third statement.

Topic Sentence in the Middle

A topic sentence can also appear somewhere in the middle of the paragraph. For example, read the following paragraph:

---

* Adapted from Joe Saltzman, "Too Much Information, Too Little Time," *USA Today,* September 1997, 67.

Copyright © Houghton Mifflin Company. All rights reserved.

An old saying in business claims that 80 percent of a company's prof-its come from 20 percent of its customers. That's why Centura Banks ranks its 650,000 customers on a scale of one to five. Those with the best ratings get better customer service. **This company and others are beginning to concentrate more on their best customers.** Continental Airlines, for instance, plans to give its agents access to each customer's history so they can give the best service to their top clients. First Union Bank codes its credit card customers. When a per-son calls for service, the bank's representatives know when they're talking to their best patrons.*

This paragraph begins with an introductory statement in the first sentence. Then, the second sentence offers the first of three examples given to explain the main idea in the fourth sentence. After the main idea is stated, the para-graph offers two more examples.

Topic Sentence as Last Sentence

A writer might choose to save the topic sentence for the end of the paragraph, offering it as the last sentence. This next paragraph is an example of one that builds up to the main point:

People who attend religious services more than once a week live seven years longer than people who never attend religious services. Spiritual people also recover more quickly from surgery. Regular church-goers are less likely to have heart disease or high blood pressure. They have lower rates of depression and anxiety, too. **Obviously, being faith-ful has positive health benefits.†**

In this paragraph, the writer offers all of her explanations first. Then, she sum-marizes the point in a topic sentence at the paragraph's end.

Topic Sentence as First and Last Sentence

Finally, the topic sentence might occur twice: once at the beginning of the paragraph and then again, in different words, at the end. Writers often restate the topic sentence to emphasize or reinforce the main idea for the reader. Here is an example:

Jigsaw puzzles, which were created in the 1760s, are still a popular pastime. Thirty million jigsaw puzzles were sold in 2000. Eighty percent of American homes contain a jigsaw puzzle for adults.

* Adapted from Diane Brady, "Why Service Stinks," *Reader's Digest*, May 2001, 161–168.
† Adapted from Elena Serocki, "Heaven Can Wait," *Reader's Digest*, May 2001, 112.

Copyright © Houghton Mifflin Company. All rights reserved.

Eighty-three percent of American homes contain at least one child's jigsaw puzzle. There's even a National Jigsaw Puzzle Championship every year. This contest offers puzzle enthusiasts $10,000 in prizes. **It's clear that many people still enjoy this centuries-old hobby.***

This paragraph identifies the main point in the first sentence, offers explanation, and then makes the same point again in the final sentence.

Steps for Locating the Topic Sentence

To find the topic sentence regardless of where it is located, look for the most general statement in the paragraph. Then, verify that the rest of the sentences in the paragraph offer information, details, or explanation for that general idea. Here's a specific step-by-step procedure you can follow when you're trying to determine the main idea and topic sentence in a paragraph:

Step 1: Read over the entire paragraph to get an idea of the subject matter included.

Step 2: Read the first sentence to see if it gives a general picture of the entire paragraph. If it doesn't, it may provide some general background or contrasting information. Or, the first sentence may pose a question that the next few sentences go on to answer.

Step 3: If the first sentence does not state the main idea, read the last sentence to see if it gives a general picture of the entire paragraph. Turn the last sentence into a question, and then see if the other sentences in the paragraph answer that question. If they do, that last sentence may be the topic sentence.

Step 4: If either the first or the last sentence gives that general overview of the paragraph, the main idea, you have found your topic sentence.

Step 5: If neither the first nor the last sentence is identified as the topic sentence, then the reader must evaluate each sentence in the middle of the paragraph to see if one of the sentences states the general idea or the main idea information. Test each possibility by turning it into a question and then determining if the other sentences in the paragraph answer that question.

Step 6: Once the topic sentence is located, then the reader must look for the general phrase located in the topic sentence that states the overall main idea.

* Adapted from John Tierney, "Playing with the Puzzle People," *Reader's Digest*, May 2001, 118–123.

Copyright © Houghton Mifflin Company. All rights reserved.

Exercise 2.14

Below each paragraph, write on the blank provided the number of the sentence (or sentences) that state(s) the main idea.

1. (1) The atmosphere in Escalante's room was much like that in the locker room at a football game. (2) Class began with warm-up exercises. (3) All the students slapped their hands against their desks and stomped their feet on the floor in rhythm while chanting an opening ritual. (4) When attention dropped, Escalante would begin the "wave," a cheer in which row after row of students, in succession, stood, raising their hands, then sat quickly, creating a ripple across the room like a pennant billowing in victory. (5) The intensity of drills and quizzes was relieved with jokes, demonstrations, and an occasional round of volleyball. (6) Just as the classroom clock never registered the correct time, the routine usually varied, keeping the team alert and focused.*

   Topic Sentence: _2(1)_

2. (1) Some years ago I had what most would call the American Dream. (2) I had a thriving construction business, a comfortable home, two new cars, and a sailboat. (3) Moreover, I was happily married. (4) I had it all.†

   Topic Sentence: _4·1_

3. (1) Cellphones are pulling drivers' attention from the road. (2) Navigation systems and e-mail are already available in vehicles. (3) Audio systems are becoming more complicated to operate. (4) Automakers are installing all kinds of potential distractions in cars. (5) There are customized information services that shower drivers with news items and shopping tips. (6) There are TVs in the backseats, too.‡

   Topic Sentence: _4_

4. (1) In the old days, kids headed off to camp with a few postcards. (2) Now a laptop might do better. (3) In today's world of camping, kids don't leave technology behind when they go off to summer camp. (4) According to Peg Smith, executive director of the American Camping Association, about 70 percent of summer camps are online and many allow e-mail. (5) Some also post daily shows of activities on Web sites; a few even have live Webcams.

   Topic Sentence: _3_

* From Ann Byers, *Jaime Escalante: Sensational Teacher*. Enslow Publishers, Inc., 1996.
† From Collin Perry, "Help Yourself Through Hard Times," *Reader's Digest*, February 1997.
‡ Adapted from Dann McCosh, "Driven to Distraction," *Popular Science*, December 2001, 86.

Copyright © Houghton Mifflin Company. All rights reserved.

5. (1) Although he is one of the highest paid ball players in history, he always takes the time to sign autographs for kids at the ball field. (2) He has his own charity organization, to which he devotes a lot of time. (3) He talks about his great family in interviews, and how much he loves his mother, father, and younger sister. (4) And, he's a great fielder and hitter. (5) That's what makes Derek Jeter one of the most popular professional athletes in America today.

Topic Sentence: ___2 (5)___

Exercise 2.15

Following each paragraph write on the blank provided the number of the sentence that is the topic sentence.

1. (1) When I was 14, I got a difficult after-school job. (2) My hometown newspaper, the Houston *Post*, hired me to sell subscriptions. (3) I was sent to some of the city's worst neighborhoods to solicit door-to-door. (4) I was often scrambling around after dark in bad areas searching for garage apartments.

Topic Sentence: _____

2. (1) The job was challenging, but I was determined to succeed. (2) People didn't like a stranger knocking on their door, especially a kid trying to get them to buy something. (3) One time, a man slammed his door in my face and screamed, "I don't want no damn paper." (4) I forced myself to knock again and was able to tell him how great the paper was. (5) I ended up selling him a subscription. (6) I was soon among the top subscription sellers and, like other successful salesmen, was given responsibility for training newcomers.

Topic Sentence: _____

3. (1) Around this time I started playing harmonica and guitar. (2) Before long I was playing in a band at chili cook-offs and other events. (3) When I turned 18, I focused my attention on becoming a professional musician. (4) I never lost sight of this dream. (5) I'm sure my perseverance in the field of music came from what I learned knocking on strangers' doors.

Topic Sentence: _____

4. (1) That experience helped me in many ways. (2) Early in my music career I was locked in a legal dispute with a former manager. (3) He pressured me to back off, but I refused. (4) Having all those doors slammed in my face

Copyright © Houghton Mifflin Company. All rights reserved.

as a kid gave me the strength to stand up to this intimidating figure. (5) Except this time there was one difference: I was the one saying no. And I won.*

Topic Sentence: _____

CHAPTER 2 REVIEW

Fill in the blanks in the following statements.

1. Paragraphs are composed of _____ and _____ statements.

2. The most general sentence in the paragraph expresses its _____, the idea or point the writer wants you to know or to believe.

3. The sentence that states the writer's main idea is called the _____.

4. The topic sentence has two parts: the _____, or subject, of the paragraph and what the writer wants to say about that topic.

5. The topic sentence can occur anywhere in the _____.

Reading Selection

important

Gossip Is Not a Trivial Pastime

1 In the beginning was the word, and the word, if the evolutionary psychologists are right, tended mainly to be used to form sentences such as "Hey, guess what I heard about Og?!," "Don't tell anyone, but I think Og and Ogga may be splitting up!" and "I shouldn't tell you this, but Og tried to get off with me at the rain-dance last night!"—or even "Ogga is still wearing that deeply uncool bone necklace—soo Lower Paleolithic, don't you think?"

2 We gossip a lot. Most of the human capacity for complex language is dedicated to gossip. Perhaps the most striking finding of recent research on human conversations is that about two-thirds of our conversation time is entirely devoted to social topics. These topics include discussions of personal relationships and experiences; who is doing what with whom; who is "in" and who is "out" and why; how to deal with difficult social situations; the behaviour and relationships of friends, family, and celebrities; our own problems with lovers, family, friends, colleagues, and neighbors; the minutiae of everyday social life—in a word, gossip.

---

* Excerpted from "My First Job: Clint Black" by Daniel L. Levine. Reprinted with permission from the *Reader's Digest,* March 2001. Copyright © 2001 by The Reader's Digest Assn., Inc.

Copyright © Houghton Mifflin Company. All rights reserved.

chismes

3   In Old English, gossip—or god-sibb—originally meant a person related to one in God, specifically referring to a woman's close female friends at the birth of a child (those she would choose to be godparents to her child, her "god-sisters," if you like). The word later came to mean more generally a close (female) friend or companion. Then, it meant the kind of talk characteristic of intimate friends; i.e., chatty talk about the details of personal matters and relationships, the sharing of secrets—more or less what we currently mean by gossip.

4   According to academics, the evaluative element of gossip is perhaps what distinguishes it from other forms of informal, chatty conversation. Gossip has been defined as "evaluative talk about a person who is not present." It has also been defined less narrowly and more accurately, as "the process of informally communicating value-laden information about members of a social setting."

5   These definitions do not imply that all gossip involves criticizing or disparaging others. One recent study showed that criticism and negative evaluations account for only five percent of gossip-time. Another five percent is devoted to asking for or giving advice on how to handle social situations. The bulk of the conversations, though, focus on "who is doing what with whom" and personal social experiences.

6   Evaluations are often positive: we may express approval of someone's choice of lover, job, car, holiday, or shoes—or of their behavior, as in "she was right to dump him; it was obvious he was never going to commit." The important point about evaluation is that gossip generally involves more than the sharing of information about people's lives and relationships. Gossip usually includes the expression of opinions or feelings

about this information. The opinions or feelings may be implied, rather than directly stated, or conveyed more subtly in the tone of voice. But we rarely share details about "who is doing what with whom" without providing some indication of our views on the matter.

7   Gossip is not necessarily confined to discussion of the doings of a third party or parties. Experts generally agree that information about one's own doings—or those of the person one is communicating with—counts as gossip, providing it meets the broad criterion of being "socially interesting" information. "My car broke down yesterday" would clearly not be an appropriate response to the question "So, what's the gossip?" But "I met this really gorgeous man at the garage . . ." would certainly qualify. Equally, "What's the latest with you and that bloke [English expression for "guy"] from the garage?" is a perfectly acceptable gossip-opener. To be "socially interesting," gossip about oneself is of course highly likely to involve some information about third parties, but a definition of gossip must include participants as subjects.

8   Many people might initially agree with the first of the two definitions of gossip quoted above. But the second ("the process of informally communicating value-laden information about members of a social setting") is more accurate and more helpful in several ways. It conveys the informal, chatty nature of gossip. It allows for forms of communication other than talk (such as letters, gossip columns, e-mails, and text messages). And it indicates the range of people about whom information may be communicated—including the people actually engaged in the gossip.

9   Although the term gossip has, relatively recently, acquired some negative connotations, earlier definitions emphasize the beneficial social and psychological functions of

Copyright © Houghton Mifflin Company. All rights reserved.

gossip. We gossip because gossip helps us to establish, develop, and maintain relationships. It helps us to bond with other members of our social circle and to clarify our social position and status. It helps us to assess and manage reputations; to learn social skills, to learn and reinforce shared values, and to resolve conflicts. And it helps us to build support networks and to win friends and influence people.

10   We may also gossip because we are genetically programmed to do so. According to the psychologist Robin Dunbar, gossip is part of our evolutionary hard-wiring—perhaps even the single most important part. Language, he argues, evolved to allow us to gossip. Gossip is the human equivalent of what is known as "social grooming" among our primate cousins. Among humans, language evolved to replace this physical mutual grooming, because physical grooming became too time-consuming for the larger human social networks (primate social groups are no larger than 50–55, while the average human social network is around 150). Language evolved to fill the "grooming gap," because it allows us to use the limited time we have available for social interaction—keeping in touch and bonding with a wide social network—more efficiently.

11   Whatever their respective evolutionary roles, it is clear that both social grooming and high social status make us feel good, and may even be good for our health. It has been shown that the mutual grooming performed by primates stimulates production of endorphins—the body's natural pain-killing opiates (sedatives)—which makes them relaxed, and reduces their heart rate and other signs of stress. It is highly likely that the "vocal grooming" of gossip among humans has similar effects. Experiments have also shown that raising of social status is associated with increased serotonin (an organic substance) in the brain, which has equally beneficial physical and psychological effects. By gossiping, we may effectively be giving ourselves the natural equivalent of small doses of morphine and Prozac.*

12   Gossip is clearly far more than just a trivial pastime: it is good for us. In fact, the research evidence would suggest that gossip is essential to our social, psychological and physical well-being.

* Morphine is a pain drug and Prozac is a mood-altering drug sometimes given to patients with depression.

From "Gossip Is Not a Trivial Pastime" from *Evolution, Alienation, and Gossip: The Role of Mobile Telecommunications in the 21st Century* by Kate Fox, Social Issues Research Centre, www.sirc.org. Reprinted by permission of the author.

VOCABULARY

Read the following questions about some of the vocabulary words that appear in the previous selection. Circle the correct responses.

1. In paragraph 2, what does *minutiae* mean?

   a. minutes   c. excess

   b. details   d. happiness

Copyright © Houghton Mifflin Company. All rights reserved.

2. What is a *characteristic,* as used in paragraph 3?

   a. trait   c. illustration
   b. qualifier   d. style

3. What does *evaluative* mean, as used in paragraph 4?

   a. measurable   c. qualifying
   b. distinguishing   d. determining

4. If something is *laden,* as used in paragraph 4, what does that mean?

   a. without   c. full of
   b. lacking   d. despised

5. In paragraph 5, what does *disparaging* mean?

   a. happy   c. damaging
   b. lighthearted   d. critical of

6. What is a *connotation?* (Paragraph 9)

   a. meaning   c. sentence
   b. word   d. phrase

TOPIC, TOPIC SENTENCE, AND MAIN IDEA

Answer the following questions.

1. The topic of paragraph 2 is

   a. complex language.
   b. personal relationships and experiences.
   c. gossip.
   d. the minutiae of everyday social life.

2. Which of the following sentences from paragraph 6 is the topic sentence?

   a. Gossip is not necessarily confined to discussion of the doings of a third party or parties.

   b. Experts generally agree that information about one's own doings—or those of the person one is communicating with—counts as gossip, providing it meets the broad criterion of being "socially interesting" information.

   c. "My car broke down yesterday" would clearly not be an appropriate response to the question "So, what's the gossip?"

   d. To be "socially interesting" gossip about oneself is of course highly likely to involve some information about third parties, but a definition of gossip must include participants as subjects.

Copyright © Houghton Mifflin Company. All rights reserved.

2

3. Which of the following sentences from paragraph 8 is the topic sentence?

    a. Many people might initially agree with the first of the two definitions of gossip quoted above.

    b. But the second ("the process of informally communicating value-laden information about members of a social setting") is more accurate and more helpful in several ways.

    c. It conveys the informal, chatty nature of gossip.

    d. It allows for forms of communication other than talk (such as letters, gossip columns, e-mails, and text messages).

4. The main idea of paragraph 10 is

    a. We are genetically programmed a certain way.

    b. Language evolved to fill the "grooming gap."

    c. We have wide social networks.

    d. We gossip because we are genetically programmed to do so.

5. The main idea of paragraph 11 is

    a. Social grooming and high social status make us feel good, and may even be good for our health.

    b. We gossip a lot.

    c. Mutual grooming performed by primates stimulates production of endorphins.

    d. We are getting morphine through gossip.

QUESTIONS FOR DISCUSSION AND WRITING

Answer the following questions based on your reading of the selection.

1. Do you agree or disagree with the statement, "Gossip is clearly far more than just a trivial pastime: it is good for us"? Why? _____

_____

2. Is gossip, in your experience, mostly composed of "informal, chatty" conversation? Have you ever had a situation where it was more than that? Explain. _____

_____

3. List any new information you learned from this selection. Did you find the selection interesting? Why or why not? _____

_____

Copyright © Houghton Mifflin Company. All rights reserved.

▶ Vocabulary: Synonyms

Synonyms are words that have the same, or similar, meanings. Synonyms serve four purposes in texts. First of all, they add variety to a reading selection. Instead of writing the same word over and over again, authors will use different words with the same meanings to keep sentences lively and interesting. For example, in the paragraph about the Slinky, the author refers to the Slinky as both a *toy* and a *plaything*.

Secondly, authors use synonyms to express their thoughts as precisely as possible. For example, the paragraph about protective netting for hockey stadiums refers to "the recent *tragedy*." The author could have used the word *situation* or *incident* or *misfortune*, but she used the more specific and emotional word *tragedy*, which clearly communicates how she feels about Brittanie Cecil's death.

A third use of synonyms is to connect ideas and sentences together and to reinforce ideas. Do you remember the paragraph about the reliability of Web sites? Notice how the italicized words are synonyms that keep the paragraph focused on the main idea:

> As much as 80 percent of Web sites on the Internet include inaccurate information. If you're doing research, how do you make sure the information you find is **true?** You can examine certain parts of a Web site to evaluate its **reliability.** Web sites with addresses that include .org, .gov, or .edu are usually **accurate.** Web sites that give the sources of their information, too, tend to be more **trustworthy.** Also, look for identification of the site's creators, as well as contact information for those people.

Finally, texts include synonyms to help readers figure out what other words mean. For example, in the sentence below, the author provides a synonym to help the reader understand what the word *artifacts* means:

> True to these ancient meanings, portfolios are movable collections of papers and artifacts, or *work products*.

Work products is another way to say *artifacts*, so it's a synonym used to define a word.

Vocabulary Exercise

The following paragraphs come from examples in this chapter. On the blanks following each paragraph, write in two synonyms used in the paragraph for the italicized, boldface word or phrase.

1. ***People who attend religious services*** more than once a week live seven years longer than people who never attend religious services. Spiritual

Copyright © Houghton Mifflin Company. All rights reserved.

2

people also recover more quickly from surgery. Regular church-goers are less likely to have heart disease or high blood pressure. They have lower rates of depression and anxiety, too.

Two synonyms for italicized phrase: _spiritual people/regular church goers_

2. Single mothers face many **challenges.** Their greatest difficulties are usually financial. They are the primary family breadwinners, so their greatest struggles, especially for those who are younger and less educated, often involve making ends meet. To make matters worse, single moms often do not receive regular child support from their children's fathers. They also must curtail their work hours due to childcare limitations, so many can't earn full-time wages.

Two synonyms for italicized word: _difficult, struggles_

3. **Cheating** in high school is very common. Three out of every four high school students admit to breaking the rules by cheating on a test at least once. Seventy-five percent of students have also confessed to handing in work that was completed by someone else. A quarter of all students say they've been dishonest by working with others when they were instructed to work by themselves.

Two synonyms for italicized word: _breaking the rules, been dishonest_

4. Developing the ability to concentrate is another important study skill. Keep your mind on what you're doing and try hard to ignore distractions. Remove the telephone and the television set, and try to eliminate any other interruptions. Find a quiet place where you'll be isolated from **things that might disturb you.** Sometimes low-level noise like instrumental music or a steady flow of traffic helps stimulate concentration. And don't try to study if you are hungry. That's a sure way to break your concentration.

Two synonyms for the italicized phrase: _interruption distractions_

5. An old saying in business claims that 80 percent of a company's profits come from 20 percent of its **customers.** That's why Centura Banks ranks its 650,000 customers on a scale of one to five. Those with the best ratings get better customer service. This company and others are beginning to concentrate more on their best customers. Continental Airlines, for instance, plans to give its agents access to each customer's history so they can give the best service to their top clients. First Union Bank codes its credit card customers. When a person calls for service, the bank's representatives know when they're talking to their best patrons.

Two synonyms for the italicized word: _clients, patrons_

Copyright © Houghton Mifflin Company. All rights reserved.

Name _____ Date _____

POST-TEST 1

A. Choose the option that puts each list of words or phrases in order from most general to most specific.

1. (1) maintaining healthy teeth   (3) daily health care
   (2) brushing teeth   (4) healthy habits
      a. 1-2-4-3   c. 3-4-2-1
      b. 4-3-1-2   d. 4-1-3-2

2. (1) facial expression   (3) showing joy
   (2) expressing emotion   (4) smiling
      a. 4-1-3-2   c. 1-2-4-3
      b. 3-4-2-1   d. 2-3-1-4

3. (1) hobby   (3) growing vegetables
   (2) gardening   (4) leisure activity
      a. 4-1-2-3   c. 4-3-1-2
      b. 3-1-4-2   d. 1-3-4-2

4. (1) *Friends* cast member   (3) entertainment personality
   (2) Jennifer Aniston   (4) TV star
      a. 1-3-2-4   c. 3-4-1-2
      b. 4-3-1-2   d. 2-4-3-1

5. (1) BIC   (3) pen
   (2) writing instrument   (4) means of communication
      a. 4-2-3-1   c. 3-2-4-1
      b. 1-3-2-4   d. 4-1-2-3

Copyright © Houghton Mifflin Company. All rights reserved.

For tests on identifying the topic sentence, see the Test Bank.

2

B. Each of the following groups of words includes one general word and three specific words. Circle the letter for the most general word in each group.

6. Writing   Drawing   Creating   Sculpting

   a. Writing   c. Creating

   b. Drawing   d. Sculpting

7. Trumpet   Instrument   Flute   Harp

   a. Trumpet   c. Flute

   b. Instrument   d. Harp

8. University   Harvard   Yale   Princeton

   a. University   c. Yale

   b. Harvard   d. Princeton

9. Lamp   Flashlight   Lantern   Lighting device

   a. Lamp   c. Lantern

   b. Flashlight   d. Lighting device

10. Anger   Emotion   Happiness   Sorrow

   a. Anger   c. Happiness

   b. Emotion   d. Sorrow

C. For each group of words, select the general category that includes all the specific items listed.

11. Newspaper   Magazine   Brochure   Book

   a. Reference materials   c. Electronic media

   b. Printed materials   d. Free information

12. Juice   Soda   Water   Milk

   a. Healthy foods   c. Nutritious drinks

   b. Energy sources   d. Things to drink

13. Forest green   Sky blue   Blood red   Flaming yellow

   a. Colors   c. Rock groups

   b. Places   d. Landscapes

14. Christmas   Easter   Chanukah   Kwanzaa

   a. School breaks   c. Holidays

   b. Societies   d. Religions

Copyright © Houghton Mifflin Company. All rights reserved.

15. Russian   French   Dutch   Portuguese

    a. Countries   c. Realms

    b. Automobiles   d. Languages

2

D. For each general idea, select the more specific idea that fits it best.

16. General Idea: Room in a house

    Specific Idea:

    a. Dishwasher   c. Hanger

    b. Kitchen   d. Back yard

17. General Idea: Means of transportation

    Specific Idea:

    a. Store   c. Train

    b. Fishing   d. Reading

18. General Idea: Earning money

    Specific Idea:

    a. Wearing a hat   c. Sleeping soundly

    b. Paying an admission price   d. Working at a job

19. General Idea: Taking a photograph

    Specific Idea:

    a. Get out the camera   c. Have fun with friends

    b. Walk to a beautiful spot   d. Cook a meal

20. General Idea: Reference sources

    Specific Idea:

    a. Hardware store   c. Shopping mall

    b. Encyclopedia   d. Novel

POST-TEST 2

A. For each group of sentences, select the option that places them in order from most general to most specific.

  1. 1. Andrea regularly goes to the dentist to avoid problems with her teeth.

    2. Good dental health is an essential part of good overall health.

Copyright © Houghton Mifflin Company. All rights reserved.

3. During Andrea's last dental appointment, her dentist filled a cavity.

4. Watching over your health is vital for achieving a happy life.

   a. 2-1-4-3   c. 3-4-2-1

   b. 4-2-1-3   d. 1-4-3-2

2. 1. The right windshield wiper doesn't work correctly anymore.

  2. My car has developed plenty of ailments in its old age.

  3. When you switch on the windshield wipers, the right one goes back and forth too fast.

  4. Old cars often have plenty of things that go wrong.

   a. 2-4-3-1   c. 1-2-4-3

   b. 4-1-3-2   d. 4-2-1-3

3. 1. In the mornings, I drink too much coffee.

  2. I have some bad habits I'd like to break.

  3. I'd like to make some improvements in my life.

  4. The caffeine leaves me feeling stressed and irritated.

   a. 3-2-1-4   c. 1-2-4-3

   b. 4-1-2-3   d. 3-4-2-1

4. 1. A PG-13 rating means the film contains a limited number of curse words and other exclamations.

  2. A panel of the Motion Picture Association of America assigns a movie's rating by using a formula that counts the frequency of particular words and body parts.

  3. *Behind Enemy Lines* contained, for instance, only seven mentions of the word *hell*.

  4. For example, the movie *Behind Enemy Lines,* which contains about fifty curse words, got a PG-13 rating.

   a. 2-3-4-1   c. 2-1-4-3

   b. 1-2-3-4   d. 2-4-3-1

5. 1. There are some things about having a baby that surprise you no matter how prepared you are.

  2. Eventually, Michael was a name of which everyone could approve.

Copyright © Houghton Mifflin Company. All rights reserved.

3. Naming our new son turned out to be much more difficult than any of us thought.

4. We wanted to name him after his grandfather, so we needed a name starting with "M."

   a. 1-2-3-4   c. 2-4-3-1

   b. 1-3-4-2   d. 3-1-2-4

2

B. Each of the following groups of sentences includes one general sentence and three specific sentences. For each group, choose the *general* sentence.

6. 1. There were many who wanted to sell magazine subscriptions.

   2. A small group wanted to sell cakes and other baked goods.

   3. For our school band's fundraiser, we decided to have a sale.

   4. Most people wanted to sell grapefruit fresh from the orchard.

      a. 1   c. 3

      b. 2   d. 4

7. 1. Mary Peterson is known for her wide selection of boots.

   2. I think more people wear sneakers than any other type of shoes.

   3. Frank Evans usually dresses casually, but he always wears black dress shoes with tassels.

   4. There's no dress code at our office, so people wear all kinds of shoes.

      a. 1   c. 3

      b. 2   d. 4

8. 1. It seems as though our kids spent most of their holiday break at the movies.

   2. They made sure to see *Harry Potter and the Sorcerer's Stone* first.

   3. Perhaps they enjoyed *The Fellowship of the Ring* most of all.

   4. *Monsters, Inc.* was another important must-see on their list.

      a. 1   c. 3

      b. 2   d. 4

9. 1. Juan liked the excitement, the culture, and the crowds of the city.

   2. Juan and Marie wanted to settle down and buy a house.

Copyright © Houghton Mifflin Company. All rights reserved.

2

3. Marie favored the comforts and convenience of the suburbs.

4. Both of them found that the simple, quiet beauty of the countryside was the best choice of all.

    a. 1   c. 3

    b. 2   d. 4

10. 1. The kids clean up and vacuum their rooms and change their beds.

    2. Frederick vacuums the rest of the house and cleans the bathrooms.

    3. Winona dusts the entire house and polishes the furniture.

    4. One day a week, the entire family does their cleaning chores.

        a. 1   c. 3

        b. 2   d. 4

C. For each item, read the three specific sentences given. Then identify the general sentence best supported by those three specific sentences.

11. The most appealing and most expensive option was tile.

A cheaper and quite practical choice was linoleum.

It was also possible to leave the carpeting that was already there.

General Sentences:

a. While renovating their new house, Sally and Bob had many arguments over how much space they needed.

b. Sally wanted to add two new rooms to the house as an extension to the kitchen.

c. Sally and Bob were having a hard time deciding on what to use for their new kitchen floor.

d. Bob was against the addition of two new rooms because he liked having a large back yard.

12. The descendants of Lewis and Clark could number in the thousands today.

A Lewis and Clark family reunion will be held at Fort Clatsop on the Oregon Coast.

Only 50 direct descendants and 18 collateral descendants have been documented so far.*

*Adapted from "Expedition Members' Descendants Sought," *USA Today*, December 11, 2001, 9D.

Copyright © Houghton Mifflin Company. All rights reserved.

2

General Sentences:

a. Neither Lewis nor Clark ever married, so they had no descendants.

b. The Lewis and Clark family reunion may have to be postponed.

c. Of the many possible descendants of Lewis and Clark, only a few have been found for a reunion.

d. Lewis and Clark were our country's greatest explorers.

13. Margie is allergic to eggs.

Terrence is allergic to lactose.

Susan is allergic to cat dander.

General Sentences:

a. Margie should never have eggs for breakfast.

b. My friends suffer from different types of allergies.

c. Cat dander is a common allergy.

d. Allergies can be annoying.

14. The company that made my computer told me it was a software problem, and I should call the software company.

I called the company that made my software, but they said it was a hardware problem.

When I called my Internet service provider, they said there was probably a problem with my telephone connection.

General Sentences:

a. The company that made my computer has excellent technical support.

b. My computer has generally been working well, so this problem doesn't bother me.

c. I think my Internet service provider had the correct solution.

d. Everyone I called for help gave me a different opinion about the problem's source.

15. Gayle canceled her cell phone service and paid all she owed, but the phone company keeps sending her more bills.

When Gayle calls the phone company, the customer service people are always polite and always say they have solved the problem.

Every time a customer service person says that Gayle owes the company nothing, Gayle receives another bill the following week.

Copyright © Houghton Mifflin Company. All rights reserved.

2

General Sentences:

a. The phone company has well-meaning customer service people but a terrible billing system.

b. Gayle should never have canceled her cell phone service.

c. The phone company has a policy of continuing to bill their customers in hopes that their customers will eventually reinstate their service.

d. The phone company's customer service people choose not to help those who cancel their phone service.

D. For each item, read the general sentence and choose three specific sentences from the list that explain or support that statement.

16. General Sentence: The Toyota Prius and Honda Insight are the first of a new breed of better automobile, the gas-electric "hybrid."*

Specific Sentences:

1. By comparison, American cars are not as advanced as these new models.

2. The Honda Insight is not the ideal trip or family car.

3. These cars combine an internal-combustion engine with an electric motor.

4. It is as much fun and as practical to drive these cars as it is to drive conventional cars.

5. They deliver exceptional gas mileage and cleaner exhaust.

6. They are the vanguard of a huge change in automobiles.

7. Both the Prius and Insight come in a wide variety of colors.

    a. 1, 4, 7   c. 3, 4, 7

    b. 2, 3, 6   d. 3, 5, 6

17. General Sentence: The city of San Francisco stretches over 45 square miles—about twice the area of the island of Manhattan—yet the economic output of Manhattan dwarfs that of San Francisco.†

Specific Sentences:

1. Workers in Manhattan generally have much longer commutes than their counterparts in San Francisco.

---

* Adapted from Ralph Kinney Bennett, "Lean, Green Driving Machines," *Reader's Digest*, December 2001, 86.

† Adapted from Thomas H. Lee, "Vertical Leap for Mankind," *Scientific American*, January, 2002, 53.

Copyright © Houghton Mifflin Company. All rights reserved.

2

2. Although San Francisco is considered the financial center of the West Coast, the New York Stock Exchange resides in an historic downtown Manhattan building and is responsible for generating billions of dollars of revenue each day.

3. To avoid long, time-wasting waits for elevators, workers in Manhattan spend more time at their desks.

4. Businesses in New York are stacked vertically into the skies.

5. As the financial capital of the country, Manhattan has documented its economic output more thoroughly than has San Francisco.

6. By building upward rather than outward, developers increase not only the value of their real estate but also the working power of the city as a whole.

7. San Francisco's more casual Western lifestyle produces much less job-related anxiety than is found among workers in Manhattan.

    a. 2, 4, 6   c. 4, 6, 7

    b. 1, 3, 4   d. 2, 3, 7

18. General Sentence: The nuclear-powered aircraft carrier *U.S.S. Enterprise* is the longest, tallest, most powerful warship ever built.*

Specific Sentences:

1. The *Enterprise* carries eight air-wing squadrons, Sea Sparrow missiles, and some of the most sophisticated electronic spying equipment ever devised.

2. Landing on the *Enterprise*'s flight deck, especially the first time, is a heart-stopping experience.

3. During a recent deployment, the crew of the *Enterprise* had 27,000 haircuts, had 1,300 wisdom teeth pulled, and bought 720,000 soft drinks from vending machines.

4. It can carry U.S. military forces within striking range of any point on the planet.

5. Even now, when every crew member has e-mail, conventional mail call is always one of the high points of shipboard life.

6. Women sailors on the *Enterprise* now make up 10 percent of the crew and 3 percent of the pilots aboard.

* Adapted from T. R. Reid, "09543-2810, The Big E," *National Geographic,* January, 2002, 114.

Copyright © Houghton Mifflin Company. All rights reserved.

7. The ship has 250 pilots, backed up by thousands of other sailors who plan each flight, maintain the planes, navigate the ship, and perform many other jobs.

    a. 4, 5, 7   c. 1, 4, 7

    b. 2, 3, 6   d. 1, 3, 4

19. General Sentence: Before you begin to paint a room, you have to make sure the room is prepared for painting.

Specific Sentences:

1. Have a good meal and get plenty of rest before you begin painting.

2. Take off the covers from all heating-air conditioning ducts to protect them from splattering paint.

3. Turn off the electricity to the room.

4. If you're new at painting, start with a small, out-of-the-way room.

5. Make sure the colors you select for the room will work well with the rest of your home.

6. Remove all nails, screws, and picture hangers from surfaces to be painted.

7. Wear gloves and old clothes you won't mind getting full of paint.

    a. 3, 5, 7   c. 2, 4, 5

    b. 1, 2, 6   d. 2, 3, 6

20. General Sentence: When buying a computer, you'll probably be more satisfied if you buy from a reputable mail order computer company than if you go to a retail store.

Specific Sentences:

1. The salespeople at retail stores often don't know much about the computers they sell.

2. Retail stores will often advertise special, time-limited sales in your local newspaper.

3. The salespeople at reputable mail order computer companies are usually polite, attentive, and very knowledgeable about their products.

4. When you call a mail order computer company, you often have to wait on hold for a long time before you get to talk with a salesperson.

5. Just about any computer you buy these days comes with a one-year warranty on parts and labor, and you can often purchase an extended warranty.

Copyright © Houghton Mifflin Company. All rights reserved.

6. Retail store salespeople are usually hard to find and too busy to spend much time with you, while mail order salespeople will usually stay with you as long as you need.

7. Many people like to buy at retail stores because they get to deal face-to-face with a salesperson, which gives them more confidence in the purchase.

a. 4, 5, 7   c. 1, 2, 5

b. 1, 3, 6   d. 3, 5, 6

POST-TEST 3

A. Read each paragraph and identify the correct topic.

1. A Web site might be thought of as a special type of publication. In some cases, the entire contents of an individual Web site are contributed by the Web author. In other instances, a Web site consists of some material developed by the Web author and connections to other resources found on computers throughout the Internet. A Web user does not have to keep track of who authored what in the Web site. The user simply follows links embedded within the content of Web pages from one topic of interest to another.*

Topic:

a. Publications   c. The World Wide Web

b. Web sites   d. Links in Web sites

2. The flower-selling business rests in no small part on human drama. One blossom can fuel a flaming passion, calm a raging jealousy, salve a sickness. Back in the 1960s you could join the social revolution just by sticking a flower in your hair. But now raw commerce is involved, too. After Los Angeles the flower market in San Francisco is the country's biggest—a fixture in this ever-changing city for more than 70 years. Aside from the sticky-sweet smell of the wares, the traders might as well be handling auto or electronic parts.†

a. Human drama   c. A 70-year tradition

b. The San Francisco flower market   d. The flower-selling business

* Adapted from Mark Grabe and Cindy Grabe, *Integrating Technology for Meaningful Learning.* Boston: Houghton Mifflin, 1998, 204.

† Adapted from Vivienne Walt, "Flower Trade," *National Geographic,* April, 2001, 106.

Copyright © Houghton Mifflin Company. All rights reserved.

3. If you're like me, you probably have one or two really close friends and a lot of great acquaintances. But that's good because that's what you need. According to Dr. John Litwac of the University of Massachusetts Medical Center, people in modern society require a variety of friends to meet their needs. And the variety of friends we need varies over time. What Dr. Litwac says in a book, *Adult Friendships,* is that the friendships we enjoy when we are young differ a lot from those we experience as we grow older. As we develop, so does the complexity and intimacy of our relationships.*

a. Friendships   c. Modern society

b. Experience   d. Complexity

4. "If I told my husband, who is not a nutritionist, to eat a varied diet, he would say, 'Aha! I can eat anything and everything and as much as I want,'" says Althea Zanecosky, M.S., R.D., a spokeswoman for the American Dietetic Association. "But eating lots and lots of food, especially foods with low nutritional quality like cake and chips, is not what 'eat a variety of foods' means." Instead, says Zanecosky, it means "eat different foods from different food groups on different days. For example, if you ate chicken on Monday night, then have beans or eggs for dinner on Tuesday night. If you tend to eat apples and oranges to satisfy your 'fruit quota,' then substitute blueberries and cantaloupe for a few days instead."†

a. Nutritionists   c. A varied diet

b. Food groups   d. Nutritional quality

5. I can accept that many people take fashion seriously, but I have never been a fashion buff. To me, dressing in style is pointless. I can, however, accept that many people love to dress in style, but there is one particular fashion "statement" that totally baffles me. I mean, specifically, wearing a fashionable watch. To me, it is beyond comprehension that multitudes pay hundreds or thousands of dollars for their watches. My watch cost me $13.00. It keeps accurate time, and it has a stopwatch, an alarm, and when I want it, a very good light for telling the time in the dark. My watch may not be "stylish," but I suppose you could say it's part of how I "dress in style."

a. Fashion statements   c. Fashionable watches

b. Dressing in style   d. Watches

* From Michael Osborn and Suzanne Osborn, *Public Speaking.* Boston: Houghton Mifflin, 2000, 356.

† From Christie Riggins Walking, "Just Say Yes," December, 2001, rd.com/common/nav/index.jhtml?articleId=9520798.

Copyright © Houghton Mifflin Company. All rights reserved.

B. For each item, decide whether the topic listed for the paragraph is too broad, too narrow, or the correct topic for the paragraph.

6. Why do people dance? The urge springs from the same desire to express that motivates the other arts, but the medium is the most accessible—the human body. Dancing is in a sense "body language." We have all felt the need to express fear, sorrow, anger, love, and joy with gesture and with movement. One can express an emotion in movement before it can be put into words and also gesture feelings beyond the limits of words.*

Topic: How people express themselves

a. Too broad   c. The correct topic
b. Too narrow

7. Many people do not achieve their full potential because they are afraid to venture outside their "comfort zone." These individuals often earn less than they deserve, exert little effort to win a promotion to a more challenging position, and refuse assignments that might enhance their career. Some people stay in their comfort zone because they fear success. This fear can stem from a variety of sources such as low self-esteem or family upbringing.†

Topic: Earning too little salary

a. Too broad   c. The correct topic
b. Too narrow

8. Otto von Bismarck (1815–1898), the most important figure in German history between Luther and Hitler, has been the object of enormous interest and debate. A great hero to some, a great villain to others, Bismarck was above all a master of politics. Bismarck had a strong personality and an unbounded desire for power. Yet in his drive to secure power for himself and for Prussia, Bismarck was extraordinarily flexible and pragmatic. He kept his options open, pursuing one policy and then another as he moved with skill and cunning toward his goal.‡

Topic: Otto von Bismarck

a. Too broad   c. The correct topic
b. Too narrow

* From Mary Ann Frese Witt et al., *The Humanities,* Vol. II. Boston: Houghton Mifflin, 1997, 181.
† From Barry L. Reece and Rhonda Brandt, *Effective Human Relationships in Organizations* 7th ed. Boston: Houghton Mifflin, 1999, 190.
‡ Adapted from John P. McKay et al., *A History of World Societies,* Vol. II. Boston: Houghton Mifflin, 1996, 834.

Copyright © Houghton Mifflin Company. All rights reserved.

2

9. There's a fine line between motivation and intimidation: A new study suggests that a woman's performance may hinge on the phrasing or type of positive feedback she receives. Indeed, praise that indicates much is expected might render women more anxious and less equipped to perform the task a second time, according to Rebecca Shulak, B.A. Shulak conducted the research as a psychology student at Sonoma State University in California. She administered word-search tests to 40 college women. One group was verbally praised and told that their performance indicated probable academic and professional success. A second group received rewards such as candy and chips. This group demonstrated no anxiety when repeating the test. However, they did not score as well as those who received verbal feedback.*

Topic: How rewards such as candy affect performance in women

a. Too broad   c. The correct topic

b. Too narrow

10. The consumers' right to safety means that the products they purchase must be safe for their intended use, must include thorough and explicit directions for proper use, and must be tested by the manufacturer to ensure product quality and reliability. There are several reasons why American business firms must be concerned about product safety. Federal agencies such as the Food and Drug Administration and the Consumer Product Safety Commission have the power to force businesses that make or sell defective products to take corrective actions. Such actions include offering refunds, recalling defective products, issuing public warnings and reimbursing consumers.†

Topic: Consumer safety

a. Too broad   c. The correct topic

b. Too narrow

C. Read each paragraph and identify the main idea.

11. That ache in your spine could be an infection. Researchers at the Royal Orthopaedic Hospital in Birmingham, England, found that a surprising number of patients with sciatica—pain extending from the back into the legs—had infectious microorganisms in the area of the sciatic nerve. In one group, 43 of 140 people had the bacteria; among 36 patients with severe sciatica, 19 carried the bug. The researchers theorize that some cases of

*Adapted from "Positive Feedback May Backfire," *Psychology Today,* January/February 2002, 16.
†Adapted from William M. Pride et al., *Business.* Boston: Houghton Mifflin, 1999, 41.

Copyright © Houghton Mifflin Company. All rights reserved.

2

lower-back pain are actually chronic low-grade infections, and that these occur when microscopic tears in spinal disks allow the organisms entry.*

Main Idea:

a. There is a research lab at the Royal Orthopaedic Hospital in Birmingham, England.

b. Sciatica is pain extending from the back into the legs.

c. Lower back pain is sometimes the result of an infection.

d. Out of 36 patients with severe sciatica, 19 carried infectious microorganisms.

12. Genetic engineering can do remarkable things to flowering of plants. Not everyone agrees it's desirable to fool Mother Nature this way, but there's no denying the potential significance of the results. Getting a plant to flower even slightly earlier or later than normal can extend the geographical range of a particularly favored variety. Fast flowering also means faster breeding.†

Main Idea:

a. Not everyone agrees that genetic engineering should be used on plants.

b. Genetic engineering can remarkably affect the flowering of plants.

c. Flowering even slightly earlier can mean faster plant breeding.

d. You can extend the geographical range of a particularly favored variety.

13. Sometimes new teachers who want to engage their students in a student-centered, activity-based science learning environment are intimidated by messy materials and by what appears to be disarray. It is true: when students are using materials, working in groups, and trying to solve their own problems, the classroom will look a bit messy and sound a little noisy. But those are good signs. They are indications that active learning is taking place and that the students are taking charge of their own experiences—with guidance and coaching from their teacher.‡

Main Idea:

a. Classroom noise and messiness are signs that active learning is taking place.

b. Messiness and disarray encourage guidance and coaching from a teacher.

* From John O'Neill, as quoted in the *New York Times,* "Bacterial Back Pain," *Reader's Digest,* January 2002, 48.

† Adapted from Rosie Mestel, "Rhythm and Blooms," *Natural History,* June, 2000, 74.

‡ From Janice Koch, *Science Stories.* Boston: Houghton Mifflin, 1999, 143.

Copyright © Houghton Mifflin Company. All rights reserved.

c. Teachers seek to establish a student-centered, activity-based science learning environment.

d. New teachers are especially known for encouraging noise and messiness in their classrooms.

14. In 1791, a study committee of the French Academy of Sciences devised the "metric system" of units, in which larger and smaller units of a given quantity are related by multiples of 10. For example, 1 kilometer is exactly 1000 meters. (By comparison, 1 mile equals 5280 feet.) The metric system is now used in most countries of the world and in all scientific work. Even the present system of units in the United States, although not a metric system, is defined in terms of the metric system. For example, the inch is exactly 0.0254 meter.*

Main Idea:

a. In the metric system, 1 kilometer is exactly 1000 meters.

b. The U.S. measurement of one inch is exactly 0.0254 meter.

c. Scientists in all but a few countries use the metric system for every calculation they make.

d. Devised in France in 1791, the metric system is now used throughout the world.

15. President Franklin Delano Roosevelt recognized the importance of radio for informing the nation and embarked on a series of radio talks to promote his administration's policies. The popular broadcasts became known as "fireside chats." Roosevelt delivered thirty-one fireside chats over the radio during his thirteen years as president. Historians agree that the chats reassured Americans during the Great Depression, and mobilized them to fight Japan and Germany during World War II.†

Main Idea:

a. Radio is an important method of informing the nation.

b. President Roosevelt's "fireside chats" were a popular and effective use of radio.

c. Americans needed reassurance during the Great Depression.

d. During Franklin Roosevelt's thirteen years as president, he delivered thirty-one "fireside chats."

* Adapted from Darrell D. Ebbing and R. A. D. Wentworth, *Fundamentals of Introductory Chemistry.* Boston: Houghton Mifflin, 1998, 17.

† Adapted from Joseph Turow, *Media Today.* Boston: Houghton Mifflin, 1999, 178.

Copyright © Houghton Mifflin Company. All rights reserved.

D. Read each paragraph and circle the main idea.

16. In calculating report card grades, teachers do not evaluate students based on a single test or sample of performance. Combining several trustworthy scores from several different tests will increase the reliability substantially. Teachers base grades on points accumulated from a variety of sources. Therefore, the final grade is likely to be reliable even though a single test may not be.*

    Main Idea:

    a. Teachers combine a variety of trustworthy scores in calculating reliable report card grades.

    b. Teachers often use a single major test as a reliable guide for calculating report card grades.

    c. There are many different methods teachers use to calculate report card grades.

    d. When scores are accumulated from a variety of sources, teachers often discard the highest and lowest scores.

17. A composer's working methods are unique to his personality. Some composers are fluent and fast: Rossini, it is said, preferred rewriting a page to picking up a leaf of manuscript fallen to the floor, and Mozart appears to have been able to keep the totality of a work in his mind's ear at every turning point. Beethoven worked with great difficulty; Mahler revised compulsively, forever tinkering with bass drum strokes and cymbal crashes.†

    Main Idea:

    a. Beethoven worked with great difficulty.

    b. Some composers work quickly, seemingly without effort.

    c. Every composer has unique working methods.

    d. Mozart could keep track of several musical parts simultaneously.

18. Earth's origins lie in the creation of the universe. Just how this came about remains unclear, but many scientists accept some version of the "big bang" theory, which goes like this. At first all energy and matter (then only subatomic particles) were closely concentrated. About 15,000 million years ago, a vast explosion scattered everything through space. Star studies prove the universe is still expanding, and background radiation hints at its initial heat.‡

* From Sharon J. Sherman, *Science and Science Teaching*. Boston: Houghton Mifflin, 2000, 183.

† Adapted from D. Kern Holoman, *Masterworks: A Musical Discovery*. New York: Prentice-Hall, 1998, 7.

‡ From David Lambert and the Diagram Group, *The Field Guide to Geology*. New York: Facts on File, 1988, 16.

Copyright © Houghton Mifflin Company. All rights reserved.

2

2

Main Idea:

a. The universe is still expanding.

b. Some scientists do not accept the "big bang" theory.

c. Energy and matter were at first subatomic materials that were closely concentrated.

d. Many scientists accept the "big bang" theory of the universe's origins.

19. The War of 1812 saw the birth of an American icon: "Uncle Sam." He appears to have arisen in 1813 in Troy, New York, but little more than that is known. The inspiration for Uncle Sam is sometimes traced to one Samuel Wilson, an army inspector in Troy, but it seems more probable that the name was merely derived from the initials U.S. The top-hatted, striped-trousered figure we associate with the name was popularized in the 1860s in the cartoons of Thomas Nast, and later reinforced by the famous I WANT YOU recruiting posters of the artist James Montgomery Flagg.*

Main Idea:

a. "Uncle Sam" possibly originated in 1813 and was later popularized by Thomas Nast and James Montgomery Flagg.

b. Americans first saw "Uncle Sam" in the top-hatted, striped-trousered cartoon figure created by Thomas Nast in the 1860s.

c. Samuel Wilson, an army inspector in Troy, was definitely the inspiration for the original "Uncle Sam."

d. It is possible that the American icon "Uncle Sam" was merely derived from the initials U.S.

20. By 1066, the English social system was elaborate and stable. There were many strata. At the bottom were serfs or slaves; next cottagers or cottars; then villeins, who farmed as much perhaps as fifty acres; then thanes, who drew rents in kind from the villeins; then earls, each ruling one of the six great earldoms that covered the country; and above all, the king.†

Main Idea:

a. There were six ruling English earldoms in 1066.

b. In 1066, villeins were people who farmed as much perhaps as fifty acres.

c. The English social system in 1066 was stable and had many strata.

d. At the top of the entire English social system in 1066 was the king.

* Adapted from Bill Bryson, *Made in America*. New York: Avon, 1994, 65.
† Adapted from David Howarth, *1066*. New York: Penguin, 1977, 14.

Copyright © Houghton Mifflin Company. All rights reserved.

CHAPTER 3
Supporting Details

GOALS FOR CHAPTER 3

▶ Describe the principles of effective time management.

▶ Define the terms *major details* and *minor details*.

▶ Recognize major and minor details in paragraphs.

▶ Define the term *transitions*.

▶ Locate transitions that often identify major details and minor details.

▶ Recognize transitions in paragraphs.

▶ Use mapping to show major and minor details in a paragraph.

▶ Use outlining to show major and minor details in a paragraph.

3

READING STRATEGY: Reading and Time Management

How often should you read? How long should you try to read in one sitting? How many times should you read a chapter? Is it better to read the whole chapter at once or just a section at a time?

There are no right or wrong answers to these questions. The most effective length, amount, and frequency of reading time will differ from student to student and from class to class. You will have to experiment to discover what works best for you, and you will probably need to make adjustments for each different course you take.

However, be aware of the following general principles of effective time management:

- Schedule time to read. Don't just try to fit reading in whenever you can; actually make an appointment to read by blocking out regular times on your calendar.

- The best time to read is the time of day or night when you are most mentally alert. If you're a night owl, read at night. If you're a morning person, try to fit in your reading time at the beginning of your day.

Continued

Copyright © Houghton Mifflin Company. All rights reserved.

- Take frequent breaks during reading sessions. Regularly stand up and stretch, walk around, and rest your eyes for a few minutes.

- Keep up with the reading assignments in a course by following the schedule provided by your instructor. Following the schedule will give you the basic understanding of the material you'll need in order to get the most out of class lectures, discussions, and activities.

- Try to schedule time for multiple readings of the same chapter. Repeated exposure to information helps increase your retention of the material. If you hurriedly read large chunks of information all at once just before a test, you probably won't remember much of it. If you digest information slowly and regularly over a longer period of time, you'll remember more.

Answer the following questions:

1. Describe the typical length, amount, and frequency of reading time that seems to work best for you.

   _____

2. Describe a time when you took a class that required you to alter significantly the length, amount, and/or frequency of your reading.

   _____

3. What time of day are you most mentally alert? Is that the time of day when you usually read?

   _____

4. Which of the guidelines listed above do you already practice?

   _____

   _____

5. Which of the guidelines above do you think you should implement in order to get more out of your reading?

   _____

Copyright © Houghton Mifflin Company. All rights reserved.

In the previous chapter, you practiced finding the main idea of a paragraph. The main idea is the general point the writer wants you to know or to believe when you've finished reading the paragraph. Often, though, readers cannot understand or accept this point as true unless they get more information. The **supporting details** in a paragraph provide this information.

Before continuing, take this pre-test to find out what you already know about supporting details.

PRE-TEST

Identify the main idea and write it on the blank following each paragraph. Then, choose one sentence that you think is a *major* detail supporting that main idea. Write the number of that sentence in the blank below your main idea statement.

1. (1) The United States is home to many highly regarded universities with an African-American tradition. (2) From a shanty and church in rural Alabama, African-American visionary Booker T. Washington built the future Tuskegee Institute, which has been around for 120 years. (3) Another example, Howard University, in Washington, D.C., is the largest of these schools. (4) It has a fine reputation as an educational institution. (5) Nashville is the home to Fisk, which was founded in 1866. (6) Fisk is noted for having W. E. B. DuBois among its graduates. (7) And finally, the state of Georgia has Morehouse University, whose graduates include Martin Luther King, Jr., and Spike Lee.*

   Main Idea: *#1*
   _____
                #2
   _____

   Major Supporting Detail: *#3 #5 #7*

2. (1) There are certain things you should do to keep children safe around cars in warm weather. (2) First, teach children not to play in, on, or around cars. (3) Second, never leave a child or pet unattended in a motor vehicle, even with the window slightly open. (4) Car temperatures can rise to 122 degrees within 20 minutes and 150 degrees within 40 minutes on a hot day. (5) Always lock car doors and trunks—even at home—and keep keys out of children's reach. (6) And finally, watch children closely around cars, particularly when loading or unloading. (7) Check to ensure that all children leave the vehicle when you reach your destination. (8) Don't overlook sleeping infants. (9) Following all of these suggestions will ensure safety when it comes to children and automobiles in hot weather.†

* Adapted from "Don't Know Much About Historically Black Colleges," *USA Weekend,* July 6–8, 2001, 14.

† Adapted from Cathy Elcik, "Summer Safety: Kids and Cars Don't Mix," *Westchester Family,* July 2001, 24.

Copyright © Houghton Mifflin Company. All rights reserved.

Main Idea: *#1* _____

_____

Major Supporting Detail: *# 2 # 3 # 5 # 6* _____

3. (1) The benefits of walking go well beyond the purely physical. (2) More than any other activity, walking is a sure way to jump-start the brain, set thoughts in motion, and calm our troubles. (3) Prompted by our modest exertions, just a few minutes into a walk the body begins to produce endorphins, chemical compounds that reduce pain and stress, enhance memory and judgment as they course through the brain. (4) Walking also produces increased levels of serotonin, an important brain neurotransmitter that increases feelings of well-being. (5) For this reason, doctors recommend walking as a treatment for mild depression and anxiety.*

Main Idea: *# 1* _____

Major Supporting Detail: *#2 #3 #4 #* _____

4. (1) Jack Lemmon was one of the finest, funniest, and most popular movie actors of the second half of the last century. (2) He was a middle-class Everyman forever tugging at his collar. (3) His shoulders hunched in anticipation of trouble on the way, and his smile was more nervous than an expression of pleasure. (4) Lemmon represented the white-collar American male, always having problems, but lovable. (5) People loved him because his characters were never larger than life; they were people most Americans could identify with.†

Main Idea: *#1* _____

_____

Major Supporting Detail: *#2 # 4 # 5* _____

5. (1) If you live with a chronic snorer, take a hard look at his habits. (2) Some simple changes could stop a snoring problem for good. (3) For example, being overweight is the most common cause of snoring, so if you can get your bedmate to take off a few pounds, the snoring may become less frequent. (4) Also, don't allow your bedmate to drink alcohol before going to bed, as that can increase the frequency of snoring during the night. (5) Sleeping on the back is another cause of snoring. (6) And finally, encourage your bedmate to quit if he smokes cigarettes; smoking is known as a leading cause of snoring in addition to being an unhealthy habit.‡

* Adapted from Gregory McNamee, "Wandering Soles," *Modern Maturity,* September/October 2001, 76.

† Adapted from David Ansen, "Nobody's Perfect, but Some Get Close," *Newsweek,* July 9, 2001, 61.

‡ Adapted from Ellie McGrath, "How to Sleep with a Snorer," *Good Housekeeping,* May 2000, 64–68.

Copyright © Houghton Mifflin Company. All rights reserved.

Main Idea: #2 _____

Major Supporting Detail: #3   #4   #5   #6 _____

3

Supporting details are the specific facts, statistics, examples, steps, anecdotes, reasons, descriptions, definitions, and so on that explain or prove the general main idea stated in the topic sentence. They support, or provide a solid foundation for, this main idea.

Supporting details should answer all of the questions raised by the topic sentence. For example, read the following statement:

> Female surgeons are treated differently from male surgeons by their colleagues, nurses, and patients.

This topic sentence immediately raises the questions *how?* and *why?* in the reader's mind. To answer the questions, the paragraph must go on to offer the reasons and other explanations that prove this point.

As you read this next paragraph, notice how the supporting details clarify the main idea, which is in boldface, and explain why it's true:

> **If you want to become rich, you must follow four important rules.** The first rule is to establish a reasonable income base. To reach and maintain that stable, middle-income base, you should earn a college degree, marry someone with an equal or higher education and stay married, and work as long as you are able to. The second rule for becoming rich is to avoid frivolous temptations. For example, don't drive expensive luxury cars; instead, buy medium-priced cars. Following rule #2 will allow you to save more money, which is rule #3. Average people who become rich often do so because they save more of their money, even if they must make sacrifices to do so. Finally, the fourth rule to becoming rich is take advantage of compound interest. If you invested $2,000 every year from age 22 to age 65, and that money earned 10 percent interest per year, you'd have over a million dollars when you retired.*

The topic sentence of this paragraph raises the question, *What are these rules for becoming rich?* Then, the paragraph goes on to answer that question by explaining the four things you must do to increase your wealth. The reader would not be able to understand the topic sentence without reading the details in the rest of the paragraph. It's important to learn to recognize supporting details, for they determine your understanding and interpretation of what you read.

---

* Adapted from Richard B. McKenzie and Dwight R. Lee, "Becoming Wealthy: It's Up to You," *USA Today,* September 1998, 16–19.

Copyright © Houghton Mifflin Company. All rights reserved.

Major and Minor Details

There are two kinds of supporting details: major details and minor details. The **major details** are the main points that explain or support the idea in the topic sentence. They offer *essential* reasons or other information that the reader must have in order to understand the main idea.

Minor details offer more explanation of the major details. Minor details are not usually critical to the reader's comprehension of the main idea, though they do offer more specific information that helps clarify even more the points in the paragraph.

To see the difference between major and minor details, read the following paragraph:

> **Many Americans believe in the supernatural.** For one thing, they believe in supernatural beings. A recent Gallup poll revealed that 69 percent of people believe in angels, half of them believe they have their own guardian angels, and 48 percent believe that there are aliens in outer space. Americans also believe in the existence of supernatural powers. For example, over 10 million people have called the Psychic Friends network to get advice about their present and future.*

The topic sentence of this paragraph, which is in boldface, raises the question, *What kinds of supernatural things do they believe in?* The second and fourth sentences of the paragraph answer that question. They tell the reader that Americans believe in supernatural beings and supernatural powers. The other sentences in the paragraph offer minor details. In this case, the minor details offer examples of the kinds of beings and powers people believe are real. Therefore, they offer nonessential information that helps explain the main idea even more.

Remember the explanation of general and specific sentences back in Chapter 2? You learned that the topic sentence is the most general statement in a paragraph, while the other sentences offer more specific information. Well, these other sentences (the supporting details) are also related to each other in general and specific ways. It might be helpful to visualize these relationships in a diagram form as shown at the top of the next page.

This diagram offers a useful visual image of the general and specific relationships among sentences in paragraphs. The major details—represented in the blocks beneath the topic sentence—provide the solid foundation of support for the main idea. You could not remove any of these blocks without significantly weakening the base on which the main idea rests. The minor details in the next row of blocks make the structure even sturdier. Though the

* Adapted from Jill Neimark, "Do the Spirits Move You?" *Psychology Today*, September 19, 1966, 48.

Copyright © Houghton Mifflin Company. All rights reserved.

```
┌─────────────────────────────────────┐
│        Many Americans believe        │
│        in the supernatural.          │
└─────────────────────────────────────┘
┌──────────────────────┬──────────────────────┐
│ For one thing, they  │ Americans also       │
│ believe in           │ believe in the       │
│ supernatural beings. │ existence of         │
│                      │ supernatural powers. │
├──────────────────────┼──────────────────────┤
│ A recent Gallup poll │ For example, over    │
│ revealed that        │ 10 million           │
│ 69 percent of people │ people have called   │
│ believe in angels,   │ the Psychic          │
│ half of them believe │ Friends network to   │
│ they have their      │ get advice           │
│ own guardian angels, │ about their present  │
│ and 48 percent       │ and future.          │
│ believe that there   │                      │
│ are aliens in outer  │                      │
│ space.               │                      │
└──────────────────────┴──────────────────────┘
```

main idea would still be supported by the major details even if the minor details were removed, the minor details make the whole base even stronger.

To better understand what you read, you may want to try to visualize the sentences in a diagram like the one above. Sorting out these relationships is critical not only to comprehending a paragraph but also to deciding whether or not you can agree with the author's ideas.

Exercise 3.1

Read the following paragraphs, and then label the list of sentences that follow as MI for main idea, MAJOR for major detail, or MINOR for minor detail.

1. (1) Walkie-talkies are becoming a fashionable way for families to stay in touch during outings at places like malls and amusement parks. (2) One reason for walkie-talkies' popularity is their low cost. (3) Cell phones charge monthly fees, but walkie-talkies cost an average of just $35 each, with no extra fees beyond the cost of batteries. (4) Another reason more parents and children are using walkie-talkies is their ease of use. (5) You don't have to dial a number; you just push a button to talk and release it to listen.*

   _____MI_____ Sentence 1

   Major 2 Sentence 2

   minor 3 Sentence 3

* Adapted from Leonard Wiener, "Hello? Can You Hear Me? Walkie-Talkies Are the Rage," *U.S. News and World Report Online,* July 2, 2001, www.usnews.com/usnews/issue/010702/tech/walkie.htm.

Copyright © Houghton Mifflin Company. All rights reserved.

2. (1) Venus Williams is one of the best tennis players in the United States today. (2) She has won many tennis tournaments, including Wimbledon. (3) She won there in spite of playing on a grass court, which is considered a difficult surface for tennis players to master. (4) She has also beaten some of the great players in the game today—Martina Hingis and Jennifer Capriati—which puts her in an elite league of players. (5) And for several years, she has been listed among the best tennis players in the world.

MI _____1_____ Sentence 1

Major _2_ Sentence 2

Major _4_ Sentence 4

3. (1) Learning to ride a motorcycle can be a very difficult thing to do. (2) First, balancing yourself on two wheels can be frightening, especially since, if you fall, a thousand-pound machine can land on top of you! (3) It is also hard to manage the coordination between the gear shift and the gas pedal, although Harley Davidson makes a motorcycle that is easier to handle than most. (4) It can be a little intimidating, too, to ride a motorcycle on a major highway with cars going past you at 60 miles an hour. (5) It is fun, however, to feel the wind whipping through your hair as you ride.

MI _1_ Sentence 1

Major _2_ Sentence 2

Major _3_ Sentence 3

4. (1) You can become a good writer if you put your mind to it. (2) The best thing to do if you want to learn to write well is to write every day. (3) Writing every day increases confidence in your skills, so you should set aside time in your schedule every day to write for fun, for school, or just for practice. (4) You should also make sure that you have a good, quiet place to write, as that can increase your concentration.

MI _1_ Sentence 1

Major _2_ Sentence 2

Minor _3_ Sentence 3

5. (1) Working with a personal trainer is a good way to begin an exercise program. (2) Personal trainers will make sure that you are in good enough health to start exercising and will tailor a program to fit your fitness level, your body type, and your schedule. (3) Furthermore, you will see results faster if you work with a trainer. (4) A trainer will encourage you to stick with your program and make it harder for you to quit.

Copyright © Houghton Mifflin Company. All rights reserved.

MI __1__   Sentence 1

Major __3__   Sentence 3

Minor __4__   Sentence 4

Exercise 3.2

Read each paragraph and rewrite an abbreviated form of each sentence in the boxes that follow to indicate their general and specific relationships.

1. Since she discovered tennis at the age of 10, Zina Garrison has encountered extraordinary, inspiring people at tennis camps and in early matches. Althea Gibson, the first great African-American tennis player, taught her about the physical and mental requirements for becoming a professional. Arthur Ashe taught her about a slice backhand and dedication to the sport. Once she had made the choice to be dedicated, Motown's Berry Gordy taught her about grace under pressure. "No matter what," he said, "win like a champion, lose like a champion."*

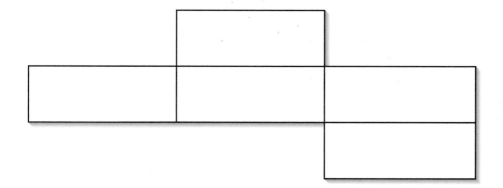

2. Cheating on tests can be a tempting choice. One benefit is that we might get a good grade without having to study. Instead of studying, we could have more time to watch TV, party, sleep, or do anything that seems like more fun. Another benefit is that we could avoid the risk of doing poorly on a test—which could happen even if we do study. And finally, by doing well on a test, we can look better to our instructors.†

* Adapted from Elizabeth Kaye, "After Youth, Then What?" *O Magazine*, June 2001, 160.

† Adapted from Dave Ellis, "Integrity in Test-Taking: The Costs of Cheating," from *Becoming a Master Student*. Boston: Houghton Mifflin, 2000, 173.

Copyright © Houghton Mifflin Company. All rights reserved.

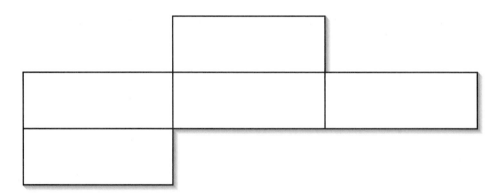

3. If you find that procrastination, or putting things off, hurts your progress, here are some ways to break the habit. First, look at the benefits of doing the work at hand. Will you feel a sense of accomplishment when the job is done, and will you feel less stressed and more relieved? Next, break the job into smaller parts. Break the work into 15-minute segments, take a break after each segment, and work slowly to build up your capacity to work. Another strategy is to reward yourself when you are done. Finally, if you simply can't break the procrastination habit, just sit down and force yourself to complete the task.*

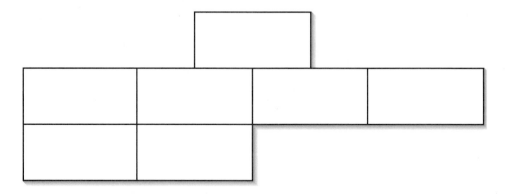

4. Life on the farm was much harder than the advertisements and railroad agents suggested because farmers often encountered scarcities of essentials they had once taken for granted. The open prairies contained little lumber for housing and fuel. As a result, pioneer families were forced to build houses of sod and to burn manure for heat. Water was sometimes as scarce as timber. Few families were lucky or wealthy enough to buy land

* Adapted from Sherman and Sherman, "Getting Yourself to Study," from *Essential Concepts of Chemistry*. Boston: Houghton Mifflin, 1999, xxxi–xxxii.

Copyright © Houghton Mifflin Company. All rights reserved.

near a stream that did not dry up in the summer and freeze in winter, and machinery for drilling wells was scarce until the 1880s.*

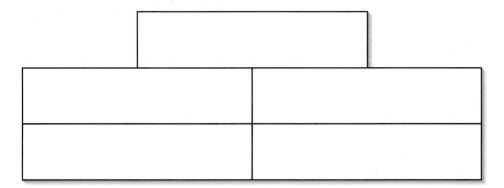

3

5. Americans tend to believe several long-standing myths about families past and present. The first myth concerns the roles of family members. Many people think that the 1950s, an era of bread-winning dads and stay-at-home moms, was the last decade in a long era of stable families, but 1950s families actually reversed a 100-year trend of rising divorce rates. A second myth concerns the best family structure. People assume that a return to roles common within a 1950s family would decrease the number of broken homes, but today, sole bread-winning males are often less competent fathers, and stay-at-home women often feel isolated and depressed. Another myth relates to the number and severity of family problems. Though people believe that modern families face worse problems, the truth is that families in all eras of history have dealt with difficulties like drug and alcohol addiction and abuse.†

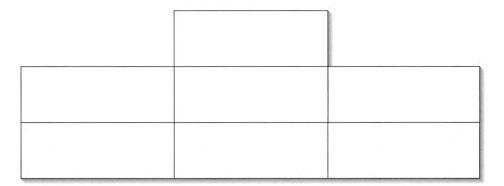

* Adapted from Norton et al., *A People and a Nation.* Vol II. Boston: Houghton Mifflin, 1998, 492.
† Adapted from "Unrealistic Family Myths," *USA Today Newsview,* December 1997, 1–2.

Copyright © Houghton Mifflin Company. All rights reserved.

Exercise 3.3

Read the paragraph below and answer the questions that follow by circling the correct response.

(1) Are you interested in the idea of vacationing at a farm? (2) Before booking your trip, there are a few important things to consider, says guidebook author Jay Golan, who stayed on farms while researching *Frommer's Philadelphia & the Amish Country,* his book about farm vacations. (3) First, he says, some people could be put off by rural America's old-fashioned ways. (4) For the most part, men do the farm work and women do the household chores. (5) If you don't want your children to experience that lifestyle, you may not want to visit. (6) Second, there are often smells that can bother city slickers who aren't used to them. (7) On farms that have cattle and chickens, there can be overpowering smells in the air that people who live in and around the city find hard to take. (8) Third, you may get dirty. (9) City people sometimes show up in designer clothing, which is not the thing to wear on the farm. (10) You have to expect that you will pick up dirt or manure on your shoes or boots if you are going to be on a farm. (11) Indeed, at one farm, the owner's one rule is that people visiting the chicken house must scrub their shoes before returning to the farmhouse. Chicken droppings, it turns out, are surprisingly sticky!*

1. The main idea is expressed in sentence

   a. 1   c. 3

   b. 2   d. 4

2. The supporting details of this paragraph relate to

   a. farms.
   b. things about a farm you may not like.
   c. cows and cattle.
   d. smells on the farm.

3. Which of the following is NOT a *major* detail in this paragraph?

   a. "Third, you may get dirty."
   b. "Second, there are often smells that can bother city slickers who aren't used to them."
   c. "City people sometimes show up in designer clothing, which is not the thing to wear on the farm."
   d. "First, he says, some people could be put off by rural America's old-fashioned ways."

* Adapted from Gene Sloan, "Farmers Are Bullish on City Tourists," *USA Today,* June 29, 2001, 4d. Copyright © 2001, *USA Today.* Reprinted with permission.

Copyright © Houghton Mifflin Company. All rights reserved.

4. Which of the following would be considered a *minor* detail in this paragraph?

   a. "First, he says, some people could be put off by rural America's old-fashioned ways."

   b. "You have to expect that you will pick up dirt or manure on your shoes or boots if you are going to be on a farm."

   c. "Second, there are often smells that can bother city slickers who aren't used to them."

   d. "Before booking your trip, there are a few important things to consider, says guidebook author Jay Golan, who stayed on farms while researching *Frommer's Philadelphia & the Amish Country,* his book about farm vacations."

5. People who are not used to farm life often show up with designer clothing because

   a. they are not prepared for the realities of farm life.

   b. they like to wear designer clothes all of the time.

   c. they think farmers wear designer clothes too.

   d. they are too materialistic.

Transitions

To help readers recognize the general and specific relationships between sentences in a paragraph, paragraphs usually include transitions. **Transitions** are words that assist readers in distinguishing between major and minor details because they make connections and distinctions between the different details. In particular, sentences that offer major details are likely to begin with words such as:

first, second, third	finally
in addition	one
and	another
also	furthermore
next	

These words signal that the sentence will offer another new point in support of the topic sentence. For an example of transitions that indicate major details, read the following paragraph. These transitions are in bold print:

Copyright © Houghton Mifflin Company. All rights reserved.

Several states are considering extending daylight savings time so that it would start earlier in the spring and end later in the fall. **One reason** for doing so is to save energy costs. With longer daylight time, need for electricity would be reduced, and both governments and individuals would pay less. **Another reason** for lengthening daylight savings time is increased safety. More daylight into the evening would reduce the number of rush-hour traffic accidents and make Halloween trick-or-treating safer for children.*

The transitions in the list above are not the only ones that identify major details. Others will be discussed later in Chapter 5. However, because they commonly introduce important supporting details, readers should be aware of their function within the paragraph.

A paragraph might also include transitions to indicate minor details. Sentences that offer minor details are sometimes introduced with words such as:

for example	to illustrate
one example	specifically
for instance	in one case

These words can indicate that the sentence is about to offer more specific information to develop the last idea further. In the next paragraph, the transitions that signal minor details are in boldface print, while those that identify major details are in italics:

Certain traits separate the good bosses from the bad bosses. *The first characteristic* is the boss's response to his or her employees. **For example,** a bad boss orders employees around, while a good boss treats employees with respect by recognizing their skills and experience. *The next characteristic* is the boss's response to his employees' ideas. A bad boss, **for instance,** is close-minded and disregards others' input, but a good boss encourages workers to contribute their ideas, and then listens to and seriously considers those ideas. *Finally,* a good boss and a bad boss differ in the way they handle their own egos. A bad boss cares only about his own power and prestige, while a good boss focuses instead on providing the best, most efficient product or service.†

It is important to note here that the transitions in the list above can also be used to introduce *major* details in a paragraph. Chapter 5 will offer more specific information about how paragraphs use transitions in different ways.

* Adapted from "More Daylight Makes Sense," *USA Today Online,* June 18, 2001. www.usatoday.com/usatonline/20010618/3408445s.htm.
† Adapted from Paul B. Hertneky, "You and Your Boss," *Restaurant Hospitality,* August 1, 1996, 78.

Copyright © Houghton Mifflin Company. All rights reserved.

Exercise 3.4

Read each paragraph and underline the topic sentence, circle the transitions that signal major details, and underline transitions that signal minor details.

1. There are some basic principles of outlining you should keep in mind when preparing an outline. First, each point in your outline should contain only one idea or piece of information. Second, your outline should accurately reflect relationships between ideas and supporting material. Third, you should use a consistent system of symbols and indentations. Fourth, write out transitions and relevant portions of introductions and conclusions.*

2. According to management experts, a business must do two things to be successful. First, it must put the customer first—by listening, understanding, and providing customer service. Second, a company—both its managers and employees—must act with speed and flexibility. In one case, Dell Computers, the company scores A+ on both counts. Specifically, in just fourteen years, Dell has made its mark in the computer industry because of its ability to see an opportunity that larger competitors like Compaq and IBM ignored.†

3. One of the brain's primary jobs is to manufacture images so we can use them to make predictions about the world and then base our behavior on those predictions. For one thing, when a cook adds chopped onions, mushrooms, and garlic to a spaghetti sauce, he has a picture of how the sauce will taste and measures each ingredient according to that picture. And, when an artist creates a painting or sculpture, he has a mental picture of the finished piece. Another example would be that of the novelist who has a mental image of the characters she wants to bring to life.‡

* Adapted from Andrews and Andrews, *Public Speaking.* Boston: Houghton Mifflin, 1999, 184–186. Copyright © 1999 by Houghton Mifflin Company. Reprinted with permission.
† Adapted from Pride et al., *Business,* 6th ed. Boston: Houghton Mifflin, 1999, 24.
‡ Adapted from Dave Ellis, "Notice Your Pictures and Let Them Go," *Becoming a Master Student.* Boston: Houghton Mifflin, 2000, 132.

Copyright © Houghton Mifflin Company. All rights reserved.

4. Denis Leary is a comedian who is also devoted to a couple of charities. One charity is called the Kerry Chesire Fund, which helps handicapped people in Ireland. Another is the Cam Neely Foundation, which provides a home away from home for cancer patients. Finally, the Leary Firefighters Foundation raises money to help firefighters get new and improved equipment that could help save their lives during a fire.*

5. Kids today are busier than ever, and Andrea Galambos is no exception. As captain of the junior-varsity volleyball team, first-chair flute in the school orchestra, a top player on the tennis team, and an honors student with three hours of homework a night, Andrea, who was also taking singing and art classes after school, put in 18-hour days. In addition, she was also dealing with the death of her father from cancer, which happened in 1997.†

Mapping and Outlining

Earlier in this chapter, you saw how you can visualize the relationships between sentences in a paragraph by inserting each one into a block. The main idea went into the block at the top, the major supporting details went into the row of blocks just beneath the main idea, and the minor details, if any, were in the third row.

	MAIN IDEA	
MAJOR DETAIL	MAJOR DETAIL	MAJOR DETAIL
Minor Detail	Minor Detail	Minor Detail

* Adapted from Frank DeCaro, "Denis Leary Gets Serious," *Rosie,* July, 2001, 88.
† Adapted from David Noonan, "Stop Stressing Me," *Newsweek,* January 29, 2001, 54.

Copyright © Houghton Mifflin Company. All rights reserved.

This diagram is a form of **mapping,** a technique that involves using lines, boxes, circles, or other shapes to show how sentences in a paragraph are related.

In mapping, you lay out a visual to help you see the main idea, major supporting details, and minor supporting details. Here are some other, different ways to visualize these relationships:

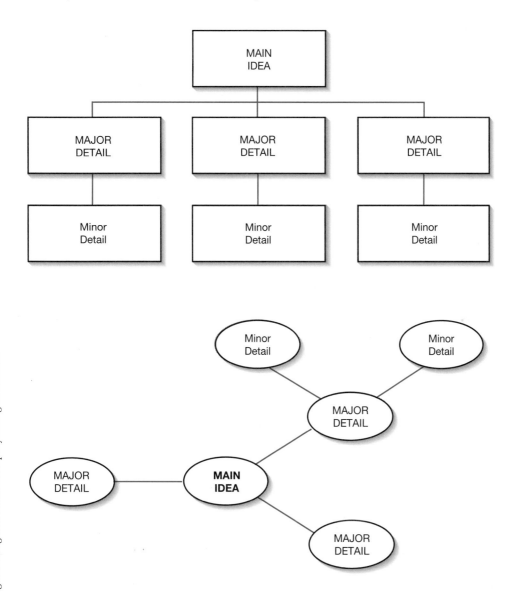

Copyright © Houghton Mifflin Company. All rights reserved.

For example, using the diagram above, you might map the paragraph about good and bad bosses on page 122 like this:

3

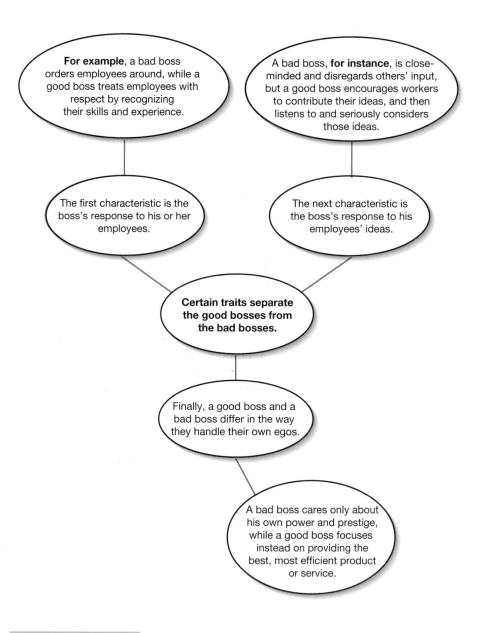

For example, a bad boss orders employees around, while a good boss treats employees with respect by recognizing their skills and experience.

A bad boss, for instance, is close-minded and disregards others' input, but a good boss encourages workers to contribute their ideas, and then listens to and seriously considers those ideas.

The first characteristic is the boss's response to his or her employees.

The next characteristic is the boss's response to his employees' ideas.

Certain traits separate the good bosses from the bad bosses.

Finally, a good boss and a bad boss differ in the way they handle their own egos.

A bad boss cares only about his own power and prestige, while a good boss focuses instead on providing the best, most efficient product or service.

Exercise 3.5

Read each paragraph and fill in the map that follows with an abbreviated form of each sentence.

1. It would be hard to imagine a place better suited for vacations than Florida. On any given day, the sun is almost guaranteed to shine in a clear blue sky. Spectacular beaches stretch a remarkable 1,200 miles.

Copyright © Houghton Mifflin Company. All rights reserved.

Parks and wildlife preserves protect millions of acres. The landscape retains the lush beauty that inspired Spanish explorers to name it La Florida, "Land of Flowers."*

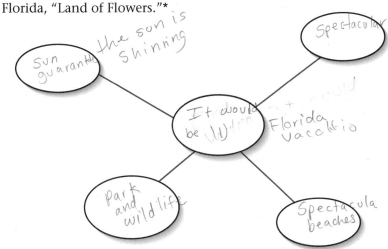

3

2. Companies are finding that business e-mail messages clog computer networks and increasingly take up employees' time, so several companies are encouraging workers to curb e-mail. Intel has recently started classes on how to manage e-mail. And IBM is increasingly using instant messaging instead of e-mail because messaging is less taxing on networks. Another company called Computer Associates asks its employees to place large files on internal networks where they can be viewed by many, and, like Intel, offers e-mail training.†

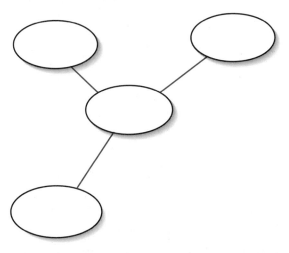

* Adapted from FLA USA, Visit Florida advertisement, from *Ladies' Home Journal*, May 2000.

† Adapted from Jon Swartz, "E-mail Overload Taxes Workers and Companies," *USA Today*, June 26, 2001, 1A.

Copyright © Houghton Mifflin Company. All rights reserved.

3. Some companies are using wireless devices in a variety of ways and reaping big benefits. One Illinois cleaning company called Service-Master, which scrubs Greyhound buses, uses its hand-held wireless network to keep track of customer satisfaction. After each bus is cleaned, a Greyhound supervisor rates the job using an electronic form on one of the company's other computers. Another company is Office Depot, which has cut the time it spends filing and searching for delivery paperwork by 50 percent thanks to a wireless system that links trunks on 22,000 delivery routes. And police officers in Coos Bay, Oregon, no longer have to make two one-hour detours back to headquarters each shift, thanks to a wireless computer in patrol cars that allows them to submit entries to the police log through a wireless network.*

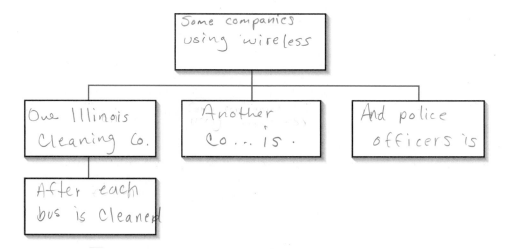

4. According to the Weber Grill-Watch survey, nearly all Americans fall into one of four categories of barbecue grilling personalities. The first category is the Gallant Grillers. These people, who make up 33 percent of barbecue grill owners, are adventurous and love to treat their guests to grilled food experiments. The next group is the Careful Cooks. These grillers—32 percent of grill owners—love to entertain, too, but they are more cautious and follow recipes closely. Busy Barbecuers are the third group. These people, who make up 19 percent of grill owners, like to cook only those foods that don't take much time, and they rarely try new things. The fourth and smallest category is the Need-It-Nows. This 12 percent of grill owners views barbecueing only as a way to produce food, not as a way to entertain or spend time with the family.†

* Adapted from Michelle Kessler, "Gadgets Give Workers on the Run a Leg Up," *USA Today*, June 26, 2001, 5E.

† Adapted from "What's Your Barbecue Profile?" *USA Today*, May 1998, 10.

Copyright © Houghton Mifflin Company. All rights reserved.

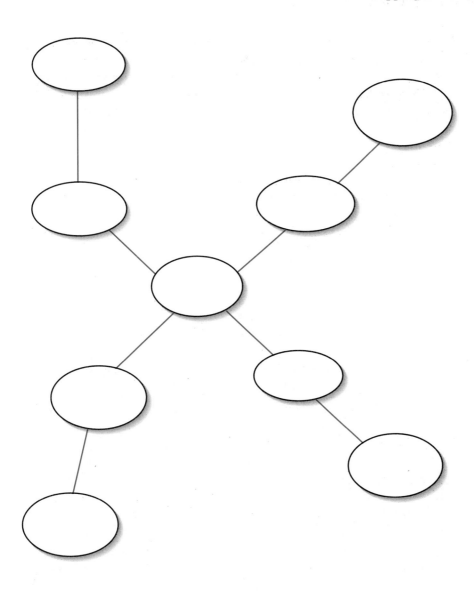

Copyright © Houghton Mifflin Company. All rights reserved.

5. There are some dos and don'ts that you should keep in mind when you are exercising with a dog. First, don't run with toy breeds or short-nosed dogs such as bulldogs, because they don't have a human's endurance. Second, don't run a dog on hot pavement. If the surface is too hot to put your hand on, it's too hot for the dog. Third, if the dog is scared of traffic, or panics next to your bicycle, neither of you will enjoy the workout. Think of alternatives—running in a park

or on side streets rather than on a busy street, for instance. Fourth, if the dog is overweight, is suspected of having heartworms or has any other health problems, check with a veterinarian before beginning an exercise program. Finally, always keep the dog's abilities and limits in mind. Set your pace to match what the dog can do, and cut the workout short if the dog looks tired or stressed.*

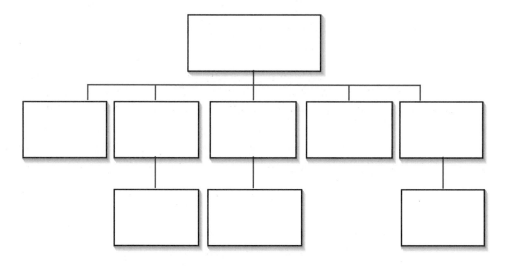

Another good way to identify the main idea and supporting details is to create an outline. An **outline** is a list of these details labeled with a system of numbers and letters that show their relationships to one another. Outlines often use the Roman numeral system, which effectively identifies the main idea and different topics or details. Outlines can be in sentence form or in topic form. The latter is useful for creating a brief summary that allows you, at a glance, to see the general and specific relationships.

   I. Main Idea
      A. Major detail
         1. Minor detail
         2. Minor detail
      B. Major detail
         1. Minor detail
         2. Minor detail

* Adapted from Aline McKenzie, "Do's and Don'ts When Exercising a Dog," *The Journal News,* June 25, 2001, 1E. © Knight Ridder Newspapers. Reprinted by permission of Knight Ridder/ Tribune Information Services.

Copyright © Houghton Mifflin Company. All rights reserved.

For example, you could outline the paragraph about daylight savings time on page 122, as follows:

I. Reasons for extending daylight savings time
   A. Save energy costs
      1. Reduce electricity needs
      2. Governments and individuals would pay less
   B. Increased safety
      1. Fewer rush-hour traffic accidents
      2. Halloween safer for children

To create an outline, line up the major details along one margin and label them with capital letters. Beneath each major detail, indent minor details with numbers: 1, 2, 3, etc.

If you do not like the formality of a Roman numeral outline, you can also outline a paragraph in a more visual way, by using a series of indented boxes in place of the numbers and letters:

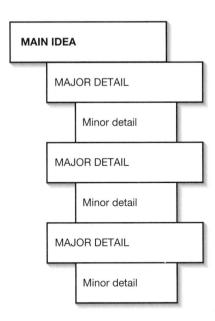

This diagram, like the Roman numeral outline, arranges major details along one margin line and indents minor details beneath each one. You could create an outline of this type for the paragraph about becoming wealthy on page 113, as follows:

Copyright © Houghton Mifflin Company. All rights reserved.

If you want to become rich, you must follow four important rules.

The first rule is to establish a reasonable income base.

To reach and maintain that stable, middle-income base, you should earn a college degree, marry someone with an equal or higher education and stay married, and work as long as you are able to.

The second rule for becoming rich is to avoid frivolous temptations.

For example, don't drive expensive luxury cars; instead, buy medium-priced cars.

Following rule #2 will allow you to save more money, which is rule #3.

Average people who become rich often do so because they save more of their money, even if they must make sacrifices to do so.

Finally, the fourth rule to becoming rich is take advantage of compound interest.

If you invested $2,000 every year from age 22 to age 65, and that money earned 10 percent interest per year, you'd have over a million dollars when you retired.

Exercise 3.6

Complete the outline that follows each paragraph.

1. Celebrities, and in particular movie stars, find it very hard to have long-term relationships for a number of reasons. For one thing, celebrity couples rarely work on movies together. This means that they are often in two different locations at the same time for extended periods of time. It is also hard to have a relationship under the

Copyright © Houghton Mifflin Company. All rights reserved.

constant eye of tabloid newspapers, television reporters, and photographers. Oftentimes, the media mistake photos taken from movies or friends seen together as romantic encounters and report on a star's unfaithfulness to his or her significant other. And finally, it is hard to stay faithful when you are surrounded by great-looking people all day long, as is the case with most movie stars. Many stars have confessed to having romantic relationships with co-stars from a movie project because of the long hours, the time away from home, and just being attracted to a co-star.

I.

   A.

   B.

   C.

2. Sean "P. Diddy" Combs is a busy man these days. In addition to releasing a new album, his Sean John fashion company will soon introduce a line of underwear to compete in department stores with the likes of Calvin Klein. His Justin's restaurants are all over the country and continue to do well. In the past 18 months, Bad Boy records, his label, has released successful debut albums from Shyne, Thomas, Dream and Black Rob, and 112's third album, Part III, is the group's biggest seller to date. He also has two sons with whom he spends a great deal of time.*

I.

   A.

   B.

   C.

   D.

3. Right after having a baby, a woman might experience one of three kinds of postpartum depression. One kind of depression is called the postpartum blues. This type affects about 85 percent of new mothers and causes mood swings for up to two weeks. The second, more severe type is called postpartum depression. This condition affects about 10 percent of mothers, especially those who don't enjoy motherhood, and can produce eating or sleeping disorders for months at a time. The third and worst kind of depression is called postpartum psychosis. Fortunately, this type occurs in only one out of 1,000 mothers because it causes a woman to experience delusions and believe the baby would be better off dead.†

* Adapted from Steve Jones, "Sean Combs' Saga Continues," *USA Today*, July 10, 2001, 1d.

† Adapted from "Most Mothers Affected by 'Blues,'" *USA Today Online*, June 22, 2001, www.usatoday.com/usatonline/20010622/3424834s.htm.

Copyright © Houghton Mifflin Company. All rights reserved.

I.

   A.

      1.

      2.

   B.

      1.

      2.

   C.

      1.

      2.

4. The U.S. justice system should not treat violent juvenile offenders as adults. First of all, these children do not yet possess the intellectual or moral capacity to understand the consequences of their actions. Also, they are not totally responsible for their crimes. They should not have access to deadly weapons such as guns. The adults who allowed them to get their hands on weapons are at least as accountable as the kids themselves. Finally, the juvenile system still gives these kids a chance to turn their lives around. Adult facilities have all but abandoned any attempt to rehabilitate inmates. Juvenile facilities, on the other hand, still offer opportunities for kids to evolve into productive members of society.*

I.

   A.

   B.

      1.

      2.

   C.

      1.

      2.

5. European-American parents tend to employ one of three distinct socialization patterns, as described by Diana Baumrind. *Authoritarian parents* tend to be strict, punitive, and unsympathetic. They value obedience from children and try to shape their children's behavior to meet a set standard and to curb the children's wills. They do not encourage independence. They are detached and seldom praise their youngsters. In contrast, *permissive parents* give their children complete freedom and lax discipline. The third group, *authoritative parents*, fall

* Adapted from Jessica Reaves, "Should the Law Treat Kids and Adults Differently?" *Time.com*, May 21, 2001, www.time.com/time/nation/printout/0,8816,110232,00.html.

Copyright © Houghton Mifflin Company. All rights reserved.

between these two extremes. They reason with their children, encouraging give and take. They allow children increasing responsibility as they get older and better at making decisions. They are firm but understanding. They set limits but also encourage independence. Their demands are reasonable, rational, and consistent.*

I.

  A.

    1.

    2.

    3.

    4.

  B.

    1.

    2.

  C.

    1.

    2.

    3.

    4.

    5.

CHAPTER 3 REVIEW

Fill in the blanks in the following statements.

1. ___Supporting details___ _(Prove the main idea)_ are the specific facts, statistics, examples, steps, anecdotes, reasons, descriptions, definitions, and so on that explain or prove the general _prove the main idea_ stated in the topic sentence.

2. There are two kinds of supporting details: _____ details and _____ details. The _____ details are the main points that explain or support the idea in the topic sentence. _____ details offer more explanation of the major details.

*Adapted from Douglas A. Bernstein et al., *Psychology.* Boston: Houghton Mifflin, 1997, 410.

Copyright © Houghton Mifflin Company. All rights reserved.

3. _____ are words that assist readers in distinguishing between major and minor details because they make connections and distinctions between the different details.

4. _____ is a technique that involves using lines, boxes, circles, or other shapes to show how sentences in a paragraph are related.

5. An _____ is a list of supporting details labeled with a system of numbers and letters that show their relationships to one another.

3

Reading Selection

College Lectures: Is Anybody Listening?
By Robert Holkeboer and Thomas Hoeksema

1 Today, American colleges and universities (originally modeled on German ones) are under strong attack from many quarters. Teachers, it is charged, are not doing a good job of teaching, and students are not doing a good job of learning. American businesses and industries suffer from unenterprising, uncreative executives educated not to think for themselves but to mouth outdated truisms the rest of the world has long discarded. College graduates lack both basic skills and general culture. Studies are conducted and reports are issued on the status of higher education, but any changes that result either are largely cosmetic or make a bad situation worse.

2 One aspect of American education too seldom challenged is the lecture system. Professors continue to lecture and students to take notes much as they did in the thirteenth century, when books were so scarce and expensive that few students could own them. The time is long overdue for us to abandon the lecture system and turn to methods that really work.

3 To understand the inadequacy of the present system, it is enough to follow a single imaginary first-year student—let's call her Mary—through a term of lectures on, say, introductory psychology (although any other subject would do as well). She arrives on the first day and looks around the huge lecture hall, taken a little aback to see how large the class is. Once the hundred or more students enrolled in the course discover that the professor never takes attendance (how can he?—calling the role would take far too much time), the class shrinks to a less imposing size.

4 Some days Mary sits in the front row, from where she can watch the professor read from a stack of yellowed notes that seem nearly as old as he is. She is bored by the lectures, and so are most of the other students, to judge by the way they are nodding off or doodling in their notebooks. Gradually she realizes the professor is as bored as his audience. At the end of each lecture he asks, "Are there any questions?" in a tone of voice that makes it plain he

Copyright © Houghton Mifflin Company. All rights reserved.

would much rather there weren't. He needn't worry; the students are as relieved as he is that the class is over.

5   Mary knows very well she should read an assignment before every lecture. However, as the professor gives no quizzes and asks no questions, she soon realizes she needn't prepare. At the end of the term she catches up by skimming her notes and memorizing a list of facts and dates. After the final exam, she promptly forgets much of what she has memorized. Some of her fellow students, disappointed at the impersonality of it all, drop out of college altogether. Others, like Mary, stick it out, grow resigned to the system and await better days when, as juniors and seniors, they will attend smaller classes and at last get the kind of personal attention real learning requires.

6   I admit this picture is overdrawn. Most universities supplement lecture courses with discussion groups, usually led by graduate students, and some classes, such as first-year English, are always relatively small. Nevertheless, far too many courses rely principally or entirely on lectures, an arrangement much loved by faculty and administrators but scarcely designed to benefit the students.

7   One problem with lectures is that listening intelligently is hard work. Reading the same material in a textbook is a more efficient way to learn because students can proceed as slowly as they need to until the subject matter becomes clear to them. Even simply paying attention is very difficult; people can listen at a rate of four hundred to six hundred words a minute, while the most impassioned professor talks at scarcely a third that speed. This time lag between speech and comprehension leads to daydreaming. Many students believe years of watching television have sabotaged their attention span, but their real problem is that listening attentively is much harder than they think.

8   Worse still, attending lectures is passive learning, at least for inexperienced listeners. Active learning, in which students write essays or perform experiments and then have their work evaluated by an instructor, is far more beneficial for those who have not yet fully learned how to learn. While it's true that techniques of active listening, such as trying to anticipate the speaker's next point or taking notes selectively, can enhance the value of a lecture, few students possess such skills at the beginning of their college careers. More commonly, students try to write everything down and even bring tape recorders to class in a clumsy effort to capture every word.

9   Students need to question their professors and to have their ideas taken seriously. Only then will they develop the analytical skills required to think intelligently and creatively. Most students learn best by engaging in frequent and even heated debate, not by scribbling down a professor's often unsatisfactory summary of complicated issues. They need small discussion classes that demand the common labors of teacher and students rather than classes in which one person, however learned, propounds his or her own ideas.

10   The lecture system ultimately harms professors as well. It reduces feedback to a minimum, so that the lecturer can neither judge how well students understand the material nor benefit from their questions or comments. Questions that require the speaker to clarify obscure points and comments that challenge sloppily constructed arguments are indispensable to scholarship. Without them, the liveliest mind can atrophy. Undergraduates may not be able to make telling contributions very often, but

Copyright © Houghton Mifflin Company. All rights reserved.

lecturing insulates a professor even from the beginner's naïve question that could have triggered a fruitful line of thought.

11   If lectures make so little sense, why have they been allowed to continue? Administrators love them, of course. They can cram far more students into a lecture hall than into a discussion class, and for many administrators that is almost the end of the story. But the truth is that faculty members, and even students, conspire with them to keep the lecture system alive and well. Lectures are easier on everyone than debates. Professors can pretend to teach by lecturing just as students can pretend to learn by attending lectures, with no one the wiser, including the participants. Moreover, if lectures afford some students an opportunity to sit back and let the professor run the show, they offer some professors an irresistible forum for showing off. In a classroom where everyone contributes, students are less able to hide and professors less tempted to engage in intellectual exhibitionism.

12   Smaller classes in which students are required to involve themselves in discussion put an end to students' passivity. Students become actively involved when forced to question their own ideas as well as their instructor's. Their listening skills improve dramatically in the excitement of intellectual give and take with their instructors and fellow students. Such interchanges help professors do their job better because they allow them to discover who knows what—before final exams, not after. When exams are given in this type of course, they can require analysis and synthesis from the students, not empty memorization. Classes like this require energy, imagination, and commitment from professors, all of which can be exhausting. But they compel students to share responsibility for their own intellectual growth.

13   Lectures will never entirely disappear from the university scene both because they seem to be economically necessary and because they spring from a long tradition in a setting that rightly values tradition for its own sake. But the lectures too frequently come at the wrong end of the students' educational careers—during the first two years, when they most need close, even individual instruction. If lecture classes were restricted to junior and senior undergraduates and to graduate students, who are less in need of scholarly nurturing and more able to prepare work on their own, they would be far less destructive of students' interests and enthusiasms than the present system. After all, students must learn to listen before they can listen to learn.

Adapted from Robert Holkeboer and Thomas Hoeksema, "College Lectures: Is Anyone Listening?" *The College Success Reader.* Boston: Houghton Mifflin, 1998, 62–65. Copyright © 1998 by Houghton Mifflin Company. Reprinted with permission.

VOCABULARY

Read the following questions about some of the vocabulary words that appear in the previous selection. Circle the correct responses.

1. In paragraph 1, what does *unenterprising* mean?

   a. not living   c. not breathing

   b. not showing initiative   d. not drinking

Copyright © Houghton Mifflin Company. All rights reserved.

2. In paragraph 5, what does *impersonality* mean?

    a. detachment   c. energy
    b. warmth   d. feeling

3. In paragraph 7, what does *impassioned* mean? *not*

    a. insensitive   c. emotional
    b. remote   d. demented

4. In paragraph 7, what does *sabotaged* mean?

    a. refunded   c. energized
    b. replaced   d. damaged

5. In paragraph 10, what does *obscure* mean?

    a. transparent   c. unclear
    b. lucid   d. damaged

6. In paragraph 10, what does *indispensable* mean?

    a. essential   c. independent
    b. not needed   d. insufficient

7. In paragraph 10, what does *atrophy* mean?

    a. wasted   c. award
    b. wither *get weak*   d. plaque

8. In paragraph 10, what does *insulates* mean?

    a. protects   c. warrants
    b. defends   d. models

9. In paragraph 11, what does *conspire* mean?

    a. plot   c. ward off
    b. determine   d. protect

10. In paragraph 11, what does *exhibitionism* mean? *nous*

    a. showing   c. mirror
    b. display   d. nakedness

but contract while

TOPIC, TOPIC SENTENCE, MAIN IDEAS, AND SUPPORTING DETAILS

Answer the following questions.

1. What is the topic of paragraph 2?

    a. American education   c. methods that really work
    b. the lecture system   d. books that are scarce

1 b   6 a
2 a   7 b
3 C   8. a
4: d   9. a
5 C   10. b

Copyright © Houghton Mifflin Company. All rights reserved.

2. Which of the following is the topic sentence of paragraph 7?

   a. One problem with lectures is that listening intelligently is hard work.
   b. Reading the same material in a textbook is a more efficient way to learn because students can proceed as slowly as they need to until the subject matter becomes clear to them.
   c. Even simply paying attention is very difficult; people can listen at a rate of four hundred to six hundred words a minute, while the most impassioned professor talks at scarcely a third that speed.
   d. This time lag between speech and comprehension leads to daydreaming.

3. What is the main idea of paragraph 10?

   a. The lecture system reduces feedback.
   b. Undergraduates ask naïve questions.
   c. Lecturing insulates a professor from questions.
   d. Lectures harm professors as well as students.

4. Which of the following is a *major* supporting detail in paragraph 11?

   a. If lectures make so little sense, why have they been allowed to continue?
   b. Administrators love them, of course.
   c. They can cram far more students into a lecture hall than into a discussion class, and for many administrators that is almost the end of the story.
   d. In a classroom where everyone contributes, students are less able to hide and professors less tempted to engage in intellectual exhibitionism.

5. Which of the following is a *minor* supporting detail in paragraph 10?

   a. The lecture system ultimately harms professors as well.
   b. It reduces feedback to a minimum, so that the lecturer can neither judge how well students understand the material nor benefit from their questions or comments.
   c. Questions that require the speaker to clarify obscure points and comments that challenge sloppily constructed arguments are indispensable to scholarship.
   d. Without them, the liveliest mind can atrophy.

QUESTIONS FOR DISCUSSION AND WRITING

Answer the following questions based on your reading of the selection.

1. In what type of environment do you learn best? Have you ever been in a college lecture like the one described? If so, does your experience match Mary's or was it different? How? _____

   _____

   _____

Copyright © Houghton Mifflin Company. All rights reserved.

2. What is one aspect of your learning experience or learning environment that you wish you could change? Why? _____

_____

3. In your opinion, is there a student population for which the types of lectures described in the selection work effectively? _____

_____

▌ Vocabulary: Context and Meaning

When you encounter an unfamiliar word as you read and go to the dictionary to look it up, you'll often find several different meanings and variations for that word. How do you know which definition is the right one? You have to look at the context—the words, phrases, and sentences surrounding that word—to determine which meaning applies.

To figure out the right definition, you may need to first determine the word's part of speech in the sentence. Many words can function as different parts of speech (for example, the word *left* can be a noun, a verb, an adjective, or an adverb), so you'll have to figure out how the word is being used before you can decide which definition applies. For example, the word *interest* is both a noun and a verb. The noun form means both "a state of curiosity" and "a charge for a loan." Which of the noun form meanings is being used in the following sentence?

> Finally, the fourth rule to becoming rich is to take advantage of compound **interest**.

You know the word refers to a charge for a loan because of the other words around it. The whole passage that contains this sentence is about becoming wealthy, so you know the word *interest* refers to money.

Vocabulary Exercise

The following sentences all come from paragraphs throughout this chapter. Look up the boldfaced, italicized words in a dictionary and determine which definition best describes how each word is being used.

1. Many people think that the 1950s, an era of bread-winning dads and stay-at-home moms, was the last decade in a long era of *stable* families, but 1950s families actually reversed a 100-year trend of rising divorce rates.

_____

Copyright © Houghton Mifflin Company. All rights reserved.

2. *Character* education programs that try to instill values and virtues in students are producing positive results in schools. _noun   qualities_

3. People loved him [actor Jack Lemmon] because his *characters* were never larger than life; they were people most Americans could identify with.

   _____

4. One kind of *depression* is called the postpartum blues. _noun   feeling sadness and a loss of hope_

5. Always lock car doors and *trunks*—even at home—and keep keys out of children's reach. _____

6. Another company is Office Depot, which has cut the time it spends filing and searching for delivery paperwork by 50 percent thanks to a wireless system that links *trunks* on 22,000 delivery routes. _____

   _____

7. Companies are finding that business e-mail messages *clog* computer networks and increasingly take up employees' time, so several companies are encouraging workers to curb e-mail. _____

8. Companies are finding that business e-mail messages clog computer networks and increasingly take up employees' time, so several companies are encouraging workers to *curb* e-mail. _____

9. Prompted by our *modest* exertions, just a few minutes into a walk the body begins to produce endorphins, chemical compounds that reduce pain and stress, enhance memory and judgment as they course through the brain. _____

10. Prompted by our modest exertions, just a few minutes into a walk the body begins to produce endorphins, chemical compounds that reduce pain and stress, enhance memory and judgment as they *course* through the brain. _____

Copyright © Houghton Mifflin Company. All rights reserved.

Name _____ Date _____

POST-TEST 1

A. Read the following paragraphs, and circle the correct answer (main idea, major supporting detail, or minor supporting detail) for each individual sentence.

(1) Athletes can become heroes. (2) Jackie Robinson suffered years of blatant discrimination that would have caused lesser men to lash out at their tormentors and postpone the racial integration of Major League Baseball. (3) Hall of Fame outfielder Roberto Clemente lost his life in a plane crash bringing food and supplies to earthquake victims in Nicaragua. (4) After serving in World War II, baseball legend Ted Williams returned to active duty in the Korean conflict, where he flew 39 combat missions. (5) The three men are heroic figures because of the courage and exemplary behavior they exhibited as human beings, not as athletes.*

1. Sentence 1 is a
   a. main idea
   b. major supporting detail
   c. minor supporting detail

2. Sentence 3 is a
   a. main idea
   b. major supporting detail
   c. minor supporting detail

3. Sentence 4 is a
   a. main idea
   b. major supporting detail
   c. minor supporting detail

(1) Unlike Hillary Clinton, First Lady Laura Bush has no overt political ambitions, but she serves an enormous strategic role. (2) The delight she takes in reading to grade-school children helps soften the image of the Administration. (3) And in November 2001, she became the first presidential wife to

* Adapted from George J. Bryjak, "Don't Call Jocks Sports 'Heroes,'" *USA Today*, February 18, 2002, 13A.

For more tests on word mapping and outlines, see the Test Bank.

Copyright © Houghton Mifflin Company. All rights reserved.

deliver the weekly White House radio address. (4) She spoke about the brutality with which the Taliban* treated women in Afghanistan, and drew plaudits all around.†

4. Sentence 1 is a

   a. main idea
   b. major supporting detail
   c. minor supporting detail

5. Sentence 2 is a

   a. main idea
   b. major supporting detail
   c. minor supporting detail

6. Sentence 3 is a

   a. main idea
   b. major supporting detail
   c. minor supporting detail

(1) Delivering painful information requires a complex set of skills—whether you're a doctor speaking to a patient, a manager firing an employee, or a teacher telling a parent "Your son is failing." (2) To start with, experts say, find a private, quiet place to begin the conversation, as opposed to conducting it in a crowded hallway or over the phone. (3) Then, open with what's called a verbal warning shot. (4) Medical students learn to say, "I'm afraid I have some difficult news that we need to talk about today," so the patient has time to steel herself for what's coming. (5) Also, avoid saying "I don't know" (a better reply is "I'll find out"), and withhold details the listener isn't ready to hear. (6) For example, a doctor should spare a cancer patient specifics about her inevitable chemotherapy and radiation treatments.‡

7. Sentence 2 is a

   a. main idea
   b. major supporting detail
   c. minor supporting detail

8. Sentence 4 is a

   a. main idea
   b. major supporting detail
   c. minor supporting detail

* Afghanistan's former rulers.

† Adapted from "The Teaching of Laura Bush," *Reader's Digest*, January 2002, 80.

‡ Adapted from Amy O'Connor, "How to Tell Hard Truths," *O*, January 2002, 144.

Copyright © Houghton Mifflin Company. All rights reserved.

9. Sentence 6 is a

    a. main idea
    b. major supporting detail
    c. minor supporting detail

(1) Men no longer dominate the workplace because women are entering in greater numbers than ever before and are achieving management positions. (2) One result of these changes has been a realization that men and women tend to speak in distinctly different "genderlects," just as people from various cultures speak different dialects. (3) Men are more likely to talk about money, sports, and business; women prefer talking about people, feelings, and relationships. (4) Even when discussing the same topic, men and women may be on different wavelengths because their gender-specific focus is different. (5) For example, if a man and woman are discussing an upcoming layoff in their organization, the man might approach it from a cost-cutting point of view, and the woman may focus on the feelings of the people involved. Neither view is wrong, but the resulting conversation can frustrate both parties.*

10. Sentence 2 is a

    a. main idea
    b. major supporting detail
    c. minor supporting detail

11. Sentence 3 is a

    a. main idea
    b. major supporting detail
    c. minor supporting detail

12. Sentence 5 is a

    a. main idea
    b. major supporting detail
    c. minor supporting detail

(1) There are two types of chemical sedimentary rocks: organic and inorganic. (2) Organic chemical sedimentary rocks are composed of minerals that were transported in a solution but were subsequently acted on by marine organisms. (3) Organic limestone, for example, consists of the remains of microscopic organisms' skeletal and shell matter, and coal is derived from the remains of plant matter. (4) Inorganic chemical rocks are formed when the evaporation of water leaves behind a residue of chemical sediment. (5) The

* Adapted from Reece and Brandt, *Effective Human Relations in Organizations*, 7th ed. Boston: Houghton Mifflin, 1999, 39.

Copyright © Houghton Mifflin Company. All rights reserved.

icicle-shaped stalactites and cone-shaped stalagmites in caves are examples of inorganic chemical sedimentary rock.*

13. Sentence 1 is a

    a. main idea
    b. major supporting detail
    c. minor supporting detail

14. Sentence 3 is a

    a. main idea
    b. major supporting detail
    c. minor supporting detail

15. Sentence 4 is a

    a. main idea
    b. major supporting detail
    c. minor supporting detail

B. Read the paragraphs below and answer the questions that follow by circling the correct response.

(1) You can use the following three techniques to stay focused as you read. (2) First, visualize the material by forming mental pictures of the concepts as they are presented. (3) For instance, if you read that a voucher system can help control cash disbursements, picture a voucher handing out dollar bills. (4) Second, read it out loud—especially complicated material. (5) Some of us remember better and understand more quickly when we hear an idea instead of seeing it in print. (6) Third, get a "feel" for your subject. (7) For example, if you're reading about a paramecium in your biology text, imagine what it would feel like to run your finger around the long, cigar-shaped body of the organism and feel the hairy little cilia as they wiggle in your hand.†

16. The topic of this selection is

    a. reading
    b. visualization
    c. techniques for staying focused while reading
    d. reading out loud

17. The main idea is stated in

    a. Sentence 1   c. Sentence 3
    b. Sentence 2   d. Sentence 4

* Adapted from Shipman et al., *An Introduction to Physical Science*, 9th ed. Boston: Houghton Mifflin, 2000, 578.

† Adapted from Dave Ellis, *Becoming a Master Student*, 9th ed. Boston: Houghton Mifflin, 2000, 112.

Copyright © Houghton Mifflin Company. All rights reserved.

18. How many major supporting details develop the main idea?

    a. 1   c. 4

    b. 3   d. 6

(1) Nothing gets in the way of Hollywood's movie machinery—even the death of the film's star. (2) *Queen of the Damned*, singer/actress Aaliyah's last movie, was released after she died in a plane crash. (3) Oliver Reed died of a heart attack while shooting 2000's Oscar-winning *Gladiator*, but director Ridley Scott used computer-generated imagery to patch him into some scenes. (4) Phil Hartman was shot and killed by his wife, Brynn, in 1998, six weeks before his action-adventure *Small Soldiers* was to open. (5) No scenes were cut or altered. (6) John Candy died in his sleep of a heart attack in March 1994 while shooting the comedy *Wagons East!* in Mexico. (7) But thanks to a body double and digital wizardry, Candy appeared in several scenes that he had never originally filmed, including one at a bar. (8) Brandon Lee's final film, *The Crow*, opened one year after he died from an accidental gunshot wound in 1993—on Friday the 13th. (9) According to producer Ed Pressman, "Everyone knew how wonderful he was, and it made more sense to continue than to destroy what he'd created." (10) A stand-in salvaged Bruce Lee's unfinished 1973 flick *Game of Death.* (11) The movie was completed six years after Lee's demise with the surviving actors and a body double.*

19. The topic of this selection is

    a. Aaliyah

    b. actors and actresses

    c. films that were released after their stars' deaths

    d. weird things that happen in the film industry

20. The main idea is stated in

    a. Sentence 1   c. Sentence 9

    b. Sentence 2   d. Sentence 11

21. How many major supporting details develop the main idea?

    a. 1   c. 6

    b. 3   d. 8

(1) American President Theodore Roosevelt and British Prime Minister Winston Churchill had much in common. (2) Both were from aristocratic families. (3) Churchill was the grandson of the Duke of Marlborough, and Roosevelt's grandfather, Cornelius Van Schaack Roosevelt, owned acres of

* Adapted from Donna Freydkin, "Even in Death, Shows Must Go On," *USA Today*, February 18, 2002, 11B.

Copyright © Houghton Mifflin Company. All rights reserved.

Manhattan real estate. (4) Both men revered their fathers, even as they tried to avoid what they regarded as their respective single flaws. (5) Specifically, Theodore Roosevelt, Sr., hired a substitute to serve in his place in the Civil War, and Lord Randolph Churchill made a political blunder that ended his career. (6) Both men wrote several books. (7) Both took part in cavalry charges in 1898; Roosevelt's was on San Juan Hill in Cuba, and Churchill's at Omdurman in the Sudan. (8) Both men worked to expand and modernize their nations' navies. (9) And both saw history as a story of the expansion of the influence of English-speaking peoples.*

22. The topic of this selection is
    a. Theodore Roosevelt
    b. Winston Churchill
    c. similarities between Roosevelt and Churchill
    d. Roosevelt's and Churchill's fathers

23. The main idea is stated in
    a. Sentence 1   c. Sentence 8
    b. Sentence 2   d. Sentence 9

24. How many major supporting details develop the main idea?
    a. 1   c. 6
    b. 3   d. 8

25. Which of the following sentences is a minor supporting detail?
    a. Sentence 1   c. Sentence 5
    b. Sentence 4   d. Sentence 6

POST-TEST 2

Read each paragraph and answer the questions that follow by circling the correct response.

(1) You can learn techniques to help you remember to do certain things. (2) One technique is to link something you need to remember to another event that you know will take place. (3) For example, if you want to remember that your accounting assignment is due tomorrow, switch your watch (or a ring) from one arm to the other. (4) Then, every time you look at your watch, it becomes a reminder that you were supposed to remember something. (5) Tie a triple knot in your shoelace to remind you to set the alarm for

* Adapted from Michael Barone, "A Big Stick," *U.S. News and World Report*, February 25–March 4, 2002, 52.

Copyright © Houghton Mifflin Company. All rights reserved.

your early morning study group meeting. (6) A second technique is to use imaginary cues. (7) For instance, to remember to write a check for the phone bill, picture your phone hanging onto the front door and picture reaching for the door knob and grabbing the phone instead. (8) When you get home and reach to open the front door, the image is apt to return to you. (9) A third way to remember something is just to tell yourself you will remember it. (10) Specifically, relax and say to yourself, "At any time I choose, I will be able to recall. . . ." (11) The intention to remember can be more powerful than any other memory technique.*

1. The topic sentence of this paragraph is
   a. Sentence 1   c. Sentence 3
   b. Sentence 2   d. Sentence 4

2. Which of the following sentences does NOT begin a transition that signals a major supporting detail?
   a. Sentence 2   c. Sentence 7
   b. Sentence 6   d. Sentence 9

3. Which of the following sentences begins with a transition that signals a minor supporting detail?
   a. Sentence 1   c. Sentence 9
   b. Sentence 2   d. Sentence 10

(1) Gretchen Grimm, who finally kicked her decades-old habit of stealing when she was 83 years old, illustrates two important truths about shoplifting. (2) The first is the powerful ego boost it can provide, especially to insecure young people. (3) To illustrate, Gretchen began shoplifting when she was just six years old, she believes, to win her mother's attention and affection. (4) The other lesson is that a crime that can be perpetrated by first graders and old ladies is pretty hard to stop. (5) Gretchen, for instance, had only one serious arrest and hid her habit from her family for almost her whole life.†

4. The topic sentence of this paragraph is
   a. Sentence 1   c. Sentence 3
   b. Sentence 2   d. Sentence 4

5. Which two sentences begin with transitions that signal major supporting details?
   a. Sentences 1 and 2   c. Sentences 2 and 4
   b. Sentences 2 and 3   d. Sentences 3 and 5

* Adapted from Dave Ellis, *Becoming a Master Student*, 9th ed. Boston: Houghton Mifflin, 2000, 87.
† Adapted from Jerry Adler, "The 'Thrill' of Theft," *Newsweek*, February 25, 2002, 53.

Copyright © Houghton Mifflin Company. All rights reserved.

6. Which of the following sentences begins with a transition that signals a minor supporting detail?

a. Sentence 1   c. Sentence 3
b. Sentence 2   d. Sentence 4

(1) The Internet provides car buyers with a wealth of information. (2) For one thing, they can look at photos and find data about comparative safety, reliability, and owner satisfaction. (3) Also, they can read independent reviews, locate dealers in their geographic area, select options, and compare prices. (4) At the Auto Channel's Web site, for example, consumers can find data on used-car prices, and the Used-Vehicle Classified Ads Web site lets shoppers design a search based on geographic area, make, model, price range, year, and desired features. (5) In addition, customers can click on another site that provides a toll-free number to VINguard, which reports on a vehicle's history and tells if a car has ever been in a collision.*

7. The topic sentence of this paragraph is

a. Sentence 1   c. Sentence 3
b. Sentence 2   d. Sentence 4

8. Which of the following sentences does NOT begin with a transition that signals a major supporting detail?

a. Sentence 1   c. Sentence 3
b. Sentence 2   d. Sentence 5

9. Which of the following sentences includes a transition that signals a minor supporting detail?

a. Sentence 2   c. Sentence 4
b. Sentence 3   d. Sentence 5

(1) Most methods of coping with stress can be classified as either problem-focused or emotion-focused. (2) Problem-focused methods involve efforts to alter or eliminate a source of stress. (3) For example, you might deal with the problem of noise from a nearby airport by forming a community action group to push for tougher noise-reduction laws. (4) Emotion-focused techniques attempt to regulate the negative emotional consequences of stress. (5) For instance, you might calm your anger when airport noise occurs by mentally focusing on the group's efforts to improve the situation.†

* Adapted from Pride et al., *Business,* 6th ed. Boston: Houghton Mifflin, 1999, 307. Copyright © 1999 by Houghton Mifflin Company. Reprinted with permission.

† Adapted from Bernstein and Nash, *Essentials of Psychology*, 2nd ed. Boston: Houghton Mifflin, 2002, 359.

Copyright © Houghton Mifflin Company. All rights reserved.

10. The topic sentence of this paragraph is
    a. Sentence 1   c. Sentence 3
    b. Sentence 2   d. Sentence 4

11. The two sentences that provide major supporting details are
    a. Sentences 1 and 2   c. Sentences 2 and 4
    b. Sentences 2 and 3   d. Sentences 4 and 5

12. Which of the following sentences begin with a transition that signals a minor supporting detail?
    a. Sentences 2 and 3   c. Sentences 4 and 5
    b. Sentences 3 and 4   d. Sentences 3 and 5

3

(1) Janice Boucher, author of *How to Love the Job You Hate*, says it's possible to recapture your love for a job gone bad. (2) One approach is to redesign your job so that it offers more challenge, more variety, or less stress. (3) For instance, you could delegate to someone else some task that you do not like to do, or you could develop a special project that gives your job greater meaning. (4) Also, you can do things that make you feel good about yourself and your job again. (5) As an illustration, a supermarket cashier might begin to pay genuine attention to customers in order to improve service, and a newspaper reporter pressured to emphasize sensationalism could establish higher standards for truth in reporting.*

13. The topic sentence of this paragraph is
    a. Sentence 1   c. Sentence 3
    b. Sentence 2   d. Sentence 4

14. Which of the following sentences begins with a transition that signals a major supporting detail?
    a. Sentence 1   c. Sentence 4
    b. Sentence 3   d. Sentence 5

15. Which of the following sentences begins with a transition that signals a minor supporting detail?
    a. Sentence 1   c. Sentence 4
    b. Sentence 2   d. Sentence 5

Copyright © Houghton Mifflin Company. All rights reserved.

* Adapted from Reece and Brandt, *Effective Human Relations in Organizations*, 7th ed. Boston: Houghton Mifflin, 1999, 190.

Copyright © Houghton Mifflin Company. All rights reserved.

CHAPTER **4**

Implied Main Ideas

GOALS FOR CHAPTER 4

▶ **Apply the steps of the SQ3R strategy to reading selections.**

▶ **Define the term *implied main idea*.**

▶ **Form generalizations based on specific details.**

▶ **State the implied main idea of a paragraph.**

4

READING STRATEGY: SQ3R

In Chapter 1, you learned how to use active reading techniques to increase your comprehension of the material you read. One specific type of active reading strategy is called the **SQ3R method.** This abbreviation stands for

S urvey

Q uestion

R ead

R ecite

R eview

This series of five steps gives you a clear, easy-to-remember system for reading actively.

 Step one is to **survey** the text. "To survey" means look over the text to preview it. Surveying gives you an overall idea of a reading selection's major topics, organizations, parts, and features. When you complete this step, you'll be able to form a mental framework that will allow you to better understand how specific paragraphs, sections, or chapters fit in. At this stage, your purpose is not to read the whole text but to get an overview of what to expect.

 If you are preparing to read a longer text, such as a book, read over the title and glance through the table of contents to understand the major topics covered and how they are organized. Flip to one of the chapters and make yourself aware of its important features. A textbook, like this

Continued

153

one, for example, may include a list of goals at the beginning of the chapter and a review summary at the end. It will probably also include headings that divide and identify sections of information. It is likely to emphasize key words or concepts with distinctive typeface such as bold print.

Prior to reading a shorter selection—such as one particular chapter, or an article, or an essay—survey it by reading any introductory material, the headings throughout, and the first sentence of each paragraph or each section. Read any review summaries or questions at the end of the chapter to get an idea of the major concepts covered in the selection. Also, glance over any illustrations and their captions.

The second step is to **formulate questions.** Turn the title and the headings into questions; then, when you read, you can actively look for the answers to those questions. For example, if the heading is "The Medieval Castle," you could turn it into "What was The Medieval Castle like?" If the heading is "The War of 1812," you could create the question "What caused The War of 1812?" or "What happened during The War of 1812?"

The next three steps are the three Rs of the SQ3R process. Step three is **read.** In this step, you read entire sentences and paragraphs in a section. However, you read only one section at a time; for example, in a textbook, you'd read from one heading to the next and then stop. As you read, look for the answers to the questions you formed in step two. Mark the text as you go. Highlight or underline those answers and other important information. You may want to write the answers or other details in the margins.

Step four is to **recite.** Reciting means saying something aloud. After you read a section of material, stop and speak the answers to the questions you created in step two. If you can't answer a question, reread the information until you can. Move on to the next section only when you can say the answers for the section you just read.

The last step of the SQ3R method is **review.** Review means "look at again." After you've read the entire selection, go back through it and see if you can still answer all of the questions you formed in step two. You don't have to reread unless you can't answer a particular question.

Practice the SQ3R active reading method with the following passage from a physical science textbook:

The tornado is the most violent of storms. Although it may have less *total* energy than some other storms, the concentration of its energy in a relatively small region gives the tornado its violent distinction. Characterized by a whirling, funnel-shaped cloud that hangs from a dark cloud mass, the tornado is commonly referred to as a *twister*.

Continued

Copyright © Houghton Mifflin Company. All rights reserved.

Tornadoes occur around the world, but are most prevalent in the United States and Australia. In the United States, most tornadoes occur in the Deep South and in the broad, relatively flat basin between the Rockies and the Appalachians. But no state is immune. The peak months of tornado activity are April, May, and June, with southern states usually hit hardest in winter and spring, and northern states in spring and summer. However, tornadoes have occurred in every month at all times of day and night. A typical time of occurrence is between 3:00 and 7:00 P.M. on an unseasonably warm, sultry spring afternoon.

Most tornadoes travel from southwest to northeast, but the direction of travel can be erratic and may change suddenly. They usually travel at an average speed of 48 km/h (30 mi/h). The wind speed of a major tornado may vary from 160–480 km/h (100–300 mi/h). The wind speed of the devastating 1999 Oklahoma tornado was measured by Doppler radar to be 502 km/h (312 mi/h), the highest ever recorded.

Because of many variables, the complete mechanism of tornado formation is not known. One essential component, however, is rising air, which occurs in thunderstorm formation and in the collision of cold and warm air masses.

As the ascending air cools, clouds are formed that are swept to the outer portions of the cyclonic motion and outline its funnel form. Because clouds form at certain heights, the outlined funnel may appear well above the ground. Under the right conditions, a full-fledged tornado develops. The winds increase and the air pressure near the center of the vortex is reduced as the air swirls upward. When the funnel is well developed, it may "touch down" or be seen extending up from the ground as a result of dust and debris picked up by the swirling winds.*

*Adapted from James T. Shipman et al., *An Introduction to Physical Science*, 9th ed. Boston: Houghton Mifflin, 2000, 540. Copyright © 2000 by Houghton Mifflin Company. Reprinted with permission.

4

Copyright © Houghton Mifflin Company. All rights reserved.

When you read Chapter 2 of this book, you learned that many paragraphs include a topic sentence that clearly states the main idea. Other paragraphs, however, do not contain a topic sentence. Does that mean they don't have a main point? No, it means that readers must do a little more work to figure out what it is. To see how much you already know about drawing conclusions about a main idea, take the following pre-test.

Copyright © Houghton Mifflin Company. All rights reserved.

4

PRE-TEST

The following paragraphs do not include a stated main idea. Read each paragraph and see if you can determine its main point. Circle the sentence from the list that best states the main idea.

1. Why do we watch reality-based shows, such as *Big Brother, Fear Factor*, and *Survivor*? Most people, when responding to a survey, answered that guessing who will be eliminated or will win is the reason they watch. Others stated that seeing real people facing challenging situations was their motivation for watching the shows, while others get a thrill out of imagining themselves in similar situations. Other respondents to the survey cited fights among contestants, making fun of contestants, watching physically attractive contestants, and emotional attachment to contestants as their main reasons for watching reality-based shows. Only 11.4 percent, however, answered that they watched only because there was nothing better on TV.*

   a. Reality-based TV shows are popular today.
   b. Reality-based TV shows present challenging situations.
   c. Reality-based TV shows interest people for a number of different reasons.
   d. Several surveys have been designed to ask people why reality-based TV shows are popular.

2. *Jurassic Park III* is only one of a handful of high-profile sequels that have popped up this summer movie season. Already, *The Mummy Returns* has gotten loads of box office action, while *Dr. Doolittle 2* has performed solidly, and *Scary Movie 2* is on its way to making a tidy profit. Out later: *American Pie 2* and *Rush House 2*. And for many first-run successes this summer, talks already are in the works for a second helping.†

   a. There are many reasons why sequels are released in the summer.
   b. Many summer movies are sequels because sequels are generally successful.
   c. *Jurassic Park III* will be a successful movie.
   d. People like sequels to movies for a lot of different reasons.

3. I have clung to a potato cart as it climbed the steep, rugged mountains to Kurdish refugee camps. I have flown in a dark, cold, windowless cargo

---

* Adapted from "We're Reality-TV Voyeurs," *USA Today*, July 18, 2001, 1D.
† Adapted from Josh Chetwynd, "Shoring Up the Sequel Craze," *USA Today*, July 18, 2001, 1D.

plane to cover a story in the Mideast desert. I have watched the most graphic and gory bone surgery, standing just inches from the carved limbs. On the other hand, my face flushes hot and my heart races before facing a person with whom I have had a major disagreement. I worry that someone won't like or admire me. I burn with anxiety when I think I'm being talked about behind my back. Nothing unnerves me more than the prospect of being humiliated. Even writing these words, I wonder what friends and family will think when they read them. My sister Leslie, who at least appears fearless, has asked me often over the years: "Why in the world do you care what any of these people think?" I've never had a good answer.*

a. The author has done many dangerous things in her life.
b. The author is not afraid to do dangerous things but is afraid of emotional things.
c. The author is concerned about what her friends and family will think of her writing.
d. The author's sister Leslie counsels her on a variety of things.

4. Who is a master student? A master student is a person who has attained a level of skill that goes beyond technique. A master student is curious about everything and the unknown does not frighten him or her. He or she can take a large body of information and sift through it to discover relationships. Mastery of skills is important to the master student and work is generally effortless; struggle evaporates. Mastery can lead to flashy results, but often the result of mastery is a sense of profound satisfaction, well-being, and timelessness.†

a. The master student has many different personalities.
b. The master student understands the importance of developing certain critical skills.
c. There are many flashy results that can be attained by a master.
d. The master student feels like he or she needs to be an expert at everything.

5. What do I have planned for the summer? Well, by August, my body fat will match that of a *Survivor* contestant. My abdominal muscles will be flat, my biceps round, my inner thighs carved, and my rear end will be jiggle-free. Oh, and I'll be smarter and far more accomplished, once I finish Plato's *Republic*, watch those French videos, hone my pastry skills, organize my closets, and embrace the power of yoga. It's going to happen. Trust me.‡

* Adapted from Tracy Chutorian Semler, "Pulse," *Rosie*, August 2001, 58. Reprinted by permission of International Creative Management, Inc. Copyright © 2001 by Tray Chutorian Semler. First appeared in *Rosie*.

† Adapted from Dave Ellis, "The Master Student," *Becoming a Master Student*. Boston: Houghton Mifflin, 2000, 26–27.

‡ Adapted from Linda Wells, "Better, Stronger, Faster," *Allure*, July 2001, 30.

Copyright © Houghton Mifflin Company. All rights reserved.

a. The author is going to change her body type by August.
b. The author is going to organize her closet by August.
c. The author has some very ambitious summer plans.
d. The author has many different skills.

Understanding Implied Main Ideas

Every paragraph contains a main idea. Sometimes, that main idea is stated outright in a topic sentence. Sometimes, though, the main idea is implied. An **implied main idea** is one that is suggested but not said. To determine the implied main idea, you examine the details presented and draw from them a conclusion about the overall point.

If you think about it, you figure out implied main ideas quite often in your daily life. For example, look at the following conversation:

Mother: How was your day, honey?

Son: Well, I overslept. As I was rushing to get to class, I slipped and fell in a mud puddle. I left an assignment at home that was due today, so I'll lose points for turning it in late. At lunch, my girlfriend told me she wants to break up with me.

The son answered his mother's question with a series of specific details. What conclusion can you draw from them? Every incident he reported caused him pain, trouble, or aggravation, so it's safe to conclude that he had a pretty bad day.

Here's another example: You're in the park. You see a dog. You notice that the dog is not wearing a collar. The dog looks dirty and wet. The dog also appears underfed because you can see its ribs through its skin. The dog appears to be alone, not with a person. What conclusion do you make? Most people would say that the animal is probably a stray.

You yourself notice details, add them together, and draw conclusions all the time. In Chapter 3 of this book, you practiced recognizing supporting details, the information that proves or explains a main idea. A paragraph with an implied main idea contains *only* supporting details. These details are the clues that you put together to figure out the author's point.

To improve your ability to draw these conclusions while you read, it's helpful to remember what you learned about the terms *general* and *specific* back in Chapter 2.

Figuring out an implied main idea requires you to form a generalization based on a series of specific items or ideas. Look at the following group of words:

Copyright © Houghton Mifflin Company. All rights reserved.

coat

pants

dress

shirt

What generalization can you make about this list of items? They're all things you wear, so the general term that describes them is *clothing*.

Now, examine another list:

paper

desk

pencil

toothpick

This group is a little trickier. When you read the first three items, you may have thought they were *things in an office* or *things you use at school*. But, the last item isn't in either of those categories. When you add up all the details and look for the similarities, you realize that these are all *products made from wood*.

Exercise 4.1

Write on the blank above each group of words a general category that includes all of the items listed.

1. General Idea: _____
   airplane
   helicopter
   bird
   kite

2. General Idea: _____
   leaf blower
   weed eater
   lawn mower
   hedge clipper

3. General Idea: _____
   steering wheel
   tire
   hula hoop
   donut

Copyright © Houghton Mifflin Company. All rights reserved.

4. General Idea: _____

rap
hip-hop
disco
alternative rock

5. General Idea: _____

ice cream
cake
pie
cookies

6. General Idea: _____

river
ocean
stream
pond

7. General Idea: _____

subway
basement
root cellar
gas station tanks

8. General Idea: _____

cheese
yogurt
cream
butter

9. General Idea: _____

dictionary
magazine
notebook paper
football field

10. General Idea: _____

e-mail   letter
phone   face-to-face

As you remember from Chapter 2, a group of specific sentences can also support a general idea. For example, read the sentences below:

Copyright © Houghton Mifflin Company. All rights reserved.

Maggie works seven days a week.

Maggie works over ten hours a day.

Maggie hasn't taken a vacation in three years.

What general statement would include all three of those specific sentences? The answer is *Maggie works too much.*

Exercise 4.2

On the blank above each group of sentences, write a general sentence that includes all of the specific details given.

1. General Sentence: _____

   Police officers sometimes drive patrol cars in high-speed chases.
   Police officers can be wounded in fights or shot by criminals.
   Police officers have to go into dark buildings or alleys to investigate crimes.

2. General Sentence: _____

   Jim has several newspapers delivered to his home every day.
   Jim belongs to several book clubs and attends book club meetings regularly.
   Jim reads six or seven books a month.

3. General Sentence: _____

   The sun doesn't shine very much in Seattle.
   Seattle has about 200 rainy days a year.
   Some streets often flood in Seattle.

4. General Sentence: _____

   _____

   Rich weeds his garden every day.
   Rich has planted four tomato plants in his garden.
   Rich spends a lot of money on flowers for his garden.

5. General Sentence: _____

   Ann Marie sends e-mail to many of her friends and family on a weekly basis.
   Ann Marie does most of her shopping on the Internet.
   Ann Marie surfs the Web for information on movies, books, and other things that interest her.

You may not have realized it, but you often form general ideas based on specific details when you read cartoons and comic strips. For instance, look at the following comic strip:

Copyright © Houghton Mifflin Company. All rights reserved.

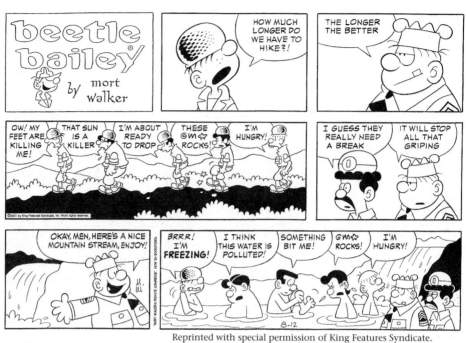

Reprinted with special permission of King Features Syndicate.

This comic strip never states a main idea. However, you can add up all of the details to conclude that these men are complainers who are not happy no matter what they're doing.

Exercise 4.3

On the blank beneath each of the following cartoons, write the idea the artist hoped to imply.

Cathy © 2001 Cathy Guisewite. Reprinted with permission of Universal Press Syndicate. All right reserved.

Copyright © Houghton Mifflin Company. All rights reserved.

1. Main Idea:

_____

_____

Grand Avenue reprinted by permission of United Feature Syndicate, Inc.

2. Main Idea:

_____

_____

© Bill Keane, Inc. Reprinted by special permission of King Features Syndicate.

3. Main Idea:

_____

_____

_____

Copyright © Houghton Mifflin Company. All rights reserved.

Cathy © 2002 Cathy Guisewite, Reprinted with permission of Universal Press Syndicate. All rights reserved.

4. Main Idea:

_____

_____

Determining Implied Main Ideas

To figure out the implied main idea in a paragraph, you can often use a methodical, step-by-step approach. Basically, this procedure involves looking for clues in the supporting details, adding them together, and drawing a logical conclusion based on the evidence. These next sections will explain and give you practice with each of the four steps in this process:

Step 1: Find the subject of each sentence.

Step 2: Determine the *type* of supporting detail in the paragraph.

Step 3: Determine a general topic based on the specific details.

Step 4: State an implied main idea that includes both the topic and what the author is saying about that topic.

As you become a more proficient reader, you will be able to complete all of these steps in your head most of the time.

Step 1: Find the Subject of Each Sentence

The first step in discovering an implied main idea is to closely examine the supporting details. The major and minor details in a paragraph will provide

Copyright © Houghton Mifflin Company. All rights reserved.

you with the clues you need to draw a conclusion about the author's point. For example, read the following paragraph:

(1) "Calvin and Hobbes," a comic strip about a little boy and his tiger, often tackles classical, philosophical, and ethical subjects. (2) The "Doonesbury" comic strip takes on political subjects, and even the "Peanuts" comic strip included social commentary on the Vietnam War. (3) "The Far Side" cartoons often focused on scientific ethics. (4) The "Dilbert" comic strip points out the illogic and insensitivity within American corporations. (5) The "For Better or Worse" comic strip often examines morality and family issues.*

Here are the subjects in each of the sentences:

Sentence 1: "Calvin and Hobbes"

Sentence 2: "Doonesbury" and "Peanuts"

Sentence 3: "The Far Side"

Sentence 4: "Dilbert"

Sentence 5: "For Better or Worse"

4

Exercise 4.4

On the blanks below each paragraph, write the subject of each sentence.

1. (1) Louisiana was named after France's King Louis XIV. (2) South Carolina comes from *Carolus*, the Latin word for Charles I, King of England. (3) Maryland was named after Queen Mary, wife of England's King Charles I. (4) Georgia was named in honor of England's King George II. (5) Both Virginia and West Virginia were named for Elizabeth I, the "virgin" queen.

Sentence 1 subject: _____

Sentence 2 subject: _____

Sentence 3 subject: _____

Sentence 4 subject: _____

Sentence 5 subjects: _____

* Adapted from *USA Today Newsview*, August 1997, 5.

Copyright © Houghton Mifflin Company. All rights reserved.

2. (1) Teachers, according to 79 percent of public high school students, are too easy on students when it comes to enforcing rules and assigning homework. (2) In addition, half of teens in public schools say their teachers and schools do not challenge them. (3) Too many disruptive students in classrooms, according to 70 percent of teenagers, are interfering with learning. (4) Schools' standards for graduation, say 70 percent of students, are too low. (5) According to three-fourths of students, diplomas are given to students even if they don't learn the required material.*

Sentence 1 subject: _____

Sentence 2 subject: _____

Sentence 3 subject: _____

Sentence 4 subject: _____

Sentence 5 subject: _____

3. (1) *Ladies' Home Journal* is a magazine that focuses on women's issues, and is generally considered appropriate for women in their thirties, forties, and fifties. (2) *Glamour* is a magazine that devotes many pages to issues facing women in their twenties and early thirties. (3) *Mode* is a new magazine devoted entirely to issues affecting "plus-size" women. (4) *Allure* magazine has the most information on beauty products and is for women who are interested in the latest information on makeup and hairstyles. (5) For the most information on home life, however, the best magazine to buy is *Better Homes and Gardens*.

Sentence 1 subject: _____

Sentence 2 subject: _____

Sentence 3 subject: _____

Sentence 4 subject: _____

Sentence 5 subject: _____

4. (1) Thomas Jefferson, who wrote the Declaration of Independence, was lean, elegant, remote, thrifty, and a bit sneaky. (2) John Adams, who contributed to the Declaration as well, was stout, cheap, and perhaps too

* Adapted from "Teenagers Want More from Public Schools," *USA Today Newsview*, August 1997, 4.

Copyright © Houghton Mifflin Company. All rights reserved.

honest about himself and everyone else. (3) Considered somewhat ecentric, or odd, Benjamin Franklin was a noted inventor and diplomat who was somewhat chubby and messy, but neither of those things interfered with his ability to help write the most important document in American history. (4) George Washington was a genius at lifting morale and knowing when to retreat to fight another day, so keeping the Founding Fathers agreeable and on task was his major contribution.

Sentence 1 subject: _____

Sentence 2 subject: _____

Sentence 3 subject: _____

Sentence 4 subject: _____

5. (1) Philadelphia is known for its "Philly cheese steak." (2) Coney Island in Brooklyn, New York, is known for its hot dogs. (3) Miami is famous for its Cuban food, particularly chicken and rice, or "arroz con pollo." (4) Chicago has made a name for itself by serving great deep-dish pizza. (5) And you can't go to Boston without getting the best clam chowder in the entire United States.

Sentence 1 subject: _____

Sentence 2 subject: _____

Sentence 3 subject: _____

Sentence 4 subject: _____

Sentence 5 subject: _____

Step 2: Determine the *Type* of Supporting Detail in the Paragraph

Once you've determined what each sentence is about, you should be able to conclude what type of supporting details they are. Common types of supporting details include the following:

reasons	causes
examples	effects
events	types

Copyright © Houghton Mifflin Company. All rights reserved.

steps	parts
points of comparison	descriptive details or features

For an illustration, read the next paragraph:

(1) If you have struggled all your life with chronic worry, dark moods, or a short fuse, are your genes to blame? (2) Only about half of your personality is inherited. (3) Even more encouraging, the genes for personality aren't like those for blue eyes or height because they merely give you a *susceptibility*, or tendency, for doom and gloom. (4) Therefore, they leave you a lot of room for self-improvement because the choice to see the glass as half empty or half full is largely up to you.*

To determine the type of details in this paragraph, first, find the subject of each sentence:

Sentence 1: Genes and personality

Sentence 2: Genes' effect on personality

Sentence 3: Genes' effect on personality

Sentence 4: Genes' effect on choice

What type of details are these? If you answered *causes and effects*, you're right. Understanding the kind of details included in the paragraph will help you formulate a more accurate statement of the main idea when you get to step 4.

Be aware that there may be more than one type of supporting detail in a paragraph. A paragraph may, for example, combine examples and reasons or causes and types. Authors can use different types of details together to develop their ideas.

Exercise 4.5

In the list below each paragraph, place a checkmark next to the correct type of supporting details in that paragraph.

1. When severe thunderstorms threaten your area, the first thing you should do is listen to your local radio or TV station. Then, get inside a home, large building, or car. Do not stand under a tall tree in an open area, on a hilltop, in an open field, or on a beach. Also get away from all metal objects, such as tractors or other metal farm equipment, motorcy-

* Adapted from Barbara K. Bruce and Denise Foley, "Is It Time for an Attitude Adjustment?" *USA Today*, September 1998, 60.

Copyright © Houghton Mifflin Company. All rights reserved.

cles, bicycles, golf carts, and scooters, and do not hold metal objects, such as golf clubs. When you get indoors, do not use the telephone, except for emergencies. Do not use bathtubs, water faucets, or sinks because metal pipes can conduct electricity.*

_____ reasons	_____ points of comparison
_____ causes and effects	_____ events
_____ steps	_____ examples

2. The Physician's Health Study in the 1980s, a long-term monitoring of 22,000 doctors, found that aspirin in small doses every other day may reduce the risk of a first heart attack by 44 percent. Other studies have shown that aspirin can lower the risk of a second heart attack by 30 percent and death during a heart attack by 23 percent. Aspirin also seems to reduce the risk of most strokes and their recurrence by about 25 percent. Research has revealed that regular aspirin use may protect against the risk of colon cancer by as much as 40 to 50 percent; esophageal, or throat, cancer by about 80 to 90 percent; and ovarian cancer by some 25 percent.†

_____ reasons	_____ points of comparison
_____ causes and effects	_____ events
_____ steps	_____ examples

3. When buying sunglasses, look for glasses that have a label or tag that indicates 99 percent ultraviolet radiation protection. Try on glasses near a store window or outside in natural light (be sure to ask first!) to decide how the color looks because you'll be wearing your sunglasses outdoors, not in store lighting. Next, if you select a strong color, go with a basic shape and a small to moderate size. If you can't decide on a color, try a lens that combines a darker tone with a lighter one. Finally, shop online for sunglasses only if you know which colors and styles work for you.‡

_____ reasons	_____ points of comparison
_____ causes and effects	_____ events
_____ steps	_____ examples

* Adapted from "Emergency Weather Information," from *The Westchester County Planning for Emergencies Booklet,* 9.

† Adapted from Jake Page, "Take Two Aspirin and Call Me in the Morning," *Smithsonian,* August 2001, 101.

‡ Adapted from Nancy Laboz, "Look Lively," *Real Simple,* August 2001, 50.

4

Copyright © Houghton Mifflin Company. All rights reserved.

4. Are all fast-food restaurants alike? That depends on what you are looking for. Wendy's has a full salad bar with fresh salads, some soups, and accompanying things like croutons and beans. Their salad dressing selection is great, too. McDonald's doesn't offer a salad bar, but does offer salads in easy-to-use cups that can be shaken to distribute dressing evenly throughout the salad. Burger King also offers salads, but they are in rectangular trays, which can be difficult to handle while eating. All of the restaurants mentioned, however, have hamburgers, chicken sandwiches, and fried sandwich selections that are comparable in price and quality.

_____ reasons   _____ points of comparison

_____ causes and effects   _____ events

_____ steps   _____ examples

5. In the early 1800s, every city and town in America kept its own time, so it might be 11:55 A.M. in New York City, 11:47 A.M. in Washington, and 11:35 A.M. in Pittsburgh. As a result, mid-19th century railroad travelers who moved from city to city began to find all of the different times confusing and inconvenient. In 1872, therefore, the Time-Table Convention searched for a solution, and Charles F. Dowd proposed the creation of time zones, imaginary divisions of the Earth's surface. In 1883, after Congress did not act to solve the problem, the railroads decided to establish four time zones: Eastern, Central, Mountain, and Pacific. On November 18, 1883, they set one standard time, and cities around the country changed their clocks to conform to it.*

_____ reasons   _____ points of comparison

_____ causes and effects   _____ events

_____ steps   _____ examples

Step 3: Determine a General Topic Based on the Specific Details

Once you've discovered the supporting details' subjects and type, you can make a generalization about them. You must make this generalization before you can complete the final step. In using logic to determine an overall category for the details, you are figuring out the overall topic of the paragraph. You'll need to be able to include this topic in your statement of the main idea.

* Adapted from John Steele Gordon, "Standard Time," *American Heritage*, July/August 2001, 22–23.

Copyright © Houghton Mifflin Company. All rights reserved.

Let's look at the paragraphs in the explanations of Steps 1 and 2 as illustrations. In the paragraph about comic strips on page 165, the subjects of each sentence were all examples of comic strips or cartoons. This is the general category that includes those specific details. Now look back at the paragraph about genes and personality on page 168. In that paragraph, the sentences were all causes or effects. What generalization can you make about those details? You might say they're all *effects of genes on personality*. That is the paragraph's overall topic.

Exercise 4.6

Read each of the following paragraphs and fill in the blanks after each one. The types of supporting details are reasons, examples, events, steps, points of comparison, causes, effects, types, parts, and descriptive details or features.

1. (1) Saving most of your income may allow you to retire early, like John Greaney, who retired at the age of 38 after saving aggressively in his twenties and early thirties. (2) Experts say that living in the smallest, least expensive home that will meet your needs will give you more money to spend during your retirement. (3) Other things to do so you can live well while retired include living more cheaply, tapping into your retirement account sooner, or arranging to work a few hours so that you still have some kind of income to help you live.*

   Sentence 1 subject: _____

   Sentence 2 subject: _____

   Sentence 3 subject: _____

   Type of supporting details: _____

   General topic of paragraph: _____

2. (1) What made Katharine Graham so special? (2) Graham, who won a Pulitzer Prize in 1998 for her autobiography, was best known for her leadership of the Washington Post Company during the Watergate scandal of 1972–1974. (3) In time, Graham became a Washington institution who hosted some of the city's most elegant and publicized social gatherings. (4) At 5 feet 9 inches tall with swept-back hair and regal bearing, Graham

* Adapted from Linda Stern, "Retire When You Want To," *Reader's Digest*, RD.com, July 17, 2001.

Copyright © Houghton Mifflin Company. All rights reserved.

was an icon, an enduring symbol to women, and a businessperson with vision. (5) The woman her friends called "Kay" was the daughter of a talented and domineering mother, then a groundbreaking newspaper reporter, then the mother of four and wife of a brilliant but tormented newspaper executive.*

Sentence 2 subject: _____

Sentence 3 subject: _____

Sentence 4 subject: _____

Sentence 5 subject: _____

Type of supporting details: _____

General topic of paragraph: _____

3. (1) Before you take any family photos, experts advise, look for a good point-and-shoot camera with a flash and a good lens. (2) Next, read the manual that comes with the camera so you can find out, for example, that your camera could, with the flip of a switch, add the date to a print. (3) Third, buy a lot of film; professional photographers might use 20 rolls of film to get one good shot. (4) And last, make sure everyone is in a good mood because good moods lead to good pictures.†

Sentence 1 subject: _____

Sentence 2 subject: _____

Sentence 3 subject: _____

Sentence 4 subject: _____

Type of supporting details: _____

General topic of paragraph: _____

4. (1) What could possibly be on a video made for cats? (2) To start, colorful bird sequences filled with stereo chirps and trills are very attractive to cats. (3) Gerbils scurrying across reddish desert rocks and a chipmunk

* Adapted from Richard Willing, "Graham, a Publishing Icon, Dies," *USA Today*, July 18, 2001, 1A.

† Adapted from S. Johanna Robledo, "Group Mug," *Real Simple*, August 2001, 45.

Copyright © Houghton Mifflin Company. All rights reserved.

darting into a grate rate more highly with other furry viewers, who watch intently from their perches until excitement finally propels them to paw the screen or to look behind the television set to find the critters they've been watching. (4) Also popular is the televised aquarium, which makes some kitties jump to the top of the television to try to dip their paws into the image on the screen.*

Sentence 2 subject: _____

Sentence 3 subject: _____

Sentence 4 subject: _____

Type of supporting details: _____

General topic of paragraph: _____

5. (1) On his own, an orangutan named Fu Manchu figured out how to use a wire lock-pick to escape from his cage at the Omaha Zoo, hiding the tool in his mouth each time he was recaptured. (2) Another orangutan at a Seattle Zoo came up with a ploy, too, by pretending to drop or lose a piece of fruit and then asking for a replacement while actually hiding it. (3) A killer whale named Corky let a keeper stand on his head—a trick he had never been taught—to help the man reach a baby whale in danger of dying in a stretcher hanging over the tank. (4) An ape named Chantek who learned to earn coins for doing chores and to trade them for treats came up with the idea to try to expand his money supply by counterfeiting extra coins from tinfoil.†

Sentence 1 subject: _____

Sentence 2 subject: _____

Sentence 3 subject: _____

Sentence 4 subject: _____

Type of supporting details: _____

General topic of paragraph: _____

* Adapted from "The Cats' Meow," advertisement, National Syndications, Inc.

† Adapted from Eugene Linden, "What Animals Really Think," *Reader's Digest*, February 2000, 116–123.

Copyright © Houghton Mifflin Company. All rights reserved.

As you complete this step, remember what you learned in Chapter 2 about topics that are too broad or too narrow. Make sure the topic you choose is neither.

Exercise 4.7

After each paragraph, label each topic N if it's too narrow, B if it's too broad, and T if it's the correct topic.

1. The mothers of today's "Generation X," the group of Americans born between 1961 and 1981, did 89 percent of the cooking in their homes, but their grown children now tend to divide evening meal preparation equally between the husband and the wife. The parents of Generation Xers usually insisted that their families sit down to eat meals together almost every day, but parents and children today eat only about five meals per week as a family. The length of meals has changed, too: in the homes of most older generation people, mealtimes usually lasted at least thirty minutes, but now only half of Generation Xers stay at the table that long.*

   _____ a. Mealtimes

   _____ b. Mealtimes in older generation and Generation X homes

   _____ c. The length of mealtimes in older generation and Generation X homes

2. In front of the house on Popham Beach, an American flag flutters in a breeze, and dunes thick with dune grass and sandpipers and plovers ripple toward the beach. Inside the house, floors creak and everywhere there are black-and-white photographs of the owner and her family. On some of the bookshelves are novels that were popular in the past ten decades. One room is devoted to books relating to sailing and all things nautical, like lobstering and knot tying. One book from the turn of the century records the early history of Popham Beach, and in it appears a photograph of the house, breasting the wind on a stormy day in the late 1800s. We marvel each time we look at it that the very same house is still here. We can make out clear as day the same rickety door to the basement, probably still swinging on the same hinges.†

   _____ a. An old house

   _____ b. The books in a house on Popham Beach

   _____ c. The contents of an old house on Popham Beach

* Adapted from "Who's Cooking in Gen X Households?" *USA Today*, July 1998, 9–10.
† Adapted from Martha McPhee, "Return to a Favorite Place," *Real Simple*, August 2001, 73.

Copyright © Houghton Mifflin Company. All rights reserved.

3. As a child with Attention Deficit Disorder (ADD), I spent so much time in my private inner world that I missed out on developing a lot of social skills children need. I heard that boys found me "weird" or "twisted" or "stuck-up" or "from a solar system other than our own." Everyone said I was really creative. I never wore "outfits" to school; it was more like "costumes." I'd show up wearing ski knickers, construction boots and earrings I had made out of discarded office supplies. Nowadays, to control kids with ADD, they simply put them on medication.*

_____ a. Boys' reactions to girls with ADD

_____ b. Attention Deficit Disorder (ADD)

_____ c. The author's childhood ADD behaviors

4. Stroll down a country lane. Meander along an ancient footpath. Picnic next to a bubbling stream or a village courtyard. Walking tours will also give you a closer look at a country and its people. You'll get to know your fellow travelers, too. Last but not least, you'll get lots of exercise because walking vacations usually involve several miles of hiking per day.†

_____ a. Vacations

_____ b. Things to see and do on walking tours

_____ c. Meeting people on walking tours

5. Shaquille O'Neal and Kobe Bryant, Los Angeles Lakers teammates, sometimes try too hard to show that there's no animosity between them, with displays of affection in front of the cameras that feel forced. But they can be genuinely friendly in private moments. Before a game in Boston they were talking near the locker room, unaware that anyone could see them. O'Neal leaned over, Bryant whispered something in his ear, and they fell against each other, laughing.‡

_____ a. Kobe Bryant and Shaquille O'Neal's relationship

_____ b. Basketball players

_____ c. Shaquille O'Neal

---

* Adapted from Stephanie Brush, "Pay Attention!" _USA Weekend,_ July 13–15, 2001, 7.

† Adapted from Judy Hammond, "In Step with the World," _The Daily News,_ July 15, 2001, 12, Travel Section.

‡ Adapted from Phil Taylor, "Double Dip," _Sports Illustrated,_ June 25, 2001, 47.

Copyright © Houghton Mifflin Company. All rights reserved.

4

Step 4: State an Implied Main Idea

If you have successfully completed Steps 1 through 3, you have systematically gone through each thinking stage necessary to state the paragraph's main idea. It is in this last step that you put together all of the clues you examined to come up with a statement of the main idea in your own words. This requires you to not only recognize the subjects in the supporting details but also to draw a general conclusion based on *what is being said about each of these subjects*. Then once more, you decide on a general category of ideas or things that include all of those statements.

Remember what you learned about main ideas and topic sentences in Chapter 2. The main idea has two parts: the topic and the point the author wants to make about that topic. The implied main idea is no different. It, too, should include both of those parts. Your statement will begin with the general topic you discovered in Step 3 of this process. Then, it will go on to express the conclusion you drew from adding together the specific supporting details.

For example, look again at the paragraph about comic strips on page 165. What is being said about each different comic strip? Each sentence points out a certain type of subject matter that the cartoonists include in their creations:

philosophy and ethics

political and social commentary

scientific ethics

illogic and insensitivity within American corporations

morality and family issues

What generalization can you make about the items in this list? Obviously, they're all serious, important, and weighty issues.

To form a statement of the main idea, begin with the topic you determined in Step 3: comic strips and cartoons. Often, you will indicate the type of details the paragraph contains, which is why you completed Step 3. Then, add the generalization above to state the main idea:

> Several examples of cartoons and comic strips are often about some serious, important, and weighty issues.

This is the overall point suggested by the paragraph's specific supporting details.

Now, let's follow the same procedure with the paragraph about the effects of genes on personality. This list briefly summarizes those causes and effects:

Cause #1:   Genes determine half of personality.

Cause #2:   Genes create susceptibility, not definite traits.

Effect: Genes leave room for choice.

Copyright © Houghton Mifflin Company. All rights reserved.

What generalization can you make based on these causes and effects? You could say that the answer to the question posed in the paragraph's first sentence is *No, genes are not solely to blame for negative personality traits.*

Next, put the generalizations you made about the topic and about the ideas together to form a statement of the main idea. Here is one possibility:

> The cause of negative personality traits is not genes alone because these traits are also determined by your attitude and choices.

As a final illustration, let's go through all four steps for another paragraph:

> (1) In 1959, the Mercury astronauts were household names, but today, few Americans can name even one of the 148 Space Shuttle astronauts currently on NASA's roster. (2) In the early days of America's space program, people were interested in astronauts because they were swaggering, bragging, boastful pilots, but now that two-thirds of them are doctors, scientists, and engineers, they're no longer "glamorous." (3) In the 1960s, astronauts were worshipped by the American public as heroes, but today, most Americans are indifferent to them. (4) People used to stop their lives to pay close attention when astronauts went into space, but now, the Space Shuttle goes up and comes back with little fanfare.*

Step 1: Sentence 1: Americans' past and present knowledge of astronauts' names

Sentence 2: Americans' past and present interest in astronauts

Sentence 3: Americans' past and present perceptions of astronauts

Sentence 4: Americans' past and present attentiveness to astronauts' missions

Step 2: Types of details: Points of comparison

Step 3: Paragraph's topic: Changes in Americans' attitudes about astronauts

Step 4: Sentence 1: Knew names → don't know names

Sentence 2: Interested → not interested

Sentence 3: Hero worship → indifference

Sentence 4: Attentive → not attentive

* Adapted from Traci Watson, "Quick: Name an Astronaut," *USA Today*, July 12, 2001, 1A.

Copyright © Houghton Mifflin Company. All rights reserved.

4

Generalization: Americans used to care about astronauts, but now they don't.

Implied main idea: Between the early days of the space program and now, Americans' attitudes toward astronauts have changed from caring to indifference.

As you can see, determining implied main ideas is not only a necessary reading skill, it also helps you sharpen your thinking skills. You must analyze and apply logic as you complete each step of this process to draw a final conclusion. This kind of practice will lead to better thinking in general.

Exercise 4.8

Complete the blanks that follow each of the paragraphs below.

1. (1) In the recent past, U.S. President Bill Clinton lied about his extramarital romantic encounters with a White House intern. (2) Executives at Sony's Columbia Pictures admitted to creating a fake movie critic to write praiseworthy quotations about their films. (3) Pulitzer Prize-winning historian Joseph Ellis was exposed as a liar who invented his whole tour of duty in Vietnam. (4) Journalist David Brock knowingly printed false information about Anita Hill, an attorney who accused Supreme Court Justice nominee Clarence Thomas of sexual harassment.*

Sentence 1 subject: _____

Sentence 2 subject: _____

Sentence 3 subject: _____

Sentence 4 subject: _____

Type(s) of supporting details: _____

General topic of paragraph: _____

Generalization: _____

Implied main idea: _____

2. (1) Ever wanted to just up and leave your spouse for an extended—but temporary—period of time? (2) Janis Kirstein is a high school art teacher

* Adapted from Karen S. Peterson, "Would I Lie to You?" *USA Today*, July 5, 2001, 8D.

Copyright © Houghton Mifflin Company. All rights reserved.

in Louisville who says she is taking a time-out at the Vermont Studio Center in Johnson, Vermont, to spend a month nurturing her creativity and learning more about art. (3) Sally Howald took a leave from her job as a creative director for an ad agency to teach advertising strategies in Holland and to get away from her life as "soccer mom and full-time working mom" and reconnect with the person she was before she married. (4) Joan Mister, however, waited until her children were grown and then drove 30,000 miles alone in six months, having her 65th birthday on the road. (5) Her trip, she says, was about self-exploration.*

Sentence 2 subject: _____

Sentence 3 subject: _____

Sentence 4 subject: _____

Type(s) of supporting details: _____

General topic of paragraph: _____

_____

Generalization: _____

_____

Implied main idea: _____

_____

3. (1) Bands that compete on the television show *Cover Wars* are hit with a rapid-fire series of song titles from the last 30 years—anything from The Mamas and The Papas (a group from the 1960s) to current star Moby— which they must start within five seconds. (2) That makes for some frantic onstage huddles, as some band members may not remember how a song goes or what key it is played in. (3) Then comes a new batch of songs, only this time the bands must transform them into styles as diverse as punk, swing, and Latin. (4) Next comes a nerve-racking version of musical chairs. (5) One band starts a song, and when it stops, the other must pick it up in the same key at the exact point in the lyrics. (6) Mess up one word and you're history.†

* Adapted from Karen S. Peterson, "Relationship Respite," *USA Today*, July 19, 2001, 1D.
† Adapted from David Hiltbrand, "Jukebox Heroes," *TV Guide*, July 21, 2001, 30–31.

Copyright © Houghton Mifflin Company. All rights reserved.

Sentence 1 subject: _____

Sentence 3 subject: _____

Sentence 4 subject: _____

Type(s) of supporting details: _____

General topic of paragraph: _____

Generalization: _____

Implied main idea: _____

_____

4. (1) Girls now outnumber boys in student government, honor societies, school newspapers, and debating clubs. (2) A recent study found girls ahead of boys in almost every measure of well-being; for example, girls feel closer to their families, have higher aspirations, and even boast better assertiveness skills. (3) Boys earn 70 percent of the Ds and Fs that teachers dole out. (4) They make up two-thirds of students labeled "learning disabled." (5) They account for 80 percent of high school dropouts. (6) And they are less likely to go to college than ever before; by 2007, universities are projected to enroll 9.2 million women to 6.9 million men.*

Sentence 1 subject: _____

Sentence 2 subject: _____

Sentence 3 subject: _____

Sentence 4 subject: _____

Sentence 5 subject: _____

Sentence 6 subject: _____

Type(s) of supporting details: _____

General topic of paragraph: _____

_____

* Adapted from Anna Mulrine, "Are Boys the Weaker Sex?" *U.S. News and World Report,* July 2, 2001.

Copyright © Houghton Mifflin Company. All rights reserved.

Generalization: _____

Implied main idea: _____

_____

5. (1) Do cops go easy on celebrities? (2) Consider the case of a high-profile politician who was linked to the disappearance of his girlfriend. (3) Despite evidence linking him to the woman, the police didn't interview him, search his apartment, or give him a lie-detector test early on in the case. (4) Or look at the circumstances surrounding a New York city publicist, who some say backed her car into a group of people waiting to get into a famous nightclub. (5) By the time the police got around to asking her some questions, her lawyer had arrived and instructed her not to say anything, arranging for her to be released on bail and back at home before dawn. (6) Then there's the case of a famous child actor who claims his wife was shot while he went into a restaurant. (7) Police declined to name him a suspect despite the fact that he had a gun in his car and it was clear that the couple was unhappily married.*

Sentence 2 subject: _____

Sentence 4 subject: _____

Sentence 6 subject: _____

Type(s) of supporting details: _____

General topic of paragraph: _____

_____

Generalization: _____

Implied main idea: _____

_____

Exercise 4.9

Read each paragraph and circle the letter next to the sentence that correctly states the paragraph's main idea.

* Adapted from Rich Hampson, "Do the Cops Go Easy on Celebrities? Maybe Not," *USA Today*, July 19, 2001, 1A. Copyright © 2001, *USA Today*. Reprinted with permission.

Copyright © Houghton Mifflin Company. All rights reserved.

1. Problems are the cutting edge that distinguishes between success and failure. Problems call forth our courage and our wisdom; indeed, they create our courage and our wisdom. It is only because of problems that we grow mentally and spiritually. When we desire to encourage the growth of the human spirit, we challenge and encourage the human capacity to deal with problems, just as in school we deliberately set problems for our children to solve. It is through the pain of confronting and resolving problems that we learn. As Benjamin Franklin said, "Those things that hurt, instruct."*

   a. Problems have both positive and negative effects.
   b. Problems produce beneficial outcomes for human beings.
   c. Too many people avoid confronting their problems.
   d. Benjamin Franklin had a lot of problems.

2. Alicia Keys, who released the album *Songs in A Minor*, was born to an Italian mother and an African-American father and grew up in New York's Hell's Kitchen,† surviving on her mother's paralegal salary in a one-bedroom apartment. Though money was tight, Keys's mother managed to pay for ballet and classical piano lessons. "She didn't care what it cost," says Keys. Alicia's talent got her into the Professional Performing Arts School in New York. After hours found Keys studying voice with a girls' group at the Police Athletic League near her home.‡

   a. Alicia Keys is very talented.
   b. Alicia Keys just released an album.
   c. Despite being poor, Alicia Keys and her mother stayed devoted to developing Alicia's musical talent.
   d. Alicia Keys went to the Professional Performing Arts School in New York.

3. She walks down the sidewalk of one of Cincinnati's meanest streets. Young toughs, pants low on their hips, slouch on the corner. As she approaches, they straighten up. "Good afternoon, Miz Mattie," they say to the 74-year-old woman. She cuts them the briefest of nods. She disapproves of idleness, but she's kind and charitable, too. She's head of "Grandma's Hands," a place where volunteers teach girls from the meaner streets of Cincinnati to cook and sew.§

   a. Mattie Johnson commands respect from everyone in her neighborhood because of the work she does.

---

* Adapted from M. Scott Peck, *The Road Less Traveled*. New York, Simon and Schuster, 1978, 16.

† Hell's Kitchen is an area in New York City that had a reputation for being a rough place to live and grow up.

‡ Adapted from Allison Samuels, "'Minor' Is Major," *Newsweek*, July 23, 2001, 54.

§ Adapted from Laura Pulfer, "Mattie's Mission," *Rosie*, August 2, 2001, 55.

Copyright © Houghton Mifflin Company. All rights reserved.

b. People are afraid of Mattie Johnson.

c. Mattie Johnson owns "Grandma's Hands."

d. Mattie Johnson dislikes the Cincinnati neighborhood where she lives and works.

4. Who do men think they are, anyway? They refuse to ask for directions, women say. And they won't talk about their feelings. They swagger and boast and take up too much oxygen in the conference room. When men are silent it's not because they have nothing to say but because they don't have to fill up the air with words. They already dominate, just by being themselves, but they're serene about it. Some men feel that the air around us is rarely improved by the sound of words, and if you're not improving on silence, why talk?*

a. Many men are silent.

b. Men have different characteristics from women, especially when it comes to communication styles.

c. Women talk too much.

d. Men and women may never be able to communicate.

5. Why is Harry Potter such a popular and likeable character? Well, for one thing, he is an orphan who was raised by mean, nasty relatives who didn't want him and still manages to succeed in life. He goes from being an abused little boy to being a star athlete at Hogwarts School of Witchcraft and Wizardry, almost overnight. He is very self-sufficient, which is a character trait that many people strive to incorporate into their own personalities. He is also a master magician and makes friends and fights mythic battles against the forces of Darkness, all of which appeal to a wide variety of readers. And, not once does he blame his miserable aunt and uncle for his troubles. Harry's never a victim, even though he does have the most powerful evil wizard of all time harboring a grudge against him, which makes Harry Potter readers root for the character.†

a. Harry Potter was an orphan, which makes a lot of readers identify with him.

b. Harry Potter has had to overcome a lot of adversity and has a lot of positive character traits, so readers identify with him and enjoy reading about him.

c. Harry Potter does not blame anyone for his troubles.

d. The Harry Potter series is very popular.

4

---

* Adapted from Amy Finnerty, "What Women Can Learn from Men," *O Magazine*, April 2001, 145–146.

† Adapted from Janette Barber, "On Being . . . a Harry Potter Fan," *Rosie*, August 2001, 42–43.

Copyright © Houghton Mifflin Company. All rights reserved.

CHAPTER 4 REVIEW

Fill in the blanks in the following statements.

1. An _____ main idea is one that is suggested but not stated.

2. An implied main idea paragraph contains specific supporting details but no _____.

3. To determine the implied main idea of a paragraph, you can follow four steps:

   a. Find the _____ of each sentence.

   b. Determine the _____ of supporting details in the paragraph.

   c. Determine a general _____ based on the specific details.

   d. Draw a _____ from the supporting details and state an implied main idea in your own words.

4. An implied main idea, like one that's stated in a topic sentence, includes both the _____ and what is being said about that topic.

Reading Selection

Greatness Knows No Color
By Angela G. King

1 I still remember it vividly. Dozens of small hands shot up into the air throughout packed classrooms and children screamed out the names Martin Luther King, Jr., George Washington Carver, and Harriet Tubman, to name a few.

2 The usual short list of well-known blacks was eagerly recited by third-, fourth-, and fifth-graders in response to my query, "Who can name a famous black person in American history?" as I went from school to school in Troy, Michigan.

3 It was 1982, I was 17 years old and, as a debutante for America's oldest black sorority, Alpha Kappa Alpha, I had decided to talk to elementary school kids in my hometown about significant black historical figures.

4 Troy was back then as it is now—a predominately white suburb of Detroit. I happened to be a black girl who lived there, and I figured that all children, not just black children down in the city, needed to know about some of the overlooked Americans who played a pivotal role in pushing this nation forward. Unfortunately, I learned then what still holds true today—that even as we commemorate Black History Month every February, many blacks who made a tremendous contribution in shaping this country languish in obscurity.

Copyright © Houghton Mifflin Company. All rights reserved.

5   That's a shame. Knowing about the inventor of the traffic light (Garrett Morgan) or how Elijah McCoy revolutionized the locomotive industry by inventing a self-lubricating oil cap for steam engines or about the partner of Howard Hughes who helped develop the first commercial communications satellite (Frank Mann) isn't just *black* history. It's *American* history.

6   Take the blacks I chose to tell those Troy school children about as my community-service project. Who has heard of Asa Spaulding, founder of the nation's oldest and largest black life insurance firm? Or Percy Lavon Julian, a chemist who synthesized physostigmine, the drug used to treat glaucoma? Or Mary McCleod Bethune, the educator and promoter of civil and women's rights who founded Bethune-Cookman College, one of this nation's oldest black colleges?

7   I'd never heard of them until I did research for my project back then as a high school senior, and very few of the young students I talked to back then—or, I dare say, their teachers—had heard of them either.

8   I'm sorry to say that it has not been until this year, at age 35, while doing research for a freelance writing project, that I've learned about Dr. Daniel Hale Williams, the first physician to successfully perform open-heart surgery; Jan Ernst Matzeliger, who automated shoe manufacturing with a machine he invented to replace the costly manual method of forming shoes; Julian Francis Abele, one of the nation's first professional black architects, who designed the Philadelphia Museum of Art; and Mary Church Terrell, who founded the National Association of Colored Women to help poor black women fight for women's rights.

9   As the old saying goes, "You can't know where you're going unless you know where you've been." Americans can't move forward together as a nation until we recognize the entire spectrum of people who have helped to shape our nation. That's a lesson not just for February, but all year round.

From Angela G. King, "Greatness Knows No Color," *Daily News*, Feb. 25, 2000. New York Daily News, L. P., reprinted with permission.

Copyright © Houghton Mifflin Company. All rights reserved.

VOCABULARY

Read the following questions about some of the vocabulary words that appear in the previous selection. Circle the correct responses.

1. In paragraph 1, the author uses the word *vividly* to describe how she recalls a memory she had about her experience in an elementary school classroom. In this context, what does *vividly* mean?

   a. cloudy   c. shaky
   b. clearly   d. faintly

2. What does the word *query* mean as used in paragraph 2?

   a. eerie   c. explanation
   b. reply   d. question

3. The author describes herself as having been a *debutante* (paragraph 3). What do you think the word *debutante* means?

   a. a poor woman
   b. a young woman who makes a formal debut into society
   c. a college student
   d. an elementary school teacher

4. In paragraph 4, the author writes, ". . . I figured that all children, not just black children down in the city, needed to know about some of the overlooked Americans who played a *pivotal* role in pushing this nation forward." What does the word *pivotal* mean as used here?

   a. significant   c. insignificant
   b. not worthy   d. happy

5. What does the word *commemorate* mean as used in paragraph 4?

   a. to begin   c. to design
   b. to acknowledge and honor d. to declare

6. What do you think the phrase to *languish in obscurity* means? In paragraph 4, the author writes ". . . many blacks who made a tremendous contribution in shaping this country *languish in obscurity*."

   a. are famous   c. are unknown
   b. remain fearful   d. stay inside

7. In paragraph 6, the author asks if you know Percy Lavon Julian, a chemist who synthesized physostigmine, the drug used to treat glaucoma. What do you think the word *synthesized* means?

   a. shook up   c. combined or produced
   b. threw out   d. deleted

8. What does the word *spectrum* mean in paragraph 9? "Americans can't move forward together as a nation until we recognize the entire *spectrum* of people. . . ."

   a. range   c. batch
   b. cluster   d. concentration

IMPLIED MAIN IDEAS, TOPICS, AND SUPPORTING DETAILS

Answer the following questions by circling the letter of the correct response.

1. What is the implied main idea of paragraphs 1–3? Circle the correct choice.

   a. Children in Troy, Michigan, are very smart.
   b. The author was a debutante and a member of a black sorority.

Copyright © Houghton Mifflin Company. All rights reserved.

   c. Children know a few names of famous African Americans.

   d. The author is from Troy, Michigan, and was a good student.

2. What is the implied main idea of paragraph 6?

   a. There are many significant figures in black history, and students should know about them.

   b. Mary McCleod Bethune founded a famous college long before women were doing things like that.

   c. Asa Spaulding faced racism in founding the oldest and largest black life insurance firm.

   d. Bethune-Cookman college is one of the nation's oldest black colleges.

3. Reread paragraph 8. What is the implied main idea?

   a. The author's research project was very difficult.

   b. These historical figures are not given proper credit for their achievements.

   c. The author wishes she had known about these important black figures in history earlier in her life.

   d. Mary Church Terrell founded the NACW.

4. The topic of paragraph 5 is

   a. traffic lights   c. communications satellites

   b. African-American inventors   d. shameful behaviors

5. The type of supporting details in paragraph 8 is

   a. examples   c. points of comparison

   b. reasons   d. steps

QUESTIONS FOR DISCUSSION AND WRITING

Answer the following questions based on your reading of the selection.

1. The author writes in paragraph 5 that "knowing about [important black figures in history] . . . isn't just *black* history. It's *American* history." Do you agree or disagree? Why? _____

_____

2. Agree or disagree with the statement, "You can't know where you're going unless you know where you've been." Explain your answer. Why do you think the author chose to end her essay with that statement?

_____

_____

Copyright © Houghton Mifflin Company. All rights reserved.

3. What do you think the author is saying about Black History Month as an event? Do you agree or disagree with her? Why? _____

_____

4

▌ Vocabulary: The Definition/Restatement Context Clue

When you encounter an unfamiliar word as you read, you may be able to figure out its meaning by using context clues. The context of a word is its relationship to the other words, phrases, and sentences that surround it. Sometimes, these nearby elements offer clues you can use to get a sense of what a particular word means.

One type of context clue is **definition** or **restatement.** In this type of clue, either the word's meaning is directly stated, or synonyms are used to restate it. The following sentence, which comes from one of the paragraphs in this chapter, uses restatement:

> Considered somewhat *eccentric,* or odd, Benjamin Franklin was a noted inventor and diplomat who was somewhat chubby and messy, but neither of those things interfered with his ability to help write the most important document in American history.

The word *odd* is a synonym for *eccentric*; therefore, it tells you what *eccentric* means.

Vocabulary Exercise

The following sentences all come from paragraphs in Chapters 3 and 4. In each one, underline the definition or restatement context clue that helps you understand the meaning of the boldfaced, italicized word:

1. Even more encouraging, the genes for personality aren't like those for blue eyes or height because they merely give you a **_susceptibility,_** or tendency, or doom and gloom.

2. Research has revealed that regular aspirin use may protect against the risk of colon cancer by as much as 40 to 50 percent; **_esophageal_** (throat) cancer by about 80 to 90 percent; and ovarian cancer by some 25 percent.

3. The mothers of today's "**_Generation X,_**" the group of Americans born between 1961 and 1981, did 89 percent of the cooking in their homes, but their grown children now tend to divide evening meal preparation equally between the husband and the wife.

Copyright © Houghton Mifflin Company. All rights reserved.

4. Both the Washington and San Francisco-Oakland areas have developed and continue to expand their passenger rail systems, but they are still leaders among cities plagued with **gridlock,** or frustrating traffic jams.

5. In 1872, therefore, the Time-Table Convention searched for a solution, and Charles F. Dowd proposed the creation of **time zones,** imaginary divisions of the Earth's surface.

6. Prompted by our modest exertions, just a few minutes into a walk the body begins to produce **endorphins,** chemical compounds that reduce pain and stress, enhance memory and judgment as they course through the brain.

7. If you find that **procrastination,** or putting things off, hurts your progress, here are some ways to break the habit.

8. At 5 feet 9 inches tall with swept-back hair and regal bearing, Graham was an **icon,** an enduring symbol to women, and a businessperson with vision.

9. Stroll down a country lane. **Meander** along an ancient footpath. Picnic next to a bubbling stream or a village courtyard. Walking tours will also give you a closer look at a country and its people.

10. In the early days of America's space program, people were interested in astronauts because they were **swaggering,** bragging, boastful pilots, but now that two-thirds of them are doctors, scientists, and engineers, they're no longer "glamorous."

4

Copyright © Houghton Mifflin Company. All rights reserved.

Name _____ Date _____

POST-TEST 1

A. Select the correct general category that includes all the specific items listed. Circle the correct response.

1. Sport utility vehicle   Convertible

   Van   Sedan

   a. Bicycles   c. Toys
   b. Automobiles   d. Publications

2. Cardinals   Orioles

   Robins   Blue Jays

   a. Foods   c. Clocks
   b. Clothes   d. Birds

3. Bedroom   Kitchen

   Den   Bathroom

   a. Rooms   c. Instruments
   b. Sports   d. Tasks

4. Dog   Parakeet

   Cat   Guinea pig

   a. Pets   c. Trees
   b. Foods   d. Places

5. Oil   Electricity

   Gas   Coal

   a. Reference materials   c. Countries
   b. Home repairs   d. Energy sources

For additional tests, see the Test Bank.

Copyright © Houghton Mifflin Company. All rights reserved.

B. For each group of sentences, select the general sentence that includes all the specific details given. Circle the correct response.

6. You can teach a dog to sit on command.

   You can teach a dog to lie down.

   You can teach a dog to come when called.

   a. Dogs know how to come when called.
   b. Dogs are friendly.
   c. Dogs know when to lie down.
   d. Dogs can be trained.

7. Eric always undercooks our eggs.

   Eric makes spaghetti that's too soft.

   Eric usually burns the meat loaf.

   a. Eric doesn't care for eggs.
   b. Eric doesn't like to cook.
   c. Eric is not a good cook.
   d. Eric doesn't cook much.

8. My watch runs too slow.

   My watch's alarm does not come on at the right time.

   Sometimes my watch stops altogether.

   a. My watch needs to be repaired.
   b. All watches have their own characteristics.
   c. My watch is interesting.
   d. New watches are expensive.

9. Lydia always talks very loudly into her cell phone.

   Lydia uses her cell phone in restaurants, theaters, and even during religious services.

   Lydia interrupts any conversation she's having in order to answer her cell phone.

   a. Lydia never misses messages that come by cell phone.
   b. Lydia needs to learn her cell phone manners.
   c. Lydia thinks her cell phone is one of her most useful appliances.
   d. Lydia is a believer in new phone technology.

10. Some people read the newspaper's sports section before everything else.

    Others are not interested in sports at all.

Copyright © Houghton Mifflin Company. All rights reserved.

And there are still others who follow their local team only when it is playing a championship game.

a. People have widely varying tastes when it comes to sports.
b. Most people like to know how their local sports teams are doing.
c. People who care deeply about sports usually dress tastefully.
d. People who don't care about sports are dull.

POST-TEST 2

A. Read each of the following paragraphs and answer the questions that follow. Circle the correct response.

(1) Domino's Pizza offers mayonnaise and potato pizza in Tokyo and pickled ginger pizza in India. (2) Heinz varies its ketchup recipe to satisfy the needs of specific markets; in Belgium and Holland, for example, the ketchup is not as sweet. (3) When Haagen-Dazs served up one of its most popular American flavors, Chocolate Chip Cookie Dough, to British customers, they left it sitting in supermarket freezers. (4) What the premium ice-cream maker learned is that chocolate chip cookies aren't popular in Great Britain, and children don't have a history of snatching raw dough from the bowl. (5) After holding a contest to come up with a flavor the British would like, the company launched "Cool Britannia," vanilla ice cream with strawberries and chocolate-covered Scottish shortbread.*

1. The subject of sentence 1 is

   a. Domino's Pizza.
   b. Tokyo.
   c. mayonnaise.
   d. India.

2. The subject of sentence 2 is

   a. Belgium and Holland.
   b. recipes.
   c. Heinz.
   d. markets.

3. The subject of sentence 4 is

   a. Haagen Dazs.
   b. ice-cream flavors.
   c. contests.
   d. Britain.

* Adapted from William M. Pride et al., *Business,* 6th ed. Boston: Houghton Mifflin, 1999, 338.

Copyright © Houghton Mifflin Company. All rights reserved.

4. The major supporting details are

   a. reasons.
   b. points of comparison.
   c. events.
   d. examples.

5. The general topic of this paragraph is

   a. pizza.
   b. food manufacturers.
   c. ice-cream preferences.
   d. delicious food.

4

(1) Before you choose a contractor to remodel your home, experts advise, look for someone who either lives in your town or has done work there before. (2) Next, meet with the contractor to see if his or her vision for your home matches yours. (3) For example, does the contractor agree with what you've planned to do? (4) If not, you might want to shop around for someone else. (5) Third, get a list of references from the contractor and find out if the people for whom he or she has done work like what was done and feel it was of good quality. (6) And last, make sure the contractor is available on the date on which you would like to start the work.

6. The subject of sentence 1 is

   a. contractors.
   b. homes.
   c. experts.
   d. towns.

7. The subject of sentence 2 is

   a. your vision.
   b. contractor's vision.
   c. homes.
   d. meetings.

8. The subject of sentence 5 is

   a. contractors.
   b. list of references.
   c. people in town.
   d. quality.

Copyright © Houghton Mifflin Company. All rights reserved.

9. The type of supporting details is

    a. examples.

    b. events.

    c. steps.

    d. points of comparison.

10. The general topic of this paragraph is

    a. your home.

    b. things to check when choosing a contractor.

    c. steps in remodeling.

    d. home improvement.

(1) Cats spend most of their day sleeping, but have been known to prance around at night, to the dismay of their owners. (2) Dogs are awake most of the day, but usually sleep all night, just like their human friends. (3) Cats have few needs in the hygiene department; they wash themselves and usually don't need to be bathed by their owners. (4) Dogs should be bathed and groomed on a regular basis in order to keep their coats healthy and free from matting. (5) Cats can be left a bowl of food that they can graze at throughout the day. (6) A dog's bowl should only be filled in the morning and at night. (7) Dogs have been known to eat more than necessary only to get sick later. (8) Cats can also be left alone for long periods of time. (9) Dogs should have regular companionship and get exercise on a regular basis.

11. The subject of sentence 1 is

    a. cats.

    b. sleep.

    c. dogs.

    d. cat owners.

12. The subject of sentence 2 is

    a. cats.

    b. dogs.

    c. sleep.

    d. dog owners.

13. The subject of sentence 6 is

    a. dogs.

    b. a dog's bowl.

    c. sick dog.

    d. feeding schedules.

Copyright © Houghton Mifflin Company. All rights reserved.

14. The type of supporting details is

    a. reasons.
    b. steps.
    c. points of comparison.
    d. examples.

15. The general topic of this paragraph is

    a. differences between cats and dogs.
    b. why pet owners buy pets.
    c. feeding cats and dogs.
    d. exercising dogs regularly.

B. After each paragraph and topic statement, select N if the topic is too narrow, B if it's too broad, and T if it's the correct one. Circle the correct choice.

16. Have you ever noticed how few people drive at the speed limit? Most drivers stretch it at least 10 miles per hour beyond the limit, and many go even faster. In fact, when someone does keep to the speed limit, it makes the motorists behind frustrated and anxious to get past so they can go at their normal fast speed. When police officers give speeding tickets, it's usually when someone is going way beyond the speed limit. But can you imagine how many tickets the police would give out if they stopped everyone who went faster than the speed limit?

    Topic: People who drive at the speed limit.

    a. N
    b. B
    c. T

17. Like the Great War, the Great Depression must be spelled with capital letters. Economic depression was nothing new. Depressions occurred throughout the nineteenth century with predictable regularity, as they recur in the form of recessions and slumps to this day. What was new about this depression? It struck the entire world with ever-greater intensity from 1929 to 1933, and recovery was uneven and slow. Only with the Second World War did the depression disappear in much of the world.*

    Topic: Economic depressions before the Great Depression

    a. N
    b. B
    c. T

* Adapted from John P. McKay et al., *A History of the World Societies*. Boston: Houghton Mifflin, 1996, 1044.

Copyright © Houghton Mifflin Company. All rights reserved.

18. When do children develop a sense of time? When young children enter elementary school, they have a fairly secure conception of "yesterday." But events that happened to them prior to yesterday—two weeks, two months, or two years ago—are usually thought of as happening "a long time ago," somewhere in a vast and undifferentiated past. However, because young children sometimes have difficulty differentiating the time span of past events does not mean that they have forgotten what happened. Children can often describe past events—vacations, birthday parties, or other experiences—in excruciating detail. They can tell what happened, but they may be unable to provide an accurate time frame for when the events took place.*

Topic: Time

a. N
b. B
c. T

4

19. One theory about the derivation of the name "chicken pox" says that it comes from the early years of diagnosis, when the pox blisters were described as looking like chickpeas. Another theory is that the blisters were said to look like chicken bites. A third states that children were once popularly called "chickens." Since the disease mainly struck that age group, the affliction was named for them.†

Topic: Theories about the origin of the name "chicken pox"

a. N
b. B
c. T

* Adapted from David A. Welton and John T. Mallan, *Children and Their World.* Boston: Houghton Mifflin, 1999, 103.
† Adapted from "FYI," *Popular Science*, September 2001, 78.

Copyright © Houghton Mifflin Company. All rights reserved.

Transitions

GOALS FOR CHAPTER 5

▶ Practice the steps involved in summarizing a reading selection.

▶ Define the term *transition.*

▶ Recognize common transitions used to indicate a series of items.

▶ Recognize common transitions used to indicate time order.

▶ Recognize common transitions used to indicate cause/effect.

▶ Recognize common transitions used to indicate comparison/contrast.

▶ Recognize common transitions used to indicate definition and examples.

▶ Recognize transitions in paragraphs organized according to more than one pattern.

5

READING STRATEGY: Summarizing

When you **summarize** a reading selection, you briefly restate, in your own words, its most important ideas. A summary usually focuses on the most general points, which include the overall main idea and some of the major supporting details. As a result, summaries are much shorter than the original material. A paragraph can usually be summarized in a sentence or two, an article can be summarized in a paragraph, and a typical textbook chapter can be summarized in a page or two.

Summarizing is an important reading skill that you will use for three specific academic purposes: studying, completing assignments and tests, and incorporating source material into research projects.

Studying. Writing summaries is an effective way to gain a better understanding of what you read. If you need to remember the information in a textbook chapter, for instance, you will know it more thoroughly after you have summarized its main ideas. Also, the act of writing down these ideas will help reinforce them in your memory.

Continued

Copyright © Houghton Mifflin Company. All rights reserved.

Completing assignments and tests. Summaries are one of the most common types of college writing assignments. Professors in a variety of disciplines often ask students to summarize readings such as journal articles. Also, "summarize" is a common direction in tests that require written responses.

Incorporating source material into research projects. You will use summaries of other sources to support your ideas in research projects such as term papers.

To write a summary, follow these three steps:

1. Using active reading techniques, read and reread the original material until you understand it.

2. Identify the main idea and major supporting points. In particular, underline all of the topic sentences. You might also want to create an outline or map that diagrams the general and specific relationships among sentences (in a paragraph) or paragraphs (in an article or chapter).

3. Using your own words, write sentences that state the author's main idea along with the most important major details. Your paraphrase should be accurate; it should not add anything that did not appear in the original or omit anything important from the original. It should also be objective. In other words, don't offer your own reactions or opinions; just restate the author's points without commenting on them. If you use a phrase from the original, enclose it in quotation marks to indicate that it is the author's words, not yours.

Follow the three steps described above to write a one-paragraph summary of the following newspaper article: .

Columbine's Lessons Learned*

Anyone who has wondered how schools can prevent a repeat of the Columbine, Colo., high school massacre need only look at New Bedford High in Massachusetts. In November 2001, police arrested three students for plotting a massacre there. Among the items seized from their homes: directions for making bombs, shotgun shells, knives and a flare gun.

* Adapted from *USA Today*, November 28, 2001, 16A. Copyright © 2001, *USA Today*. Reprinted with permission.

Continued

Copyright © Houghton Mifflin Company. All rights reserved.

The school's success at foiling this twisted plan was no accident. For years [the school] has worked to create a culture of trust. The 3,000-plus students are broken up into four houses, essentially mini-schools with their own housemasters. Students are encouraged to talk to teachers about problems. The effort paid off when one student told a teacher last month that she overheard boys talking about planting bombs in the school. That sparked a police investigation, which helped stop the attacks from occurring.

New Bedford's experience lines up with advice from a Secret Service study released in 2000. This study provides a blueprint for schools eager to prevent other Columbine-like tragedies. Such acts of violence are almost always planned out, the Secret Service found. More importantly, the shooters almost always tell someone else about their plot in advance. At least four schools nationwide have averted similar disasters in the past year, after students alerted school officials about what they'd heard from fellow students.

The good news is that several schools across the country are recognizing that their best weapon against violence is students themselves. They've set up anonymous tip lines, put in "student relations officers," set up e-mail accounts for tips and looked to create mini-schools within larger buildings.

Still, violence remains an all-too-common threat. In the 2001 school year alone, there were nine bombs or bomb threats and four cases of murder/suicide, according to National School Safety and Security Services. And many schools are only just beginning to address causes of school violence. The Secret Service report found, for instance, that bullying played a role in two-thirds of all school attacks. But much of the advice on dealing with bullying simply tells kids how to cope with it, when cracking down on bullies is what's needed.

Even as memories of Columbine fade, schools can't lose sight of the need for constant vigilance. New Bedford showed that with careful plans in place, murderous acts by students can be thwarted before anyone gets hurt.

In Chapters 3 and 4, you learned how to recognize supporting details within paragraphs. To help you understand how those details are related to one another, paragraphs include transitions that help you follow the author's train of thought. To discover what you already know about transitions, take the following pre-test.

Copyright © Houghton Mifflin Company. All rights reserved.

PRE-TEST

Circle the transition words in the following paragraphs.

1. Starting a vegetable garden can be a rewarding experience, but you have to spend a lot of time tending your plants in order to be able to have a crop at the end of summer. At first, your plants will be small and will not yield any vegetables or fruit. But don't get discouraged! Before long, you will begin to see small sprouts growing, which means that the work you have done is paying off. Eventually, after spending time weeding and trimming your garden, you are sure to have many things to eat from your garden and you will understand the joys of gardening.

2. Five minutes after I arrive home, I have to cook dinner for my family. My children are old enough to boil a pot of water, yet dinner has become my nightly duty. Consequently, we end up getting take-out on many nights because I am just too tired to cook. As a result, I feel like our diet is not as healthy as it should be.

3. When Janis Klein became a school nurse 15 years ago, one-sixth of the children in her elementary school had head lice. As a result, they couldn't go to school. So, Klein, who has worked in hospitals and summer camps, quickly became an expert in recognizing head lice. In time, she started her own business to help families through the area recognize, treat, and deal with head lice.*

4. Long-standing bases of identity and the problems they sometimes gave rise to were becoming less important as a new society emerged. At the same time, new questions about identity appeared. By the 1980s, an awareness of gender roles in society became important to women and

* Adapted from M. K. Fottrell, "No Nits Here," *Westchester Parent*, August 2001, 16.

Copyright © Houghton Mifflin Company. All rights reserved.

helped create the women's, or feminist, movement. <u>As</u> it matured, the feminist movement that had grown in popularity in the 1960s found it necessary to expand its focus beyond the quest for equal opportunity.*

5. Geology is the science of the Earth, the study of its composition, structure, and history. <u>In particular,</u> it is the study of those processes that shaped the Earth of the past and those that continue to mold the Earth of the present. <u>Also,</u> it is a science concerned with everything from the migration of sand dunes across the desert to the migration of continents across the globe and from the flow of molten rock down the sides of volcanoes to the flow of rivers to the sea. Geology even goes outside of the Earth's boundaries. Planetary geology has become a thriving branch of the science.†

5

Transitions are words and phrases whose function is to show the relationships between thoughts and ideas. The word *transition* comes from the Latin word *trans*, which means "across." Transitions bridge the gaps across sentences and paragraphs and reveal how they are related.

Transitions make sentences clearer, so they help readers understand the ideas in a passage more easily. Without them, the readers have to figure out relationships on their own. For example, read these two sentences:

> She was afraid of guns. She bought a gun and learned to use it to protect herself.

When you read these two sentences, which are not connected, the second one seems to contradict the first one. If someone fears guns, why would she buy one? In the absence of a transition, the reader has to pause and mentally fill in that gap on his or her own. Now look at how the addition of a transition more clearly reveals the contrast between the two thoughts:

> She was afraid of guns. ***But*** she bought a gun and learned to use it to protect herself.

* Adapted from Noble et al., *Western Civilization*. Boston: Houghton Mifflin, 1999, 711.
† Adapted from Dolgoff, *Essentials of Physical Geology*. Boston: Houghton Mifflin, 1998, 3.

Copyright © Houghton Mifflin Company. All rights reserved.

Characteristics of Transitions

You should be aware of three characteristics of transitions:

1. Some of them are synonyms. In other words, they mean the same thing. For instance, the transitions *also, in addition,* and *too* all have the same meaning. Therefore, they are usually interchangeable with one another.

2. Some transitions can be used to show more than one kind of relationship between details. For example, you may see the word *next* in both series of items and in a paragraph that explains the steps in a process.

   The **next** component of love is commitment. (series of items)

   Next, prepare an agenda for the meeting. (steps in a process)

3. Different transitions can create subtle but significant changes in the meanings of sentences. For example, reread an earlier example that includes a contrast transition:

   She was afraid of guns. *But* she bought a gun and learned to use it to protect herself.

The transition *but* suggests that she bought a gun *in spite of* her fear. Notice, however, how a different transition changes the relationship between the two sentences.

   She was afraid of guns. *So* she bought a gun and learned to use it to protect herself.

Substituting the transition *so,* which is a cause/effect word, suggests that she bought the gun *to overcome* her fear. Altering that one transition significantly alters the meaning of those two sentences.

As you read, then, you'll need to pay attention to transitions so you can accurately follow the train of thought within a reading selection. The remainder of this chapter explains and illustrates the different types of transition words that accompany various patterns of organization.

Transition Words That Indicate a Series

Certain transition words show readers that the sentence will add another item to a series. A series may consist of examples, reasons, or some other kind of point. Here are some common series transitions:

Copyright © Houghton Mifflin Company. All rights reserved.

Series Transitions

also	furthermore	finally
in addition	first, second, third	lastly
too	first of all	most importantly
another	and	moreover
one	for one thing	next

The following pairs of sentences illustrate the use of series transitions:

When you travel in a recreational vehicle, kids feel at home no matter where you go. *And*, parents love the freedom, the conveniences, and the relatively low cost.

Hummingbirds are among the smallest warm-blooded animals on earth. *Also*, they are among the meanest.

A sincere apology can have a tremendous amount of healing power. *In addition*, it can set the stage for better communication in the future.

Now, read a paragraph that includes series transition words (boldfaced, italicized). Notice how each transition indicates the addition of another item in the series:

Your credit score is determined by five factors. ***The first factor*** is your payment record. Thirty-five percent of your score depends on whether you pay your bills on time. ***The second factor*** is the amount you owe. Your total amount of debt accounts for 30 percent of your score. ***The third determinant*** of your score is your credit history. The length of time you've been borrowing and paying back money influences 15 percent of your score. Your credit application history is ***the fourth factor.*** Ten percent of your score is based on how much new debt you try to acquire. ***The fifth and final factor*** is your credit mix. This last ten percent of your score is based on what kinds of debts you have incurred.*

This paragraph presents a series of five factors that determine an individual's credit score. The series transitions *first, second, third*, etc., indicate each new factor.

* Adapted from Paul J. Lim, "They Know Your Credit Score," *Reader's Digest*, July 2001, 164–166.

Copyright © Houghton Mifflin Company. All rights reserved.

5

Exercise 5.1

Fill in the blanks in the following sentences and paragraphs with appropriate series transitions. Choose words or phrases from the box on page 205. Try to vary your choices.

1. Reba McEntire is a very successful country music star. *also/In addition*, she is winning critical acclaim for her performance in the Broadway musical *Annie Get Your Gun*.

2. There are a few things you'll need to bake a cake. *first/second/Fanally/third* you will need the right ingredients. *Second*, you will need the proper baking dish. And *fanally*, you will need an oven.

3. A low-fat diet has many benefits. *for one thing*, it can help you stay at a weight that is appropriate for your height and age. *another*, it can reduce your risk of heart disease.

4. *One* example of an Alfred Hitchcock movie is *Vertigo,* starring Jimmy Stewart and Kim Novak. *another* example is *The Birds*, which made Tippi Hedren a big star.

5. Buddha gave some good advice about what to say and what not to say to others. The founder of Buddhism recommended that a person ask three vital questions before saying anything to another person. *first*, ask yourself if the statement is *true*. *Second/next*, ask if the statement is *necessary*. *third*, ask if the statement is *kind*. If a statement falls short on any of these counts, Buddha advised that we say nothing.*

6. My mother always gave me a lot of tips before I went out on a date. *first of all/for one thing*, I was never to order spaghetti. She thought that eating spaghetti on a date was too messy and had the potential for disaster. *also/Furthermore/in addition/moreover*, I was never to wear patent-leather shoes. She was so old-fashioned that she thought that patent-leather shoes could reflect what you were wearing under your dress or skirt! *Furthermore*, I was always supposed to let my date open the door for me. *fanally*, her last tip was to never let a boy kiss me on the first date. My mother was certainly behind the times!

* Adapted from Barry L. Reece and Rhonda Brandt, *Effective Human Relations in Organizations,* 7th ed. Boston: Houghton Mifflin, 1999, 213.

Copyright © Houghton Mifflin Company. All rights reserved.

7. Many people say that there is nothing worth watching on television. Television critics disagree and give several examples of worthwhile programs. _One example_ of a good program is _Seinfeld_. Even though it doesn't air in prime time on a weekly basis anymore, it is still shown daily on television stations across the United States and remains extremely popular because of the excellent script writing that defined the show. _another example_ of a worthwhile program is _The West Wing_. Although some people do not like the liberal focus of the show, most agree that it has good plots, characters, and story lines. _the last example_ [A third ex] of a great program is _60 Minutes_. Called the "grandad of news programming," it has been on for over twenty years and remains high quality and groundbreaking.

Transition Words That Indicate Time Order

Some transition words signal that the sentence is providing another event, step, or stage within a chronological order of details. Here is a list of common time order transitions:

5

Time Order Transitions			
first, second, third	next	as	finally
before	soon	when	over time
now	in the beginning	until	in the end
then	once	later	during, in, on,
after	today	eventually	_or_ by (_followed_
while	previously	last	_by a date_)
	often	meanwhile	

The following pairs of sentences illustrate the use of time order transitions:

On July 29, 1981, Diana Spencer married England's Prince Charles and became the Princess of Wales. **In 1992,** Charles and Diana officially separated.

High-fiber foods take longer to eat and increase your satisfaction. **Then,** when they get to the intestines, fiber-rich foods act as an appetite suppressant.

Copyright © Houghton Mifflin Company. All rights reserved.

Almost thirty years ago, boxer Muhammad Ali was named *Sports Illustrated's* Sportsman of the Year. *Now,* at age 59 and suffering from Parkinson's disease, he shakes uncontrollably and slurs his words when he speaks.

Now, read a paragraph that uses time order transition words (boldface italicized). Notice how each transition indicates another event in the timeline:

The famous Leaning Tower of Pisa has been tilting for over 800 years, and recent improvements should allow it to continue tilting for another 300 more. *On August 9, 1173,* construction began on this well-known Italian bell tower. *Almost immediately,* it began leaning because it was being erected on the soft silt of a buried riverbed. *Between 1178 and 1360,* work stopped and started two more times as workers tried to continue the project and figure out how to compensate for the tilt. *Over the next six centuries,* the tower's lean continued to increase, although tourists were still allowed to visit. *Then, in 1990,* Italy's prime minister feared the tower would collapse and closed it to the public. *From 1999 to 2001,* engineers excavated soil from beneath the tower. *Now,* the tower still leans out about 15 feet beyond its base, but it should remain stable for several more centuries.*

This paragraph tells the story of the Leaning Tower of Pisa, arranging the details using time order. Each new detail is introduced with a time order transition to help the reader easily follow the progression of events.

Exercise 5.2

Fill in the blanks in the following sentences and paragraphs with appropriate time order transitions. Choose words or phrases from the box on page 207. Try to vary your choices.

1. Twenty years ago, patients got most medical information from their doctors. _____now_____, they can access some 70,000 health-care-related Internet sites.

2. Tiger Woods has won just about every golf tournament that is played. _____eventually_____, he has to lose, don't you think?

3. Yesterday, I had my eyes checked at the eye doctor's office. _____today_____, I get the results of my eye exam.

* Adapted from Richard Covington, "The Leaning Tower Straightens Up," *Smithsonian*, June 2001, 41–47.

Copyright © Houghton Mifflin Company. All rights reserved.

4. ~~during~~ *In* _____ colonial times, many children died due to disease and poor medical care.

5. You just won big money in the lottery. Now what do you do? *first* _____, protect your ticket. Seal it in an envelope and stash it in a safe deposit box until you can claim your prize. _*then / second*_, contact lottery headquarters within the time limit. You probably have from 180 days to one year to show up with your winning ticket. _*before / third*_, you'll have to decide how you want to receive your money. You can either get one lump-sum payment, or you can arrange to be paid a portion every year for, say, twenty years. _*third / next / after that*_, hire a financial advisor and an accountant to help you manage and invest your money. _*Fanally / last*_, you'll need to decide whether or not you want to keep your job. Many people think they'd quit right away, but to make the money last through wise investments, you may need to keep on working.*

6. Franklin Roosevelt was not eager to enter World War II, according to many historians. _*on / always (on) a date*_ December 7, 1941, however, his position changed. *When / After* the Japanese invaded the military base at Pearl Habor, FDR found that he had no choice but to enter the war. *after* _____ much thought, he addressed the American people and gave them his decision.

7. _*Before / previously*_, the volunteer program known as "Friends for Life" was a small organization run by four people. _*now / today*_, it is a successful program that pairs senior citizens with dog friends and has a staff of over 100 people nationwide. _*now / over time*_, the head of "Friends for Life," John Baker, wants to expand the program overseas. _*In / by / Before*_ 2010, he hopes to have programs operating in France, Belgium, and Germany.

Transition Words That Indicate Cause/Effect

Certain transition words indicate that an occurrence about to be presented in a sentence is either a reason for or a result of an occurrence presented in a previous sentence. These are the transitions that reveal cause or effect

* Adapted from Jack R. Fay, "Wow! I Just Won the Lottery: Now What Do I Do?" *USA Today*, November 2000, 26–27.

Copyright © Houghton Mifflin Company. All rights reserved.

relationships between thoughts. The most common cause/effect transition words are listed below:

Cause/Effect Transitions

so	consequently
therefore	as a consequence
as a result	due to
thus	hence
because of	for this reason
in response	

The following pairs of sentences illustrate the use of cause/effect transitions:

High protein/low carbohydrate diets produce dramatic weight loss. ***As a result,*** many people are cutting bread, pasta, and cereal out of their meals.

Most head-on vehicle collisions occur when distracted drivers drift into oncoming traffic. ***So,*** to reduce your risk of such an accident, drive more on divided highways with medians.

Many Americans choose to live in urban and suburban neighborhoods. ***Consequently,*** they separate themselves from a deep connection to the land and become indifferent to the environment.

Next, read a paragraph that uses cause/effect transition words (boldfaced, italicized). Notice how each transition indicates another effect:

Mother England made the mistake of withholding liberty too long from her "children" in the American colonies. They grew to be rebellious "teenagers" who demanded their freedom. ***In response,*** their "mother" refused to release them, and a war had to be fought. ***As a consequence,*** though, England did learn a valuable lesson from a painful experience, which is why she later granted a peaceful and orderly transfer of power to another tempestuous offspring named India.*

This paragraph is arranged according to the chain reaction type of cause/effect paragraphs. Each transition indicates that the detail is the result of a previous occurrence.

* Adapted from Dr. James Dobson, "Focus on the Family," *The News Herald*, Morganton, NC, July 22, 2001, 11C.

Copyright © Houghton Mifflin Company. All rights reserved.

Exercise 5.3

Fill in the blanks in the following sentences and paragraphs with appropriate cause/effect transitions. Choose words or phrases from the box on page 210. Try to vary your choices.

1. Female elected officials are gaining more political power along with the public's trust. _as a result / for this reason / consequently, thus_, the United States will probably elect its first woman president during the 21st century.

2. There have been a few incidents involving children slipping under the water at the town pool this year. _For this reason, Therefore, so_, the town representatives are making it mandatory for children to wear safety vests at all times while at the pool.

3. _Do to / Because of_ the increase in West Nile virus cases, the health department is recommending that you wear long-sleeve shirts outside to prevent getting bitten by a mosquito that may carry the disease.

4. I have been eating more than I should, especially when it comes to dessert. _as a result / consequently_, I have gained five pounds!

5. Many Americans are locked into a work-and-spend cycle. Their debts increase. _as a result / therefore / consequently_, they give up leisure time to make more money. The treadmill continues to roll, and some people become too tired to enjoy active leisure activities such as hiking, swimming, or playing a round of golf. _So / Thus_, they engage in less satisfactory activities, such as sitting passively in front of the television set. _hence / As a result_, this work-and-spend cycle reduces quality of life.*

6. My grandfather's name was Charlie Bundrum, a tall, bone-thin man who worked with nails in his teeth and a roofing hatchet in his fist. He died in the spring of 1958, one year before I was born. _As a result / consequently_, I knew almost nothing about him growing up, because nobody in my mother's family talked about him. _So / Thus_, I made it my life's work to try to find out what kind of man Charlie Bundrum was.†

7. I was in high school when I realized my own possibilities. I had started a volunteer organization that matched students with senior citizens, and

---

* Adapted from Barry L. Reece and Rhonda Brandt, *Effective Human Relations in Organizations,* 7th ed. Boston: Houghton Mifflin, 1997, 462.

† Adapted from Rick Bragg, "Charlie and the River Rat," from "Ava's Man," *Reader's Digest,* August 2001, 149.

Copyright © Houghton Mifflin Company. All rights reserved.

my teacher told me I was a good person. ___As a result/consequently___, I felt very good about myself and those few words literally changed how I saw myself. ___for this reason___, I try to help young people understand the power they have to change the world. I co-founded the national organization Do Something based on the idea that life is most rewarding when we're helping others.*

Transition Words That Indicate Comparison/Contrast

Paragraphs include comparison transitions to help readers see similarities between two or more things. They include contrast transitions to point out differences.

First, let's examine the comparison transitions, which appear in the list below:

Comparison Transitions		
also	similarly	similar to
too	in like manner	in the same way
likewise	just like, just as	along the same line
	need a noun or	in both cases

The following pairs of sentences illustrate the use of comparison transitions:

When you shop for a car, you look for the color, style, and features you want. **Similarly,** new genetic research may allow future parents to choose the characteristics they want in their children.

In the 19th century, large numbers of Irish, Italian, and Jewish immigrants struggled to blend into American society. **Likewise,** today's Latinos and Asians are weaving themselves into this country's diverse cultural mix.

Today's parents are objecting to the skimpy, skin-baring clothes their pre-teens are wearing. **In the same way,** 1960s parents were horrified by their girls' hip-huggers and halter tops.

The following paragraph uses comparison transition words (boldfaced, italicized). Notice how each transition indicates another point of comparison:

* Adapted from Andrew Shue, "A Message from Andrew Shue," Special Advertising Section, *Reader's Digest*, August 2001, 160.

Copyright © Houghton Mifflin Company. All rights reserved.

The disputed presidential elections of 1876 and 2000 shared some striking similarities. The 1876 election between Samuel Tilden and Rutherford Hayes was so close that the victory hinged upon just a few electoral votes. ***Likewise,*** in 2000, the race between Al Gore and George W. Bush depended upon only a handful of electoral votes. In 1876, the state of Florida played a major part in the election's outcome. ***Similarly,*** Florida was cast into the national spotlight in 2000 when the election depended upon that state's poll results. The media of 1876 prematurely assumed that Hayes had won. The media in 2000, ***too,*** presumed George W. Bush the winner before they had all of the facts. ***In both cases,*** the Supreme Court had to get involved to help settle the matter.*

Exercise 5.4

Fill in the blanks in the following sentences and paragraphs with appropriate comparison transitions. Choose words or phrases from the box on page 212. Try to vary your choices.

1. World War I changed the nature of war by introducing gas, trench warfare, tanks, submarines and aircraft. _Similarly / likewise,_ World War II changed fighting by adding rockets and atomic bombs.

2. Many antibiotics and drugs have been discovered in European rivers and tap water. _Similarly / likewise,_ low levels of three antibiotics are present in West Virginia waters.

3. My biology textbook is colorful and breaks down information into small sections. _in the same way,_ my economics textbook offers a chapter summary and beautiful illustrations to make the concepts easier to understand.

4. _Just like_ you, I try to exercise at least a half an hour every day.

5. Many observers feared for the future of America's families at the ends of both the 19th and 20th centuries. In the 1890s, the U.S. divorce rate was the highest in the world. _Also similar,_ the 1990s divorce rate was very high. In the 1890s, there was an epidemic of sexually transmitted diseases. _likewise,_ such diseases were a problem in the late 1990s. Late 19th century urban areas were plagued by drug abuse. _Also_,

* Adapted from Jeremy F. Plant, "Déjà vu: Revisiting the 1876 Presidential Election," *USA Today*, May 2001, 16–18.

Copyright © Houghton Mifflin Company. All rights reserved.

many late 20th century Americans struggled with drug addiction and the crime it caused.*

6. *Murder in Small Town X* is the Fox network's latest twist on the reality-TV trend. In this experimental, formally unscripted eight-week series, the investigation is real, but the crime is not. ~~Just like / similar to~~ *Survivor* and *The Real World, Murder in Small Town X* takes ten real people and puts them in a tense situation, in this case a crime scene. And ~~similar to~~ *Survivor,* unpopular contestants are voted off by one of their housemates. ~~Similar to~~ *Survivor* and *The Real World,* the contestants have their lives filmed all day, every day, to see what they do in every situation they encounter.†

7. Although the positions they play couldn't be more different, pitchers and catchers share many of the same traits and characteristics. ~~Just as~~ a pitcher can hold the fate of the whole ballgame in his hands, a catcher can do the same by either tagging someone out at home and preventing a run from scoring or just the opposite—dropping the ball and letting the run score. ~~also/like wise~~ pitchers and catchers share the pain of sustaining major injuries, pitchers to their arms and shoulders, and catchers to any part of their body that can be hit by a bat or a ball. And ~~in the same way~~ pitchers are lifelong pitchers and never play another position, catchers are very loyal to the position, only moving if injury or the team manager makes them move.

Now, let's look at the contrast transitions:

<table>
<tr><td colspan="3" align="center">Contrast Transitions</td></tr>
<tr><td>however</td><td>nevertheless</td><td>unfortunately</td></tr>
<tr><td>but</td><td>on the one hand</td><td>in contrast</td></tr>
<tr><td>yet</td><td>on the other hand</td><td>conversely</td></tr>
<tr><td>although</td><td>unlike</td><td>even though</td></tr>
<tr><td>instead</td><td>rather</td><td>still</td></tr>
<tr><td>in opposition</td><td>on the contrary</td><td>nonetheless</td></tr>
<tr><td>in spite of</td><td>actually</td><td>whereas</td></tr>
<tr><td>just the opposite</td><td>despite</td><td>in reality</td></tr>
<tr><td>though</td><td>while</td><td>as opposed to</td></tr>
</table>

* Adapted from Stephanie Coontz, "The American Family," *Life*, November 1999, 79.
† Adapted from Shawna Malcolm, "A View to a Kill," *TV Guide*, July 21–27, 2001, 33–34.

Copyright © Houghton Mifflin Company. All rights reserved.

The following pairs of sentences illustrate the use of contrast transitions:

Scientists agree that exercising the mind keeps it functioning well. **_However,_** they disagree about the best way to go about achieving mental fitness.

For a while, eggs fell out of favor because of their high cholesterol content. **_But_** the latest studies show they are both healthy and nutritious.

Photos of President John Kennedy's family at play only looked casual and spontaneous. **_In reality,_** they were professionally lit, and the people in them were styled and posed.

Next, read a paragraph that includes contrast transition words (boldfaced, italicized). Notice how each transition indicates another point of contrast.

"Fast-food" law firm franchises differ from traditional law firms in a number of ways. Traditional law firms often take up residence in expensive office buildings or complexes. Law firm franchises, **_however,_** are usually located in storefronts at strip or shopping malls. Traditional law firms handle all types of legal matters, both easy and complex. **_But_** law firm franchises focus only on simple, straightforward matters such as wills, uncontested divorces, or name changes. A third difference is price. Traditional firms' fees are often high. **_Conversely,_** law firm franchises' fees are usually affordable.*

Exercise 5.5

Fill in the blanks in the following sentences and paragraphs with the appropriate contrast transition. Choose words or phrases from the box on page 214. Try to vary your choices.

1. Friendship ranks with marriage and kinship as one of the most important relationships in our lives. _however_ / _nevertheless_ _(but)_ _on the other hand._ it can be the most neglected.

2. _dispite_ _aren_ being one of the most beautiful and admired women in the world, Marilyn Monroe suffered from depression.

3. You would think that a team with the high salary budget of the New York Rangers hockey team would have many championships in its history. _____ _but_ _____ the Rangers have only won two Stanley Cup championships in the last 100 years.

* Adapted from "Fast-Food Legal Services," *USA Today Newsview,* December 1996, 16.

Copyright © Houghton Mifflin Company. All rights reserved.

5

4. Charles called to see if I was available to go to dinner. _unfortunate_ , I had
another commitment.
   However

5. Golf is really more of a game than a sport. Sports—such as basketball or
tennis—require aerobic activity that increases the heart rate and makes
players sweat. Golf, ___however___ , requires about the same physical
conditioning necessary for stamp collecting. In sports like soccer and
hockey, fans cheer, boo, and scream at the players. _in the other_ _hand_, in golf,
the announcers whisper, and the spectators have to be quiet, clapping po-
litely when a player hits a good shot. Sports—such as baseball and football—require uniforms, cheerleaders, and most importantly, real oppo-
nents. Golf, _on contrary_ _however_, has none of these things.*

6. Some people say that reading the newspaper is a better way to get information than watching television. _however_ , studies have shown that
people who get their news exclusively from television news shows know
almost as much about current affairs as people who read newspapers.
vevertheless/none the less
___, the debate rages on with some people favoring newspapers
and some favoring television news shows.

7. The original *Planet of the Apes* movie has a lot of fans who think it is a great
movie that never should have been remade. _however_ , a remake was
released in the summer of 2001. Why do fans of the original think it is
better? The original starred actor Charlton Heston, who brought power and
credibility to the role of the astronaut. The remake, _though/however_ stars
former rap singer and underwear model Mark Wahlberg as Leo Davidson,
the time-traveling space man. The original movie had a great ending
that no one expected. ___But___ the remake has an ending that is not
as surprising and, as a result, not as good. _despite_ a few flaws,
though, the remake was a box office hit.
   is it was a comma you can put However

Transition Words That Indicate Definition

One final set of transition words signals examples. Because the definition pattern or organization often includes one or more examples, this type of transition will often appear in definition paragraphs. However, transitions that in-

* Adapted from Bill Geist, "Planet Golf," *Reader's Digest*, August 2001, 121–122.

Copyright © Houghton Mifflin Company. All rights reserved.

dicate example can appear in other types of paragraphs, too. Anytime authors want to illustrate an idea or make it clearer, they often identify the beginning of an example with one of the following transitions:

Definition (Example) Transitions		
for example	as an illustration	in one case
for instance	in one instance	more precisely
to illustrate	such as	specifically

The following pairs of sentences illustrate the use of example transitions:

Volcanic explosions can be devastating. ***One illustration*** is Indonesia's Tambora Volcano, which killed 10,000 people when it exploded in 1815.

An autoimmune disease is one in which a person's immune system attacks the body's healthy tissue and organs. Lupus, ***for instance,*** is one of about 80 such diseases.

Thousands of employers are attempting to reduce the cost of employee health insurance by regulating their employees' lifestyles. ***For example,*** many companies require that employees don't smoke.

Now, read a paragraph that includes example transition words (boldfaced, italicized). Notice how the transition introduces the example:

When you reveal wrongdoing within an organization to the public or to those in positions of authority, you are a whistle blower. Whistle blowers are sounding alarms in industries from tobacco companies to airlines. ***For example,*** Sylvia Robins reported that she knew about a procedural flaw at Unisys, a National Aeronautics and Space Administration subcontractor that produces software programs for the space shuttle program. Robins came forward to stop any further endangerment of space shuttle crews.*

This definition paragraph explains the meaning of the term *whistle blower.* After defining the term, it presents an illustration of one specific person who acted as a whistle blower.

---

* Adapted from Barry L. Reece and Rhonda Brandt, *Effective Human Relations in Organizations,* 7th ed. Boston: Houghton Mifflin, 1999, 139–140.

Copyright © Houghton Mifflin Company. All rights reserved.

Exercise 5.6

Fill in the blanks in the following sentences and paragraphs with appropriate example transitions. Choose words or phrases from the box on page 217. Try to vary your choices.

1. One study of multivitamins found that one-third of brands don't contain what the label promises. _____, two brands of multivitamins for adults contained only 40 percent of the amount of Vitamin A listed on the package.

2. There are many cars available today that are considered safe. _____, the Volvo S70 scored extremely well in crash tests, making it one of the safest cars you can buy.

3. Dolphins have been shown to have superior thinking abilities and more than a little extrasensory perception, or ESP. _____, a dolphin swimming beside a young woman sensed that the woman was pregnant by nudging her abdomen, even though the woman herself did not know she was carrying a baby at the time!

4. The scientific method can be narrowly defined as a series of steps that begins with a question or problem to be solved and ends with an answer or solution. _____, the scientific method is less a procedure than a way of thinking.

5. I'm a nerd. While the Internet boom has lent some respectability to the term, narrow-minded stereotypes of nerds still linger. _____, nerds are supposed to be friendless bookworms who suck up to authority figures. _____, we're sissies.*

6. The categories of people to which you see yourself belonging and to which you always compare yourself are called *reference groups*. The performance of people in a reference group can influence your self-esteem. _____, if being a good swimmer is very important to you, knowing someone in your reference group swims much faster than you do can lower your self-esteem.†

---

* Adapted from Tom Rogers, "My Kids Are Smarter Than Yours," (originally printed in *Newsweek*), *Reader's Digest*, August 2001, 69.

† Adapted from Douglas A. Bernstein et al., *Psychology*, 5th ed. Boston: Houghton Mifflin, 2000, 605. Copyright © 2000 by Houghton Mifflin Company. Reprinted with permission.

Copyright © Houghton Mifflin Company. All rights reserved.

5

7. Exporting is selling and shipping materials and products to other nations.

_____, the Boeing Company exports its airplanes to a number of countries for use by their airlines. Importing is purchasing materials or products from other nations and bringing them into one's own country.

_____, American stores may purchase rugs in India or raincoats in England and have them shipped back to the United States for resale.*

Transition Words in Combinations of Patterns

Supporting details in paragraphs can be organized according to more than one pattern. For example, a paragraph may include *both* time order details and effect details. In such paragraphs, it will be particularly important for you to notice transition words and phrases, for they will provide clues about the various relationships among different kinds of details. For an example of a paragraph that includes more than one pattern and, therefore, different kinds of transitions, read the following:

> Xenotransplantation is the use of animal organs as replacement for human organs. **For example,** surgeons have removed diseased livers from human patients and substituted livers taken from baboons. Such animal-to-human transplants began **in the 1900s** when doctors tried but failed to transplant kidneys from pigs, goats, apes, and lambs. **In the 1960s,** a number of primate-to-human transplants were attempted, and several patients who received chimpanzee or baboon kidneys lived up to nine months following the operation. **In 1983,** a baby received a baboon heart, but her body rejected it 20 days later. **During the early 1990s,** doctors made three more attempts at liver xenotransplantation. **Today,** researchers are still studying xenotransplants and trying to make them a viable option for people suffering from organ failure.†

This paragraph begins with the definition pattern, including an example. Then, it switches to the time order pattern as it explains the history of xenotransplant attempts. Therefore, it includes both example and time order transitions.

* Adapted from Pride/Hughes/Kapoor, *Business*, 6th ed. Boston: Houghton Mifflin, 1999, 60.

† Adapted from John J. Fung, "Transplanting Animal Organs into Humans Is Feasible," *USA Today*, November 1999, 54–55.

Copyright © Houghton Mifflin Company. All rights reserved.

5

Exercise 5.7

Read each of the following paragraphs and circle the transition words or phrases. Then, in the list below the paragraph, place a checkmark next to each of the two patterns used to organize the details.

1. Although Columbus was a great navigator and sailor, he was not a particularly good leader. Spanish officials and settlers were never loyal to him, and King Ferdinand and Queen Isabella of Spain eventually tired of him. However, unlike Columbus, Hernando Cortés was a great leader and was able to help Ferdinand and Isabella realize their goals. In 1519, he and an army of 600 Spanish soldiers landed in Mexico. Within three years, Cortés and his small force had defeated the mighty Aztec empire. Establishing themselves in Mexico City, the Spanish took over the empire, bringing the Indian groups to the south under their rule.*

_____ series

___✓___ time order

_____ cause/effect

___✓___ comparison/contrast

_____ definition

2. Because of the influence of *The Matrix*, which was a very successful movie that combined traditional martial arts with the latest computerized film technology, many of the new movies out today are trying to recreate some of those action scenes. One example of a movie that does that is *The Mummy Returns*, which shows two characters engaged in combat using swordlike weapons. Another example is the funny *Cats & Dogs*, which features cats dressed like ninjas leaping and kicking with kung fu expertise. And then there's *Osmosis Jones*, in which a white blood cell and an evil virus duel in a midair battle.†

* Adapted from Berkin et al., *Making America*, Brief 2nd ed. Boston: Houghton Mifflin, 2001, 26.
† Adapted from Claudia Puig, "Karate Enters Age of 'Matrix,'" *USA Today*, August 1, 2001, 1d.

Copyright © Houghton Mifflin Company. All rights reserved.

_✓__ series

_____ time order

_✓__ cause/effect

_____ comparison/contrast

_____ definition

3. A minority is a racial, religious, political, national, or other group regarded as different from the larger group of which it is a part and that is often singled out for unfavorable treatment. African Americans, for example, are considered a minority. During the 1960s and 1970s, the federal government passed a number of laws forbidding discrimination in the workplace. In 1965, the first of these acts, entitled The Civil Rights Act, was passed. Now more than thirty-five years after passage of the Civil Rights Act, abuses still exist.*

_____ series

_✓__ time order

_____ cause/effect

_____ comparison/contrast

_✓__ definition

5

4. Because so many children play at the Lexington Avenue Park every day, many children lose the toys they bring to play with, such as trucks, dolls, and balls. There are a few things you can do to avoid losing your children's toys at the park. Before you come to the park, label everything with your child's name and address. It is also a good idea to bring as few toys as you can and make a list of the things that you bring with you. While you are at the park, keep your child's toys in a pile where he or she is playing, if possible. Before you leave, make a quick sweep of the park to see if your child has left anything behind. This will ensure that you leave with your child's toys.

* Adapted from Pride/Hughes/Kapoor, _Business_, 6th ed. Boston: Houghton Mifflin, 1999, 44.

Copyright © Houghton Mifflin Company. All rights reserved.

_____ series

__✓__ time order

__✓__ cause/effect

_____ comparison/contrast

_____ definition

5. The Spanish crown supported many exploratory ventures to the "New World" by hiring _conquistadors_. A conquistador was the name given to the Spanish explorers who set out to overtake parts of the New World both in Mexico and what is now the United States. For example, Ponce de Leon, Hernando de Soto, and Francisco Pizarro were all conquistadors. In 1513 and again in 1521, Juan Ponce de Leon led expeditions to Florida. In 1539, the Spanish sent Hernando de Soto to claim the Mississippi River. In 1533, Francisco Pizarro conquered the Inca Empire, an advanced civilization that glittered with gold.*

_____ series

__✓__ time order

_____ cause/effect

_____ comparison/contrast

__✓__ definition _for example_

Exercise 5.8

The following groups of sentences have been scrambled. Number them in the order they should appear (1, 2, 3, etc.) so that they make sense. Use the transitions to help you figure out the right order. Then, in the list below each group, place a checkmark next to the pattern used to organize the details.

1. __2__ First, write your positive statements—sentences like "I am intelligent," "I can handle my problems," and "I am creative"—on 3 × 5 index cards.

* Adapted from Berkin et al., _Making America_, Brief 2nd Edition. Boston: Houghton Mifflin, 2001, 26.

Copyright © Houghton Mifflin Company. All rights reserved.

___1___ One technique for improving self-esteem is designing positive self-talk statements.

___4___ Then, each time you see one of these cards, review its message and believe the words.

___3___ Next, attach your cards to your bathroom mirror, your refrigerator, your car dashboard, and your desk.*

Pattern of organization:

_____ series

___✓___ time order

_____ cause/effect

_____ comparison/contrast

___✓___ definition

2. _____ Another example is that the teachers who participated reported working very hard, getting to school first and being the last to leave, working weekends, and sometimes feeling completely overworked.

topic ___1___ The individual characteristics and temperaments of certain teachers explain their success as professionals.

___2___ A person's disposition is his or her usual temperament and frame of mind.

___3___ For instance, the teachers who participated in the study were highly dedicated.†   *Another*

Pattern of organization:

_____ series

_____ time order

_____ cause/effect

_____ comparison/contrast

___✓___ definition

* Adapted from Barry L. Reece and Rhonda Brandt, *Effective Human Relations in Organizations*, 7th ed. Boston: Houghton Mifflin, 1997, 111.

† Adapted from Garcia, *Student Cultural Diversity*. Boston: Houghton Mifflin, 2000, 303.

Copyright © Houghton Mifflin Company. All rights reserved.

5

3. __4__ Consequently, town residents who want to swim will have to join either the Silver Lake swim club or the Charles Cook Pool in Cortlandt Manor.

__2__ As a result, no swimming will be allowed during July and August.

__1__ Due to high levels of algae, the Duck Pond in the center of town has tested positive for a dangerous microbe.

__3__ Because swimming won't be allowed, the Duck Pond in the center of town is being closed for the summer.

Pattern of organization:

_____ series

_____ time order

__✓__ cause/effect

_____ comparison/contrast

_____ definition

4. __3__ In the early 1960s, Irving refined his storytelling skills at the University of Iowa, where he got a master's degree in creative writing.

__1__ John Irving grew up in Exeter, New Hampshire, where his step-father taught at exclusive Phillips Exeter Academy.

__2__ He took up wrestling at age 14 to provide a much-needed outlet for his energy.

__3__ In 1964, he married photographer Shyla Leary, whom he met in college, and became a father at the age of 23.*

Pattern of organization:

_____ series

__✓__ time order

_____ cause/effect

_____ comparison/contrast

_____ definition

* Adapted from Kim Hubbard and Natasha Stoynoff, "Hands Full," *People* Magazine, July 30, 2001, 96–97.

Copyright © Houghton Mifflin Company. All rights reserved.

CHAPTER 5 REVIEW

Fill in the blanks in the following statements.

1. _transitions_ are words and phrases whose function is to show the relationships between thoughts and ideas.

2. Some transitions are _synonyms_; in other words, they mean the same thing.

3. Some transitions can be used in more than one _way/patter_ of organization.

4. Different transitions can create subtle but significant changes in the _meaning_ of sentences.

5. _series_ transitions indicate the addition of another reason, example, type, or other point.

6. _time order_ transitions signal another event, step, or stage within a chronological order of details.

7. _cause affec_ transitions indicate either a reason for or a result of an occurrence presented in a previous sentence.

8. _comparison_ transitions point out similarities, and _contrast_ transitions point out differences.

9. _defination_ transitions illustrate ideas in definition paragraphs as well as other types of paragraphs.

10. _paragraph_ organized according to more than one pattern will often include different kinds of transitions.

Reading Selection

Barbara Jordan, a Self-Portrait

1 Years ago, I was at Boston University in this new and strange and different world, and it occurred to me that if I was going to succeed at this strange new adventure, I would have to read longer and more thoroughly than my colleagues at law school had to read. I felt that in order to compensate for what I had missed in earlier years, I would have to work harder, and study longer, than anybody else. I did my reading not in the law library, but in a library at my graduate dorm, upstairs where it was very quiet, because apparently nobody else studied there. So, I would go there at night after dinner. I would load my

Copyright © Houghton Mifflin Company. All rights reserved.

books under my arm and go to the library, and I would read until the wee hours of the morning and then go to bed.

2   I was always delighted when I would get called upon to recite in class. But the professors did not call on the "ladies" very much. There were certain favored people who always got called on, and then on some rare occasions a professor would come in and announce: "We're going to have Ladies' Day today." And he would call on the ladies. We were just tolerated. We weren't considered really top drawer when it came to the study of law.

3   At some time in the spring, Bill Gibson, who was dating my new roommate, Norma Walker, organized a black study group, as we blacks had to form our own. This was because we were not invited into any of the other study groups. There were six or seven in our group—Bill, and Issie, and I think Maynard Jackson—and we would just gather and talk it out and hear ourselves do that. As a result, I learned that you had to talk out the issues, the facts, the cases, the decisions, the process. You couldn't just read the cases and study alone in your library as I had been doing; and you couldn't get it all in the classroom. But once you had talked it out in study group, it flowed more easily and made a lot more sense.

4   Finally I felt I was really learning things, really going to school. I felt that I was getting educated, whatever that was. I became familiar with the process of thinking. I learned to think things out and reach conclusions and defend what I had said.

5   In the past I had got along by spouting off. Whether you talked about debates or oratory, you dealt with speechifying. But I could no longer orate and let that pass for reasoning because there was not any demand for an orator in Boston University Law School. You had to think and read and understand and reason. I had learned at twenty-one that you couldn't just say a thing is so because it might not be so, and because somebody brighter, smarter, and more thoughtful would come out and tell you it wasn't so. Then, if you still thought it was, you had to prove it. Well, that was a new thing for me. I cannot, I really cannot describe what that did to my insides and to my head. I thought: I'm being educated finally.

(Excerpt from *Barbara Jordan: A Self-Portrait* by Barbara Jordan and Shelby Hearon. Reprinted by permission of The Wendy Weil Agency, Inc. Copyright © 1978, 1979 by Shelby Hearon and Barbara Jordan.)

VOCABULARY

Read the following questions about some of the vocabulary words that appear in the previous selection. Circle the correct responses.

1. In paragraph 1, the author uses the word *compensate* as follows: "I felt that in order to *compensate* for what I had missed in earlier years, I would have to work harder, and study longer, than anybody else." What do you think the word *compensate* means as used in this context?

   a. pay for   c. change

   b. make up for   d. rearrange

Copyright © Houghton Mifflin Company. All rights reserved.

2. What does the word *debates* mean as used in paragraph 5? "Whether you talked about *debates* or oratory, you dealt with speechifying."

    a. talks

    b. discussions meant to persuade

    c. fights

    d. letters

3. The author uses the following words in paragraph 5: *oratory*, *orate*, and *orator*. *Oratory* and *orator* are from the infinitive word *to orate*. What does *to orate* mean?

    a. to communicate by talking

    b. to communicate by writing a letter

    c. to study

    d. to do research

4. When the author uses the word *speechifying* in paragraph 5, what does it mean?

    a. discussing

    b. writing

    c. orating

    d. explaining

MAIN IDEAS, SUPPORTING DETAILS, AND TRANSITIONS

Answer the following questions.

1. In paragraph 1, how many sentences begin with transitions?

    a. 1

    b. 2

    c. 3

    d. 4

2. How many sentences begin with transitions in paragraph 3?

    a. 1

    b. 2

    c. 3

    d. 6

3. Which of the following sentences from paragraph 3 includes a transition?

    a. "At some time in the spring . . ."

    b. "This was because . . ."

    c. "There were six or seven . . ."

    d. "You couldn't just read . . ."

4. What is the main idea of paragraph 1?

    a. Boston University was a strange place.

    b. I liked to study in the law library.

    c. I wish I had read more books before going to law school.

    d. I learned that I would have to work harder than my colleagues in law school in order to succeed.

5. What is the implied main idea of paragraph 3?

    a. By studying with other students, Barbara Jordan found that she began to understand the material in her law books for the first time.

    b. It's difficult to date and attend law school at the same time.

    c. The workload in law school is overwhelming.

    d. Joining a study group is a great way to meet new friends.

Copyright © Houghton Mifflin Company. All rights reserved.

5

QUESTIONS FOR DISCUSSION AND WRITING

Answer the following questions based on your reading of the selection.

1. Barbara Jordan, an African-American woman, attended Boston University Law School at a time when neither many African Americans nor many women attended law school. In the essay, where does Jordan outline the discrimination she faced as both a woman and an African American? Have you ever had a similar experience? If so, describe. _____

_____

_____

_____

_____

2. What was the turning point in her law school education that made Jordan write (in paragraph 4), "Finally I felt I was really learning things, really going to school"? What event led her to this conclusion?

_____

_____

_____

_____

_____

3. Have you ever had an experience where you felt that in order to prove yourself, you would have to work harder than those around you? If so, describe. _____

_____

_____

4. Why does the author focus on the whole concept of oratory and speechifying in paragraph 5? What is she trying to say by describing herself as someone who "had got along by spouting off"? How did she change in law school? _____

_____

_____

_____

_____

Copyright © Houghton Mifflin Company. All rights reserved.

5

Vocabulary: The Explanation Context Clue

In Chapter 4, you learned about the definition/restatement context clue. A second type of context clue is **explanation.** In this type of clue, the words, phrases, or sentences near an unfamiliar word will explain enough about that word to allow you to figure out its meaning. For example, read this next sentence, which comes from one of the paragraphs in this chapter:

> Almost immediately, it began leaning because it was being erected on the soft *silt* of a buried riverbed.

What is *silt*? Well, you get several explanation clues in this sentence. First of all, it's soft, and secondly, it's found in buried riverbeds. It also caused the tower to lean. Therefore, you can conclude that it must be some type of wet, unstable sand.

Vocabulary Exercise

The following examples all come from paragraphs in Chapters 4 and 5. In each one, use the explanation context clue to help you determine the meaning of the boldfaced, italicized word, and write a definition for this word on the blank provided.

1. From 1999 to 2001, engineers ***excavated*** soil from beneath the tower.

   _____

   _____

2. So, to reduce your risk of such an accident, drive more on divided high ways with ***medians.*** _____

   _____

3. Mother England made the mistake of withholding liberty too long from her "children" in the American colonies. They grew to be rebellious "teenagers" who demanded their freedom. . . . As a consequence, though, England did learn a valuable lesson from a painful experience, which is why she later granted a peaceful and orderly transfer of power to another

   tempestuous offspring named India. _____

   _____

4. The ***disputed*** presidential elections of 1876 and 2000 shared some striking similarities. The 1876 election between Samuel Tilden and Rutherford Hayes was so close that the victory hinged upon just a few electoral votes.

Copyright © Houghton Mifflin Company. All rights reserved.

Likewise, in 2000, the race between Al Gore and George W. Bush depended upon only a handful of electoral votes. _____

_____

5. Sports—such as basketball or tennis—require **aerobic** activity that increases the heart rate and makes players sweat. _____

_____

6. As the ascending air cools, clouds are formed that are swept to the outer portions of the **cyclonic** motion and outline its funnel form. Because clouds form at certain heights, the outlined funnel may appear well above the ground. Under the right conditions, a full-fledged tornado develops. _____

_____

7. New Bedford showed that with careful plans in place, murderous acts by students can be **thwarted** before anyone gets hurt. _____

_____

8. He is also a master magician and makes friends and fights **mythic** battles against the forces of Darkness, which appeals to a wide variety of readers.

_____

_____

9. By the 1980s, an awareness of **gender** roles in society became important to women and helped create the women's, or feminist, movement.

_____

_____

10. Also, it is a science concerned with everything from the migration of sand dunes across the desert to the migration of continents across the globe and from the flow of **molten** rock down the sides of volcanoes to the flow of rivers to the sea. _____

_____

Copyright © Houghton Mifflin Company. All rights reserved.

Name _____ Date _____

POST-TEST 1

Choose the transition that would best fill in the blank. Circle the appropriate choice.

1. Phil spends a lot of time at the library. _____, his wife has never been there.

   a. Also
   b. Due to
   c. On the other hand
   d. Finally

2. Recent court cases involving unethical behavior have helped make business ethics a matter of public concern. _____, the Copley Company pled guilty to charges of faking drug reports to a government agency.

   a. Often
   b. Due to
   c. However
   d. For instance

3. *Court TV* is a popular cable television station because it shows reruns of popular television crime shows, such as *Law and Order*. _____, it broadcasts famous trials, such as the O. J. Simpson trial, which bring in high ratings.

   a. In addition
   b. Another
   c. As a result
   d. While

4. _____ the exceptionally cold weather this winter, many lakes have frozen over, making it possible for people to skate and play hockey.

   a. In contrast to
   b. Therefore
   c. As a result of
   d. For example

5. _____ Wegman's now offers prepared foods for take-out, the Food Emporium has a wide selection of heat-and-eat dinners that busy people can buy and serve for dinner.

   a. Just as =like
   b. Yet
   c. Due to
   d. First

For additional tests, see the Test Bank.

Copyright © Houghton Mifflin Company. All rights reserved.

6. Russell Watson, known as "the Voice" because of his soaring tenor, has been a very busy man lately. He has just released an album entitled *The Voice*. _____, he has contributed many songs to the sound-track of the movie *Captain Corelli's Mandolin*.

   a. Then   c. Furthermore
   b. Such as   d. In contrast

7. Yahoo offers many great sites if you are interested in using the Internet for research. _____, Alta Vista brings you good sites and interesting information that will help you do research.

   a. Conversely   c. After
   b. First   d. Similarly

8. _____ the concert ran late, the Tates were still able to make our dinner reservation.

   a. Although   c. First
   b. For example   d. Finally

9. Brainstorming is a technique for finding solutions, creating plans, and discovering new ideas. _____, when you are stuck on a problem, brainstorming can help you clear your mind.*

   a. Instead   c. Eventually
   b. For example   d. In contrast

10. I locked my keys in the car. _____, we'll miss the beginning of the concert.

    a. Due to   c. Often
    b. As a consequence   d. Previously

11. My minivan is great because I can pack lots of groceries in the back when I go to the store. _____, there is plenty of room for my four children.

    a. First   c. Next
    b. In addition   d. Despite

12. Jack had used the local service station many times while he lived in Statesville. _____, he decided that their service was not very good and that their rates were high, so he changed service stations.

    a. Before   c. While
    b. Over time   d. Next

in addi
Also

* Adapted from Dave Ellis, *Becoming a Master Student*. Boston: Houghton Mifflin, 2000, 228.

6= C   7: D   8 = A   9 = B   10 = B   12 = B

Copyright © Houghton Mifflin Company. All rights reserved.

13. Polaner offers a low-fat strawberry jelly that has a lot of flavor.

    _____, Smucker's has a reduced-fat blueberry jam that can't be beat!

    a. Consequently   c. To illustrate
    b. Along the same line   d. While

14. There are many advantages to maintaining your car. _____,
    your car will last longer than a car that is not maintained.

    a. Also   c. First of all
    b. In spite of *Along the same time/similarly*   d. Finally

15. Danielle read a book to two of her children before dinner.

    _____, her husband took the other child to the park.

    a. First   c. Meanwhile
    b. As   d. When

16. Children's movies seem to be more for adults. _____, *Shrek*
    has a lot of jokes that children wouldn't understand but that have adults
    howling with laughter.

    a. As an illustration *for example*   c. As a result
    b. In the beginning   d. On the contrary

17. Leanne Nakamura saw huge nets that had washed ashore from fishing

    boats digging into the sand on the island of Oahu. _____,
    damage was done to the beach and the coral reefs, and fish and sea turtles
    were dying.*

    a. While   c. Second
    b. Before   d. Consequently

18. Jane's health club has a pool that members can use just by showing their

    membership card. _____, Frank's club has a pool that caters
    exclusively to club members.

    a. In like manner *like wise*   c. Second
    b. First   d. Similar to

19. Many people use the Internet for a variety of activities including shop-

    ping, gathering information, and sending messages. _____,
    you will be able to send video messages to loved ones with just the click
    of a button!

    a. Eventually   c. While
    b. Before   d. As a result

* Adapted from Maile Carpenter, "The Girl Who Helped Preserve Paradise," originally published
  in *Teen People, Reader's Digest*, August 2001, 163–164.

13 B   14 - C   15 = C   16 = a   17 = D   18 = A   19 = A

5

Copyright © Houghton Mifflin Company. All rights reserved.

20. There are only a few parking spaces left on campus. _____,
    you should get over to the security office and get a parking pass as soon as
    possible.
    a. For this reason   c. Meanwhile
    b. Now   d. During

21. Everyone at the dinner party praised Janet's attempt at baking a chocolate
    soufflé. _____, it was soggy and tasteless.
    a. In opposition   c. Nevertheless _However_
    b. Before   d. In addition

22. There are a lot of new soft drinks on the market with extra vitamins for
    health. _____, any of the "Fresh Samantha" drinks are packed
    with vitamins.
    a. However   c. In spite of
    b. After   d. For example

23. How are you doing today? _____, have you recovered from
    your recent bout of strep throat?
    a. In addition   c. Third
    b. Specifically   d. Though

24. I'm going to go swimming. _____ that I'm going to take a
    shower.
    a. While   c. Eventually
    b. After   d. Once

25. _____ he makes a lot of money, Donald never seems to have
    a dime to spare!
    a. However   c. Before
    b. In opposition   d. Even though

POST-TEST 2

Read each of the following paragraphs and answer the questions that follow.
Circle the correct choice.

A. (1) Here's a concept that everyone will applaud but few will put into practice: start a regular savings program at a very early age. (2) To begin, a
   child could put a certain percentage of his or her allowance into a savings

Copyright © Houghton Mifflin Company. All rights reserved.

20=A   21=C   22=D   23=B   24=B   25=D

account (or a piggy bank). (3) Later on, as the youngster receives payment for chores completed, this percentage would continue to be socked away. (4) When he or she gets a job, that same percentage can be put aside for the savings account. (5) Although the amount of money saved will vary from year to year, over time it will accumulate surprisingly quickly. (6) By the time the youngster has grown into a retiree, you will be astounded at how much money is now available!

1. Which of the following sentences begins with a contrast transition?

   a. Sentence 1   c. Sentence 5
   b. Sentence 3   d. Sentence 6

2. Which of the following sentences does NOT start with a time order transition?

   a. Sentence 3   c. Sentence 5
   b. Sentence 4   d. Sentence 6

B. (1) I have a word of advice for college students: consult a counselor. (2) When I went through college, I never spoke with a counselor to plan my future courses. (3) As a result, when graduation time came around, I was two credits short. (4) I had to take an extra semester just to obtain those two credits. (5) From then on, I was a semester behind all of the classmates with whom I'd gone through college. (6) For example, I couldn't apply for graduate school until a semester after they had applied.

3. Which of the following sentences begins with a cause/effect transition?

   a. Sentence 2   c. Sentence 5
   b. Sentence 3   d. Sentence 6

4. Which of the following sentences begins with a definition/example transition?

   a. Sentence 2   c. Sentence 5
   b. Sentence 3   d. Sentence 6

C. (1) Some people take the process of buying a new computer step by step. (2) They begin by educating themselves about computers and which components would be right for them. (3) Next, they shop around by comparing computer sales ads and visiting the Web sites of computer companies. (4) Then they make a list of the features they need in a computer and try to match that list with the computers being offered in ads. (5) Finally, they call the computer company to order their computer. (6) On the other hand, there are also people who simply walk into the nearest computer store and buy the computer the salesperson recommends.

Copyright © Houghton Mifflin Company. All rights reserved.

5. Which of the following sentences does NOT begin with a time order transition?

   a. Sentence 3   c. Sentence 5
   b. Sentence 4   d. Sentence 6

6. Which of the following sentences begins with a contrast transition?

   a. Sentence 3   c. Sentence 5
   b. Sentence 4   d. Sentence 6

D. (1) My first mistake was registering my e-mail address with a few Web sites that interest me. (2) After I did that, I started getting unwanted e-mails with advertisements all the time. (3) I then registered with a direct mail association to have my e-mail address put on a list of addresses not wanting advertising e-mail. (4) As a consequence, I seem to be getting more advertising e-mail than ever before. (5) Help!

7. Sentence 4 begins with a

   a. cause/effect transition.   c. time order transition.
   b. series transition.   d. comparison/contrast transition.

8. Sentence 2 begins with a

   a. definition/example transition. c. series transition.
   b. cause/effect transition.   d. time order transition.

E. (1) Different people have different types of living styles. (2) You can look right on our block for perfect illustrations of this. (3) For example, the Hammonds' house down the block is a ramshackle affair. (4) The paint is peeling, the driveway has ruts in it, and some windows are broken. (5) By contrast, just next door, the Rubellas' house is a model of upkeep. (6) It is freshly painted, all the fixtures look like new, and the greenery seems almost manicured.

9. Sentence 3 begins with a

   a. series transition.   c. definition/example transition.
   b. cause/effect transition.   d. time order transition.

10. Sentence 5 begins with a

   a. cause/effect transition.   c. time order transition.
   b. comparison/contrast transition. d. series transition.

Copyright © Houghton Mifflin Company. All rights reserved.

Patterns of Organization

GOALS FOR CHAPTER 6

▶ Take notes on a reading selection.

▶ Define the term *pattern* as it relates to paragraphs.

▶ Name the five broad patterns for organizing supporting details
 in paragraphs.

▶ Recognize words in topic sentences that indicate certain patterns.

▶ Recognize supporting details within a series pattern.

▶ Recognize supporting details within a time order pattern.

▶ Recognize supporting details within a cause/effect pattern.

▶ Recognize supporting details within a comparison/contrast pattern.

▶ Recognize supporting details within a definition pattern.

6

READING STRATEGY: Taking Notes

Learning how to take notes effectively is a vital skill for college students.
You will often be tested on the information in reading selections such as
textbook chapters, so you will need to make sure you're using all of the
tools at your disposal to understand and retain this information. One of
those tools is an active reading technique known as note taking.
Taking notes means recording in writing the major information and
ideas in a text. You might choose to take these notes in the margins of
the book itself, or in a notebook, or on separate sheets of paper.

Regardless of where you write them, notes offer two important benefits. First of all, writing down information and ideas helps you to
remember them better. For many people, taking the extra time to hand-
write the main points helps implant those points in their memory more
securely. As a result, retention and test performance tend to improve.
Second, good notes are often easier to study because they provide the
student with a condensed version of the main points.

Continued

Copyright © Houghton Mifflin Company. All rights reserved.

Good notes always begin with highlighting or underlining main ideas or key terms as you read, just as you learned to do in Chapter 1. When you write notes, they might take one or more of the following forms:

- **A list of the main ideas in all of the paragraphs.** Put them in your own words and condense them whenever possible. Don't try to include all of the details, just the most important points.

- **A summary of the chapter or article** (for an overview of this strategy, see Chapter 5).

- **An outline.** In previous chapters of this book, you've practiced filling out outlines that reveal the relationships between the details. You can use a Roman numeral outline, but the notes are usually for your eyes only, so you could also adopt or create a more informal system. No matter what kind of outline you use, though, make sure it clearly demonstrates the general and specific relationships between the ideas.

No matter what form they take, effective notes always possess three important characteristics. They should be:

1. *Neat.* Skip lines between points and write legibly.

2. *Clearly organized.* Group related points together so they're easier to remember.

3. *Factual and objective.* Like summaries, notes should be free of your own opinions.

Actively read the following section from a textbook. Then, take notes by creating a list of the paragraphs' main ideas, by writing a summary, or by outlining the selection.

Cooperative Learning: Studying with People

Education often looks like competition. We compete for entrance to school, for grades when we're in school, and for jobs when we leave school. In that climate, it's easy to overlook the power of cooperation.

Consider the idea that competition is not necessary for success in school. In some cases, competition actually works against your success. It is often stressful. It can strain relationships. According to staff members at the Institute for Cooperative Learning at the University of Minnesota, people can often get more done by sharing their skills and resources than by working alone.

Continued

Copyright © Houghton Mifflin Company. All rights reserved.

Copyright © Houghton Mifflin Company. All rights reserved.

We are social animals, and we draw strength from groups. Study groups feed you energy. Aside from offering camaraderie, fellowship, and fun, study groups can elevate your spirit on days when you just don't want to work at your education. You might be more likely to keep an appointment to study with a group than to study by yourself. If you skip a solo study session, no one may know. If you declare your intention to study with others who are depending on you, your intention gains strength. In addition to drawing strength from the group when you're down, you can support others.

Almost every job is accomplished by the combined efforts of many people. For example, manufacturing a single car calls for the contribution of designers, welders, painters, electricians, marketing executives, computer programmers, and many others. Jobs in today's economy call for teamwork—the ability to function well in groups. That's a skill you can start developing by studying with others.

Study groups are especially important if going to school has thrown you into a new culture. Joining a study group with people you already know, as well as with people from other cultures, can ease the transition. Promote your success in school by refusing to go it alone.

In forming a study group, look for dedicated students. Find people you are comfortable with and who share some of your academic goals. You can include people who face academic or personal challenges similar to your own. For example, if you are divorced and have two toddlers at home, you might look for other single parents who have returned to school.

To get the benefit of other perspectives, also include people who face challenges different from yours. Studying with friends is fine, but if your common interests are beer and jokes, beware of getting together to work.

Look for people who pay attention, ask questions, and take notes during class. Ask them to join your group. Choose people with similar educational goals but different backgrounds and methods of learning. You can gain from seeing the material from a new perspective.

Ask two or three people to get together for a snack and talk about group goals, meeting times, and other logistics. You don't have to make an immediate commitment. Limit groups to five or six people. Larger groups are unwieldly. Test the group first by planning a one-time session. If that session works, plan another. After several successful sessions, you can schedule regular meetings.

Continued

> Another way to get into a group is to post a note on a bulletin board asking interested students to contact you. Or pass around a sign-up sheet before class. The advantage of these methods is that you don't have to face rejection. The disadvantages are that this method takes more time and you don't get to choose who applies.*
>
> * Adapted from Dave Ellis, *Becoming a Master Student*, 9th ed. Boston: Houghton Mifflin, 2000, 190–191.

Now that you've practiced examining supporting details and transitions, you're ready to look at some common patterns for arranging details. To find out what you already know about patterns of organization in paragraphs, take the pre-test below.

PRE-TEST

Read each of the following paragraphs and decide which pattern of organization arranges the details. Check the correct pattern in the list below each paragraph.

1. Smoking is the single most preventable risk factor for fatal illnesses in the United States. Indeed, cigarette smoking accounts for more deaths than all other drugs, car accidents, suicides, homicides, and fires combined. Further, nonsmokers who inhale smoke from other people's cigarettes face an elevated risk for lung cancer and other illnesses related to the lungs, a fact that has given rise to a nonsmokers' rights movement in the United States.*

   _____ series

   _____ time order

   _____ cause/effect

   _____ comparison/contrast

   _____ definition

* Adapted from Bernstein et al., *Psychology*, 5th ed. Boston: Houghton Mifflin, 1999, 473.

Copyright © Houghton Mifflin Company. All rights reserved.

2. Therapists often teach clients desirable behaviors by demonstrating those behaviors. In modeling, the client watches other people perform desired behaviors to learn new skills without going through a lengthy process. In fear treatment, for example, modeling can teach the client how to respond fearlessly while getting rid of the fear responses the patient has.*

_____ series

_____ time order

_____ cause/effect

_____ comparison/contrast

_____ definition

3. In April of every year almost everyone in the United States files a tax return. There are a few things you can do during the year to make the process easier for next year and years to come. First, keep copies of your tax return, W-2 statement and 1099 forms, and records of tax deductions and investment income for three years. Second, keep seven years' worth of documentation in your files so that in case you are audited, the information is right at your fingertips. Third, compare the figures on your tax returns to your Social Security statement, which is sent each year just before your birthday and lists the amount of Social Security taxes you have paid. Fourth, start a file for this year's medical expenses. And finally, make sure all of your permanent records are stored in an impregnable place, such as a fireproof strongbox.†

_____ series

_____ time order

_____ cause/effect

_____ comparison/contrast

_____ definition

4. Just before I went to college, I remember telling my father that I wanted to be an actress and to major in speech and drama. My father grew up poor in rural Mississippi, where being a teacher was the highest calling—the most honorable position a black person could hold, other than being a doctor, so he was not happy with my choice. Before I left, I got a scholarship so that

* Adapted from Bernstein et al., *Psychology*, 5th ed. Boston: Houghton Mifflin, 1999, 572.

† Adapted from Suze Orman, "Spring Cleaning," *O* Magazine, April 2001, 64.

Copyright © Houghton Mifflin Company. All rights reserved.

6

my daddy wouldn't have to pay my tuition—and so that I would have control over my decision. Then, I attended college and majored in speech and drama. From there, I went on to become a newscaster and host of my own television show.*

_____ series

_____ time order

_____ cause/effect

_____ comparison/contrast

_____ definition

5. My two children are so different that it surprises me every day. For one thing, my older child is a girl, and my younger child is a boy. My daughter loves reading, going to the movies, and writing in her journal. My son, on the other hand, loves running, jumping, and swimming—anything that requires using energy. My daughter loves all different kinds of foods, but my son likes to eat only pizza. And while my son can't go a day without watching some kind of sporting event on television, my daughter will only watch a baseball game if nothing else is on.

_____ series

_____ time order

_____ cause/effect

_____ comparison/contrast

_____ definition

To help readers find and comprehend supporting details more easily, paragraphs are usually organized according to at least one particular pattern. A **pattern** is a consistent, predictable form or method of putting something together. So, if you learn the most common patterns found within paragraphs, you'll be able to:

1. Recognize supporting details more quickly and accurately.

2. Better understand the relationships between supporting details.

* Adapted from Oprah Winfrey, "Set Yourself Free," *O Magazine*, April 2001, 37.

Copyright © Houghton Mifflin Company. All rights reserved.

Both of these skills are essential to good reading comprehension.

This chapter presents five broad patterns of organization: **series, time order, cause/effect, comparison/contrast,** and **definition.** Each pattern type is illustrated by itself first, but it's important to realize that paragraphs often combine two or more of these patterns. The end of this chapter presents some examples of paragraphs that are organized according to two or more patterns.

Topic Sentences

As you read the example paragraphs and learn to recognize each pattern, note how the **topic sentence** often indicates the paragraph's pattern of organization. Alert readers know how to watch for clues within topic sentences, clues that indicate how the information is arranged. When you can see these clues, you'll be able to predict the paragraph's framework and see more easily how the details fit into it as you read.

Series

Many paragraphs organize supporting details as a series of items. A **series** is a number of things that come one after the other in succession. Series within paragraphs are often in the form of examples, reasons, types, or some other kind of point. Series of items all equally support the paragraph's topic sentence. For example, read the following paragraph:

> Many modern people are turning themselves into social victims. One example is a Tennessee woman who is suing McDonald's because she was badly burned on the chin by a hot pickle in her hamburger. A Canadian woman is another example. She wants to ban the *South Park* television show because her son Kenny is victimized by the show's Kenny character, who is killed in each episode. A third example is a group of European and Australian women who want to ban urinals in men's restrooms because they require men to stand in a way that suggests violence toward women. Another victims group called the American Association for Single People claims that single people are victimized because society ignores them.*

* Adapted from John Leo, "Victims of the Year," *U.S. News and World Report*, December 4, 2000, 24.

Copyright © Houghton Mifflin Company. All rights reserved.

6

This paragraph offers a series of four equal examples to explain the topic sentence:

Example #1: Tennessee woman burned by a pickle

Example #2: Canadian woman who believes *South Park* damages her son

Example #3: Women who object to urinals

Example #4: Single people who feel ignored

Here's another paragraph that uses a series pattern:

I hit the beach with my new electronic book in hand, but e-books and the outdoors don't mix. They're impossible to read because bright sun reflects off the glass screen, turning it into a mirror. And they're fragile, too. I had to shield mine from sand and surf, but a computer just doesn't belong on the beach. Plus, I had to worry about my e-book being stolen while I took a dip in the ocean.*

The details in this paragraph are organized into a series of reasons. The main idea is "E-books and the outdoors don't mix," and the paragraph gives three reasons to support that idea:

Reason #1: They're difficult to read in a sunny setting

Reason #2: They're too fragile

Reason #3: They might be stolen

If you were to map this paragraph, it might look like this:

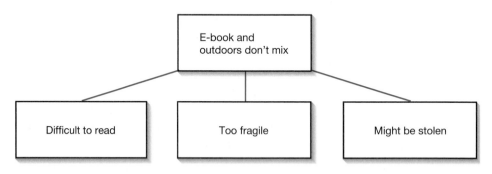

Series of supporting details all equally develop the topic sentence, so they can often be presented in any order. Authors, however, may choose to arrange them according to their order of importance so they can emphasize one of the points by either presenting it first or saving it for last.

A paragraph's topic sentence will often indicate that the details will appear as a series of items. For example:

* Adapted from Jim Louderback, "E-books: Hot or Not?" *USA Weekend,* July 13–15, 2001, 4.

Copyright © Houghton Mifflin Company. All rights reserved.

We should eliminate pennies for a ***number of reasons.***

There are ***four major forms*** of child abuse.

I began the New Year with ***three major goals*** in mind.

As you read, look for the following topic sentence words that indicate a series to follow.

Words and Phrases That Indicate a Series Pattern

Quantity word	*plus*	*Series word*
several		examples
many		reasons
two, three, four, etc.		points
a number of		classes
numerous		types
		categories
		groups
		goals
		kinds
		characteristics
		methods
		advantages
		ways
		forms
		tips

Copyright © Houghton Mifflin Company. All rights reserved.

6

Exercise 6.1

Read each of the paragraphs below and fill in the blanks that follow. Then, insert abbreviated versions of the paragraph's sentences in the outline or map to indicate the series of *major* supporting details.

1. Isabelle Tihanyi, the founder and owner of the first and only for-women-only surfing schools, called Surf Diva, has a few goals for her surfers. First, she wants them to have fun. Second, she wants them to learn to surf. And third, she wants them to enjoy the whole process of learning to surf, which means falling down, going under the water, and working hard to achieve something.*

Word(s) in the topic sentence that indicate a series: _____

* Adapted from David Leon Moore, "Surf Divas," *USA Today*, 1C.

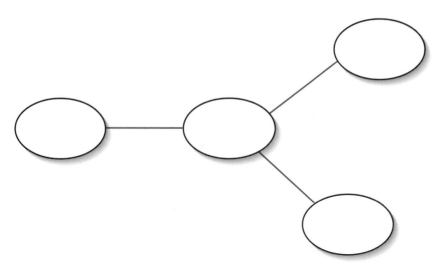

2. Several animated programs on television today are designed to appeal specifically to adults. One example, *The Simpsons*, which started as short animated segments on *The Tracy Ullman Show*, is the oldest of the animated situation comedies for adults and deals with adult themes but in a lighthearted manner. Another example is *King of the Hill*, which focuses on a family and, again, deals with their problems and adult themes in a comedic way. Finally, *South Park*, although originally designed to appeal to and be viewed by adults, has found a following with the preteen and teen set, who memorize and recite lines from the program.

Word(s) in the topic sentence that indicate a series: _____

_____

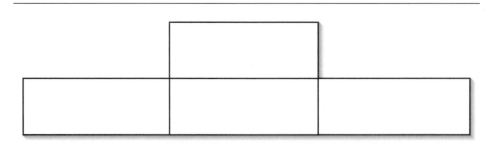

3. For several reasons, *The Bold and the Beautiful*, a popular daytime drama, or soap opera, recently made the decision to add a Spanish-language simulcast (the first in soap history) and a major story line featuring Latino characters. One reason is that the Hispanic population in the United States has surpassed 35 million, and that vast audience, already a strong viewing base for Spanish-language soaps, or *telenovelas*, has American producers taking notice. Another reason is that the network that broadcasts the show is pres-

Copyright © Houghton Mifflin Company. All rights reserved.

suring the producers to add Latino characters to make the show more eth-
nically diverse. The network is also hoping that by adding some exciting
Latino characters, it will expand its viewing base to include younger viewers whom advertisers seek when they buy time during a show.*

Word(s) in the topic sentence that indicate a series: _____

    I. _____

       A. _____

       B. _____

       C. _____

4. There are four advantages to joining a weight loss program or group like
Weight Watchers or Jenny Craig. First, if you choose a program suited to
your personality and lifestyle, your chances of success are much higher.
For instance, if you like to eat out a lot, a program that requires that you
buy its food may not be for you, but one where you can eat what you like,
in moderation, may be the answer. Second, some weight loss programs
often offer different classes on portion control, exercise, and eating habits
that may help you understand why you overeat at times. Third, weight
loss programs are attended by a lot of different people, so you may find a
built-in support group that can help you overcome the tough times when
you are dieting. Finally, studies have shown that people who join weight
loss programs often have greater success at losing weight and often keep
the weight off longer than those who diet on their own.

Word(s) in the topic sentence that indicate a series: _____

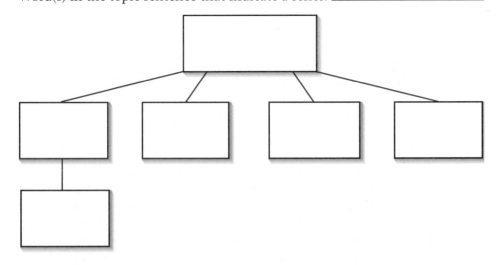

* Adapted from Michael Logan, "Haute Tamale," *TV Guide,* July 21, 2001, 36.

Copyright © Houghton Mifflin Company. All rights reserved.

5. Family rules typically fall into five categories. The first category is safety rules such as "Stay in your car seat while riding in the vehicle." The second category is health, which includes hygiene and nutrition. For example, a common hygiene rule might be "Brush your teeth every morning." A third category of rules covers appropriate and inappropriate behaviors such as "Don't burp at the table." Next is the rights category, which includes rules like "Knock before you enter the bathroom." Finally, the fifth category concerns values. "We respect people's feelings" is an example of a values-type rule.*

Word(s) in the topic sentence that indicate a series: _____

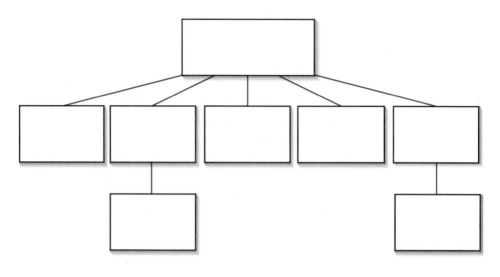

Time Order

The next common pattern for organizing details is time order. In **time order** paragraphs, the details are arranged according to their chronological relationships. In other words, time order paragraphs present details in the order they happened or should happen. Like the series pattern, the time order pattern includes items that follow each other in succession to support a main idea. However, these series are events, stages, or steps presented in the order they occurred or should occur. Unlike series paragraphs, these details cannot be rearranged because they would no longer make sense.

Two types of time order paragraphs are narrative and process. A **narrative** paragraph tells a story or recounts a sequence of events. Here is an example of a narrative paragraph that arranges details according to the time order pattern:

* Adapted from Nancy Seid, "How to Set Rules Your Kids Won't Break," *Parents,* August 2001, 109.

Copyright © Houghton Mifflin Company. All rights reserved.

The Lindbergh baby kidnapping was one of the biggest crime stories of the 20th century. On March 1, 1932, Charles Lindbergh, Jr., the beloved 20-month-old son of the flying ace, was put to bed, as usual, at 7:30 P.M. But when a nurse checked on the blond, curly-haired boy at 10 P.M., his crib was empty, and the window to his second-floor bedroom was open. Police found a ransom note on the sill. Whoever took the child wanted $50,000 to bring him back. Charles Lindbergh paid the money in marked bills. But on May 12, the baby's body was found in the woods near the Lindbergh house, and police believed he was killed the night he was kidnapped. In September 1934, detectives arrested Bruno Richard Hauptmann after finding thousands of dollars of the marked bills in his house. Hauptmann was convicted of the crime and executed in 1936 by electric chair.*

In this paragraph, the supporting details are all events presented in the order they occurred:

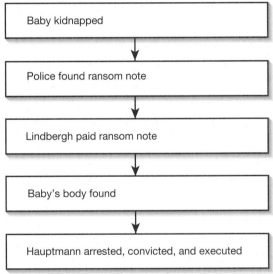

LINDBERGH BABY KIDNAPPING

Baby kidnapped

↓

Police found ransom note

↓

Lindbergh paid ransom note

↓

Baby's body found

↓

Hauptmann arrested, convicted, and executed

The second type of time order paragraph is **process.** A process paragraph explains how something is done or could be done. Its details are organized in the steps or stages, in the order they occur. Here is an example:

The new gasoline-electric hybrid cars work by transferring power back and forth between a gasoline engine and an electric motor. First, the

---

* Adapted from Angie Cannon and Kate V. Forsythe, "Crime Stories of the Century," *U.S. News and World Report,* December 6, 1999, 41ff.

Copyright © Houghton Mifflin Company. All rights reserved.

car's batteries feed power to the electric motor to start the car. When the car accelerates to about 15 miles per hour, the gasoline engine takes over. It also sends backup power to a generator, which either feeds it back to the electric motor or sends it to recharge the batteries. As the car continues to accelerate, the batteries contribute power to the electric motor to help the gasoline engine. When the car slows down, the electric motor captures the energy from the spinning axles and sends it to recharge the batteries.*

HOW A HYBRID CAR WORKS

Step 1: Batteries start car

Step 2: Gasoline engine takes over and powers electric motor or recharges batteries

Step 3: Batteries and engine both supply power

Step 4: Electric motor recharges batteries

Topic sentences in time order paragraphs will often indicate that a chronology will follow:

To cope with stress more effectively, follow *six steps.*

According to William Shakespeare, a person's life moves through *seven stages.*

Over the last 100 years, women's swimwear has undergone *several developments.*

As you read, look for topic sentence words that indicate a time order pattern:

---

* Adapted from William Holstein, "Green Cars and Red Ink," *U.S. News and World Report,* November 6, 2000, 42.

Copyright © Houghton Mifflin Company. All rights reserved.

Words and Phrases That Indicate a Time Order Pattern

Quantity word	*plus*	*Time Order word*
several		events
two, three, four, etc.		steps
a number of		stages
over time		developments
in just one year		procedures
		processes

Exercise 6.2

Read each of the paragraphs below and fill in the blanks that follow. Then, write abbreviated versions of the paragraph's sentences in the outline or map to indicate the *major* time order details.

1. Bozo the Clown, whose career spanned over fifty years, was the longest-running children's TV star in the country. He was created in 1946 by Capitol Records and debuted on television in 1949. Though he never appeared on network TV, one local TV station after another began producing its own Bozo show with games, circus acts, and comedy. At the height of his popularity in the 1960s, Bozo appeared on 183 TV stations around the world, and fans put their names on waiting lists for years to get tickets to a show. By the 1990s, though, kids had access to cable TV and channels like the Cartoon Network and Nickelodeon, and stations began canceling their Bozo shows. The final Bozo show was taped in Chicago in June 2001, ending a long era of clowning around.*

Word(s) in topic sentence that indicate time order: _____

I. _____

    A. _____

    B. _____

    C. _____

    D. _____

    E. _____

2. For many years, National Zoo curator Lisa Stevens concentrated on the health and well-being of two giant pandas, Ling Ling and Hsing Hsing,

* Adapted from Marc Peyser, "It's Bedtime for Bozo," *Newsweek,* June 25, 2001, 81.

6

Copyright © Houghton Mifflin Company. All rights reserved.

that came from China. On June 23, 1987, Ling Ling gave birth to twins. Within minutes, one died, but the other survived. Stevens, dubbed the Panda Lady by the media, closely tracked the baby's condition for several days. When the cub died on the fourth day, it was she who tearfully faced the press with the news. Ling Ling died in 1992, and Hsing Hsing in 1999. In 2000, after months of negotiations, China loaned the zoo two new pandas, and the Panda Lady was back in business.*

Word(s) in topic sentence that indicate time order: _____

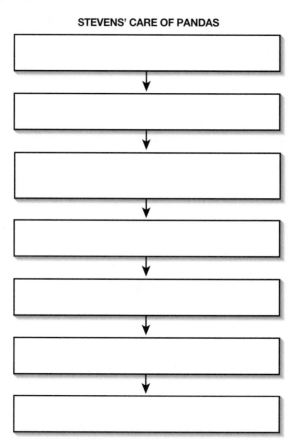

STEVENS' CARE OF PANDAS

3. Many experienced cooks shy away from baking bread because it is a time-consuming task with many steps. The first step is to buy all of the necessary ingredients, including yeast and flour, the two main ingredients in any bread. The second step is to put your ingredients together. Then, the time-consuming part begins because the dough, or the combination of all of your ingredients, must sit for an extended period of time—anywhere from one hour to four hours—to allow the yeast in the dough to rise. After the dough-

* Adapted from Andrew Ferguson, "Pandamonium's Keeper," *Reader's Digest*, August 2001, 31.

Copyright © Houghton Mifflin Company. All rights reserved.

rising step has been completed, you must take the time to knead the dough, which can also take a long time, depending on how much dough you have prepared. Finally, your risen, kneaded dough should be shaped and baked at the appropriate temperature for the period of time specified in your recipe.

Word(s) in topic sentence that indicate time order: _____

    I. _____

        A. _____

        B. _____

        C. _____

        D. _____

        E. _____

4. Building on the disillusionment of the 1960s, Americans' distrust of the federal government has deepened over the last several decades. In the 1970s, the Watergate scandal and Richard Nixon's resignation from the presidency convinced many that politics was inherently corrupt. In the 1980s, the administration of Ronald Reagan added the Iran-Contra scandal to the public's concerns about government corruption and cover-ups. And in the 1990s, Bill Clinton's White House was tainted by a variety of special investigations and trials, as well as allegations about his character, like the one that he had extramarital affairs.*

Word(s) in topic sentence that indicate time order: _____

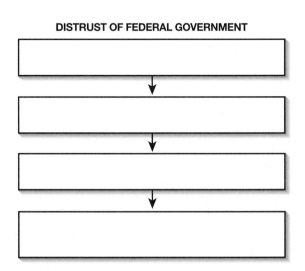

DISTRUST OF FEDERAL GOVERNMENT

6

* Adapted from Norton et al., *A People and a Nation*, Vol. II, 5th ed. Boston: Houghton Mifflin, 1998, 1002.

Copyright © Houghton Mifflin Company. All rights reserved.

5. Christopher Columbus's journey to the New World took just over two months. On August 3, 1492, in command of three ships—the *Pinta,* the *Niña,* and the *Santa Maria*—Columbus set sail from the southern Spanish port of Palos. The first part of the journey must have been very familiar, for the ships steered down the Northeast Trades to the Canary Islands. There Columbus refitted his square-rigged ships, adding triangular sails to make them more maneuverable. On September 6, the ships weighed anchor and headed out into the unknown ocean. Just over a month later, pushed by the favorable trade winds, the vessels found land approximately where Columbus had predicted. On October 12, he and his men landed on an island in the Bahamas, which its inhabitants called Guanahani, but which he renamed San Salvador. Later he went on to explore the islands now known as Cuba and Hispaniola.*

Word(s) in the topic sentence that indicate time order: _____

    I. _____

        A. _____

        B. _____

        C. _____

        D. _____

6

Cause/Effect

When details are arranged in the **cause/effect** pattern, the paragraph intends to show how the details relate to or affect each other. Like a narrative paragraph, a cause/effect paragraph presents a series of occurrences. However, unlike a narrative, the cause/effect pattern reveals how one occurrence led to another. It might also demonstrate how a series of causes produced one particular effect, or result. The diagram on page 255 will help you visualize some common types of cause/effect patterns.

The first diagram shows a chain reaction of causes and effect, while the second one indicates a separate series of effects that are not related. The third diagram shows a pattern in which several unrelated causes together produce one particular effect.

* Adapted from Norton et al., *A People and a Nation,* Vol. I, 5th ed. Boston: Houghton Mifflin, 1998.

Copyright © Houghton Mifflin Company. All rights reserved.

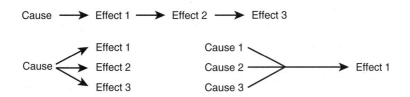

For an example of the cause/effect pattern, read the following paragraphs:

Several outcomes depend upon the results of the population census conducted in the United States every ten years. Political representation is affected by the census because population determines how many Congressional representatives each state can have. The census numbers are also given to local governments, which determine how many schools, hospitals, and firehouses to build to accommodate the number of people living in the area. The census results are given to businesses, too. They use the data to decide where to open businesses, where to close them, and even what kind and how many products to put on stores' shelves.*

In this paragraph, one cause produces three different effects:

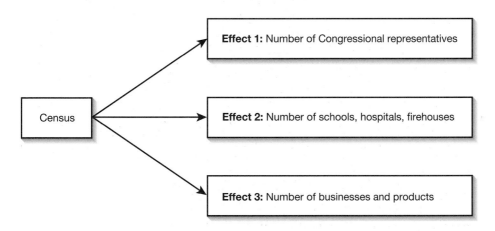

Here's a second example that is arranged according to a different cause/effect pattern:

The saga of fiber and its protection against colon cancer reveals how uncertain science can lead to consumer confusion. In 1971, a British surgeon observed that Africans in rural areas had fewer bowel disorders than Americans. He theorized that the Africans' high-fiber diet

* Adapted from Calvin Baker, "The Uncounted," *Life,* March 2000, 64.

Copyright © Houghton Mifflin Company. All rights reserved.

made the difference. So, scientists began experimenting with rats and mice, and the results seemed to indicate that fiber might help prevent colon cancer. Therefore, in 1984, the American Cancer Society recommended that people eat more fiber. That led to the Kellogg Company's printing a claim on All-Bran cereal boxes that suggested their product could reduce the risk of colon cancer. Other cereals followed suit even though it wasn't clear that *cereal* fiber was responsible. In the late 1980s and early 1990s, however, more clinical trials found that fiber's protection was much weaker than earlier studies had predicted.*

This paragraph explains a chain reaction. The British doctor's observation about Africans was the cause, and then a series of effects occurred as a result. You might map this paragraph as follows:

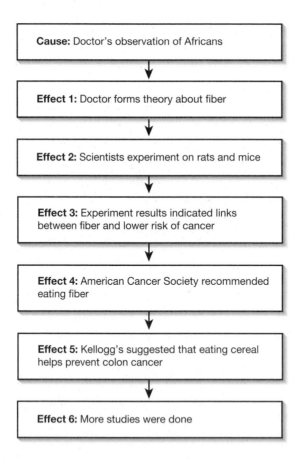

Cause: Doctor's observation of Africans

↓

Effect 1: Doctor forms theory about fiber

↓

Effect 2: Scientists experiment on rats and mice

↓

Effect 3: Experiment results indicated links between fiber and lower risk of cancer

↓

Effect 4: American Cancer Society recommended eating fiber

↓

Effect 5: Kellogg's suggested that eating cereal helps prevent colon cancer

↓

Effect 6: More studies were done

* Adapted from Linda Kulman, "Food News Can Get You Dizzy, So Know What to Swallow," *U.S. News and World Report*, November 13, 2000, 70.

Copyright © Houghton Mifflin Company. All rights reserved.

Topic sentences in cause/effect paragraphs will often indicate that an explanation of related occurrences will follow:

Stereotyping often **leads to** prejudice and discrimination.

The **results** of hypnosis can be fascinating.

A **chain reaction** of events **led** to the Great Depression of the 1930s.

As you read, look for the following topic sentence words that signal a cause/effect pattern.

Words and Phrases That Indicate a Cause/Effect Pattern

consequences	was caused by
effects	causes
results	chain reaction
outcomes	leads to
affect	factors
because	

Exercise 6.3

Read the paragraphs below and fill in the blanks that follow. Then, write abbreviated versions of the paragraph's sentences in the map to indicate the cause/effect relationships between the *major* supporting details.

1. Because of their negative effects, multiple births are frowned upon even by fertility doctors. One of the drawbacks to having four, five, or six babies at one time is poor health for the infants. Multiple births are often premature, and premature babies usually require long periods of intensive care. Even if the babies are not born prematurely, they are more likely to suffer from afflictions, such as heart problems or genetic disorders, that can affect their lifelong health. These health problems lead to a second disadvantage: financial problems. Multiple birth babies can run up expensive medical bills. These bills, along with the daily demands of caring for several infants at one time, usually result in high levels of stress for the whole family.*

Word(s) in topic sentence that indicate cause/effect order: _____

---

* Adapted from Rita Rubin, "Little Safety in Numbers," *USA Today,* July 19, 2001, 8D.

Copyright © Houghton Mifflin Company. All rights reserved.

6

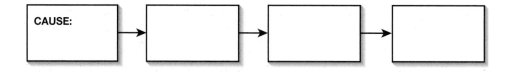

2. Because of several beneficial outcomes, frequent traveler Mike Hermens doesn't get in a line and wait for a ticket agent when he arrives at the airport but goes straight for the airline's automated kiosk to conduct his check-in business. Doing business with a machine allows him to avoid airport lines and inexperienced airline agents. When he doesn't have to deal with slow airline agents he saves time and reduces his own level of aggravation.*

Word(s) in topic sentence that indicate cause/effect order: _____

_____

3. There are a number of factors that may be contributing to your getting sunburned every summer. If you wear sunscreen but still get sunburned, you may not be using a sunscreen with enough "SPF," the ingredient that shields your skin and indicates how long you can stay in the sun with protection. For instance, if you wear a sunscreen with SPF 30, you can stay in the sun 30 times longer than you could without protection. Second, you may not be reapplying sunscreen after every dip in the pool, ocean, or lake, and after intense physical activity. Third, in addition to sunscreen, you may not be wearing a hat and sunglasses to protect your face and eyes.

Word(s) in topic sentence that indicate cause/effect order: _____

_____

* Adapted from Marilyn Adams, "Tech Takes Bigger Role in Air Service," *USA Today*, July 18, 2001, 1B.

Copyright © Houghton Mifflin Company. All rights reserved.

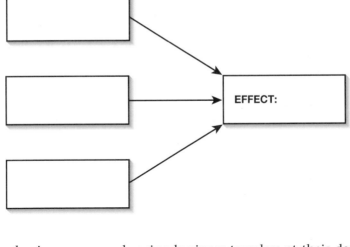

4. With a slowing economy keeping business travelers at their desks, high-end hotels in major cities are trying to get customers, and the results are staggering. For example, many famous and usually exorbitant hotels, such as The Plaza in New York City, are cutting prices to under $200 a night, which is a sharp drop from their usual rate. Other hotels are offering such value-added perks as room upgrades, spa treatments, and "buy one night, get another free" deals. And hotel employees are now able to "cut deals" with hotel guests by offering lower rates when customers ask for them.*

Word(s) in topic sentence that indicate cause/effect order: _____

6

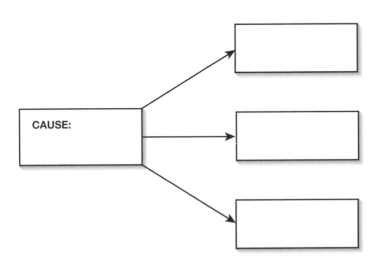

* Adapted from Laura Bly, "Luxe Hotels Lose Their Reservations About Discounting," *USA Today*, July 13, 2001, 1D.

Copyright © Houghton Mifflin Company. All rights reserved.

5. Researchers have found that the average American is driving 15 to 20 miles per hour faster than ten years ago, with serious consequences. As a result, the number of speeding tickets issued has risen by about 20 percent in the last ten years. More serious is the number of deaths associated with car accidents. Studies show that more people die as a result of speeding than any other driving-related factor, such as bad weather, driver neglect, or driving under the influence of alcohol. Consequently, many states are considering lowering the speed limit by five or ten miles per hour.

Word(s) in topic sentence that indicate cause/effect order: _____

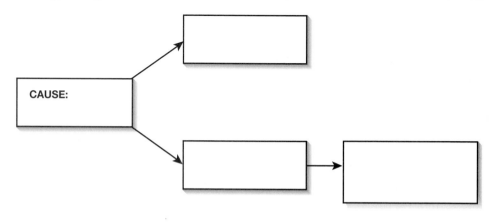

CAUSE:

Copyright © Houghton Mifflin Company. All rights reserved.

Comparison/Contrast

A third common pattern is comparison/contrast. **Comparison** means explaining the *similarities* between two or more things. **Contrast** means examining the *differences* between things. A paragraph can compare or contrast, or do both.

In comparison/contrast paragraphs, the supporting details are in the form of points of comparison. In other words, the paragraph concentrates on certain aspects or features of the subjects and explores their likenesses and/or differences in those areas. For example, a comparison of two different male singing groups might focus on the similarities in their style, the subjects of their songs, and the audiences they attract. Paragraphs arrange these details in one of two ways. One option is to focus on each subject in turn. The following paragraph, which deals only with similarities, provides an example of this pattern:

Because of their many similarities, it's difficult to tell all-male groups 'N Sync and the Backstreet Boys apart. 'N Sync is composed of five young white men who harmonize in catchy pop tunes. In performances, they dance in routines choreographed for their songs. They're popular with adolescent girls, and they've sold millions of albums. The group, which originates from Florida, was created by manager Louis Pearlman. The Backstreet Boys group, too, includes five young white men who sing catchy pop tunes. Their performances, like 'N Sync's, include dance routines, and they, too, have sold millions of albums. Like 'N Sync, the group was formed in Orlando by the same manager, Louis Pearlman.

This paragraph groups the points of comparison by subject, discussing first 'N Sync and then the Backstreet Boys. It would be outlined like this:

I. Similarities between 'N Sync and Backstreet Boys

  A. 'N Sync
    1. Number, race, and age of members
    2. Type of songs
    3. Performances
    4. Fans
    5. Number of albums sold
    6. State of origin and creator

  B. Backstreet Boys
    1. Number, race, and age of members
    2. Type of songs
    3. Performances
    4. Fans
    5. Number of albums sold
    6. State of origin and creator

A comparison/contrast paragraph can also be arranged so that it focuses on the points of comparison, alternating back and forth between the two subjects.

Even in preschool, boys and girls fall into very different play patterns. Boys tend to gather in larger groups, while girls, early on, gather in small groups. Boys play games that have clear winners and losers and bluster through them, boasting about their skills. Girls play theatrical games, such as playacting roles as members of a pretend family, that don't feature hierarchy or winners. One study of children aged three to four found they were already resolving conflict in separate ways—boys resorting to threats, girls negotiating verbally and often reaching a compromise.*

* Adapted from Deborah Blum, "What's the Difference Between Boys and Girls?" *Life*, March 1999, 52.

Copyright © Houghton Mifflin Company. All rights reserved.

This paragraph contrasts three aspects of preschool play groups: their size, type of games played, and ways conflict is resolved. You could outline the organization of these three points of comparison as follows:

I. Play patterns of boys and girls
   A. Size of play groups
      1. Boys
      2. Girls
   B. Types of games
      1. Boys
      2. Girls
   C. Conflict resolution
      1. Boys
      2. Girls

Topic sentences in comparison/contrast paragraphs often indicate that an explanation of similarities and/or differences is to follow:

Public schools and private schools ***differ*** in four significant aspects.

Although they share a few ***similarities,*** football and rugby are more ***different*** than ***alike.***

In comparison to Japanese cars, American cars give you more for your money.

As you read, look for the following topic sentence words that indicate a comparison/contrast pattern.

Words That Indicate a Comparison/Contrast Pattern

similarities	differences
alike	different
likenesses	

Exercise 6.4

Read the following comparison/contrast paragraphs and answer the questions that follow.

Though there are some differences between today's teenagers and those of previous generations, they are very much the same in many respects. It's true that modern teens must deal with problems—such as school shootings

Copyright © Houghton Mifflin Company. All rights reserved.

and AIDS—unknown to teens in other eras. Anorexia, bulimia, and teen sui- cide are more prevalent, too. But the teens of today still struggle with the same emotions and daily dramas as teens of yesterday. Teens still see adults as too critical. They still define themselves as different through their out- ward appearance. In previous generations, it was bell-bottoms and long hair. Today, it's green hair and body piercings. But what was true then and is today is that to be a teen is to be on the search for self. "Who am I?" and "How do others perceive me?" are two big questions for teenagers of any era.*

1. This paragraph (circle one):

   a. compares
   b. contrasts
   c. compares and contrasts

2. What two subjects are being compared and/or contrasted?

   _____ and _____

3. On what four similarities between the two subjects does the paragraph focus?

   1. _____
   2. _____
   3. _____
   4. _____

6

Although *USA Today* and the *New York Times* are both daily newspapers, they couldn't be more different. For one thing, *USA Today* caters to the reader who wants lots of news about a lot of different subjects and who doesn't have a lot of time to devote to reading. The *New York Times* fea- tures in-depth articles on fewer subjects and is known for its ground- breaking stories on news in the United States and abroad. *USA Today* is heavy on sports and entertainment reporting, while the *New York Times* is noted for its number of articles on political issues. Finally, *USA Today* is a daily paper that is only published Monday through Friday, while the *New York Times* is published seven days a week, with an extensive weekend supplement most noted for its magazine section.

4. This paragraph (circle one):

   a. compares
   b. contrasts
   c. compares and contrasts

* Adapted from Kimberly Kirberger, "Are Today's Teens That Different?" *Life*, March 1999, 48.

Copyright © Houghton Mifflin Company. All rights reserved.

5. What two subjects are being compared and/or contrasted?

_____ and _____

6. On what three differences between the two subjects does the paragraph focus?

1. _____

2. _____

3. _____

Princess Diana and Sarah Ferguson were similar in many ways. Both women came from royalty, even though their royal heritage went back many hundreds of years. At the time they married, both women were considered "commoners," or women who lived a nonroyal life, when they met their prospective husbands, Charles and Andrew. Both Diana and Sarah had well-publicized affairs after their breakups with their husbands and experienced terrible embarrassment as a result. And eventually, both women experienced the pain of separation or divorce, leaving Charles and Andrew and raising their children alone in homes away from the royal palace.

7. This paragraph (circle one):

a. compares
b. contrasts
c. compares and contrasts

8. What two subjects are being compared and/or contrasted?

_____ and _____

9. On what four similarities between the two subjects does the paragraph focus?

1. _____

2. _____

3. _____

4. _____

George Clooney and Brad Pitt share many of the same characteristics but couldn't be more different. Both have been named to *People* Magazine's "50 Most Beautiful People" list, and both are adored by women in the United States and abroad. Both men have made a name for themselves acting as leading men in some highly publicized movies. However, Brad Pitt is a stay-at-home kind of guy, spending most, if not all, of his time by

Copyright © Houghton Mifflin Company. All rights reserved.

the side of his wife, Jennifer Aniston. George Clooney is known for being a bit of a playboy, having been seen around Hollywood with different women. One woman, who has known him for years, claims he will never settle down and get married, whereas Pitt's friends say that he is doing exactly what he has always wanted to do by being married.

10. This paragraph (circle one):

    a. compares

    b. contrasts

    c. compares and contrasts

11. What two subjects are being compared and/or contrasted?

    _____ and _____

12. How are the two men compared? List three similarities:

    1. _____

    2. _____

    3. _____

13. How are they contrasted? _____

Swimming in a lake and a pool are two different experiences. For one thing, swimming in a lake does not involve swimming in chemicals like chlorine, which you need in a pool to keep it clean. Another thing that makes the swimming experience different is that lake water is often very cold, whereas pool water can get warm and stay warm due to the fact that it is in a closed container or area. Lake water is often very clear, whereas pool water, if you don't maintain it properly, can get cloudy and full of leaves and bugs. Finally, often you can see small fish and eels swimming with you in a lake, which is something you would never see in a pool!

6

14. This paragraph (circle one):

    a. compares

    b. contrasts

    c. compares and contrasts

15. What two subjects are being compared and/or contrasted?

    _____ and _____

16. On what four differences between the two subjects does the paragraph focus?

    1. _____

    2. _____

Copyright © Houghton Mifflin Company. All rights reserved.

3. _____

4. _____

Definition

One last pattern you should learn to recognize is the definition pattern. **Definition** usually states the meaning of a particular word, term, or concept, and then goes on to illustrate it with one or more examples. Textbooks often use this pattern to explain a term being introduced for the first time. The following paragraph is organized according to the definition pattern.

> Job sharing (sometimes referred to as work sharing) is an arrangement whereby two people share one full-time position. One job sharer may work from 8 A.M. to noon and the other from 1 to 5 P.M., or they may alternate workdays. For example, at a financial institution in Cleveland, two women share the position of manager of corporate communications. One works Tuesdays and Thursdays, and the other works Mondays, Wednesdays, and Fridays. They communicate daily through computers, voice mail, and fax machines to handle their challenging administrative position.*

The example or examples within a definition paragraph may be arranged according to one of the other patterns. For example, the definition might be followed by an example that contains details organized with a *time order* pattern. Or, the definition might be followed by *a series* of two or more examples. This next paragraph is a good example:

> Punishment involves the presentation of an unpleasant stimulus or the removal of a pleasant stimulus in order to decrease the frequency of an undesirable behavior. One example is shouting "No!" and swatting your dog when it begins chewing on the rug. That illustrates a negative stimulus that follows a behavior you want to eliminate. Another example is taking away a child's TV privileges following a demonstration of rude behavior. This is a punishment, or penalty, that removes a positive stimulus.†

Topic sentences will often indicate that a definition will follow:

> Money *can be defined as* anything a society uses to purchase products, services, or resources.

* Adapted from William M. Pride et al., *Business*. Boston: Houghton Mifflin, 1999, 237.
† Adapted from Douglas A. Bernstein, *Psychology*. Boston: Houghton Mifflin, 1997, 209.

Copyright © Houghton Mifflin Company. All rights reserved.

Personality *is* an individual's unique pattern of psychological and behavioral characteristics.

To understand what a Republican believes, you must first know what the word "conservative" *means.*

As you read, look for the following topic sentence words that may indicate a definition pattern:

Words That Indicate a Definition Pattern

means	definition
meaning	is/are
define	

Exercise 6.5

Read each of the following definition paragraphs and answer the questions that follow.

Culture shock is the feeling of dislocation that people experience when they first encounter a foreign culture.   Peace Corps volunteers, foreign students, tourists, and newly arrived immigrants often report culture shock. When they first experience the strange life patterns of a foreign culture, they feel disoriented, forced to assimilate much too soon, and afraid they have made a drastic mistake by going to a strange country.*

1. What term is defined in this paragraph? _____

2. Which sentence states the definition? _____

3. How many examples are given as illustrations? _____

Astronomers follow the rules of logic, a set of mental procedures that provide a more general formula for drawing valid conclusions about the world. For example, each step in the astronomers' thinking uses a formula of "if-then" propositions: *If* we know how much energy comes from one part of the sun's surface, and *if* we know how big the whole surface is, *then* we can calculate the total energy output.   You use the same logical reasoning processes when you conclude, for example, that *if* your friend Jovan is two years older than you are, *then* his twin brother Jermaine is two years older, too.†

* Adapted from Ryan/Cooper, *Those Who Can, Teach,* 9th ed. Boston: Houghton Mifflin, 2000, 32–33. Copyright © 2000 by Houghton Mifflin Company. Reprinted with permission.
† Adapted from Bernstein et al., *Psychology,* 4th ed. Boston: Houghton Mifflin, 1997, 272.

Copyright © Houghton Mifflin Company. All rights reserved.

4. What word is defined in this paragraph? _____

5. Which sentence states the definition? _____

6. How many examples are given as illustrations? _____

7. Which pattern organizes the examples? _____

(1) Whereas case studies provide close-up views of individuals, surveys give broad portraits of large groups. (2) In a survey, researchers use interviews or questionnaires to ask people about their behavior, attitudes, beliefs, opinions, or intentions. (3) For example, opinion polls help politicians and advertisers determine the popularity of policies or products. (4) Also, psychological surveys gather data on just about everything related to behavior and mental processes, from parenting practices to interpersonal behavior.*

8. What word is defined in this paragraph? _____

9. Which sentence states the definition? _____

10. How many examples are given as illustrations? _____

11. Which pattern organizes the examples? _____

(1) Many companies in the United States are adopting a "business casual policy" regarding how their employees dress. (2) What is business casual? (3) Business casual means that employees, who formerly wore suits and ties in the case of men, and suits and dresses in the case of women, are now permitted to wear more comfortable, less formal attire to the office. (4) An example of this would be khaki pants and a polo shirt for men. (5) For women, perhaps linen pants and a blouse would be appropriate.

12. What term is defined in this paragraph? _____

13. Which sentence states the definition? _____

14. How many examples are given as illustrations? _____

15. Which pattern organizes the examples? _____

(1) Opportunities refer to favorable conditions in the environment that could produce rewards for the organization if acted upon properly. (2) That is, opportunities are situations that exist but must be acted upon if the firm is to benefit from them. (3) Amazon.com, for example, acted quickly when new technology made it possible to sell books on the Internet.†

* Adapted from Bernstein et al., *Psychology*. Boston: Houghton Mifflin, 2000, 33.

† From Pride/Ferrell, *Marketing*. Boston: Houghton Mifflin, 2000, 43.

Copyright © Houghton Mifflin Company. All rights reserved.

16. What word is defined in this paragraph? _____

17. Which sentence states the definition? _____

18. How many examples are given as illustrations? _____

Combination of Patterns

Often, paragraphs include more than one pattern of organization. The major supporting details may be arranged according to one pattern, and minor details are arranged according to another. For example, read the following paragraph:

> Quitting smoking is difficult because of the effects of nicotine in cigarettes. Nicotine produces pleasurable feelings and acts as a depressant. As the nervous system adapts to nicotine, smokers tend to increase the number of cigarettes they smoke and, thus, the amount of nicotine in their blood. Therefore, when a smoker tries to quit, the absence of nicotine leads to two types of withdrawal. The first type of withdrawal is physical, which may include headaches, increased appetite, sleeping problems, and fatigue. The second type of withdrawal is psychological. Giving up a habit can result in depression, irritability, or feelings of restlessness.*

This paragraph begins with the *effects* of nicotine and ends with a *series* of two types of nicotine withdrawal.

Here is one more example:

> There are very different ways that men and women handle stress. Because women have a very different hormonal balance from men, researchers are finding that women are more prone to take on more stress in their daily living than men. The reasons are varied, but one reason is that women seem to have more stress in their lives. They "multi-task," or do many things at once, to keep their family life coordinated and running smoothly. Men, on the other hand, focus on one task at a time. Another reason women have more stress than men is that women worry a lot more than men and about more things. While men may worry about one or two things in a day—their immediate

6

Copyright © Houghton Mifflin Company. All rights reserved.

* Adapted from American Cancer Society, www.cancer.org/tobacco/quitting.html.

family or money—women worry about their own families, their friends' families, their extended families, and other things.

Most of the details in this paragraph are arranged using the comparison/contrast pattern of organization. However, the paragraph also includes the causes of stress for both men and women, so the paragraph combines the comparison/contrast and cause/effect patterns.

Exercise 6.6

In the list following each paragraph, check off each pattern used to organize the supporting details.

1. *Retrograde amnesia* involves a loss of memory for events prior to some critical injury. Often, a person with this condition is unable to remember anything that took place in the months, or even years, before the injury. In most cases, the memories return gradually. For example, one man received a severe blow to the head after being thrown from his motorcycle. After regaining consciousness, he claimed that he was eleven years old. Over the next three months, he gradually recalled more and more of his life. He remembered when he was twelve, thirteen, and so on—right up until the time he was riding his motorcycle the day of the accident. But he was never able to remember what happened just before the accident.*

   _____ series

   _____ time order

   _____ cause/effect

   _____ comparison/contrast

   _____ definition

2. It was evident in the early 1970s that the United States was beginning to suffer economic decline. Recessions—which economists define as at least two consecutive quarters of no growth in the gross national product—began to occur more frequently. An eleven-month recession struck the country in

* Adapted from Bernstein, *Psychology.* Boston: Houghton Mifflin, 1997, 242.

Copyright © Houghton Mifflin Company. All rights reserved.

1969 and 1979, the first recession in almost a decade. Between 1973 and 1990, there were four more, and two were particularly long and harsh.*

_____ series

_____ time order

_____ cause/effect

_____ comparison/contrast

_____ definition

3. Mainly because they live at or near the poverty level, about 30 percent of families in the United States, and even greater numbers in many other countries worldwide, have poor access to medical care. In the United States, minor illnesses combined with malnourishment put children's health at risk for additional illnesses, both minor and major. Similiarly, in Kenya, where malnutrition is a major problem, even a temporary food shortage hurt children's health and school performance two years later.†

_____ series

_____ time order

_____ cause/effect

_____ comparison/contrast

_____ definition

4. The Great Lakes contain over 30 percent of all the fresh liquid water on the Earth's surface. About ten thousand years ago, the Great Lakes basins were filled by the North American ice sheet. An ice sheet refers to giant masses of ice that spread outward and eventually melted, forming bodies of water. As the ice retreated, the streams draining the Great Lakes flowed first to the Gulf via the Mississippi River. Then, they flowed to the Atlantic via the Hudson River. Finally, they flowed out to the Atlantic via the Saint Lawrence River.‡

* Adapted from Norton et al., *A People and a Nation*, Vol. II, 5th ed. Boston: Houghton Mifflin, 1998, 958.

† Adapted from Siefert/Hoffnung, *Child and Adolescent Development*. Boston: Houghton Mifflin, 2000, 241.

‡ Adapted from Dolgoff, *Essentials of Physical Geology*. Boston: Houghton Mifflin, 1998, 295.

Copyright © Houghton Mifflin Company. All rights reserved.

6

_____ series

_____ time order

_____ cause/effect

_____ comparison/contrast

_____ definition

5. Business is an organized effort of individuals to produce and sell, for a profit, the goods and services that satisfy society's needs. The general term *business* refers to all such efforts within a society. However, a business is a particular organization, such as American Airlines, or Cracker Barrel Old Country Store. To be successful, a business must perform three activities. First, it must be organized. Second, it must satisfy needs. And third, it must earn a profit.*

_____ series

_____ time order

_____ cause/effect

_____ comparison/contrast

_____ definition

Exercise 6.7

In each of the following topic sentences, circle the clue words that suggest a particular pattern of organization. Then, put a checkmark next to the pattern indicated by those clue words.

1. Long-term overuse of aspirin can cause significant health risks.

_____ series

_____ time order

_____ cause/effect

_____ comparison/contrast

_____ definition

* Adapted from Pride/Hughes/Kapoor, *Business*. Boston: Houghton Mifflin, 1999, 7.

Copyright © Houghton Mifflin Company. All rights reserved.

2. For three reasons, fly-fishing is a great hobby.

_____ series

_____ time order

_____ cause/effect

_____ comparison/contrast

_____ definition

3. The personal computer's 20-year history can be divided into four major eras.

_____ series

_____ time order

_____ cause/effect

_____ comparison/contrast

_____ definition

4. Biometeorology is the new science of studying how the human body interacts with the weather.

_____ series

_____ time order

_____ cause/effect

_____ comparison/contrast

_____ definition

5. Hearing and listening are very different actions.

_____ series

_____ time order

_____ cause/effect

_____ comparison/contrast

_____ definition

6. Shopping downtown and shopping in a mall differ significantly.

_____ series

_____ time order

6

Copyright © Houghton Mifflin Company. All rights reserved.

_____ cause/effect

_____ comparison/contrast

_____ definition

7. A rude cell phone user exhibits three inconsiderate behaviors.

_____ series

_____ time order

_____ cause/effect

_____ comparison/contrast

_____ definition

8. A search engine is defined as a program that searches the Internet for documents that contain certain specified keywords.

_____ series

_____ time order

_____ cause/effect

_____ comparison/contrast

_____ definition

9. Canning your own vegetables requires following six steps.

_____ series

_____ time order

_____ cause/effect

_____ comparison/contrast

_____ definition

10. MTV's effects on the music industry cannot be underestimated.

_____ series

_____ time order

_____ cause/effect

_____ comparison/contrast

_____ definition

Copyright © Houghton Mifflin Company. All rights reserved.

CHAPTER 6 REVIEW

Fill in the blanks in the following statements.

1. A _____ is a consistent, predictable form or method for putting something together.

2. Patterns help readers find _____ and understand their relationships.

3. Five broad patterns for organizing details include _____, _____, _____, _____, and _____.

4. _____ often include clues to a paragraph's pattern of arrangement.

5. A _____ is a number of things that follow each other in succession. Series in paragraphs may be examples, reasons, types, or other points.

6. _____ paragraphs, which include narratives and processes, arrange details chronologically.

7. _____ paragraphs explain how supporting details are related to each other.

8. _____ paragraphs examine two or more subjects' similarities, differences, or both.

9. The _____ pattern includes a term's meaning plus one or more examples as illustration.

10. Paragraphs often use a combination of _____ to organize supporting details.

Reading Selection

Mr. Cleanup
by Nick Charles and Kristin Baird Rattini

1 As a boy in East Moline, Illinois, Chad Pregracke spent much of his time in or on the mighty Mississippi. Fishing almost daily, cruising the waterway in a family canoe or just leaping in to cool off, he was the consummate river rat. When he was 15, he even started making a few bucks on the side diving for clams with his older brother Brent. "They were a classic Huck Finn-Tom Sawyer combination," says his mother, KeeKee. "It was their life."

2 But resting up on river islands between dives in the mid-1990s, Pregracke, then a professional clammer, or someone who

Copyright © Houghton Mifflin Company. All rights reserved.

takes clams out of the water to sell to different fish markets, saw a lot of trash stacking up on the banks of the river. One day, as he was guiding his boat home after work, he saw what should have been a pretty sight: a yacht sitting near the marina. "But onshore was a pile of barrels that had been there for 30 years," recalls Pregracke, now 25. "My thought was, 'I have to change that.' "

3   And he has. He started in 1997 as a one-man volunteer mission with no more equipment than a 20-foot flat-bottomed boat and his own two hands. The operation has since grown into a major year-round effort called the Mississippi River Beautification and Restoration Project. So far Pregracke has tidied up more than 1,000 miles of the Mississippi and another 435 miles of the Illinois River, pulling almost 800,000 pounds of debris from the riverbank. Says environmental activist Robert Kennedy, Jr., who hopes to enlist Pregracke's help in river cleanup efforts elsewhere: "Chad is doing a job that most would consider impossible—which is literally piece by piece cleaning up the river."

4   In the beginning, finding financial backing was tougher than the job itself. With no contacts, Pregracke cold-called area corporations, only to be asked, "What garbage?" "I got to thinking, 'They're sitting at their desks, they don't know,'" he recalls. Assembling photos of trash strewn along the river, he met with Tim Wilkinson, the vice president at Alcoa Mill Products in Bettendorf, Iowa. "The more he talked, the more I realized he was serious," says Wilkinson. "I thought, 'Here's a young man with a dream.' " With his black Lab Indy and $8,400 from Alcoa, Pregracke took to the river in June 1997 to load his first haul. "I was stoked," he says.

5   Pregracke, still very much a fish out of water when pitching corporations for support, raised an impressive $100,000 last year and hopes to double that this year. In addition, he persuaded companies to donate equipment and even extra barges. And he can still count on a little help from his parents. "When I tell someone, 'I'll have my people contact your people,'" says Pregracke, "that means, 'My mom will give you a call.' "

6   With more money, he has been able to bring aboard a volunteer crew of four. They not only work together, they all live in Pregracke's 42-foot houseboat *The Miracle*. They go ashore only a couple of times a week for supplies or a laundry run; previous volunteers have been known to quit because they couldn't deal with the close-quartered communal living. Or the hard labor, which begins daily about 8, when Pregracke dismounts from his bunk and rousts the crew. One of his crew members says, "He wakes up full of energy. You have no choice but to follow."

7   Admiring his beloved river one recent afternoon, Pregracke wonders what Huck Finn creator Mark Twain would have thought of his cleanup job. "I guess he'd say that it was all right," he says. "His characters were into adventures. Likewise, that's what I'm doing. It's an adventure."

* From Nick Charles and Kristin Baird Rattini, *People Weekly* © 2000 Time, Inc. All rights reserved.

Copyright © Houghton Mifflin Company. All rights reserved.

Vocabulary

Read the following questions about some of the vocabulary words that appear in the previous selection. Circle the correct responses.

1. In paragraph 1, the authors write that Chad Pregracke was a "*consummate river rat*." In this context, what does *consummate* mean?

   a. dirty
   b. total
   c. goofy
   d. lazy

2. What does the word *debris* mean in paragraph 3?

   a. garbage
   b. jewels
   c. tires
   d. boxes

3. The authors write in paragraph 4 that Chad had assembled "photos of trash *strewn* along the river." What does the word *strewn* mean?

   a. compiled
   b. arranged neatly
   c. scattered
   d. raised

4. In paragraph 4, the authors describe Chad as being "stoked." What does *stoked* mean in this context?

   a. depressed
   b. sad
   c. moody
   d. excited

5. What is communal living? Reread paragraph 6 where the authors describe Chad's boat and living arrangements. What do you think *communal* means?

   a. everyone living in separate quarters
   b. people living together
   c. everyone living on land
   d. everyone staying up all night

6. In paragraph 6, when the authors write, "Pregracke dismounts from his bunk and *rousts* the crew," what do they mean by *roust*?

   a. Chad makes everyone angry.
   b. Chad wakes everyone up.
   c. Chad yells at the top of his lungs.
   d. Chad jumps onto another bunk.

6

MAIN IDEAS, SUPPORTING DETAILS, AND PATTERNS OF ORGANIZATION

Answer the following questions.

1. What pattern organizes the details in paragraph 1 of the selection?

   a. time order
   b. series
   c. cause/effect
   d. definition

Copyright © Houghton Mifflin Company. All rights reserved.

2. What pattern organizes the details in paragraph 4?

   a. time order
   b. series
   c. cause/effect
   d. definition

3. In paragraph 2, what word or phrase is defined?

   a. river islands
   b. dives
   c. marina
   d. professional clammer

4. In paragraph 7, Chad compares himself to which fictional literary character?

   a. Tom Sawyer
   b. Mark Twain
   c. Huck Finn
   d. Oliver Twist

5. What is the main idea of paragraph 1?

   a. Chad grew up in East Moline.
   b. Chad was the consummate river rat.
   c. Chad had a brother who looked like Tom Sawyer.
   d. Chad dove for clams with his brother.

6. What is the implied main idea of paragraph 6?

   a. Chad is full of energy in the morning.
   b. Working with Chad and living on the boat can be challenging.
   c. Chad and his crew mates sleep in bunks.
   d. Chad is just like Huck Finn.

6

QUESTIONS FOR DISCUSSION AND WRITING

Answer the following questions based on your reading of the selection.

1. This selection describes how one young man with limited resources and a dream was able to attain his goal. What is one of your major goals? Is it attainable? What will you have to do to attain this goal? _____

   _____

   _____

2. Visit the Mississippi River Beautification and Restoration Project Web site at www.cleanrivers.com and find one piece of new information about the project that was not in the selection. Write a brief summary of this new information that you found. _____

   _____

   _____

Copyright © Houghton Mifflin Company. All rights reserved.

3. Do you think that it is Chad's responsibility to take care of the Mississippi River by himself? Why or why not? What do you think of his commitment to the project? _____

_____

_____

▶ Vocabulary: The Example Context Clue

You've learned that a *context clue* is a word, phrase, or sentence that helps you understand the meaning of an unfamiliar word you encounter as you read. In Chapter 4, you practiced recognizing the definition/restatement context clue. In Chapter 5, you learned about the explanation context clue. The **example** is a third type of context clue that can give you a sense of a particular word's definition. In this type, an example somewhere near a word provides an illustration that allows you to draw a conclusion about the word's meaning. For example, read the following sentence, which comes from one of the paragraphs in this chapter:

And finally, make sure all of your permanent records are stored in an *impregnable* place, such as a fireproof strongbox.

What does the word *impregnable* mean in this sentence? You get a clue in the form of the phrase *such as a fireproof strongbox*. If a box is strong and fireproof, it must be a secure, tightly protected place that's difficult to get into. Therefore, you can conclude that *impregnable* means "impossible to enter."

6

Vocabulary Exercise

The following sentences all come from paragraphs in Chapters 3, 4, and 6. In each one, underline the example context clue that helps you understand the meaning of the boldfaced, italicized word. Then, on the blank provided, write a definition for the boldfaced, italicized word.

1. For example, a common ***hygiene*** [noun] rule might be "Brush your teeth every morning."

   <u>Keeping yourself clean</u>

2. And in the 1990s, Bill Clinton's White House was tainted by a variety of special investigations and trials, as well as ***allegations*** [noun] about his character, like the one that he had extramarital affairs.

   <u>discouting unproven statement you don't know if its true</u>

Copyright © Houghton Mifflin Company. All rights reserved.

3. Even if the babies are not born prematurely, they are more likely to suffer from **afflictions,** such as heart problems or genetic disorders, that can affect their lifelong health.

disease (noun)

4. For example, many famous and usually **exorbitant** hotels, such as The Plaza in New York City, are cutting prices to under $200 a night, which is a sharp drop from their usual rate.

expensed   Exorbitant -very expensive

5. Girls play **theatrical** games, such as playacting roles as members of a pretend family, that don't feature hierarchy or winners.

dramatic, play games

6. The ship carried 1,257 passengers, 702 crewmen, and **contraband** such as 4,200 cases of rifle cartridges destined for the Western Front of World War I.

7. Ask two or three people to get together for a snack and talk about group goals, meeting times, and other **logistics.**

8. One room is devoted to books relating to sailing and all things **nautical,** like lobstering and knot tying.

9. Then comes a new batch of songs, only this time the bands must transform them into styles as **diverse** as punk, swing, and Latin.

10. The second rule for becoming rich is to avoid **frivolous** temptations. For example, don't drive expensive luxury cars; instead, buy medium-priced cars.

Copyright © Houghton Mifflin Company. All rights reserved.

Name _____ Date _____

POST-TEST 1

Read each paragraph and answer the question that follows. Circle the correct response.

1. There is one primary reason that tetrapods—four-legged animals such as birds and mammals—have been able to adapt to a salt-water environment, while other groups of animals, such as insects, have not. All animals must make many adaptations if they move from land to water. The advantage of birds and the ancestors of sea mammals is that they are active. An animal that enters a new environment must compete for food and other resources with the animals that are already there. An insect spends much of its time hiding, while a bird or mammal spends much of its time looking for food. The animal that is more active is better able to compete with creatures that are already present in the environment.

   Which word in the topic sentence indicates a cause/effect pattern?

   a. reason   c. is
   b. tetrapods   d. adapt

2. Synthesis means the creative meshing of elements to form a new and unique entity. Because its key is creativity, the synthesis category may be the most distinctive and one of the easiest to recognize—but it may also be the most difficult to teach. Synthesis is the process of combining parts in such a way as to constitute a pattern or structure that did not exist before. For example, if the writer of a research paper puts ideas together in new or unique patterns or creates new idea configurations, then we would consider the writer to be engaging in a synthesis-level activity.*

   Which word or phrase in the topic sentence indicates a definition pattern?

   a. means   c. form
   b. creative meshing   d. new and unique

---

* Adapted from Orlich et al., *Teaching Strategies: A Guide to Better Instruction*, 5th ed. Boston: Houghton Mifflin, 1998, 85.

For additional tests on patterns of organization, see the Test Bank.

Copyright © Houghton Mifflin Company. All rights reserved.

6

3. There are numerous ways to begin the webbing process. One is to brainstorm by listing anything you can think of related to the topic. A second technique is to identify questions and possible teaching techniques you could use to teach the topic. A third is to collect hands-on materials that are likely to pique your interest and, eventually, that of your students.*

Which word or phrase in the topic sentence indicates a series?

a. numerous ways   c. begin

b. are   d. process

4. Although Vygotsky and Piaget are both considered to be major theorists of children's cognitive development, their bodies of work are different. Piaget lived a long and productive life, published widely, and had time to modify and perfect his early ideas. His theory is thus whole and complete. Vygotsky, on the other hand, died young and published very little. He is known for only a few major ideas, but those ideas are among the most seminal in all of developmental psychology.

Which word in the topic sentence indicates a comparison/contrast pattern?

a. considered   c. theorists

b. major   d. different

5. Dutch elm disease (actually, the disease came from Asia by way of the Netherlands) occurs in a number of stages. First, tiny beetles burrow into the bark of a tree, carrying the spores of the disease-causing fungus. The fungus spreads through the tree's system of tubes, blocking the dispersal of fluids and nutrients. The fungus eventually plugs the tubes, resulting in, at first, a few yellowed leaves but, eventually, death of the tree.†

Which word or phrase in the topic sentence indicates time order?

a. disease   c. actually

b. occurs   d. a number of stages

6. For a juicy and delicious roast chicken, follow these simple steps. First, coat the entire chicken before roasting with fat, such as olive oil. Cover the chicken breast with cheesecloth, dipped in olive oil, before roasting, and place the chicken, on its back, on a rack in a roasting pan. Preheat the oven to 500 degrees, but turn the oven down to 350 degrees as soon as you put the chicken in. Baste the chicken every 15 or 20 minutes, and roast for no more than 15 minutes per pound.

* Adapted from Welton and Mallan, *Children and Their World: Strategies for Teaching Social Studies.* Boston: Houghton Mifflin, 2002, 231.

† Adapted from Bernd Heinrich, *The Trees in My Forest.* New York: Harper Perennial, 1998, 52.

Copyright © Houghton Mifflin Company. All rights reserved.

Which word or phrase in the topic sentence indicates time order?

a. roast

b. chicken

c. these

d. simple steps

7. There are several steps in matching your topic to your audience's interests. First, list your personal interests, and make a similar listing of the presumed interests of your classmates. Do this by considering what topics spark class discussions. Study the two lists together, looking for shared interests. Then use those shared interests to generate possible speech topics.*

Which word or phrase in the topic sentence indicates time order?

a. there

b. several steps

c. topic

d. interests

8. What happened to America's banks illustrates the widespread consequences of bank failure. Banks tied to the stock market or foreign investment were badly weakend by the decline in stock prices. When nervous people withdrew money from banks, panic set in. In 1929, 659 banks folded; in 1930, the total was 1,350. The Federal Reserve Board drastically raised interest rates, tightening the money markets just when loosening was needed. In 1931 and 1932, more than 3,600 banks shut their doors.†

Which word in the topic sentence indicates a cause/effect pattern?

a. happened

b. illustrates

c. consequences

d. failure

6

9. Dissociative disorders are defined as abrupt changes in a person's memory, consciousness, or identity. For example, dissociative fugue consists of sudden loss of memory and the adoption of a new identity, usually in a new locale. Dissociative amnesia also involves loss of memory of personal identifying information, but without moving to a new place. In the most famous type of dissociative disorder, multiple personality disorder, the person displays more than one distinct identity.

Which phrase in the topic sentence indicates a definition pattern of organization?

a. dissociative disorders

b. are defined as

c. abrupt changes

d. memory, consciousness, or identity

* Adapted from Osborn/Osborn, *Public Speaking*, 5th ed. Boston: Houghton Mifflin, 2000, 129–130.

† Adapted from Norton et al., *A People and a Nation*, Vol. II, 5th ed. Boston: Houghton Mifflin, 1999, 722.

Copyright © Houghton Mifflin Company. All rights reserved.

10. The German states were locked in a political stalemate as a result of certain factors. After Austria and Russia had blocked Frederick William's attempt to unify Germany "from above," tension grew between Austria and Prussia as each power sought to block the other within the German Confederation. Stalemate and reaction also prevailed in the domestic politics of the individual German states in the 1850s.*

Which word or words in the topic sentence indicate a cause/effect pattern?

a. result; factors   c. locked
b. were   d. stalemate

11. Tree buds can take a number of different forms. Some are clusters of bare miniature leaves (as in hickory and butternut). Others hold only tiny unfurled flowers (as in alder and hazelnut). A third kind includes both tiny new leaves and flowers, encased together in a protective package (as in apple, cherry, and shadbush). Some are sticky, some smooth, but all are packed with nutrients and are eagerly sought out as food by deer, birds, and other wildlife during the lean winter months.†

Which word or phrase in the topic sentence indicates a series?

a. tree buds   c. a number of different forms
b. can take   d. different

12. All teachers believe in the importance of authentic activities, but their definitions of those activities differ greatly. Is an activity authentic just because it involves building something rather than filling out a classroom worksheet? In that case, the infamous building-an-igloo-out-of-sugar-cubes activity would classify as authentic, and we believe it is not. No, authentic activities are those that incorporate the ordinary practices of a culture. These might include setting up a play store or any of the imaginary play activities that children engage in spontaneously.

Which word in the topic sentence indicates a comparison/contrast pattern?

a. all   c. differ
b. definitions   d. greatly

13. Some schools have had success with a particular process of teaching students to drive. Students begin by taking a driver's education course in school. During the course, they begin taking driving lessons with a qualified instructor in the passenger seat. Then, they take the state's written

* Adapted from McKay et al., *A History of World Societies*, Vol. II, 4th ed. Boston: Houghton Mifflin, 1998, 833.

† Adapted from Bernd Heinrich, "Grand Opening," *Natural History*, February 2002, 26.

Copyright © Houghton Mifflin Company. All rights reserved.

driving test. Once they pass the written test, they receive a six-month learner's permit, which allows them to drive only with an adult licensed driver in the car. After six months, they may take a driving test at a state driving examination center. If they pass the driving test, they receive a full driver's license. But even then, they are not allowed to drive with other teens in the car for six months.

Which word in the topic sentence indicates a time order pattern?

a. particular   c. drive
b. teaching   d. process

14. Modern scientists see many similarities between early modern humans and Neanderthals. Certainly, the bodies of the two are very similar, and Neanderthals had, if anything, the advantage in brain size. Both used fire, made tools, and lived in social groups. Even more significant, the fossil record shows that both buried their dead and cared for the elderly and sick among them.

Which word in the topic sentence indicates a comparison/contrast pattern?

a. scientists   c. similarities
b. many   d. between

15. Sculptures of the archaic period are defined by a number of characteristics. They appear natural to some degree, but they are still confined to the stone block out of which they are carved. Their bodies are perceived as columnar shapes in which anatomical details are arranged in a symmetrical, stylized way. Each feature of the head is seen as an almost separate flat section that flows as a series of smooth planes. The total impression is of a compact, sculptural solid, not of a body in motion.*

Which word in the topic sentence indicates a definition/example pattern?

a. characteristics   c. defined
b. period   d. number

16. The Navigation Acts, passed between 1651 and 1673, established three main principles. First, only English or colonial merchants could trade in the American colonies. Second, certain particularly valuable products, such as wool, sugar, and tobacco, could be sold only in the mother country or in other British colonies. Third, all foreign goods to be sold in the colonies had to be shipped by way of English ports. Later, a fourth principle was added: that the colonies could not export items that competed with English goods.†

* Adapted from Witt et al., *The Humanities*, Vol. I, 6th ed. Boston: Houghton Mifflin, 2001, 97.
† Adapted from Norton et al., *A People and a Nation*, Vol. I, 5th ed. Boston: Houghton Mifflin, 1999, 83.

Copyright © Houghton Mifflin Company. All rights reserved.

Which word or phrase in the topic sentence indicates a series?

a. passed
c. three main principles
b. between
d. established

17. Although the phrase "oral literature" seems like a contradiction in terms, it actually has a distinct meaning to scholars. Many societies in Africa, the Middle East, and early Europe relied on an oral tradition to transmit their most important works of literature. An oral tradition relies, first and foremost, on the memory of those who transmit the works to each new generation. This memory is aided by repetition of key words and phrases and by other poetic formulas that make the work pleasing to the ear. When such a work is written down and read, most likely in translation, much of its unique flavor is lost.

Which word in the topic sentence indicates a definition pattern of organization?

a. phrase
c. terms
b. contradiction
d. meaning

18. Katherine Sherwood's career as an artist has proceeded through a number of surprising stages. Fearful of bad reviews, Sherwood did not originally intend to become a painter. However, she created a unique body of work that incorporated found objects into painted canvases. In 1997, a stroke paralyzed Sherwood's right side and made her unable to paint with her right hand. Gradually, Sherwood learned to walk and talk again and finally forced herself to begin painting again with her left hand. In the process, her creativity was freed and her work became richer, deeper, and more eagerly sought after by collectors.*

Which phrase in the topic sentence indicates time order?

a. Katherine Sherwood's career
c. has proceeded
b. as an artist
d. a number of surprising stages

19. The use of appropriate reinforcers often leads to surprising improvements in children's behavior. A child who does not routinely raise her hand to answer questions will often begin to do so if she knows the result will be a star or happy face sticker. Other appropriate reinforcers include praise (verbal or in writing), sending a note home to parents, and allowing the child to tutor other children or to run errands.

---

* Adapted from Thomas Fields-Meyer and Lyndon Stambler, "A Near Brush," *People* Magazine, December 3, 2001, 111–114.

Copyright © Houghton Mifflin Company. All rights reserved.

Which phrase in the topic sentence indicates a cause/effect pattern?

a. use of
b. appropriate reinforcers
c. leads to
d. improvements in

20. One important difference between physical development of girls and boys is timing. Girls tend to reach puberty around age 12, while the average age of puberty for boys is approximately 14. Children of both sexes undergo a growth spurt during the one and two years that precede sexual maturity. The growth spurt of boys is more extreme, resulting in taller adult stature.

Which word in the topic sentence indicates a comparison/contrast pattern?

a. important
b. difference
c. physical
d. development

POST-TEST 2

Read each of the following topic sentences and then circle the letter of the clue words that suggest a particular pattern of organization. Then, circle the letter of the correct pattern indicated by those clue words.

Comparisons of narrative and script versions of the same stories can help students see the differences in writing styles and help them to learn to look for information in the right places.*

1. What clue word(s) indicate(s) a pattern?

a. comparisons/differences
b. narrative/script
c. versions
d. to learn

2. What pattern is indicated by this topic sentence?

a. comparison/contrast
b. definition
c. cause/effect
d. time order

Categorizing is defined as the grouping together of ideas that have common features.†

3. What clue word(s) indicate(s) a pattern?

a. categorizing
b. is defined as
c. group together
d. features

* From Burns/Roe, Ross, *Teaching Reading,* 7th ed. Boston: Houghton Mifflin, 1999, 436.
† From Burns/Roe, Ross, *Teaching Reading,* 7th ed. Boston: Houghton Mifflin, 1999, 436.

Copyright © Houghton Mifflin Company. All rights reserved.

4. What pattern is indicated by this topic sentence?

   a. comparison/contrast   c. series

   b. cause/effect   d. definition

The protection of people with severe psychological disorders, when they are accused of crimes, takes two forms.*

5. What clue word(s) indicate(s) a pattern?

   a. the protection   c. two forms

   b. with severe   d. when they are accused

6. What pattern is indicated by this topic sentence?

   a. cause/effect   c. time order

   b. definition   d. series

Certain illnesses can lead to severe damage to the placenta and embryo if a woman contracts an illness while pregnant.†

7. What clue word(s) indicate(s) a pattern?

   a. certain illnesses   c. if a woman

   b. severe damage   d. can lead to

8. What pattern is indicated by this topic sentence?

   a. comparison/contrast   c. time order

   b. cause/effect   d. series

There were several developments in the area of cancer research in the 1990s.

9. What clue word(s) indicate(s) a pattern?

   a. there were   c. in the area

   b. several developments   d. in the 1990s

10. What pattern is indicated by this topic sentence?

   a. comparison/contrast   c. time order

   b. definition   d. series

POST-TEST 3

In the list following each paragraph check off the pattern(s) used to organize the supporting details.

* Adapted from Bernstein/Nash, *Essentials of Psychology,* 2nd ed. Boston: Houghton Mifflin, 2002, 444.
† Adapted from Bernstein/Nash, *Essentials of Psychology,* 2nd ed. Boston: Houghton Mifflin, 2002, 303.

Copyright © Houghton Mifflin Company. All rights reserved.

Copyright © Houghton Mifflin Company. All rights reserved.

1. Rather than basing the price of a product on its cost, companies sometimes use a method known as demand-based pricing. Demand-based pricing is defined as pricing based on the level of demand for the product. This method results in a high price when product demand is strong and a low price when demand is weak. Most long-distance telephone companies use demand-based pricing. To use this method, a marketer estimates the amount of a product that customers will demand at different prices and then chooses the price that generates the highest total revenue. Obviously, the effectiveness of this method depends on the firm's ability to estimate demand accurately.*

_____ series

_____ time order

_____ cause/effect

_____ comparison/contrast

_____ definition

2. Specific human resource management activites are assigned to those who are in the best position to perform them. The result is that human resources planning and job analysis are usually done by staff specialists, with input from line managers. In a similar way, recruiting and selection are generally handled by staff experts, although line managers are involved in the actual hiring decisions. Orientation programs are usually devised by staff specialists, and the orientation itself is carried out by both staff specialists and line managers. Compensation systems (including benefits) are most often developed and administered by the HRM staff.†

_____ series

_____ time order

_____ cause/effect

_____ comparison/contrast

_____ definition

3. Several factors contributed to the fact that many people in many parts of Europe lived on the edge of disaster in 1300. Growing numbers of people competed for land to farm and for jobs. Also, farm sizes declined throughout Europe as parents tended to divide their land among their children.

* Adapted from Pride/Hughes/Kapoor, *Business*, 6th ed. Boston: Houghton Mifflin, 1999, 351.

† Adapted from Pride/Hughes/Kapoor, *Business*, 6th ed. Boston: Houghton Mifflin, 1999, 248.

Rents for farmland increased as landlords found they could play one land-hungry farmer against another. Competition for jobs kept wages low, and when taxes were added to high rents and low wages, many peasants and artisans found it difficult to marry and raise families.*

____ series

____ time order

____ cause/effect

____ comparison/contrast

____ definition

4. Social studies is defined as the study of people and their ideas, actions, and relationships. It is different from a discipline such as mathematics or physics because it draws on various disciplines such as history, geography, political science, economics, psychology, sociology, and anthropology, as well as on religion, literature, and the arts, for its content and methods of inquiry. History has traditionally been the leading discipline of the social studies at both the elementary and secondary levels, and remains dominant.†

____ series

____ time order

____ cause/effect

____ comparison/contrast

____ definition

5. How can you as a regular education teacher be effective in teaching children with disabilities in your classroom? There are a number of ways. First, be open to the idea of including students with disabilities in your classroom. Learn about each child's limitations and potential, and about available curriculum methodologies and technologies to help the child learn. Insist that any needed services be provided. Pair students with disabilities with children who can help them. Use a variety of teaching strategies, including hands-on activities, peer tutoring, and cooperative learning strategies. The outcome will be a rich, diverse classroom filled with learning.‡

---

* Adapted from Noble et al., *Western Civilization*. Boston: Houghton Mifflin, 2002, 370.

† Adapted from Ryan/Cooper, *Those Who Can, Teach,* 9th ed. Boston: Houghton Mifflin, 2000, 263.

‡ Adapted from Ryan/Cooper, *Those Who Can, Teach,* 9th ed. Boston: Houghton Mifflin, 2000, 127.

Copyright © Houghton Mifflin Company. All rights reserved.

_____ series

_____ time order

_____ cause/effect

_____ comparison/contrast

_____ definition

6

Copyright © Houghton Mifflin Company. All rights reserved.

Reading Visual Aids

GOALS FOR CHAPTER 7

- Write a reading journal entry.
- Define the term *visual aid*.
- Summarize the reasons authors incorporate visual aids into texts.
- Describe three general steps to follow to interpret a visual aid.
- Define the term *table* and identify its purpose and parts.
- Define the term *organizational chart* and identify its purpose and parts.
- Define the term *flow chart* and identify its purpose and parts.
- Define the term *pie chart* and identify its purpose and parts.
- Define the term *line graph* and identify its purpose and parts.
- Define the term *bar graph* and identify its purpose and parts.
- Define the term *diagram* and identify its purpose and parts.
- Define the term *map* and identify its purpose and parts.

READING STRATEGY: Keeping a Reading Journal

In Chapter 1 of this book, you learned that active readers are those who interact with the text by thinking about what they read. Active researchers also consciously try to connect the text's information to their own experiences and beliefs. One useful strategy for understanding and absorbing new information you read is to keep a reading journal, a notebook in which you record your thoughts about the things you read. These thoughts could include a brief summary of the selection, a list of new ideas or new information you learned, or your reactions to or opinions about the text.

Keeping a reading journal offers two important benefits. First of all, the act of writing helps your thoughts become clearer. You may have some vague ideas or reactions after finishing a text. When you write them down, however, you'll find that trying to find the right words to express

Continued

Copyright © Houghton Mifflin Company. All rights reserved.

7

what you think will actually result in a better understanding of those thoughts. Therefore, the act of writing your response becomes a tool for learning about what that response is. A second benefit comes from creating a written record of your ideas. An entry for each article, chapter, or essay you read for a class, for example, can provide you with a handy reference for study. Later, when you're preparing for a test or completing an assignment, you can simply reread your entries to refresh your memory about the content of each text.

To keep a reading journal, obtain a notebook with blank pages inside. Immediately after you read a text, first write down its title, the author's name, and the date you read it or finished reading it. Then, let your purpose for reading the text determine the type of response you compose. If you'll be expected to discuss the content of the selection in class or write about its topic for an assignment, you may want to record several or all of the following:

- A brief summary of the text.

- Your reaction (your feelings or your own opinions about the subject).

- Your judgment of the selection's merit or accuracy.

- A comparison of this work to other works you've read.

- Your experiences or observations that either support or refute the text's ideas and conclusions.

- Your questions about the text.

If you are reading for your own pleasure or to expand your general knowledge about a particular topic, you might want to focus on just one or two of the items in the list above. No matter what your purpose, though, plan to put forth the little bit of extra effort it takes to better understand what you've read.

Read the following article and then write a reading journal entry that includes at least three of the items in the bulleted list above.

Love Your Problems (and Experience Your Barriers)*

We all have problems and barriers that block our progress or prevent us from moving into new areas. Often, the way we respond to our prob-

* Adapted from Dave Ellis, *Becoming a Master Student*, 9th ed. Boston: Houghton Mifflin, 2000, 98–100.

Continued

Copyright © Houghton Mifflin Company. All rights reserved.

Copyright © Houghton Mifflin Company. All rights reserved.

lems puts boundaries on our experiences. We limit what we allow our-selves to be, do, and have.

Our problems might include fear of speaking in front of a group, anx-iety about math problems, or reluctance to sound silly trying to speak a foreign language. We might have a barrier about trying a new thing and looking silly. Some of us even have anxiety about being successful.

Problems often work like barriers. When we bump up against one of our problems, we usually turn around and start walking along a differ-ent path. And all of a sudden—bump!—we've struck another barrier. And we turn away again.

As we continue to bump into problems and turn away from them, our lives stay inside the same old boundaries. Inside these boundaries, we are unlikely to have new adventures. We are unlikely to improve or make much progress.

The word *problem* is a wonderful word coming from the ancient Greek word *proballein*, which means "to throw forward." In other words, problems are there to provide an opportunity for us to gain new skills. If we respond to problems by loving them instead of resisting them, we can expand the boundaries in which we live our lives. When approached with acceptance and even love, problems can "throw" us forward.

Three Ways to Handle a Barrier

It's natural to have barriers, but sometimes they limit our experience so much that we get bored, angry, or frustrated with life. When this hap-pens, consider the following three ways of dealing with a barrier. One way is to pretend it doesn't exist. Avoid it, deny it, lie about it. It's like turning your head the other way, putting on a fake grin, and saying, "See, there's really no problem at all. Everything is fine. Oh, that prob-lem. That's not a problem, it's not really there."

In addition to looking foolish, this approach leaves the barrier in-tact, and we keep bumping into it. We deny the barrier and might not even be aware that we're bumping into it. For example, a student who has a barrier about math might subconsciously avoid enriching experi-ences that include math.

A second approach is to fight the barrier, to struggle against it. This usually makes the barrier grow. It increases the barrier's magnitude. A person who is obsessed with weight might constantly worry about being fat. He might struggle with it every day, trying diet after diet. And the more he struggles, the bigger the problem gets.

Continued

7

The third alternative is to love the barrier. Accept it. Totally experience it. Tell the truth about it. Describe it in detail. When you do this, the barrier loses its power. You can literally love it to death.

The word *love* might sound like an overstatement. Here, the word means to accept your problems, to allow and permit them. When we fight a problem it grows bigger. The more we fight against it, the stronger it seems to become. When we accept the fact that we have a problem, we are more likely to find effective ways to deal with it.

Suppose one of your barriers is being afraid of speaking in front of a group. You can use any of these three approaches.

First, you can get up in front of the group and pretend you're not afraid. You can fake a smile, not admitting to yourself or the group that you have any concerns about speaking—even though your legs have turned to rubber bands and your mind is jelly. The problem is, everyone in the room will know you're scared, including you, when your hands start shaking and your voice cracks and you forget what you were going to say.

The second way to approach this barrier is to fight it. You could tell yourself, "I'm not going to be scared," and then try to keep your knees from knocking. Generally, this doesn't work. In fact, your knee-knocking might get worse.

The third approach is to go to the front of the room, look out into the audience, and say to yourself, "I am scared. I notice that my knees are shaking, my mouth feels dry, and I'm having a rush of thoughts about what might happen if I say the wrong thing. Yup, I'm scared and that's OK. As a matter of fact, it's just part of me, so I accept it and I'm not going to try to fight it. I'm going to give this speech even though I'm scared."

You might not actually eliminate the fear; however, your barrier about the fear—which is what stops you—might disappear. And you might discover that if you examine the fear, love it, accept it, and totally experience it, the fear itself also disappears.

Applying This Process

Applying this process is easier if you remember two ideas. First, loving a problem is not necessarily the same as enjoying it. Love in this sense means total and unconditional acceptance.

Second, unconditional acceptance is not the same as unconditional surrender. Accepting a problem is different from giving up or escaping from it. Rather, this process involves escaping from the grip of the problem by diving *into* the problem head first and getting to know it in detail.

Continued

Copyright © Houghton Mifflin Company. All rights reserved.

> Loving a problem does not need to keep us stuck in the problem. When people first hear about this process, they often think it means to be resigned to the problem. Actually, loving a problem does not stop us from acting. Loving a problem does not keep us mired in it. In fact, fully accepting and admitting the problem usually assists us in taking effective action—and perhaps in freeing ourselves of the problem once and for all.

As you read, you will often encounter visual aids such as graphs, tables, and diagrams. Learning how to read and interpret these visuals will improve your overall comprehension of a text. To discover what you already know about visuals, complete the following pre-test.

PRE-TEST

A. Look at the following visual from *USA Today* and answer the questions that follow.

Favorite Life Saver Flavors

Flavor	Percentage
Cherry	32%
Butter rum	17%
Wint-o-green	17%
Pineapple	11%
Pep-o-mint	10%

Source: *USA Today*, July 30, 2001, 1D. Copyright © 2001, *USA Today*. Reprinted with permission.

1. What does this visual describe? _____

_____

2. What percentage of people enjoy pineapple Life Savers? _____

3. Are butter rum or pep-o-mint Life Savers more popular? How can you tell?

_____

_____

Copyright © Houghton Mifflin Company. All rights reserved.

7

4. What flavor Life Saver is the least favorite among the people surveyed?

_____

5. What flavor Life Saver is the most popular? _____

B. Study the pie chart entitled "Cultural Diversity in the United States"* and answer the questions below.

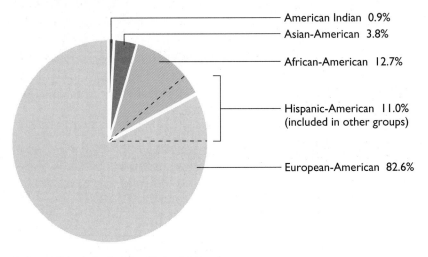

American Indian 0.9%
Asian-American 3.8%
African-American 12.7%
Hispanic-American 11.0%
(included in other groups)
European-American 82.6%

Cultural Diversity in The United States.

Source: Data from U.S. Bureau of the Census, 1997.

6. How many ethnic groups are included in the pie chart? _____

7. What percentage of U.S. citizens are European-Americans? _____

8. What percentage of U.S. citizens are Hispanic-Americans? _____

9. What is the source of the data for this pie chart? _____

10. What is the smallest percentage listed on the pie chart and to which ethnic group does it refer? _____

Visual aids, which are also known as *graphics*, are types of illustrations that represent data or information in a visual form. Visual aids include tables, charts, different types of graphs, diagrams, or maps. You will often encounter all of these kinds of visuals when you read, especially when the purpose of a reading selection is to inform or explain. Publications such as textbooks, magazines, journals, and instruction manuals will often include visuals to aid, or help, the

*From Bernstein et al., *Psychology.* Boston: Houghton Mifflin, 2000, 24.

Copyright © Houghton Mifflin Company. All rights reserved.

reader in understanding the information. Many job-related documents will also contain visual aids.

Texts include visual aids for many reasons. For one thing, they can summarize a lot of information or complex information in a relatively small space. Think about a flow chart, for instance. A flow chart provides a visual summary of the steps in a process. It allows you to see a condensed version of even a complicated procedure.

Another reason for visual aids is their ability to clarify and reinforce textual explanations. In most publications, visual aids do not substitute for written presentation of information. Instead, they provide another way of "seeing" what the words are saying. A diagram in an instruction manual is one example. When you are assembling something like a grill or a child's swing set, it's helpful to check your understanding of the directions by looking at a diagram that labels the parts and shows how they fit together. You use both the written explanation and the visual aid to figure out what you need to do.

Visual aids also allow readers to see quickly the important data or facts. For instance, a graph reveals, at a glance, trends over time. An organizational chart allows readers to quickly grasp the chain of command within a company.

Finally, visual aids provide a way for readers to find a particular detail quickly and easily. A table, for example, that organizes facts into columns and rows allows a reader to easily locate one specific piece of information he or she needs.

General Tips for Reading Visual Aids

The following tips will help you improve your comprehension of reading selections that include visuals:

- **Don't skip a visual aid.** Passive readers ignore visual aids because they don't want to take the time to read them. Skipping visual aids, however, robs you of chances to improve and/or reinforce your understanding of the information in the text. When authors invest the time and effort necessary to create a visual, they do so because they believe a visual representation is particularly important. Therefore, get in the habit of reading over each visual as well as the text.

- **Look at a visual aid when the text directs you to do so.** As you read, you'll come across references to visual aids. Resist the urge to "save them for later." Instead, when a sentence mentions a visual, as in "See Figure 2," or "Table 1 presents the results . . ." and tells you where to find it (below, to the left, on page 163, etc.), find the visual and read it before going any further. Remember, most visuals reinforce information in a text.

Copyright © Houghton Mifflin Company. All rights reserved.

7

The writer's explanation will often state the conclusion you should draw from the visual, and the visual provides more insight into the textual explanation. So, you'll get more out of both of them when you read a passage and its corresponding visual together.

- **Follow a three-step procedure for interpreting the information in a visual aid:**

  1. First, read the title, the caption, and the source line. The title and caption, or brief description, will usually identify the visual aid's subject and main point. They will help you understand what you're seeing. The source line, which identifies where the information comes from, will help you decide whether the information is accurate and trustworthy.

  2. Next, study the information represented in the visual, and try to state the relationships you see in your own words. For example, you might say, "This graph shows that sales of sport utility vehicles have been growing since 1985," or "This table shows that teachers in the Midwest earn higher salaries than teachers in the rest of the country."

  3. Finally, check your understanding of the relationship against its corresponding explanation in the text. Locate where the visual is mentioned, and verify that the conclusion you drew is accurate.

The remainder of this chapter will cover the most common types of visual aids and provide you with more specific tips for improving your understanding of each kind.

Common Types of Visuals

As you read, you'll most often encounter tables, charts, graphs, diagrams, and maps.

Tables

A *table* is a visual aid that organizes information or data in rows and columns. A table might list types, categories, figures, statistics, steps in a process, or other kinds of information. Its purpose is to summarize many related details in a concise format so that readers can read them easily and find specific facts quickly.

Tables contain the following parts:

- **Title.** The title states the visual aid's subject.

- **Column headings.** These labels identify the type of information you'll find in the vertical lists.

Copyright © Houghton Mifflin Company. All rights reserved.

1

- **Row headings.** These labels identify the type of information you'll find in each horizontal list.

- **Source line.** The source line identifies who collected or compiled the information in the table.

These parts are labeled in the following table:*

Table 7.1 Fastest Growing Types of Small Businesses, 1993–1994 — Title

Business	Employment Increase (thousands)	Employment Increase (%)
Boat building and repairing	9.4	20.2
Medical-equipment rental and leasing	5.8	16.9
Dairy-product stores	2.6	15.5
Carpentry and floor work	25.5	13.3
Masonry, stonework, tile setting, and plastering	51.0	12.9
Aluminum foundries	2.8	12.4
Equipment rental and leasing	16.5	11.4
Employment agencies	27.0	11.0
Nonferrous foundries	8.6	10.9
Painting and paperhanging	17.3	10.6
Automotive repair shops	24.5	10.4
Heavy construction equipment, rental and leasing	3.8	10.3
Child day care services	53.8	10.3
Heating equipment manufacture	2.0	10.0
Furniture stores	28.4	10.0
Total	279.0	11.4

Source: From *The State of Small Business: A Report of the President,* Washington, D.C., U.S. Government Printing Office, 1996, 59. — Source line

   To understand the information in a table, first read the title, which will identify the kind of information the table includes. Next, familiarize yourself with the column and row headings. They will identify the kind of details included. Then, form an understanding of the relationships first by moving your eyes down each column to see how details compare, and then across each row to see how those details are related. Finally, try to state in your own words the overall point revealed by the table's lists.

*From Pride et al., *Business,* 6th ed. Boston: Houghton Mifflin, 1999, 117.

Copyright © Houghton Mifflin Company. All rights reserved.

In the table on page 301, the title states that this visual aid will focus on the growth of small businesses between the years 1993 and 1994. These different types of businesses are listed in the first column. The second and third columns include corresponding numerical data. The units in parentheses—(thousands) and (%)—indicate the type of quantities listed. To find information, locate the business that interests you, and follow the row across to find the corresponding numbers. For example, you can see that child day care services increased by 53,800 employees in 1993–1994, which amounts to a 10.3 percent increase in that type of business. That made it the one in the list that experienced the largest increase of employees, although the masonry, stonework, tile setting, and plastering business grew almost as much. The business with the least amount of increase was heating equipment manufacture, although it tied with furniture stores as having the lowest percentage of increase.

Exercise 7.1

Study the table* below and then answer the questions that follow.

Table 7.2   Growth of World Population

Year	Population
1825	1.0 billion
1925	2.0 billion
1976	4.0 billion
1990	5.3 billion
2025 (projected)	8.5 billion

Source: Paul Kennedy, *Preparing for the Twenty-first Century* (New York, 1993), 22–23.

1. How many years are listed in the table for comparison? _____

2. In what year did the world's population reach 2 billion? _____

3. What is the projected world population for the year 2025? _____

4. In what year was the world's population at 1 billion? _____

5. What was the world's population in 1990? _____

*From Bulliet et al., *The Earth and Its Peoples,* Brief Edition. Boston: Houghton Mifflin, 2000, 596.

Copyright © Houghton Mifflin Company. All rights reserved.

Charts

There are different types of charts. Three of the more common are organizational charts, flow charts, and pie charts. Each kind presents a different kind of relationship.

An **organizational chart** is one that shows the chain of command in a company or organization. It uses rectangles and lines to show the managerial relationships between the individuals within a group. Its purpose is to represent the lines of authority and responsibility in the organization.

An organization chart contains the following parts:

- **Title.** The title usually identifies the organization or the part of an organization being described.

- **Boxes.** Each box, or rectangle, represents one entity within the organization. That entity might be an individual or a group of individuals, such as a department. Each box will be labeled with a name, a job title, or a department name. These boxes are arranged in a hierarchy, or ranking: the person or group with the most authority and responsibility is at the top of the chart. Each subsequent row of boxes represents the next layer of authority, a group of people or groups who are equal in rank and who all report to the individual(s) in the layer above.

- **Lines.** The lines connect boxes to show managerial relationships. They indicate who reports to whom. The source line, if applicable, identifies who collected or compiled the information in the chart.

These parts are labeled in the following organizational chart:

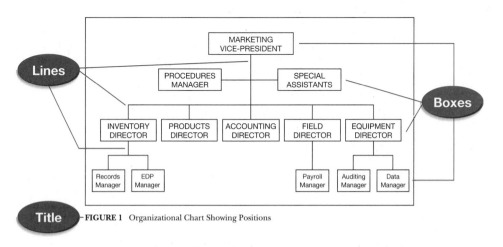

FIGURE 1 Organizational Chart Showing Positions

Source: From Brusaw et al., *The Business Writer's Handbook*, 5th ed. New York: St. Martin's Press, 1997, 422. Copyright © 1997 by Bedford/St. Martin's. Reprinted with permission of Bedford/St. Martin's.

Copyright © Houghton Mifflin Company. All rights reserved.

7

To understand an organizational chart, begin at the top. Read the label in the box at the top, and then follow the lines to see which individuals and groups are related to each other.

The portion of the organizational chart on page 303 shows a company structure that places the marketing vice-president at the top of the hierarchy. That individual has the most authority and responsibility. The staff positions listed beneath the vice-president advise him and report to him, but they do not supervise the different directors who make up the next layer of authority. Those directors report to the vice-president. The branching lines that descend from each box in the chart indicate the number and titles of individuals who are managed by that person.

Exercise 7.2

Study the organizational chart and then answer the questions that follow.

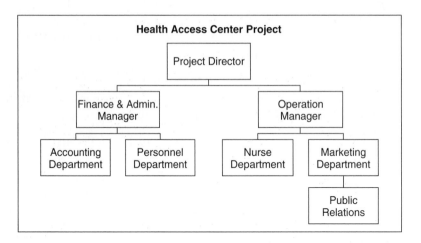

Source: William Murdick, *The Portable Business Writer.* Boston: Houghton Mifflin, 1999, 129. Copyright © 1999 by Houghton Mifflin Company. Reprinted with permission.

1. What is the title of the person in charge of the Health Access Center Project? _____

2. List the two departments that report to the Finance and Administration Manager. _____

3. List the two departments that report to the Operation Manager. _____
_____

Copyright © Houghton Mifflin Company. All rights reserved.

4. To what department does the Public Relations department report?

_____

_____

5. Who reports directly to the Project Director? _____

_____

A **flow chart** is a visual aid composed of boxes, circles, or other shapes along with lines or arrows. The purpose of a flow chart is to represent the sequence of steps or stages in a process.

The parts of a flow chart are:

- **Title.** The title identifies the process or procedure summarized in the chart.

- **Boxes or other shapes.** Each box contains one step in the process. They are arranged either top to bottom or left to right.

- **Lines or arrows.** These show the sequence of steps.

- **Source line.** The source line, if applicable, identifies who collected or compiled the information in the chart.

These parts are labeled in the following flow chart:

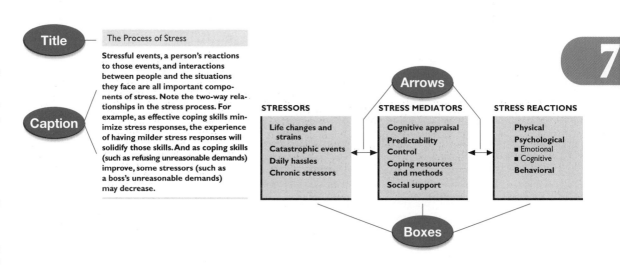

Source: From Bernstein et al., *Psychology,* 4th ed. Boston: Houghton Mifflin, 1997, 431.

Copyright © Houghton Mifflin Company. All rights reserved.

To interpret a flow chart, first read the chart's title so you'll know what process is being summarized. Next, begin with the box at the top, if the chart is organized vertically, or the box at the far left, if the chart is organized horizontally. Read each step in order, following the lines and arrows to understand their sequence.

As the title indicates, the simple flow chart on page 305 summarizes the process of stress. The process begins with stressors, which are listed in the box at the far left. The arrow indicates that the next step is the addition of stress mediators, or factors that lower the stress response. The third step lists the types of reactions that can occur as the result of the stressors and/or mediators. As the caption explains and the arrows in the chart indicate, the process moves backward as well as forward. In other words, certain reactions can improve or strengthen the mediators, which, in turn, actually lessen the stressors.

Exercise 7.3

Study the flow chart below and then answer the questions that follow.

Three Functions of the Nervous System

The nervous system's three main functions involve receiving information (input), integrating that information with past experiences (processing), and guiding actions (output). These functions work in various situations in the service of your motivational state and your goals, helping you do everything from satisfying hunger to getting a job.

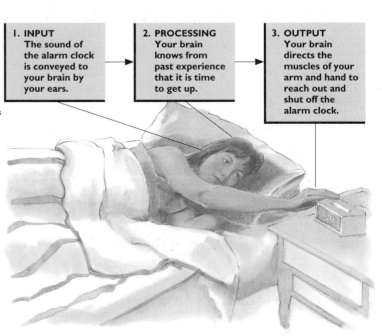

1. INPUT The sound of the alarm clock is conveyed to your brain by your ears.

2. PROCESSING Your brain knows from past experience that it is time to get up.

3. OUTPUT Your brain directs the muscles of your arm and hand to reach out and shut off the alarm clock.

Source: Bernstein et al., *Psychology.* Boston: Houghton Mifflin, 2000, 53.

Copyright © Houghton Mifflin Company. All rights reserved.

1. What are the three major functions of the nervous system? _____

   _____

2. What example is used to illustrate the three functions of the nervous system on the flow chart? _____

   _____

3. As illustrated on the flow chart, what happens during the "input" stage?

   _____

   _____

4. According to the chart, what happens during step #2, or during the "processing" part illustrated on the flow chart? _____

   _____

5. During what stage illustrated on the flow chart does your "brain direct the muscles of your arm and hand to reach out and shut off the alarm clock"?

   _____

A third kind of chart is called a **pie chart**. This visual aid is a circle that is divided into wedges or slices, like the pieces of a pie. The purpose of a pie chart is to show the composition of something; it indicates the amounts of each part that make up the whole. Each part is identified with a percentage or other quantity that indicates its size in relation to all of the other parts. One common use of pie charts is to represent financial information such as budgets or expenditures.

Pie charts contain the following parts:

- **Title.** The title identifies the whole entity that is being divided into parts.

- **Lines.** The lines radiate from the center of the circle, dividing the pie in pieces that represent the amount of each part. These pieces are different sizes because they are designed to be proportional to the whole.

- **Labels for names of parts.** Each piece is labeled to identify one part and its quantity in relation to the whole.

- **Source line.** The source line identifies who collected or compiled the information.

Copyright © Houghton Mifflin Company. All rights reserved.

7

These parts are labeled in the following pie chart:*

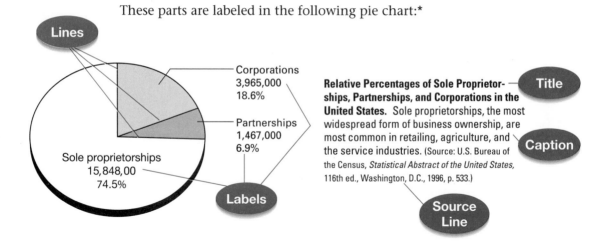

To read a pie chart, first look at its title so you'll know the whole entity that is being divided. Then, read each label and amount. Try to summarize in your own words the relationships you see and notice the biggest part, the smallest part, and parts that are about equal.

The pie chart above shows the amounts of three forms of business ownership. The largest piece of the pie represents sole proprietorships, which account for almost 75 percent of all businesses. Corporations are the next biggest group, and partnerships are the smallest. The percentages all add up to 100 percent to represent the whole. The caption provides more information by naming some examples of specific sole proprietorship businesses.

Exercise 7.4

Study the pie chart on page 309 and then answer the questions below.

1. What percentage of people spend between 16 and 30 minutes with their doctor during an office visit? _____

2. What percentage of people spend the least amount of time with their doctor during an office visit? _____

3. What percentage of people spend the most amount of time with their doctor during an office visit? _____

4. What percentage of people spend between 6 and 10 minutes with their doctor during an office visit? _____

*From Pride et al., *Business,* 6th ed. Boston: Houghton Mifflin, 1999, 87.

Copyright © Houghton Mifflin Company. All rights reserved.

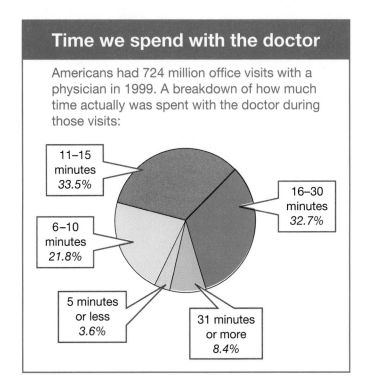

Time we spend with the doctor

Americans had 724 million office visits with a physician in 1999. A breakdown of how much time actually was spent with the doctor during those visits:

11–15 minutes *33.5%*

16–30 minutes *32.7%*

6–10 minutes *21.8%*

5 minutes or less *3.6%*

31 minutes or more *8.4%*

Source: From *USA Today*, July 24, 2001, 1A. Copyright © 2001, *USA Today*. Reprinted with permission.

5. According to the caption that accompanies the pie chart, how many office visits did Americans have with a physician in 1999? _____

Graphs

A **graph** is a visual aid composed of lines or bars that correspond to numbers or facts arranged along a vertical axis, or side, and a horizontal axis. The purpose of a graph is to show changes or differences in amounts, quantities, or characteristics. Two types of graphs are the line graph and the bar graph. Each one presents information differently.

A **line graph** is composed of points plotted within a vertical axis and a horizontal axis and then connected with lines. Line graphs typically reveal changes or trends in numerical data over time. They demonstrate how two factors interact with each other. The horizontal axis is labeled with increments of time, such as years or minutes. The vertical axis is labeled with quantities. For each point in time, a dot on the graph indicates the corresponding quantity. Then, these dots are all connected to show upward and downward movement.

Line graphs contain the following parts:

Copyright © Houghton Mifflin Company. All rights reserved.

- **Title.** The title points out the type of numbers being examined. It corresponds to the label of the vertical axis.

- **Vertical axis.** This line, which runs up and down, is divided into regular increments of numbers that correspond to the type of data being tracked. This axis is labeled to identify the type of data.

- **Horizontal axis.** This line, which runs from left to right, is divided into segments of time. It, too, is labeled to identify the kind of time factor being used.

- **Points.** Numerical data are plotted at the points where numbers and time factors intersect on the grid. These points may be labeled with specific amounts.

- **Lines.** Points are connected with lines to show trends.

- **Source line.** The source line identifies who collected or compiled the information in the graph.

These parts are labeled on the following line graph:

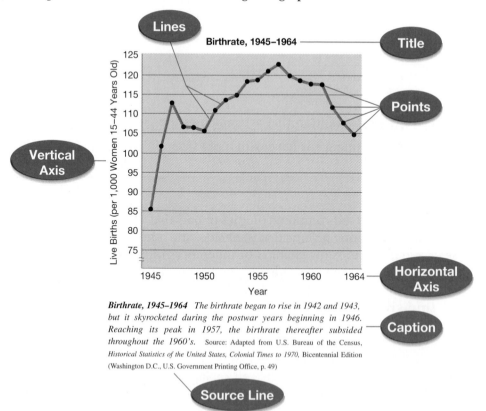

Birthrate, 1945–1964   *The birthrate began to rise in 1942 and 1943, but it skyrocketed during the postwar years beginning in 1946. Reaching its peak in 1957, the birthrate thereafter subsided throughout the 1960's.*   Source: Adapted from U.S. Bureau of the Census, *Historical Statistics of the United States, Colonial Times to 1970,* Bicentennial Edition (Washington D.C., U.S. Government Printing Office, p. 49)

From Norton et al., *A People and a Nation,* 5th ed., Vol. II. Boston: Houghton Mifflin, 1998, 830.

Copyright © Houghton Mifflin Company. All rights reserved.

To read a line graph, begin with the title. Read it carefully to understand the numerical value on which the graph focuses. Then, read the labels on the vertical and horizontal axes to understand what two factors are interacting. Finally, examine the line that connects the points and try to state in your own words the trends being revealed by the numbers. Do the numbers increase, decrease, or both? When? How much overall change has occurred during the time span indicated on the horizontal axis?

As the title indicates, the line graph on page 310 illustrates the birthrate in America between 1945 and 1964. The vertical axis is divided into numbers of live births. The horizontal axis is divided into years. The points plotted on this grid are connected, which clearly reveals, among other things, that the birthrate climbed steadily between 1950 and 1957, the year it reached its peak, and then began a steady decline.

Exercise 7.5

Study the line graph below and then answer the questions that follow.

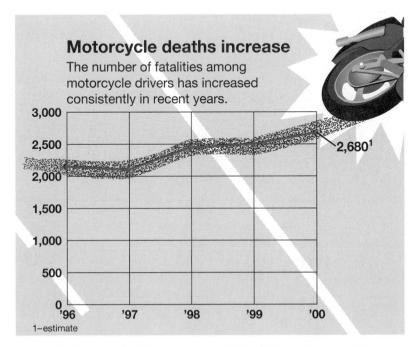

Source: *USA Today,* July 30, 2001, 1A. Copyright © 2001, *USA Today.* Reprinted with permission.

Copyright © Houghton Mifflin Company. All rights reserved.

1. In 1997, did motorcycle deaths increase or decrease? _____

2. In 1998, did motorcycle deaths increase or decrease? _____

3. How many people died as a result of a motorcycle accident in the year 2000? _____

4. In what year were the number of motorcycle deaths the highest? _____

5. In what year were the number of motorcycle deaths the lowest? _____

A second kind of graph is a **bar graph**. Bar graphs indicate quantities of something with bars, or rectangles. These bars can run upward from the horizontal axis, or sideways from the vertical axis of the graph. Each bar is labeled to show what is being measured. While the line graph includes a time factor, the bar graph may not; it focuses on varying quantities of some factor or factors, although it may include several sets of bars that correspond to different time periods.

A bar graph includes the following parts:

- **Title.** The title reveals the entity that's being measured. Depending on how the graph is arranged, this subject may correspond to either the vertical or the horizontal axis.

- **Vertical axis.** This line, which runs up and down, is labeled with either a kind of quantity or the entities being measured.

- **Horizontal axis.** This line, which runs from left to right, is labeled to identify either a kind of quantity or the entities being measured.

- **Bars.** Each bar rises to the line on the grid that matches the quantity it represents. Each bar may be labeled with a specific number.

- **Key.** If entities are broken down into subgroups, the graph may include bars of different colors to represent each group. In that case, a key, or explanation of what each color signifies, may accompany the graph.

- **Source line.** The source line identifies who collected or compiled the information in the bar graph.

These parts are labeled on the bar graph on page 313.

To interpret the information in a bar graph, read the title first to find out what is being measured. Next, read the labels of the vertical and horizontal axes to understand how the graph is arranged and what type of quantity is being used. Finally, examine each bar, and try to state, in your own words,

Copyright © Houghton Mifflin Company. All rights reserved.

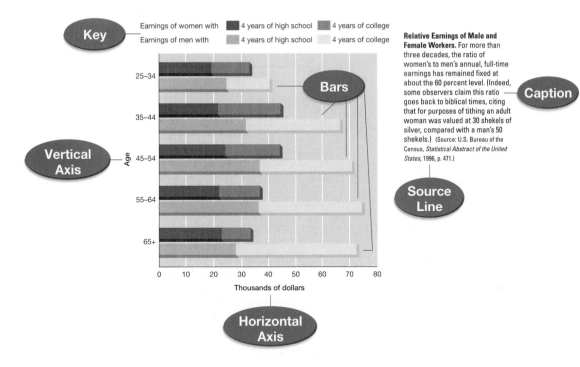

Key
Earnings of women with ▮ 4 years of high school ▮ 4 years of college
Earnings of men with ▮ 4 years of high school ▮ 4 years of college

Relative Earnings of Male and Female Workers. For more than three decades, the ratio of women's to men's annual, full-time earnings has remained fixed at about the 60 percent level. (Indeed, some observers claim this ratio goes back to biblical times, citing that for purposes of tithing an adult woman was valued at 30 shekels of silver, compared with a man's 50 shekels.) (Source: U.S. Bureau of the Census, *Statistical Abstract of the United States*, 1996, p. 471.)

Caption

Bars

Vertical Axis

Age
25–34
35–44
45–54
55–64
65+

Source Line

0 10 20 30 40 50 60 70 80
Thousands of dollars

Horizontal Axis

the relationship among them. Which entity is largest? Smallest? Are there large discrepancies between two or more of the entities?

The bar graph above* shows how much money men and women with different levels of education earn at different ages. Among the notable relationships indicated by the bars are the following:

- College-educated men and women always earn more than high school graduates.

- At any age or education level, men always earn more than women earn.

- Men aged 55 to 64 with only a high school education earn almost as much as women of the same age who have a college education.

- Men earn their highest salaries—up to $75,000—when they are between 55 and 64 years of age.

- Women earn their highest salaries—up to $45,000—when they are between 35 and 44, although the 45–54-year-old age group is a close second.

Notice how the four different shades are identified in a key at the top to help you understand all of the different groups represented in this one graph.

*From Pride et al., *Business*, 6th ed. Boston: Houghton Mifflin, 1999, 45.

7

Copyright © Houghton Mifflin Company. All rights reserved.

Copyright © Houghton Mifflin Company. All rights reserved.

Exercise 7.6

Study the bar graph below and then answer the questions that follow.

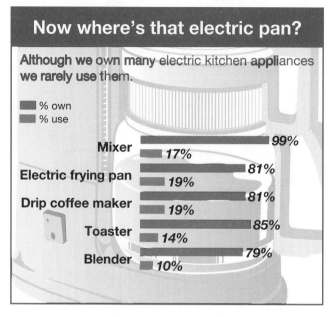

Source: From *USA Today*, July 24, 2001, 1D. Copyright © 2001, *USA Today*.
Reprinted with permission.

1. What percentage of Americans owns an electric frying pan? _____

2. What percentage of Americans uses a toaster? _____

3. Of all of the appliances listed, which one is owned by the largest percentage of Americans? _____

4. Of all the appliances listed, which two appliances are used by the largest percentage of Americans? _____

5. How many Americans actually use their blender? _____

Diagrams

A **diagram** is a visual aid that includes a pictorial illustration, usually in the form of a drawing created by hand or by computer. The purpose of diagrams is to clarify and condense written information through images, so they are very common in instruction manuals and textbooks. They often illustrate processes or sequences of information.

A diagram typically contains these parts:

- **Title.** The title identifies the subject of the drawing.

- **A picture or series of pictures.** Diagrams communicate information through images.

- **Labels.** Parts or areas of the images will often be labeled to identify what they are.

- **Key.** A diagram that contains special symbols, colors, or shading will usually include a key to explain what these features represent.

These parts are labeled on the following diagram:

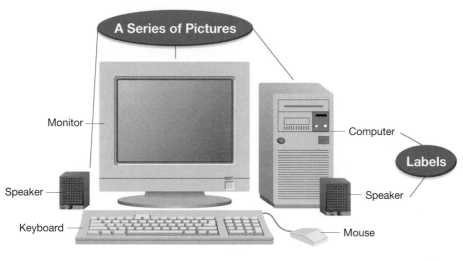

Source: From William Murdick and Jonathan C. Bloemker, *The Portable Technical Writer.* Boston: Houghton Mifflin, 2001, 170.

Reading a diagram begins with understanding the subject and main point identified in the title. Then, you can examine the labeled parts of the diagram to understand how they illustrate that point. Also, make sure you review the key, if applicable, to help you draw accurate conclusions.

The diagram illustrates the components of a standard computer. It includes line drawings of the various parts along with labels to identify each part.

Copyright © Houghton Mifflin Company. All rights reserved.

Exercise 7.7

Study the diagram below and then answer the questions that follow.

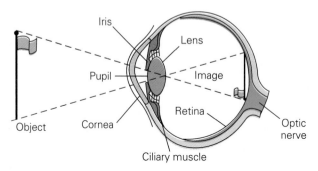

The Human Eye

The lens of the human eye forms an image on the retina, which contains rod and cone cells. The rods are more sensitive than the cones and are responsible for light and dark "twilight" vision; the cones are responsible for color vision.

Source: From Shipman, et al., *An Introduction to Physical Science*, 9th ed. Boston: Houghton Mifflin, 2000, 166. Copyright © 2000, by Houghton Mifflin Company. Reprinted with permission.

1. What is the topic of this diagram? _____

2. What is the object that the eye sees in this diagram? _____

   _____

3. According to the text accompanying the diagram, which are more sensitive, rods or cones? _____

4. Which parts of the eye are responsible for color vision? _____

5. What part of the eye, according to the graph, is at the back of the eye?

   _____

Maps

A **map** is a visual depiction of an area and its physical characteristics. Maps illustrate spatial relationships; for example, they show sizes and borders and distances from one place to another. They can also be used to make compar-

Copyright © Houghton Mifflin Company. All rights reserved.

isons. For instance, a map of the United States may color in the states that apply the death penalty in red and color those that don't blue.

Here are the parts of a map:

- **Title.** The title identifies either the area itself or the relationship between different areas.

- **A diagram of the area.** A map includes a proportionate drawing that represents the geographical features and spatial relationships.

- **Key.** Many maps incorporate symbols, so the key explains what these symbols mean.

- **Labels.** Maps will usually label parts or features that help the reader understand the overall point stated in the title.

- **Source line.** The source line identifies who collected or compiled the information shown in the map.

The map below labels all of these parts:

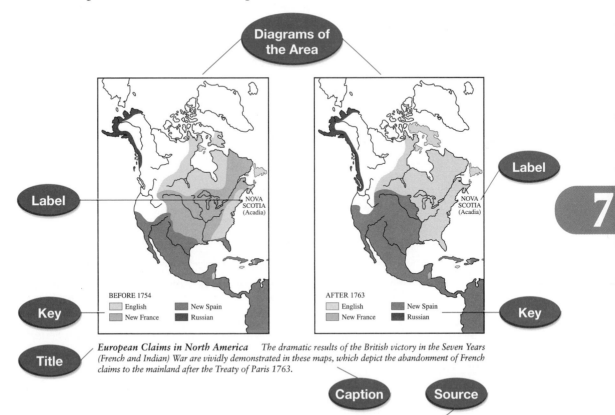

European Claims in North America The dramatic results of the British victory in the Seven Years (French and Indian) War are vividly demonstrated in these maps, which depict the abandonment of French claims to the mainland after the Treaty of Paris 1763.

Source: From Norton et al., *A People and a Nation*, 5th ed., Vol. I. Boston: Houghton Mifflin, 1998, 126.

Copyright © Houghton Mifflin Company. All rights reserved.

To interpret a map, read the title first to understand the idea or information on which you should focus. Then, familiarize yourself with symbols in the key (including the scale that indicates distance, if applicable) and read the labels that name different areas. If the map is illustrating some comparison, try to state in your own words a conclusion based on that comparison.

The visual aid on page 317 is composed of two maps that illustrate several different sets of relationships. In the first map, as the key indicates, the English claims in North America before 1754 were roughly equal to those of the French and Spanish. Notice how the continent is shaded with different shadings that correspond to the four different nations. These shadings show the relationship of the areas to each other. The second map, which represents these same countries' claims after 1763, reveals a much different distribution. France (represented by a light shading) has been virtually eliminated, and the English and Spanish have overtaken France's former areas. Taken together, the two different maps show the significant changes that occurred in less than ten years in North America.

Exercise 7.8

Study the map on page 319 and then answer the questions below.

1. Name three cities that qualify as Federal Reserve branch cities. _____

   _____

   _____

   _____

   _____

2. Name three cities that qualify as Federal Reserve Bank cities. _____

   _____

   _____

3. What city is home to the Board of Governors of the Federal Reserve System? _____

4. How would you classify Boston: as a Federal Reserve Bank city or a Federal Reserve branch city? _____

5. How would you classify El Paso: as a Federal Reserve Bank city or a Federal Reserve branch city? _____

Copyright © Houghton Mifflin Company. All rights reserved.

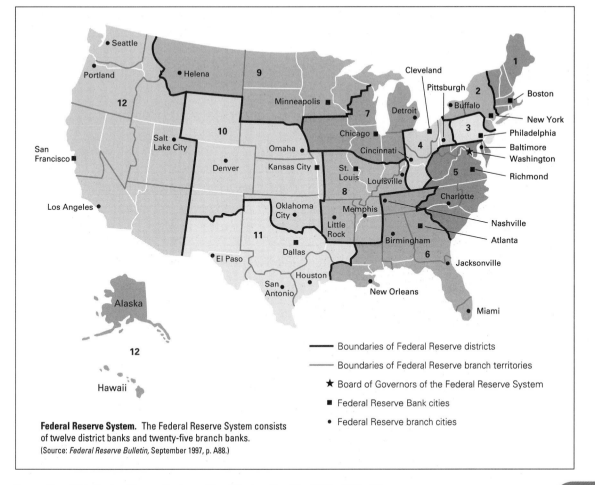

Federal Reserve System. The Federal Reserve System consists of twelve district banks and twenty-five branch banks.
(Source: *Federal Reserve Bulletin,* September 1997, p. A88.)

Source: From Pride/Hughes/Kapoor, *Business,* 6th ed. Boston: Houghton Mifflin, 1999, 483.

CHAPTER 7 REVIEW

Fill in the blanks in the following statements.

1. _____ are types of illustrations that represent data or information in a visual form.

2. Visual aids _____ information in a small space, clarify and reinforce _____, allow readers to see important _____ easily, and provide a way for readers to find a particular _____ quickly.

Copyright © Houghton Mifflin Company. All rights reserved.

3. To interpret the information in a visual aid, first read the _____, caption, and _____. Next, try to state in your own words the relationships you see. Finally, check your understanding of those relationships by reviewing the corresponding explanation in the _____.

4. A _____ is a visual aid that organizes information or data in rows and columns. It summarizes related details so readers can find them quickly and easily.

5. An _____ is a hierarchy of boxes and lines that are connected to show lines of authority and responsibility in an organization.

6. A _____ represents the sequence of steps in a process.

7. A _____ is a circle divided into wedges that indicate the amounts of each part that make up a whole.

8. A _____ plots points on a grid and then connects them to show changes or trends in numerical data over time.

9. A _____ identifies quantities of something.

10. A _____ is a pictorial illustration, usually in the form of a drawing created by hand or by computer.

11. A _____ is a visual depiction of an area and its physical characteristics. It illustrates spatial relationships and/or makes comparisons.

7

Copyright © Houghton Mifflin Company. All rights reserved.

Reading Selection

Encouraging Ethical Behavior

1 Codes of ethics that companies provide to their employees are perhaps the most effective way to encourage ethical behavior. A code of ethics is a written guide to acceptable and ethical behavior as defined by an organization. It outlines uniform policies, standards, and punishments for violations. Employees know what is expected of them and what will happen if they violate the rules. So, a code of ethics goes a long way toward encouraging ethical behavior. However, codes cannot possibly cover every situation. Companies must also create an environment in which employees recognize the importance of complying with the written code. Managers must provide direction by fostering communication, actively modeling and encouraging ethical decision making, and training employees to make ethical decisions.

2 During the 1980s, an increasing number of organizations created and implemented ethics codes. In a recent survey of *Fortune* 1000 firms, 93 percent of the companies that responded reported having a formal code of ethics. Some companies are now even taking steps to strengthen their codes. For example, to strengthen its accountability, the Health-care Financial Management Association recently revised its code to designate contact persons who handle reports of ethics violations. This organization's new code also clarifies how its board of directors should deal with violations of business ethics. It guarantees a fair hearing process, too. S. C. Johnson & Son, makers of Pledge, Drano, Windex, and many other household products, is another firm that recognizes it must behave in ways the public perceives as ethical. Its code includes expectations for employees and its commitment to consumers, the community, and society in general. Included in the ethics code of electronic giant Texas Instruments are issues relating to policies and procedures; laws and regulations; relationships with customers, suppliers, and competitors; conflicts of interest; handling of proprietary information; and code enforcement. For an example of a code of ethics, see NCR Corporation's "Shared Values" that follows on the next page. (NCR is the world leader in manufacturing of automated teller machines and bar code scanners.)

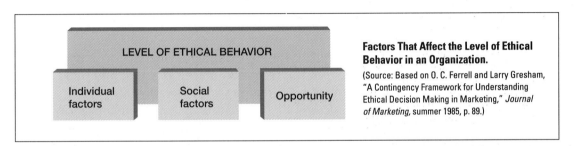

Factors That Affect the Level of Ethical Behavior in an Organization.
(Source: Based on O. C. Ferrell and Larry Gresham, "A Contingency Framework for Understanding Ethical Decision Making in Marketing," *Journal of Marketing,* summer 1985, p. 89.)

From Pride/Hughes/Kapoor, *Business.* Boston: Houghton Mifflin, 1999, 34–36.

Copyright © Houghton Mifflin Company. All rights reserved.

NCR

NCR's Shared Values

NCR Shared Values provides a global consistent framework for conducting business. They define our business relationships with our customers, partners, suppliers, and employees by being the foundation of NCR's reputation. Therefore, we use NCR Shared Values to direct our behavior, guide our decisions, and achieve our business objectives.

▶**Respect for Each Other**

We base our working relationship upon trust and respect. To be successful, we team globally across boundaries, valuing individual differences. We communicate openly and candidly with each other and extend our team spirit to partners, customers, and the communities in which we live and work.

▶**Customer Dedication**

We are dedicated to serving customers by leading our industry in understanding and anticipating customer needs. We create long-term customer relationships by consistently delivering quality, innovation, and value that meet or exceed expectations.

▶**Highest Standards of Integrity**

We are honest and ethical in all our business dealings. We keep our commitments and admit our mistakes. We know our company's reputation is built upon our conduct. We make the NCR name worthy of trust.

▶**Commitment of Excellence**

We are committed to uncompromising excellence. We set ever-higher quality standards and work together to continuously improve. We embrace creativity, encourage a growth-oriented culture, and apply innovation in our processes, ideas, products, and services—to achieve best-in-class performance.

▶**Accountability for Success**

We take personal ownership for the success of our company. We are accountable for the resources entrusted to us. We perceive profit as the means to fuel new solutions for our customers, create opportunities for each other, and reward the financial trust of our shareowners, while applying all of our Shared Values.

Defining Acceptable Behavior: NCR Shared Values. NCR encourages ethical behavior through and extensive training program and a written code of ethics and shared values. (Source: Courtesy of NCR Corporation.)

3   Assigning an ethics officer who coordinates ethical conduct gives employees someone to consult if they aren't sure of the right thing to do. An ethics officer meets with employees and top management to provide ethical advice. He or she also establishes and maintains an anonymous confidential service to answer questions about ethical issues, and takes action on ethics-code violations.

4   It is difficult for an organization to develop ethics codes, policies, and procedures to deal with all relationships and every situation. When no company policy or proce-

Copyright © Houghton Mifflin Company. All rights reserved.

dure exists or applies, a quick test to determine if a behavior is ethical is to see if others—coworkers, customers, suppliers—approve of it. Ethical decisions will always

withstand scrutiny. Openness and communication about choices will often build trust
and strengthen business relationships.

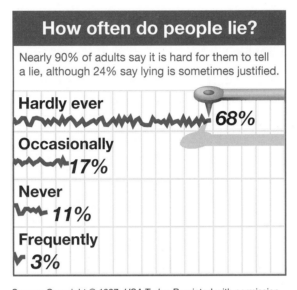

Source: Copyright © 1997, *USA Today*. Reprinted with permission.

(From Pride/Hughes/Kapoor, *Business*. Boston: Houghton Mifflin, 1999, 34–36. Copyright © 1999
by Houghton Mifflin Company. Reprinted with permission.)

VOCABULARY

Read the following questions about some of the vocabulary words that appear
in the previous selection. Circle the correct responses.

1. As used in paragraph 1, what does the word *complying* mean? "Companies
   must also create an environment in which employees recognize the importance of *complying* with the written code."

   a. going along with   c. gluing together
   b. disagreeing with   d. combining

2. "Managers must provide direction by *fostering* communication, actively
   modeling and encouraging ethical decision making . . ." In paragraph 1,
   what does *fostering* mean?

   a. discouraging   c. talking about
   b. encouraging   d. denying

Copyright © Houghton Mifflin Company. All rights reserved.

7

3. "During the 1980s, an increasing number of organizations created and *implemented* ethics codes." What does *implemented* mean in paragraph 2?

   a. destroyed
   b. put into place
   c. ruled out
   d. talked about

4. What does the word *accountability* mean as used in paragraph 2?

   a. trustworthiness
   b. happiness
   c. responsibility
   d. lack of responsibility

5. In paragraph 2, the authors used the word *proprietary* to describe information. What does *proprietary* mean?

   a. public
   b. in the media
   c. private
   d. nonexclusive

6. Paragraph 4 states, "Ethical decisions will always withstand *scrutiny*." What does *scrutiny* mean as used in this sentence?

   a. microscopes
   b. reading
   c. discussion
   d. close inspection or examination

TOPICS, MAIN IDEAS, SUPPORTING DETAILS, TRANSITIONS, AND VISUAL AIDS

Answer the following questions.

1. What is the topic of this selection?

   a. ethical managers
   b. ethical employees
   c. codes of ethics
   d. business

2. What is the main idea of paragraph 1?

   a. A code of ethics is a written document.
   b. Codes of ethics are the best way to encourage ethical behavior in the workplace.
   c. Many employees lie.
   d. Many employees are ethical.

3. Which of the following is NOT one of the companies used in paragraph 2 as an example of a corporation with a code of ethics?

   a. NCR
   b. S. C. Johnson & Son
   c. Pledge Company
   d. Healthcare Financial Management Association

4. Which of the following is NOT an example of a transition used in this selection?

Copyright © Houghton Mifflin Company. All rights reserved.

a. however   c. during the 1980s
b. by the way   d. for example

5. What percentage of people surveyed in the *USA Today* visual entitled "How Often Do People Lie?" say that they hardly ever lie?
   a. 3 percent   c. 17 percent
   b. 11 percent   d. 68 percent

6. How many points are there in NCR's "Shared Values"?
   a. 3   c. 5
   b. 4   d. 6

7. Which of the following is NOT one of the factors that affect the level of ethical behavior in an organization, as seen in the first visual that accompanies the selection?
   a. individual factors   c. motivational factors
   b. social factors   d. opportunity

QUESTIONS FOR DISCUSSION AND WRITING

Answer the following questions based on your reading of the selection.

1. Have you ever worked for a company that had a code of ethics? If so, describe some of the things that were included. If not, list a few items that you would include in a code of ethics. _____

   _____

2. Have you ever encountered unethical behavior in the workplace? What was your reaction to it? _____

   _____

3. Do you think the idea of having a company code of ethics is a good idea? Why or why not? _____

   _____

7

▶ Vocabulary: The Contrast Context Clue

In Chapters 4, 5, and 6, you learned about the three different types of context clues: definition/restatement, explanation, and example. One last type of context clue is **contrast.** In this type of clue, nearby words, phrases, or sentences may give the *opposite* meaning of the unfamiliar word, allowing you to conclude what it means by noticing this contrast. For example, read this next sentence, which comes from one of the paragraphs in Chapter 4:

Copyright © Houghton Mifflin Company. All rights reserved.

Shaquille O'Neal and Kobe Bryant, who play on the Los Angeles Lakers basketball team, sometimes try too hard to show that there's no *animosity* between them, with displays of affection in front of the cameras that feel forced.

If you're wondering what *animosity* means, you can look to the remainder of the paragraph, which includes a contrast clue. The word is contrasted with "displays of affection"; therefore, it must mean the opposite: "hatred or hostility."

Vocabulary Exercise

The following examples all come from paragraphs in Chapters 4, 5, and 6. In each one, use the explanation context clue to help you determine the meaning of the boldfaced, italicized word, and write a definition for this word on the blank provided.

1. People used to stop their lives to pay close attention when astronauts went into space, but now, the Space Shuttle goes up and comes back with little ***fanfare.*** _____

2. Unlike the old electric-only cars, the new gasoline-electric ***hybrid*** cars work by transferring power back and forth between a gasoline engine and an electric motor. _____

3. Authoritarian parents tend to be strict, ***punitive,*** and unsympathetic. They value obedience from children and try to shape their children's behavior to meet a set standard and to curb the children's wills. They do not encourage independence. They are detached and seldom praise their youngsters. In contrast, permissive parents give their children complete freedom and lax discipline. _____

4. Authoritarian parents tend to be strict, punitive, and unsympathetic. They value obedience from children and try to shape their children's behavior to meet a set standard and to curb the children's wills. They do not encourage independence. They are detached and seldom praise their youngsters. In contrast, permissive parents give their children complete freedom and ***lax*** discipline. _____

5. By loving your enemy and responding with grace and dignity, you can increase the chances of disempowering the ***antagonism*** while inviting productive communication. _____

6. To a potential employer, your portfolio gives observable evidence of your skills and achievements. In both cases, a portfolio also documents something more ***intangible***—your levels of energy, passion, and creativity.

_____

Copyright © Houghton Mifflin Company. All rights reserved.

Name _____ Date _____

POST-TEST 1

Study the table below and then answer the questions that follow. Circle the correct choice.

Periods of Egyptian History

Period	Dates	Significant Events
Archaic	3100–2660 B.C.	Unification of Egypt
Old Kingdom	2660–2180 B.C.	Construction of the pyramids
First Intermediate	2180–2080 B.C.	Political chaos
Middle Kingdom	2080–1640 B.C.	Recovery and political stability
Second Intermediate	1640–1570 B.C.	Hyksos "invasion"
New Kingdom	1570–1075 B.C.	Creation of an Egyptian empire Akhenaten's religious policy

From McKay et al., *A History of World Societies,* Vol. I. Boston: Houghton Mifflin, 2001, 21. Copyright © 2001 by Houghton Mifflin Company. Reprinted with permission.

1. What was the period of the Middle Kingdom?
   - a. 3100–2660 B.C.
   - b. 2080–1640 B.C.
   - c. 1570–1075 B.C.
   - d. 2180–2080 B.C.

2. Which significant event occurred during the Archaic period?
   - a. Unification of Egypt
   - b. Hyksos "invasion"
   - c. Recovery and political stability
   - d. Political chaos

3. Which of the following periods came first, according to the table?
   - a. Second Intermediate
   - b. New Kingdom
   - c. Middle Kingdom
   - d. Old Kingdom

4. The period from 1570–1075 B.C. is called the
   - a. Archaic period
   - b. First Intermediate period
   - c. New Kingdom
   - d. Old Kingdom

For tests on flow charts, bar graphs, diagrams, and maps, see the Test Bank.

Copyright © Houghton Mifflin Company. All rights reserved.

7

5. Political chaos occurred during the

   a. First Intermediate period   c. Archaic period
   b. New Kingdom   d. Middle Kingdom

POST-TEST 2

Study the organizational chart below and then answer the questions that follow. Circle the correct choice.

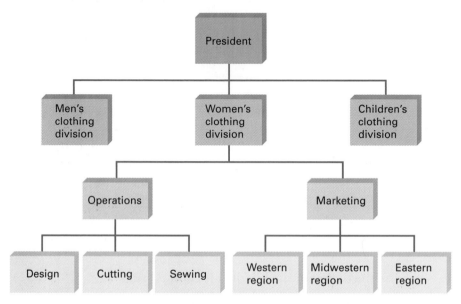

Multibase Departmentalization for New-Wave Fashions, Inc. Most firms use more than one basis for departmentalization to improve efficiency and to avoid overlapping positions. From Pride et al., *Business,* 6th ed. Boston: Houghton Mifflin, 1999, 172.

1. To what division does Marketing directly report?

   a. Children's clothing division   c. Women's clothing division
   b. President   d. Midwestern region

2. The Sewing department is on the same organizational level as

   a. Operations   c. President
   b. Marketing   d. Cutting

3. What are two of the three departments that report to Marketing?

   a. Eastern Region and Midwestern Region
   b. Children's clothing division and Women's clothing division
   c. Midwestern Region and Operations
   d. Cutting and Sewing

Copyright © Houghton Mifflin Company. All rights reserved.

7

4. The Men's clothing division reports directly to

   a. Women's clothing division.   c. Operations.

   b. the President.   d. Children's clothing division.

5. Design, Cutting, and Sewing report directly to

   a. the President.   c. Marketing.

   b. the Men's clothing division.   d. Operations.

POST-TEST 3

Study the flow chart below and then answer the questions that follow. Circle the correct choice.

▼ **Flow Chart for a Writing Plan**

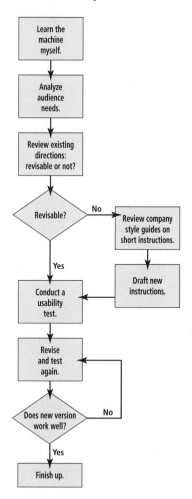

From Murdick/Bloemker, *The Portable Technical Writer.* Boston: Houghton Mifflin, 2001, 72.

Copyright © Houghton Mifflin Company. All rights reserved.

7

1. The third step in the writing plan is
    a. review company style guidelines on short instructions.
    b. learn the machine myself.
    c. analyze audience needs.
    d. review existing directions: revisable or not?

2. The final stage in the writing plan is
    a. revise.   c. finish up.
    b. edit.   d. draft new instructions.

3. If the existing directions are not revisable, what is the first thing you should do?
    a. Draft new instructions
    b. Review company style guides on short instructions
    c. Conduct a usability test
    d. Revise and test again

4. The first thing you should do before you begin writing is
    a. examine the guidelines.   c. look at the instructions.
    b. learn the machine.   d. analyze audience needs.

5. If the new version does not work well, you should
    a. revise and test again.   c. conduct a usability test.
    b. finish up.   d. draft new instructions.

POST-TEST 4

Study the pie chart* on page 331 and then answer the questions below. Circle the correct response.

1. What percentage of businesses are wholesale businesses?
    a. 22.7%   c. 1.7%
    b. 37.6%   d. 8.0%

2. 22.7% of small businesses are
    a. construction businesses.   c. service businesses.
    b. retailing businesses.   d. transportation businesses.

3. According to the chart, besides the "Other" category, small businesses have the smallest percentage in which two industries?
    a. transportation and manufacturing c. retailing and services
    b. financial and insurance   d. wholesale and manufacturing

*From Griffin, *Management*, 7th ed. Boston: Houghton Mifflin, 2000, 294.

Copyright © Houghton Mifflin Company. All rights reserved.

7

Small Businesses (Businesses with Less Than Twenty Employees) by Industry

Small businesses are especially strong in certain industries such as retailing and services. On the other hand, there are relatively fewer small businesses in industries such as transportation and manufacturing. The differences are affected primarily by factors such as the investment costs necessary to enter markets in these industries. For example, starting a new airline would require the purchase of large passenger aircraft and airport gates and hiring an expensive set of employees.

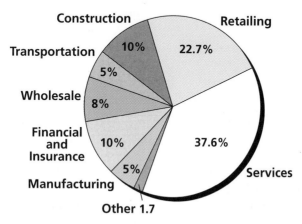

Source: U.S. Census Bureau, Statistical Abstract of the United States: 1999 (119th edition), Washington, D.C., 1999.

4. The "Other" category of small businesses accounts for what percentage on the pie chart?

a. 22.7%   c. 1.7%
b. 5%   d. 37.6%

5. After retailing, the largest percentage of small businesses are

a. construction
b. wholesale
c. wholesale and construction
d. construction and financial and insurance

POST-TEST 5

Study the line graph on page 332 and then answer the questions that follow. Circle the correct response.

Copyright © Houghton Mifflin Company. All rights reserved.

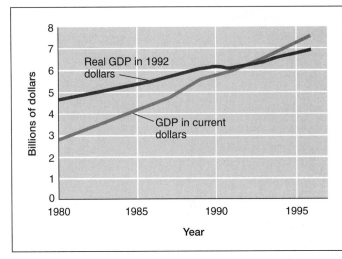

GDP in Current Dollars and in Inflation-adjusted Dollars. The changes in real gross domestic product for the United States from one year to another year can be used to measure economic growth. (Source: U.S. Department of Commerce, *Survey of Current Business,* April 1997, pp. D-4, D-34; and U.S. Bureau of the Census, *Statistical Abstract of the United States,* 116th ed., 1996, p. 443.)

From Pride/Hughes/Kapoor, *Business,* 6th ed. Boston: Houghton Mifflin, 1999, 15.

1. This chart represents
   a. the Gross National Product.
   b. the GDP in current dollars and in inflation-adjusted dollars.
   c. real GDP in 1992 dollars.
   d. the GDP in current dollars.

2. In 1985, the GDP in current dollars was about
   a. 8 million.   c. 3 million.
   b. 8 billion.   d. 4 billion.

3. In 1985, the real GDP in 1992 dollars was a little over
   a. 3 billion.   c. 5 billion.
   b. 3 million.   d. 8 billion.

4. The real GDP in 1992 and the GDP in current dollars were about the same in approximately what years?
   a. 1992–1993   c. 1995
   b. 1985–1986   d. 1990

5. The difference between the real GDP in 1992 dollars and the GDP in current dollars in 1980 was about
   a. 5 billion dollars.   c. 3 billion dollars.
   b. 2 billion dollars.   d. 8 billion dollars.

Copyright © Houghton Mifflin Company. All rights reserved.

POST-TEST 6

Study the bar graph below and then answer the questions that follow. Circle the correct response.

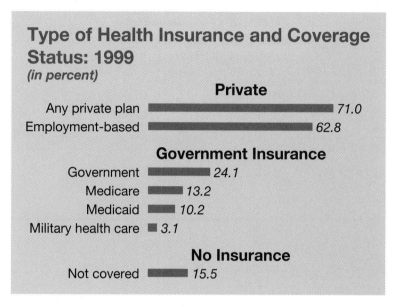

From Type of Health Insurance and Coverage Status, 1999, Issued September 2000, U.S. Census Bureau, Current Population Survey, March 2000.

1. What type of health insurance do most people have?

   a. Government insurance   c. Private
   b. Not covered   d. Personal

2. What percentage of people have Medicaid insurance?

   a. 13.2   c. 62.8
   b. 10.2   d. 3.1

3. The type of insurance that 62.8% of people have is

   a. Employment-based   c. No insurance
   b. Private   d. Military health care

4. In 1999, more people had Medicaid than had which type of insurance?

   a. Private   c. Government
   b. Employment-based   d. Military health care

5. According to the graph, 15.5% of people have

   a. employment-based insurance   c. no health insurance
   b. medicare   d. military health care

Copyright © Houghton Mifflin Company. All rights reserved.

7

POST-TEST 7

Study the diagram below and then answer the questions that follow. Circle the correct choice.

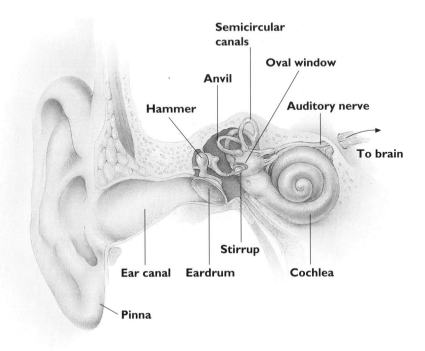

From Bernstein and Nash, *Essentials of Psychology.* Boston: Houghton Mifflin, 1999, 86.

1. What is the topic of this diagram?
   a. How we use our ears to hear   c. The eardrum
   b. The structures of the ear   d. The ear canal

2. Which component of the ear is nearest the stirrup?
   a. Hammer   c. Brain
   b. Auditory nerve   d. Oval window

3. The only part of the ear that we normally see is the
   a. cochlea.   c. anvil.
   b. pinna.   d. semicircular canals.

4. The part of the ear that leads directly to the brain is the
   a. auditory nerve.   c. stirrup.
   b. semicircular canals.   d. ear canal.

5. The ear canal joins the pinna to the
   a. oval window.   c. eardrum.
   b. hammer.   d. brain.

Copyright © Houghton Mifflin Company. All rights reserved.

7

POST-TEST 8

Study the map below and then answer the questions that follow. Circle the correct response.

From Noble et al., *Western Civilization,* Brief Edition. Boston: Houghton Mifflin, 1999, 36. Copyright © 1999 by Houghton Mifflin Company. Reprinted with permission.

Copyright © Houghton Mifflin Company. All rights reserved.

1. According to the map, Marathon would be considered which of the following?
   a. A sanctuary
   b. Part of the mountains
   c. Anatolia
   d. A major battle site of the Persian Wars

2. Which area is located closest to the Sea of Marmara?
   a. Macedonia
   b. Byzantium
   c. Thrace
   d. Chalcidice

3. What do Dodona and Delos have in common?
   a. They were both sanctuaries.
   b. They were both sites of major battles of the Persian Wars.
   c. They are both located in Thessaly.
   d. They are both in the Sea of Crete.

4. Which of the following is not a sea on this map?
   a. The Mediterranean Sea
   b. The Ionian Sea
   c. The Black Sea
   d. The Aegean Sea

5. In what year did the war of Salamis take place?
   a. 580 B.C.
   b. 479 B.C.
   c. 490 B.C.
   d. 480 b.c.

7

Copyright © Houghton Mifflin Company. All rights reserved.

Copyright © Houghton Mifflin Company. All rights reserved.

CHAPTER **8**

Inferences

GOALS FOR CHAPTER 8

▶ Explain and apply the steps of the REAP strategy.

▶ Define the term *inference.*

▶ Explain how inferences are made.

▶ State three reasons for asking readers to make inferences.

▶ Use guidelines to make accurate inferences from reading selections.

READING STRATEGY: REAP

REAP (Read-Encode-Annotate-Ponder) is a strategy that guides you to respond to a text to improve your reading and thinking skills. This method provides you with a system of four steps. When you follow these steps, you'll be training yourself to look deeper into the texts you read so you can more fully understand and evaluate them. As a result, your comprehension and critical thinking skills will improve.

STEP 1: Read. The first step involves carefully reading the text to understand the author's ideas and information.

STEP 2: Encode. Next, you translate the text's message into your own words. This step asks you to paraphrase the ideas or information to put them in language you understand.

STEP 3: Annotate. To annotate means to write notes or comments about a text. You can record these in the margins of the text, or in a notebook, or on separate sheets of paper. These notes can take the form of objective summaries, or more subjective reactions to the ideas and information. For example, you could jot down your own feelings, opinions, or judgments.

STEP 4: Ponder. Finally, you continue to reflect on what you have read and the notes you have written. In this stage, you also read or discuss other people's responses to the same text in order to more fully

Continued

8

explore its content. This sharing can take place formally in classroom settings, or informally, outside of the classroom.

Here is a sample passage annotated according to the REAP method:

Street Art

It's been called trash, scratching (by the ancient Greeks) and a crime (in today's society). Although many people see graffiti as a sign of gang activity or plain old defacement, this very American grassroots art form blossomed in New York in the late 1960s, when inner-city kids just wanted to get noticed. Now a new book shows there's more to crafting graffiti than just spraying your name on a wall in black Rust-Oleum.

The work of one such artist is chronicled in *Dondi White Style Master General: The Life of Graffiti Artist Dondi White* (Regan Books). Dondi, aka Donald White—who died of AIDS in 1998 at age 37—was one of the first "taggers," who used spray paint to transform subway cars and tunnels into irreverent art galleries. What easier audience to capture than thousands of commuting strap-hangers?

"His work looked like it had been taped off or die-cut. Dondi made it look easy when, in fact, his planning was meticulous and exhaustive," says Andrew "Zephyr" Witten, a friend who cowrote the book with the artist's brother, Michael.

Yesterday's trash has become today's treasure. While billions of dollars are spent each year to remove graffiti from public property, the works of White and other early taggers sell for thousands in galleries. And "bombing"—creating graffiti in one spurt—is sporadic now, Witten says.*

*Reading strategy adapted from "Street Art" by Robin Reid, as first appeared in *USA Weekend,* November 23–25, 2001, 17. Reprinted with permission of the author.

Continued

Copyright © Houghton Mifflin Company. All rights reserved.

Now, practice the REAP method yourself by reading and annotating the following passage. Then, discuss your reactions with a partner or a group of your classmates.

Choose Your Conversations

We can choose our conversations. Certain conversations create real value for us. They give us fuel for reaching our goals. Others distract us from what we want. They might even create lasting unhappiness and frustration.

We can choose more of the conversations that exhilarate and sustain us. Sometimes we can't control the outward circumstances of our lives. Yet no matter what happens, we retain the right to choose our conversations.

Before choosing whether to participate in a particular conversation, we can pay attention to several characteristics of that conversation: *time frame, topic,* and *attitude*. When we choose conversations that are more balanced within each of these areas, our lives will be more balanced as well.

First, we can notice the *time frame* of the conversation—whether it is about the past, the present, or the future. Most people spend most of their conversation time talking about the past. Often, they are blaming ("If he wasn't such a jerk, I wouldn't be in this mess"), justifying ("I would have been on time, but between my crazy kids and the crazy traffic, I had a terrible morning") or regretting ("If only I had bought that land before they started to develop it").

Conversations about the past can be fun and valuable. These conversations can help us learn from our mistakes, celebrate our successes, grieve over our losses, and enjoy fond memories. The problem arises when our conversations are out of balance. When the majority of our con-

8

Continued

Copyright © Houghton Mifflin Company. All rights reserved.

versations are about the past, then both our thoughts and our actions become predominantly influenced by the past. With so much focus and attention on the past, our future could be little more than a repetitive variation of the past.

An alternative is to balance our conversations. We can limit our conversations about the past to approximately one-third of our time. Then we can devote a third of our conversation space to the present, and another third to the future. Shifting conversation to the present offers many benefits. Much of our pleasure comes from paying attention to what we're doing in the present moment—enjoying great food, performing well in sports, or becoming lost in captivating music. As we engage in conversations about the present, we enhance the richness and quality of our lives.

Benefits also come from conversations about the future. These conversations help us create the most wonderful life possible. Instead of worrying about the future, we can create ways to live the life of our dreams. We can enjoy our creativity and use our planning skills.

In looking for ways to balance our conversations, we can select among the *topics* of things, others, self, or "us." Most conversations fall into one of these four categories. Like the time frame of conversations, the topics of most conversations are unbalanced. Most people talk about things (cars, houses, trips, football games, weather) and others (politicians, actors, neighbors, kids, coworkers) far more than they talk about themselves or about their relationships.

Of course, there is no problem in having conversations about things and others. But when we talk mostly about things and others, we neglect the rich intimacy that comes from revealing ourselves to another person. When we choose

Continued

Copyright © Houghton Mifflin Company. All rights reserved.

our conversations thoughtfully, we can share our heartfelt desires, fears, joys, and celebrations. We can also choose to talk about the quality of our relationships and how they can be improved.

Depending on our *attitude,* we might choose to dwell in conversations about problems, or we might prefer to engage mostly in conversations about solutions. Most people's conversations are out of balance in this area. They spend about 90 percent of their time complaining and talking about what is not working. And they spend only about 10 percent looking for solutions and celebrating what *is* working.

We can reverse these percentages. We can spend about 10 percent of our conversation space looking at and defining problems. Then we can invest the rest of our time discussing solutions, exploring new possibilities, discovering exciting new passions and potentials, and achieving amazing results.*

*Adapted from Dave Ellis, *Becoming a Master Student,* 9th ed. Boston: Houghton Mifflin, 2000, 217–218.

Reading selections don't always state everything you should know about a subject. Instead, you're expected to figure out information that's not actually in the text. To see how well you already do this, take the pre-test below.

PRE-TEST

8

Read the following sentences and answer the questions that follow. Circle the correct response.

1. I threw the stick and he fetched it.

   What can you infer about the "he" in the sentence?
   a. He is my son.   c. He is a tree.
   b. He is a dog.   d. He is a squirrel.

Copyright © Houghton Mifflin Company. All rights reserved.

2. Frank pulled the car over and asked the driver for his license.

What can you infer about Frank from this sentence?

a. Frank is a car thief.   c. Frank is a police officer.
b. Frank needs a ride home.   d. Frank's car has broken down.

3. The "flawed masterpiece" *Apocalypse Now* was one of the most talked-about screen undertakings—even before anyone had seen it—since *Gone with the Wind*.

What can you infer about *Apocalypse Now*?

a. It is a book.   c. It is a movie.
b. It is a television show.   d. Francis Ford Coppola directed it.

4. Billy Joel is considering expanding to compositions for piano with cello, violin, or clarinet, and later tackling chamber and orchestral projects. But the author of "Uptown Girl" and "Just the Way You Are" hasn't abandoned pop songs entirely.*

What can you infer about Billy Joel from this passage?

a. Billy Joel is one of the most famous singers alive today.
b. Billy Joel, in addition to playing pop tunes, can also play classical piano.
c. Billy Joel likes things "just the way they are."
d. Billy Joel enjoys living on Long Island.

5. What Bob Stoops will make as the University of Oklahoma football coach this season is more than the average American wage earner will see in a lifetime.†

What can you infer about Bob Stoops from this sentence?

a. Bob Stoops has to move to Stillwater, Oklahoma.
b. Bob Stoops lives in Oklahoma City.
c. Bob Stoops is going to be a very rich man.
d. Bob Stoops will earn about $30,000 per year.

8

Inferences

Writers do not write down everything they want you to understand about a topic, but they expect you to figure out this information anyway. How? They know you make inferences while you read. An **inference** is a conclusion you

*From Edna Gunderson, "Billy Joel's First Love," *USA Today,* August 3, 2001, 1D.
†From Steve Wieberg, "Top Dollar, Top Coaches," *USA Today,* August 3, 2001, 1A.

Copyright © Houghton Mifflin Company. All rights reserved.

draw that's based upon the stated information. You made one type of inference when you learned how to determine implied main ideas in Chapter 4. When you consider a group of related supporting details and draw a conclusion about the point they suggest, you're inferring that main idea. But you make many more kinds of smaller inferences, too, as you read. For example, read the following sentences.

> A mother thought her three-year-old child was playing too quietly, so she went into the living room to check on the youngster. The child was not in the room and the front door was wide open. Their dog was gone, too. She panicked and called the police. When they arrived, they began searching the neighborhood. One of the searchers saw a dog barking and running into and out of a wooded area beside the road. He followed the excited dog and found the three-year-old, crying and trembling, hiding behind a tree.

Did you conclude that the child left home and got lost but was rescued when the family dog revealed his or her whereabouts? If you did, you made quite a few inferences to reach that conclusion. For instance, the passage never says that the child was at home, so how do you know that? You figure that out because the child, the child's mother, and the dog are all there, and the child is in the living room. Therefore, you conclude that they're all in the house where they live. How did you—and the mother—know the child had wandered off? You get three clues: the child is gone, the door is open, and the mother panics. You add these three pieces of information together to make your conclusion. How do you know that the dog helps rescuers find the child? The animal tries to attract their attention by barking and running back and forth, and the child is found where the dog is exhibiting these behaviors. You put those clues together to figure out the dog was "telling" rescuers where they could find the child. Therefore, even though the passage does not tell you exactly what happened, you still understand because of your ability to make inferences. "To infer" means "to read between the lines." You see more than what is actually there because you bring your own knowledge, experiences, and observations to your reading, allowing you to fill in the gaps. For instance, you've noticed before that a burning building sends black smoke into the sky, and you know that fire trucks rush to a fire with their sirens on. Therefore, when you see smoke and hear sirens, you conclude that something is on fire. You apply these same experiences and observations as you read.

Here is another example that illustrates how you use your previous knowledge to make inferences:

> Some people ask me if I worry about my girlfriend getting off work late at night. I don't, though, because she has her black belt in karate.

Copyright © Houghton Mifflin Company. All rights reserved.

8

These two sentences ask you to make a couple of inferences. The first sentence assumes that you know why people would worry; it asks you to access your memory of news stories, observations, or your own personal experiences that have taught you that a woman alone at night can be vulnerable to an attack. Then, the second sentence assumes you know that someone who possesses a black belt in karate is a practiced fighter who can defend herself against attackers. Even though these two pieces of information are never stated, you easily infer the meaning of these sentences because you use your previous knowledge to understand.

As you read this next group of sentences, think about what knowledge you must possess in order to make the right conclusions:

> In New York, former Mafia boss John Gotti had his hair trimmed daily by a barber as he sat in a professional barber's chair installed in his Queens headquarters. In prison, he gets a haircut once a month from an inmate barber paid 40 cents an hour by the Bureau of Prisons.*

First of all, the passage asks you to interpret what having your hair trimmed daily means. Do you have your hair trimmed that often? Probably not. You might conclude, therefore, that John Gotti was very concerned about his looks and that he had plenty of money to pay for a service that most people can afford only occasionally. This passage also expects you to know that 40 cents an hour is far less than most people make for the work they do. Finally, then, you are expected to conclude that Gotti fell from the heights of luxury and pampering to the no-frills lows of prison life.

Exercise 8.1

Look at the following comic strips and photographs and place a check next to the statement that expresses an accurate inference.

Calvin and Hobbes
by Bill Watterson

Calvin and Hobbes © 1988 Watterson. Reprinted with permission of Universal Press Syndicate. All rights reserved.

*Adapted from Rick Hampson, "Curtains Descend on Gotti Family," *USA Today,* July 25, 2001, 3A.

Copyright © Houghton Mifflin Company. All rights reserved.

1. _____ Calvin doesn't like to take baths.

   _____ Calvin spends a lot of time on the roof.

   _____ Calvin's mother is having a good time.

   _____ Calvin lives in a very expensive house.

THE FAR SIDE® BY GARY LARSON

8

2. _____ The woman is driving the car.

   _____ The owner of the eyeball is very close to the car.

   _____ The driver is driving very slowly.

   _____ The woman is frightened.

Copyright © Houghton Mifflin Company. All rights reserved.

© Will Hart / PhotoEdit

3. _____ These two boys live in Atlanta.

   _____ These two boys fight a lot.

   _____ The boys are brothers.

   _____ The younger boy attends a private school.

© Elizabeth Crews

4. _____ These three people are students.

   _____ The woman in the middle is the teacher and the other people are her students.

   _____ The students have just taken a test.

   _____ The woman in the middle is angry at the other two people.

Copyright © Houghton Mifflin Company. All rights reserved.

© Hans Pennink, *The Daily Gazette*

5. _____ The truck is going too fast.

_____ The "Daddy" mentioned in the sign's message is a road construction worker.

_____ A child made the sign.

_____ It is rush hour on this highway.

Exercise 8.2

Read the following paragraphs and answer the questions that follow by circling the correct response.

1. Anyone inclined to dismiss Bon Jovi as a relic of the hair-happy late '80s needed only to survey the packed arena. There, teenagers too young to remember the group's heyday cheered alongside couples in their 30s and 40s toting excited tots. Many of these children knew the words to numerous songs.*

*Adapted from Elysa Gardner, "Bon Jovi in Jersey Is No '80s Throwback," *USA Today,* July 30, 2001, 4D.

Copyright © Houghton Mifflin Company. All rights reserved.

8

The author assumes that you know that Bon Jovi is

a. a rock band.
b. an organization for hairstylists.
c. a sports team.
d. a union for day care teachers.

2. Thirty years after the first Ali-Frazier fight, Laila Ali, daughter of Muhammad Ali, and Jacqui Frazier-Lyde, daughter of Smokin' Joe Frazier, reignited the family feud with a bout in upstate New York in June of 2001.*

The author assumes that you know that the women mentioned in the sentence are daughters of

a. famous scientists.
b. famous fireworks specialists.
c. famous heavyweight boxers.
d. famous Civil Rights activists.

3. Their 1981 wedding made the cover of *Newsweek*. The ceremony drew a crowd of almost 30 million. Now soap's most celebrated couple, Luke and Laura from *General Hospital,* are divorcing.†

The author assumes that you know that Luke and Laura are

a. two people who work in a hospital.
b. fictional characters who appear on a daytime soap opera.
c. a real-life couple who are divorcing.
d. two *Newsweek* journalists.

4. There are guys in my neighborhood who still sport their college's name on their car window. And they're in their 60s.‡

The author wants you to infer that

a. the men to whom he is referring are too old to be displaying their college's name on their car windows.
b. the men to whom he is referring own cars.
c. the men to whom he is referring have gray hair.
d. the men to whom he is referring went to his college.

5. Sundee Hughes, 23, who has been working since she was 15, was laid off from a local hosiery plant and has been looking in vain for full-time work for four months. She has applied at factories, convenience stores, and restaurants and has employment services helping her look. So far, all she's managed are some temporary stints at a furniture plant.§

*Adapted from Alisha Davis, "Newsmakers," *Newsweek,* June 11, 2001, 53.

†Adapted from Alisha Davis, "Newsmakers," *Newsweek,* June 25, 2001, 94.

‡From Craig Wilson, "Picking a Future Alma Mater Is Anything but Academic," *USA Today,* July 25, 2001, 1D.

§Adapted from George Hager, "Portrait of a Town in Trouble," *USA Today,* July 30, 2001, 3B.

Copyright © Houghton Mifflin Company. All rights reserved.

The author wants you to infer that Sundee Hughes

a. wants to return to work at the hosiery plant.
b. wants and needs to find a full-time job.
c. is named after a day of the week.
d. is homeless.

Writers rely on readers' ability to make inferences for three reasons. First of all, passages that spelled out every detail would be boring and tedious to read. Second, they would be unnecessarily long. And finally, they would deprive readers of the pleasure they experience in figuring out some things for themselves.

Guidelines for Making Accurate Inferences

How can you make sure you're drawing the right conclusions from information in a text? Follow these guidelines:

- **Focus only on the details and information provided, and don't "read in" anything that's not there.** It's surprisingly easy to take just a little bit of information and jump to unfounded conclusions. For example, think back to the earlier example about the three-year-old who wandered away from home. Would you say that the child's mother was careless in allowing the child to get away? Many people would; they would say that she should have been watching her child more carefully. Can you really make that assumption, though? Could there have been someone else in the house who may have been responsible for looking after the child? The passage did not say that anyone else was in the house, but it also didn't say that the mother and child were the only ones home. We read that into the story. Because we know that the mother is often the primary caretaker in a household, we also assume that it's her fault when something happens to the child. Now, without looking back at the passage, answer this question: Who rescued the child? Did you answer "a police officer"? Why? Because the mother called the police, who came and searched the neighborhood. But the person who found the child was actually referred to simply as a "searcher." That person could have been a neighbor rather than a police officer. We don't get enough information to be able to answer that question, so we should not leap to inaccurate conclusions.

Next, read another passage:

Michele Fricheteau was waiting inside the hotel she and her husband owned for 170 British musicians who had booked rooms for the

8

Copyright © Houghton Mifflin Company. All rights reserved.

night. She heard the roar of the supersonic Concorde jet plane lifting off, as it did every afternoon. But then came the deafening bang and the anguished screams, as flames ripped through the building, searing her face.*

Would it be accurate to infer from the last two sentences that the Concorde hit the hotel Michele Fricheteau owned? Yes, that's correct. Why? Because she was inside the hotel, and the flames from the crash burned her face. Could you infer that the 170 British musicians she was waiting for were on the Concorde when it crashed? No, nothing in the passage says they were, and besides, the Concorde was taking off when it crashed. The musicians would not have been flying away from the hotel if they were scheduled to stay there that night. Was Michele killed by the crash? No, the passage says only that she was burned. Could you infer that the plane was on fire when it hit the hotel? No, the passage says that flames were present, but it does not say if the plane was burning when it crashed, so we should not make that particular conclusion.

- **Don't ignore any details.** The details provide the important clues. For instance, in the earlier example, was the missing three-year-old child enjoying his or her time out of the house? Of course not. The paragraph says the child was "crying and trembling," two details that indicate the child's fear.

Here's another paragraph in which you must notice the details to make the right inferences:

When students were asked to warm up with ten minutes of simple writing exercises while soothing classical music played, hundreds of them made fewer mistakes on their homework. And Hungarian researchers found that students who warmed up this way could concentrate harder for longer periods of time. The reason? Handwriting activates the logical mind, and the music calms the emotional mind, so the logical mind can take over. Kids become instantly more attentive to new information and better able to retain it. The result is higher grades.†

Now, try to recall the details as you consider whether or not the following inferences are correct:

*Adapted from Vivienne Walt, "In Gonesse, Concorde Crash Is 'Always a Presence,'" *USA Today,* July 25, 2001, 11A.

†Adapted from Barbara Hustedt Crook, "Your Child Can Write Her Way to Better Grades," *Woman's World,* January 9, 2001, 44.

Copyright © Houghton Mifflin Company. All rights reserved.

Any kind of music provides the necessary calming effect for the emotional mind.

The act of handwriting seems to activate the whole brain.

To improve concentration, you should write as long as possible.

Think about how the details affect the inferences you make. The first statement is incorrect because the paragraph states that *classical* music is the kind researchers played during their experiment. You should not infer, then, that other kinds of music have the same effect. The second statement is also incorrect. The passage says that writing activates the logical mind only; it is the *music* that calms the emotional mind. Finally, the third statement is incorrect, too. The passage clearly states that the experiment lasted only ten minutes, and it makes no indication that longer periods of handwriting produce other results.

- **Make sure nothing contradicts your conclusion.** Try not to overlook one or more details that may conflict with any preliminary conclusion you make about a passage. For example, read the following:

    Years ago a professor overheard me talking with other engineers about the engineering dropouts who then go into business. "Don't laugh," he said. "In five years, one of them will be your boss."*

In this passage, you can infer that the writer is an engineer because he's talking with "other engineers." Next, you're supposed to infer how these engineers feel about engineering dropouts. Are they sympathetic? Are they sad for the people who can't make it through the engineering program? If you answer yes to either of those questions, you are overlooking one important detail: the professor tells them not to "laugh." If you miss that detail, you won't accurately conclude that the engineers are making fun of those who failed.

- **Don't let stereotypes and/or prejudices color your interpretation.** When you think back to that story about the missing three-year-old and try to picture the child in your mind, do you picture a boy or a girl? The passage never identifies the child's gender, but many readers think of the child as male. Why? Because we rely upon the stereotype that little boys are, in general, more adventurous and more disobedient. Therefore, a boy would be more likely to wander off and get lost. However, we should resist making that inference if there is no information in the passage that supports it, and we recognize that some of our assumptions are based on generalizations that may be incorrect.

8

*Adapted from Steven Parish, "'Show and Style' vs. Experience," *USA Today*, July 30, 2001, 11A.

Copyright © Houghton Mifflin Company. All rights reserved.

For example, read the following passage:

> Keiko the killer whale, who starred in the 1992 film *Free Willy*, may never be freed, his caretakers said. After years in captivity, Keiko was moved to Iceland in 1998 in an attempt to reintroduce him to the seas. But after 60 trips out of his pen, Keiko appears reluctant to rejoin wild whales.*

Would you say that the caretakers were cruel to hold Keiko in captivity for so long? Do you believe that he can't rejoin the wild whales because he's unsure of what to do? If you answered yes to either question, you're letting your opinions about holding sea creatures captive color your interpretation of the information. Actually, the passage never states a reason for Keiko's behavior. It also never suggests that the length of his captivity is causing his refusal to be set free. Yet, many people who oppose keeping whales in captivity might make these conclusions even though there is no information in the passage to support them.

Exercise 8.3

Read the following passages and circle the correct answer for each of the questions that follow.

Twenty-four-hour service is catching on all across America. In Milwaukee, for example, Joe Valenti operates Valenti's Hair Studio, a 24-hour hair salon. He lives upstairs from the shop near downtown. He'll give you a new 'do at 3 A.M. But it'll cost you. He doubles his prices after 10 P.M., when a $16 haircut becomes a $32 job. The night work adds 15 percent to his earnings. He started it on a whim only to discover that people wanted it.†

1. What can you infer from the information that Joe Valenti "lives upstairs from the shop near downtown"?
   a. Because Joe Valenti lives in the downtown area, he is obviously a hip and trendy person.
   b. Because Joe lives so close to his salon, he can get to work easily at any hour of the day or night.
   c. Because Joe lives so close to his salon, he obviously can't afford a house.
   d. Because Joe lives so close to his salon, he must not have anything else to do besides work.

8

*Adapted from "Whale Called 'Willy' Isn't Cooperating," *USA Today*, July 30, 2001, 1A.
†Adapted from Bruce Horovitz, "24/7 Almost a Way of Life," *USA Today*, August 1, 2001, 2A.

Copyright © Houghton Mifflin Company. All rights reserved.

2. Based on the details in this paragraph, which of the following inferences is most accurate?

   a. Joe wasn't making enough money, so he had to open for business 24 hours a day.
   b. Many people find it convenient to get their hair done in the middle of the night.
   c. Joe has more customers at night than he does in the daytime.
   d. People who pay double for a haircut are wasting their money.

3. The reader can infer that Joe doubles his prices after 10 P.M. because:

   a. He's greedy.
   b. Only rich customers want their hair done after 10 P.M.
   c. He's better at his job during nighttime hours.
   d. He works all day, too, so he has to charge extra to make the additional service worth his time.

On the bank of the Ottawa River, at 6 A.M., Colorado Avalanche hockey coach Bob Hartley removed the championship Stanley Cup trophy from its case like a father cradling a baby out of a crib, joking that he thought it was still sleeping. If the 108-year-old Stanley Cup did start its day well rested, it was unlike most of Hartley's friends. About 60 showed up at the docks starting at 5:30 A.M. to fish with Hartley and the Cup, or at least to help launch his official day with what is arguably professional sports' most storied trophy and the Holy Grail of hockey. While Hartley fished, the crowd started to build at the PPG Industries plant, a windshield manufacturing facility where Hartley worked in the 1980s. By 11 A.M., about 1,200 employees and their family members had gathered to have a photo snapped with Hartley and the Cup.*

4. What can you infer from the fact that Bob Hartley had the Stanley Cup in his possession?

   a. The Colorado Avalanche won the Stanley Cup.
   b. Bob Hartley had stolen the Stanley Cup.
   c. Bob Hartley is a hockey fan.
   d. The Colorado Avalanche had borrowed the Cup.

5. What can you infer from the fact that Bob Hartley once worked at a windshield manufacturing plant but now is in possession of the Stanley Cup?

   a. He loved his job at the plant.
   b. He didn't want to move to Colorado.
   c. He has had great success as a hockey coach since leaving the plant.
   d. He was always a fan of the Colorado Avalanche.

*Adapted from Kevin Allen, "At Home with the Cup," *USA Today,* August 2, 2001, 1C.

Copyright © Houghton Mifflin Company. All rights reserved.

8

6. The reader can infer that Bob Hartley's "official day" is a result of his

   a. coaching a Stanley Cup–winning team.
   b. retirement from the windshield manufacturing plant.
   c. having grown up in Canada.
   d. being a great fisherman.

Six months after taking office, the president will begin a month-long vacation Saturday that is significantly longer than the average American's annual getaway. If the president returns as scheduled on Labor Day, he'll tie the modern record for presidential absence from the White House. That was held by Richard Nixon at 30 days. Ronald Reagan took trips as long as 28 days.*

7. What can you infer from the term "president" as used in the paragraph?

   a. The author is referring to Jack Welch, president of General Electric.
   b. The author is referring to Bill Gates, president of Microsoft.
   c. The author is referring to the president of the United States.
   d. The author is referring to Martin Sheen, who plays the president on a popular television show.

8. What can you infer about the length of time the president is taking for vacation?

   a. The president is using his position to justify taking a vacation longer than the average American would take.
   b. The president is not really going to be away that long.
   c. The president is going to see Ronald Reagan while on vacation and that's why he needs a month.
   d. The president might not return on Labor Day, as promised.

9. What can you infer about other presidents not mentioned in the paragraph and the length of time that they took for vacation?

   a. You can infer that they took vacations, too.
   b. You can infer that they took less time than the presidents mentioned in the paragraph.
   c. You can infer that they didn't take vacations.
   d. You can infer that their vacations were longer than the ones taken by presidents mentioned in the paragraph.

They got up with the birds, fought traffic on the Pennsylvania Turnpike, crowded four into a hotel room and spent hours dressing up to look like their idol, singer Madonna. They paid $336 apiece for a package that included concert tickets, hotel, preconcert party, and transportation to the show. For good luck, they brought a shrine: a framed picture of Madonna and a little altar

*Adapted from Laurence McQuillan, "White House to Move to Texas for a While; President Takes Month Off for Working Vacation at His Ranch," *USA Today,* August 3, 2001, 10A.

Copyright © Houghton Mifflin Company. All rights reserved.

with candles. They decorated their hotel rooms with Madonna banners, posters, and even a Madonna throw rug.*

10. What you can you infer about the people referred to in the paragraph?

    a. They are fans of Madonna.
    b. They became fans of Madonna when they were children.
    c. They own birds.
    d. They like driving on the Pennsylvania Turnpike.

11. What is one other thing that you can infer about the people referred to in the paragraph?

    a. They like to wear costumes.
    b. They dress up like Madonna on Halloween.
    c. They would have done just about anything to see Madonna in concert.
    d. They have seen the movie *Desperately Seeking Susan* a hundred times.

12. What can you infer from the statement, "They got up with the birds"?

    a. The people going to the Madonna concert slept late.
    b. The people going to the Madonna concert overslept.
    c. The people going to the Madonna concert got up very early.
    d. The people going to the Madonna concert stayed up late the night before.

Last month, nine women wearing black caps and gowns walked onto a podium here and received their college diplomas as their friends and family members wept and cheered. It was an unusual ceremony, because all the graduates were convicted felons, and it took place in a gym embraced by locked metal gates and razor wire at the Bedford Hills Correctional Facility, a maximum security women's prison.†

13. What can we infer about the graduates from the paragraph?

    a. They had committed serious crimes.
    b. They were going to be in jail for life.
    c. They all had children.
    d. They didn't care about the graduation ceremony.

14. What can we infer from the statement, "It was an unusual ceremony"?

    a. There was no music at the ceremony.
    b. Graduation ceremonies usually don't take place at prisons.
    c. It was unusual because the graduates were wearing caps and gowns.
    d. It was unusual because all of the graduates were women.

8

*Adapted from Maria Puente, "Mad About Madonna," *USA Today,* July 25, 2001, 1D.

†From Robert Worth, "Bringing College Back to Bedford Hills," *New York Times,* June 24, 2001, Sec. 14,1.

Copyright © Houghton Mifflin Company. All rights reserved.

15. What can we infer about the friends and families of the graduates and the fact that they "wept and cheered"?

    a. They were very saddened by the event.
    b. They had come long distances to see the graduation.
    c. They were very proud of the graduates.
    d. They were not proud of the graduates.

Exercise 8.4

Read the following passages and then check all of the accurate inferences in the list.

1. Upset that your husband forgot to call? Think telling him off will make you feel better? Not so, says psychologist Brad Bushman, Ph.D., whose research shows that venting anger actually ends up making people unhappy. Why? We often say things we later regret, studies show. A better idea, according to Bushman, is reading a good book, watching a funny TV show, or listening to a favorite CD. You'll soon calm down enough to deal more productively with the situation by having a calm discussion with whoever made you angry.*

    _____ 1. Women vent their anger more than men do.

    _____ 2. Venting anger often involves hurtful verbal criticism.

    _____ 3. Venting anger can damage the relationship between two people, leading to more unhappiness.

    _____ 4. Women have a right to feel angry when their husbands forget them.

    _____ 5. A primary goal of the media is to help people better manage their anger.

2. Medical experts have warned for years that anorexia and bulimia can be deadly, but a growing number of teens are celebrating their eating disorders on the Web and sharing their tips and strategies for losing weight and exercising. It's a trend that worries and disturbs eating-disorder experts. "I love the feeling I get when I can feel my bones sticking out. I love feeling empty, like a hollow gourd. I love knowing I went the whole day without eating." So says a posting on one Web site promoting eating disorders as a lifestyle.†

*From Barbara Hustedt Crook, "Feel Happier Just by Doing These Six Simple Things," _Woman's World,_ July 10, 2001, 21.

†Adapted from Nanci Hellmich, "Super-thin, Super-troubling," _USA Today,_ July 25, 2001, 7D.

Copyright © Houghton Mifflin Company. All rights reserved.

_____ 1. Teens don't take eating disorders as seriously as medical experts do.

_____ 2. Medical experts think that teens are stupid.

_____ 3. Medical experts are disturbed by how teens are dealing with eating disorders.

_____ 4. Teens think that medical experts don't know what they are talking about.

_____ 5. Teens with eating disorders don't care about other people.

3. His toe may be crushed, but _San Francisco Chronicle_ editor Phil Bronstein's ego should be very healthy. Wife Sharon Stone has been calling him a hero ever since their private tour of the Los Angeles Zoo ended when a Komodo dragon, which is like a small Godzilla, bit him in the foot. According to Stone, the man known at the _Chronicle_ as "El Macho" always wanted to get up close and personal with the seven-foot lizard, so she arranged a private visit as a Father's Day gift.*

_____ 1. Phil Bronstein is an outstanding father.

_____ 2. Sharon Stone was angry at her husband, so she set him up to be bitten by a Komodo dragon.

_____ 3. A Komodo dragon is a playful animal.

_____ 4. The Los Angeles Zoo is being sued by Sharon Stone.

_____ 5. A Komodo dragon is a dangerous animal.

4. Computer-savvy teenagers are creating millions of fake driver's licenses despite the high-tech security features that states now put on licenses to discourage forgers. Using the Internet, anyone willing to break a few laws can be a mass producer of fake IDs, the gateways to underage drinking that received new attention in May of 2001, when President Bush's 19-year-old twin daughters were cited in Austin, Texas, on charges of alcohol violations.†

_____ 1. Teens are not using fake IDs to get into bars and buy alcohol.

_____ 2. The Bush twins were using fake IDs when they were cited for alcohol violations.

_____ 3. Teens are finding ways around high-tech security features on licenses and are making fake IDs anyway.

*From Alisha Davis, "Newsmakers," _Newsweek_, June 25, 2001, 94.
†Adapted from Donna Leinwand, "Fake IDs Swamp Police," _USA Today_, July 2, 2001, 1A.

Copyright © Houghton Mifflin Company. All rights reserved.

_____ 4. President Bush's daughters are identical twins.

_____ 5. President Bush's daughters like being famous.

5. Resisting slavery seemed second nature to Harriet Tubman. Born a slave on a Maryland plantation in 1820, she quickly developed a fiery spirit and was not shy about protesting bad treatment. One such incident so angered the plantation overseer that he hit her over the head with a lead weight, inflicting a permanent brain injury that would cause her to suddenly lose consciousness several times a day for the rest of her life. To overcome this disability, she worked on building herself up physically, becoming an uncommonly strong woman. It was said that she could single-handedly haul a boat fully loaded with stones, a feat deemed impossible for all but the strongest men.*

_____ 1. Harriet Tubman was an African American.

_____ 2. Harriet Tubman is now dead.

_____ 3. Harriet Tubman stood up for herself.

_____ 4. Men were frightened of Harriet Tubman.

_____ 5. Harriet Tubman freed herself from slavery.

Exercise 8.5

Read the following Aesop fable. This fable is written in the style of a parable, or a story written to make a point. Answer the questions that follow. Circle the correct response.

The tortoise and the hare argued over which was the swifter. So, as a result, they agreed on a fixed period of time and a place and parted company. Now the hare, trusting in his natural speed, didn't hurry to set out. He lay down at the side of the road and fell asleep. But the tortoise, well aware of his slowness, didn't stop running, and, overtaking the sleeping hare, he arrived first and won the contest.†

8

*From Berkin et al., *Making America*. Boston: Houghton Mifflin, 2001, 276.

†Aesop fable from *The Complete Fables*, translated by Olivia and Robert Temple. New York: Penguin, 1998. Copyright © 1998 by Olivia and Robert Temple. Reprinted by permission of the authors.

Copyright © Houghton Mifflin Company. All rights reserved.

1. What can you infer about the hare from this selection?

    a. He assumed that he could beat the tortoise.
    b. He was very tired.
    c. He had won many speed contests.
    d. He did not like the tortoise.

2. What can you infer about the tortoise from this selection?

    a. The tortoise assumed that he could beat the hare without too much effort.
    b. The tortoise was aware of his slowness and worked hard to win the race.
    c. The tortoise wasn't as tired as the hare.
    d. There is nothing to infer about the tortoise from this selection.

3. What inference can you make about what the author is trying to convey in this selection?

    a. The author is warning against thinking too much of oneself.
    b. The author is saying that speed wins over intellect any day.
    c. The author is saying that hard work often prevails over talent if the talents are not used effectively.
    d. The author isn't really saying anything worth mentioning.

CHAPTER 8 REVIEW

Fill in the blanks in the following statements.

1. An _____ is a conclusion you draw that's based upon the stated information.

2. _____ use their knowledge, experiences, and observations to help them make inferences.

3. Writers ask readers to make inferences to keep their writing _____ _____, and fun for the reader.

4. To make accurate inferences, readers should avoid _____ information that's not in a text. Conversely, they should not ignore any details provided.

5. To make accurate inferences, readers should make sure nothing _____ _____ a conclusion, and they should avoid letting stereotypes or _____ affect their conclusions.

Copyright © Houghton Mifflin Company. All rights reserved.

8

Reading Selection

What a Way to Live, What a Way to Die!
By Al Neuharth

1 He reminded people of all ages how to live with life's little disappointments. And to laugh about them. For 50 years.

2 Now he has shown us how to die. Charles Schulz died in his sleep just when his farewell comic strip of *Peanuts* was being inserted and distributed in the Sunday papers.

3 Schulz was much more than a cartoonist. He was a philosopher. His teachings were more useful than those of such noted philosophers as Aristotle or Confucius or Plato or Socrates. Here's why: He knew life is not always fair, but it can still be fun.

4 He and his *Peanuts* gang took life very seriously, but never took themselves too seriously. So, Charlie Brown always missed the football and always got his kite stuck in a tree. So, Linus always sucked his thumb and carried his comfort blanket. So, Snoopy was a sleepy-eyed beagle who dozed at the typewriter. So, Lucy's curbside psychiatric clinic didn't offer a nickel's worth of good advice. So what? That's life. It made kids of all ages laugh, because they could relate.

5 Some Schulz critics suggested he should create winners, not just losers. His response: "You can't create humor out of happiness." Yet, the few times I was in his presence, I sensed a serene sort of happiness about him.

6 My feeling of kinship goes back to our Midwestern upbringing. His father was a barber in Minnesota; mine, a farmer in South Dakota. We both entered the army at Fort Snelling, in St. Paul, in 1943 for World War II. He served as a sergeant in the 20th Armored Division in Europe. I was a sergeant in the 86th Infantry Division in Europe and the Pacific.

7 After the war, we returned home, both hoping to find fame and fortune in newspapering. He began by drawing comics for the *St. Paul Pioneer Press*. I wrote news stories for the *Rapid City* (South Dakota) *Journal*. The rest, as they say, is history.

8 Charles Schulz showed me and the 355 million of you around the world who read him regularly how to live. Now he has shown us how to die. What a way to be and to go!

(Al Neuharth, "What a Way to Live, What a Way to Die!" *USA Today,* March 21, 2000. Reprinted by permission of the authors.)

Peanuts reprinted by permission of United Feature Syndicate, Inc.

Copyright © Houghton Mifflin Company. All rights reserved.

VOCABULARY

Read the following questions about some of the vocabulary words that appear in the previous selection. Circle the correct responses.

1. As used in paragraph 2, what does the word *distributed* mean?
   a. taken away
   b. given out
   c. cleaned up
   d. put together

2. "Schulz was much more than a cartoonist. He was a *philosopher*" (paragraph 3). What does *philosopher* mean?
   a. professor
   b. artist
   c. wise person
   d. painter

3. "I sensed a *serene* sort of happiness about him" (paragraph 5). What does *serene* mean?
   a. disturbed
   b. happy
   c. calm
   d. sad

4. When someone has a "feeling of *kinship*" what does that mean (paragraph 6)?
   a. a feeling of being connected or friends with someone
   b. a feeling of being unhappy with someone
   c. a feeling of being like a child
   d. a feeling of being out of place

TOPICS, TOPIC SENTENCES, AND INFERENCES

Answer the following questions by circling the correct responses.

1. The topic of paragraph 3 is
   a. cartoonists.
   b. philosophers.
   c. Charles Schulz.
   d. cartoons.

2. What is the topic sentence of paragraph 4?
   a. Sentence 1
   b. Sentence 2
   c. Sentence 3
   d. Sentence 4

3. Based on the information presented in the selection, which of the following statements best expresses an inference that you can make from reading the selection?
   a. *Peanuts* was not a popular cartoon.
   b. Charles Schulz had a hard life.

Copyright © Houghton Mifflin Company. All rights reserved.

8

   c. Schulz had a lot of critics.

   d. The author of this selection has a great deal of respect for Charles Schulz and his work.

4. What is another inference you can make about Al Neuharth and Charles Schulz as people, based on the last few paragraphs of the selection?

   a. Neuharth and Schulz had nothing in common, but Neuharth still respected Schulz as an artist.

   b. Neuharth and Schulz had a lot in common, from their upbringing to different events that took place in their lives.

   c. Neuharth and Schulz were very patriotic.

   d. Neuharth enjoyed serving in World War II but Schulz did not.

5. Look at the cartoon that accompanies the reading selection. What can you infer from the cartoon?

   a. People shouldn't try to tame wild birds.

   b. All children like birds.

   c. The birds get a lot of satisfaction from being patted on their heads by Linus.

   d. The birds leave because they do not like being patted on their heads.

QUESTIONS FOR DISCUSSION AND WRITING

Answer the following questions based on your reading of the selection.

1. Why do you think the selection is called "What a Way to Live, What a Way to Die"? What does the author want to say about Charles Schulz?

   _____

   _____

   _____

2. Do you agree or disagree with the statement in paragraph 5, "You can't create humor out of happiness"? Why? _____

   _____

3. Based on the information in paragraph 4, why do you think that the comic strip "made kids . . . laugh, because they could relate"? _____

   _____

   _____

Copyright © Houghton Mifflin Company. All rights reserved.

8

▶ Vocabulary: Formal vs. Informal Language

When you read, you should be able to distinguish between formal and informal language. **Formal language** is usually serious, businesslike, and often sophisticated. This is the type of language that is most prevalent in scholarly, academic, and business writing. Most textbooks, college assignments, and business reports, for example, are written using formal language. **Informal language** is closer to that of conversation. It is more casual, often including colloquial (everyday) words, slang terms, idioms (expressions like "She's trying to butter me up"), and even humor.

The level of formality in a reading selection helps the reader know how the author feels about his or her subject. A passage or document written in a formal style communicates the author's belief that the subject is important and significant. A more informal style can suggest that the author is more lighthearted about the topic.

To understand the difference between formal and informal language, first take a look at an informal statement from one of the examples in this chapter:

> There are ***guys*** in my neighborhood who still ***sport*** their college's name on their ***car*** window.

The boldfaced, italicized words are colloquial and casual. Notice, though, how the substitution of different words increases the sentence's formality:

> There are ***gentlemen*** in my neighborhood who still ***affix*** their college's name to their ***vehicle*** window.

Vocabulary Exercise

Use the boldfaced, italicized words in each of the following sentences to decide whether the language is formal or informal, then on the blank after each sentence, write FORMAL or INFORMAL.

1. There, teenagers too young to remember the group's ***heyday*** cheered alongside couples in their 30s and 40s ***toting*** excited ***tots.*** <u>h informal</u>   *[handwritten: carrying, baby]*

2. When ***students*** were asked to warm up with ten minutes of simple writing ***exercises*** while ***soothing*** classical music played, hundreds of them made fewer mistakes on their ***homework.*** <u>formal</u>

3. He'll give you a new ***'do*** at 3 A.M. <u>informal</u>

8

Copyright © Houghton Mifflin Company. All rights reserved.

4. Last month, nine **women** wearing black caps and gowns walked onto a **podium** here and **received** their **college diplomas** as their friends and family members **wept** and cheered. _formal_

5. One such **incident** so **angered** the plantation overseer that he hit her over the head with a lead weight, **inflicting** a permanent brain injury that would cause her to suddenly **lose consciousness** several times a day for the rest of her life. _formal_

6. **Mess up** one word and **you're history.** _informal_
   you will fell

7. Bedding, or **stratification,** is the **arrangement** of sediment particles into distinct layers having different **sediment compositions** and/or grain sizes. A clear break, or bedding plane, is generally **visible** between **adjacent** beds. _formal_

8. First, the **staff** of successful programs **regard** themselves as **competent** observers of **children's educational needs** and as being capable of making important decisions in **tailoring** a **curriculum** to particular children. _formal_

9. **Nerds** are supposed to be friendless **bookworms** who **suck up** to authority figures. Furthermore, we're **sissies.** _informal_
   afraid of going things

Copyright © Houghton Mifflin Company. All rights reserved.

8

Name _____ Date _____

POST-TEST 1

Read the following sentences and answer the questions that follow. Circle the correct response.

1. It took me a long time to clean the house today.

   What can you infer about the state of the house from this statement?

   a. The house was very neat and tidy before it was cleaned.
   b. The house was very dirty and needed to be cleaned.
   c. The house is old.
   d. The house is very small.

2. Patrick likes his mother to read books to him before he goes to bed.

   What can you infer about Patrick's age from this statement?

   a. Patrick is very young.
   b. Patrick is a teenager.
   c. Patrick is an old man.
   d. Patrick is a second grader.

3. With all the new rules at airports these days, you'd think that Americans would have figured out a way to travel lighter.*

   What can you assume about the number of bags Americans bring onto airplanes these days?

   a. They bring on fewer bags.
   b. They bring on heavier bags.
   c. They bring on lighter bags.
   d. They bring on as many bags as they did before, if not more.

4. I've seen an 80-year-old lady in a wheelchair have her tennis shoes removed and checked for explosives at the airport. A five-year-old girl's doll carrier was hand-searched. A flight attendant's bag was emptied and her clean and neatly folded clothes scrambled.†

*From Gene Sloan, "Americans Carry a Lot of Baggage," *USA Today,* March 8, 2002, 1D.
†Adapted from Al Neuharth, "Hassle, Not Fear, Is Crippling Air Travel," *USA Today,* March 8, 2002, 11A.

For additional tests on inferences, see the Test Bank.

Copyright © Houghton Mifflin Company. All rights reserved.

What can you infer about airline security from this passage?

a. It is very lax.
~~b.~~ It is very strict with nobody above being searched.
c. It is for the very old.
d. It is only for the very young.

5. Six months after <u>Pearl Harbor</u>, June 7, 1942, Americans did not have the luxury of wallowing in self-obsessed thoughts on the meaning of it all. The pivotal Battle of Midway had ended just the day before.*

What can you infer about America in 1942 from this passage?

a. The country was in a recession.
b. The country was in the midst of good economic times.
c. The country was at war.
d. The country was in the midst of a presidential election.

6. James Joyce had Dublin, Saul Bellow claimed Chicago, William Faulkner distilled the Southern quintessence into his fictional Yoknapatawpha County, and William Kennedy owns Albany, New York. Though such comparisons would appear to put Kennedy at a cultural disadvantage, he somehow approaches Faulkner's mythic dimensions, Bellow's comic realism, and Joyce's rapturous romance with language. Where literature and Albany are concerned, if you can make it there, you can make it anywhere.†

The author assumes you know that William Kennedy is

a. a writer.   c. a cab driver.
b. a chef.   d. a criminal.

7. Lynn Cheney never forgets her sleek laptop when she travels. The author of four books and several reports, with a Ph.D. in English literature, whose dissertation analyzed the influence of Immanuel Kant's philosophy on Matthew Arnold's poetry, Cheney is the first woman to hold a paying job while her husband served as vice president. When he was elected, she gave up six of the corporate boards on which she sat, but retained two. She is also a senior fellow at a conservative think tank, the American Enterprise Institute, where she is working on a book about education reform.‡

*Adapted from Walter Shapiro, "Americans Strangely Fixated on Tragic Anniversary," *USA Today*, March 8, 2002, 6A.

†From Don McLeese, "A City All His Own," *Book*, January–February 2002, 64.

‡From Ann Gerhart, "Second-in-Command," *More*, February 2002, 87.

Copyright © Houghton Mifflin Company. All rights reserved.

What can you infer about Lynn Cheney from this passage?

a. She is extremely intelligent and very busy.
b. She has a lot of time on her hands to engage in her hobbies.
c. She likes to knit.
d. She is married to the president of the United States.

8. Believe it or not, filmmakers try to avoid having their work slapped with an R rating. By banning unchaperoned teens, the R automatically stunts a movie's box office potential. But Robert Altman is different. When he heard that *Gosford Park,* his 1930s comedy of British manners and murder, had earned an R for its curse words, his reaction could be summed up with a four-letter word: Cool.*

What can you infer about Robert Altman from this passage?

a. He is a producer.
b. He is a director and filmmaker.
c. He is British.
d. He is a poet.

9. On a cold afternoon about a week before Valentine's Day, Meichelle Jackson, 41, sits with 18 other students in a classroom in rural Caddo County, Oklahoma, and listens to a lecturer discuss communication and conflict resolution in marriage. The course is part of Oklahoma's Marriage Initiative, a controversial $10 million program that uses welfare money to lower the state's sky-high divorce rate. Many of the students doodle and giggle, but Jackson listens courteously.†

What can you infer about Meichelle Jackson from this passage?

a. She is interested in making friends with her 18 classmates.
b. She is married.
c. She is interested in learning new skills in the program.
d. She doesn't want to become friends with anyone in her class.

10. She was signed by the Elite modeling agency when she was 13. Last year she showed up clad in an American flag on the cover of the British magazine *Tatler.* The Pirelli tire company put her on the cover of its 2002 calendar, and designer Tommy Hilfiger made her his latest Tommy Girl—the focus of his print ads. But now 17-year-old Lauren Bush has really hit her size-4 stride as the girl on the April cover of—what else?—*W.*‡

8

*Adapted from Jim Jerome, "Inside Outsider," *People,* March 18, 2002, 109.
†From Peg Tyre, "Giving Lessons in Love," *Newsweek,* February 18, 2002, 64.
‡From Cathleen McGuigan, Lorraine Ali, Malcolm Jones, and Peter Plagens, "A Bipartisanly Beautiful Bush," *Newsweek,* March 18, 2002, 71.

Copyright © Houghton Mifflin Company. All rights reserved.

What can you infer about Lauren Bush from this passage?

a. She is the president's favorite niece.
b. She is the president's daughter.
c. She lives in Texas.
d. She is a very popular model.

POST-TEST 2

Read the following passages and answer the questions that follow. Circle the correct response.

A. Earthwatch recruits volunteers to help scientists conduct field research in locations throughout the world. Most of the trips are for two weeks and cover everything from excavating a Roman fort in England to studying manatees in Florida. The cost of these expeditions averages $1,600–$1,800, without airfare. Participants stay in dorms or guesthouses and generally cook meals together.

Earthwatch has fared well considering the downturn in travel, with just over two dozen cancellations out of an expected 4,000 volunteers this year, according to Earthwatch spokesperson Blue Magruder. "They know that the scientists need them badly," she says.

Two-thirds of Earthwatch participants are from the United States, and the other third come from 46 other countries. Magruder emphasizes that this diversity plays an important role in building much-needed global camaraderie.*

1. Based on the passage, the people who spend their vacations with Earthwatch prefer

   a. relief from a stressful life.
   b. to do something meaningful.
   c. to get away from other people.
   d. to relax in luxury.

2. According to spokesperson Magruder, diversity in Earthwatch participants

   a. creates many problems due to language barriers.
   b. gives Earthwatch scientists a large talent pool to utilize.
   c. is one of the reasons for the downturn in Earthwatch involvement.
   d. helps build worldwide support for Earthwatch efforts.

camaraderie = cooperation

*Adapted from Kathy McCabe, "Volunteer Vacations Benefit Many," usatoday.com Travel Guide, November 30, 2001.

Copyright © Houghton Mifflin Company. All rights reserved.

3. What would you most expect to experience on an Earthwatch vacation?

   a. golf, tennis, and swimming
   b. plenty of hard work
   c. music and dancing
   d. two weeks of complete leisure

B. We came in 1970. No minister visited to encourage us to worship on Sunday, no neighbor dropped in with a plate of brownies. Several times I stopped at neighboring farms to say hello and announce our presence and was met in the yard by the farmer, and we spent an uncomfortable few minutes standing beside my car, making small talk about the weather, studying the ground, me waiting to be invited into the house, him waiting for me to go away, until finally I went away. In town the shopkeepers and the man at the garage were cordial, of course, but if I said hello to someone on the street, he glanced down at the sidewalk and passed in silence. I lived south of Freeport for three years and never managed to have a conversation with anyone in the town. I didn't have long hair or a beard, didn't dress oddly or do wild things, and it troubled me. I felt like a criminal.*

4. Which of the following inferences is accurately based on the information given?

   a. People in this town are cruel to strangers.
   b. Shopkeepers don't like conversation.
   c. People in this town do not welcome strangers.
   d. New people were welcomed here.

5. Which of the following inferences is accurately based on the information given?

   a. The writer was a criminal.
   b. The writer was friendly, and looked similar to the people who lived in the town.
   c. The writer is a churchgoing person.
   d. The writer did favors for the townspeople.

6. Which of the following inferences is accurately based on the information given?

   a. The writer tried to make friends in the town.
   b. The townspeople sensed something unusual about the writer.
   c. The writer did not like making small talk.
   d. The writer came to hate the townspeople.

8

*From Garrison Keillor, "In Search of Lake Wobegon," *National Geographic*, December 2000, 102.

Copyright © Houghton Mifflin Company. All rights reserved.

C. It was almost like a hallucination. Immediate. A sense of dislocation. Something was awry. A few seconds earlier, seen from the surface, everything had looked normal. The midday sun shot arrows of light through the dappled water, illuminating a routine reef in an isolated backwater of an exhausted sea. But no sooner had I submerged—my bubbles had had no time to disperse nor the mist to clear from my mask—than I knew I was in the grip of the weird. Time was out of joint. I had flopped overboard from a dinghy on a glassy Caribbean sea in the summer of the year 2000 and in an instant, apparently, slipped backward nearly half a century into an underwater realm that had not existed, so far as I knew, since the 1950s.

Residents swarmed over me, welcoming me to the neighborhood, animals in numbers and diversity I hadn't seen in decades, not since Lyndon Johnson was president and man had yet to set foot on the moon. Groupers of all description and sizes lumbered around me: Nassau groupers, black groupers, even the patriarch of the grouper clan, the gigantic jewfish (aka the goliath grouper), creatures widely assumed to have almost disappeared from the Caribbean long ago—speared, hooked, netted, poisoned by men driven by poverty, hunger, and need.*

7. What can you infer when the author says that "Time was out of joint"?
   a. The author is a time traveler.
   b. The author feels that quoting Shakespeare is impressive.
   c. Something very unusual was happening.
   d. The author did not know what time it was.

8. Who were the "residents" the author says are swarming over him?
   a. Many different types of fish
   b. Strange people who were inhabiting the water
   c. Ghosts he was seeing
   d. People he hadn't seen in many years

9. Why does the author feel that time had slipped backward?
   a. He is in the middle of a science fiction story in which he is visiting another era.
   b. He is merely saying that his watch had stopped.
   c. Fish were there that he'd expected to have disappeared long ago.
   d. The fish he was seeing were actually killed many years ago.

D. "The Delaware people have lost so much," says Lucy Parks Blalock of Quapaw, Oklahoma. "Our language is almost gone and our culture forgotten. When I was a girl, the white kids teased us so much that some were ashamed

*From Peter Benchley, "Cuba Reefs," *National Geographic,* February 2002, 50. Reprinted by permission of the National Geographic Society.

Copyright © Houghton Mifflin Company. All rights reserved.

to be Indian. . . . It is hard now for many Delawares to imagine how to do things the traditional way. They no longer remember."

Mrs. Blalock, also known as *Oxeapanexkwe,* or "Early Dawn Woman," does remember. Born on June 14, 1906, in Indian Territory shortly before it became the state of Oklahoma, she is one of a handful who can still speak her native tongue (the Unami dialect of the Delaware language) and who attended important ceremonies that died out during the 1920s and 1930s.*

10. What can you infer about how Mrs. Blalock feels when she says, "It is hard now for many Delawares [*Native*] to imagine how to do things the traditional way"?

   a. She has no feeling one way or the other about it.
   b. She thinks it's a good thing that the traditional ways are being forgotten.
   c. She does not like observing the traditions.
   d. She is sorry that the traditional ways are being forgotten.

11. From the information, do you think Mrs. Blalock is "ashamed to be Indian"?

   a. Yes; it was because she was teased as a child.
   b. On the contrary; she is proud of her heritage.
   c. She doesn't have any opinion about it.
   d. She has forgotten her heritage.

12. From the information, what can you infer that Mrs. Blalock would like to do?

   a. Enjoy living in the present
   b. Change all the bad memories of the past into happy ones
   c. Forget the present day and relive the past so she can improve on it
   d. Help remember the traditions and native language of her heritage

8

*From David M. Oestreicher, "Lucy Blalock: Rescuing a Language from Oblivion," *Natural History,* October 1996, 20.

10 = d   11 = b   12 = d

Copyright © Houghton Mifflin Company. All rights reserved.

CHAPTER 9
Critical Reading

GOALS FOR CHAPTER 9

▶ Explain the three purposes for skimming, and describe the steps involved in skimming a text.

▶ Define the term *critical reading.*

▶ Explain the difference between a fact and an opinion.

▶ Label statements either facts or opinions.

▶ Explain why a reader should pay attention to an author's background and goals.

▶ Define the term *bias.*

▶ Explain why readers should learn to detect bias in texts.

▶ Identify examples of positive and negative bias.

▶ Define the term *tone.*

▶ Recognize different types of tone in reading selections.

▶ List the characteristics of a sound main idea.

▶ Define the term *evidence.*

▶ List the two essential qualities of sound evidence.

READING STRATEGY: Skimming

When you look at an Internet Web site for the first time, do you read every word on your computer screen? Of course not. Instead, your eyes probably flick around over the pictures and text, reading individual words or phrases as you try to form a general impression of the site and its content. You do the same thing when you're standing in a store, deciding whether to buy a magazine. You flip through the pages, glancing at the titles of the articles and at the pictures, as you try to determine if the magazine is worth your money. This is called *skimming,* and it's also a useful strategy for reading printed materials.

Continued

Copyright © Houghton Mifflin Company. All rights reserved.

9

When you skim a text or a passage, you're not looking for specific details or information (that's called *scanning,* which is discussed in another chapter). Instead, you're trying to get some sense of the content and organization. In particular, you skim a reading selection to get an idea of the author's subject, main point, overall focus, or purpose.

Skimming should never be a substitute for reading. It will not give you a full understanding of a text or a passage. However, skimming is useful for three particular purposes: previewing, evaluating a source's worth or relevancy, and reviewing.

Previewing. Skimming a reading selection—for instance, a chapter in a textbook or a journal article—will provide you with a "big picture" of what you're about to read. As a result, when you do finally read the text, you'll have a framework for understanding the specific details.

Evaluating. Skimming is also useful for research. You don't have time to read every single article you find when you're looking for information about a research topic. Skimming gives you a way to determine if a particular book or article relates to your project and is worth reading in detail later.

Reviewing. Finally, you can skim a text after reading it as a way of reviewing the information. Therefore, skimming can be a valuable technique for studying and remembering information.

To skim a text or a passage, follow these steps:

1. Glance over the title and all of the headings.

2. Quickly read the first sentence of each paragraph. Authors often state their main ideas at the beginnings of paragraphs, so reading these first sentences can help you get a sense of the major points.

3. Quickly move your eyes in a zigzag pattern over the words in the text. At the same time, ask yourself, *What's this about?* and *What's the point?* Try to answer those questions by noticing words or phrases that are highlighted with bold print, italics, or some other kind of distinctive typeface. As you practice skimming, you'll become better at noticing key words or concepts even when they're not highlighted. You'll find that, after a while, these words will begin to jump out at you as you run your eyes over the passage.

Follow the three steps described above to skim the following passage from a psychology textbook. Then, answer the questions after the passage.

Continued

Copyright © Houghton Mifflin Company. All rights reserved.

Thinking Critically: Are There Drugs That Can Make You Smarter?

Drugs intended to improve cognitive functioning are called nootropics (pronouned "no-oh-TROH-pix"), a word that comes from *noos,* which is Greek for "mind." In some circles, nootropics are seen as "smart drugs" and sold at "smart bars." Are smart drugs really effective, or are they modern-day snake oil, giving only an illusion of a sharpened mind?

What Am I Being Asked to Believe or Accept?

The belief that certain drugs can improve memory was popularized in the 1990s by John Morgenthaler and Ward Dean, who wrote two books, *Smart Drugs and Nutrients* and a sequel called *Smart Drugs II: The Next Generation.* One online reviewer of the second book wrote, "And the results have been nothing less than a total transformation. My life has come together finally and I am advancing my work."

Is There Evidence Available to Support the Claim?

Some drugs can improve mental performance under some conditions. For instance, animals given the drugs that Morgenthaler and Dean wrote about show improvements in performance on tasks requiring attention and memory. These drugs have also been shown to facilitate recalling old memories and forming new ones. Nootropic drugs also have biochemical effects on brain metabolism in elderly people: Some increase the blood flow in the brain, and others affect specific neurotransmitters.

One study of elderly people with general brain impairment found improvement after twelve weeks of treatment with smart drugs. Other studies have shown memory improvement in elderly people with memory problems due to poor blood circulation to the brain. Some studies have also found positive effects on memory in normal persons. For example, young adult college students improved on tests of memory after taking some of these drugs.

Can That Evidence Be Interpreted Another Way?

Glowing testimonials from people who feel that these drugs helped them may reflect their belief in the drugs, not the effectiveness of the drugs themselves. For example, in 1894, when the scientist Charles Edouard Brown-Sequard was feeling old and tired, he gave himself injections of extract of ground-up dog testicles. He reported a return to youthful energy and sharpened cognitive abilities. It was all probably a

Continued

Copyright © Houghton Mifflin Company. All rights reserved.

9

placebo effect. Only carefully controlled double-blind studies can separate the effect of a participant's expectations from the specific effects of drugs or other treatments.

Some of the controlled studies previously cited show that nootropic drugs have positive effects on memory and cognitive ability, but the effects tend to be small and inconsistent. Often, the drugs primarily affect attentiveness, and the improvements are no greater than those caused by drinking a cup of coffee. Overall, evidence from well-designed studies shows nootropic drugs to be a major disappointment.

What Evidence Would Help to Evaluate the Alternatives?

Researchers are testing several promising new categories of nootropic drugs in animals. It will take years of studies to determine which ones are truly effective, and under what circumstances. Research on side effects will also be needed. For example, one of the more effective drugs for Alzheimer's patients was found to cause serious liver damage in about a third of those who took it. And one of the chemicals occasionally found to improve memory in humans may create nausea and increased blood pressure.

What Conclusions Are Most Reasonable?

In spite of their unimpressive showing overall, nootropic drugs are sometimes used with Alzheimer's patients, mainly for lack of better alternatives. As for the drinks you can buy in smart bars, be sure they taste good, because their effect on your mental powers is likely to be minimal. Instead of smart drugs, try education: Educational achievement and a life of working at a job that engages your mind are more likely to lower the risk for Alzheimer's disease.*

1. What is the topic of this entire passage? _____

2. According to the headings, what five aspects of the topic are discussed in this passage? _____

_____

3. Skim the section labeled "Can That Evidence Be Interpreted Another Way?" by reading the topic sentences and then running your eyes in a zigzag pattern over the rest of the paragraphs. Then,

*From Douglas A. Bernstein and Peggy W. Nash, *Essentials of Psychology*, 2nd ed. Boston: Houghton Mifflin, 2002, 45–46. Copyright © 2002 by Houghton Mifflin Company. Reprinted with permission.

Continued

Copyright © Houghton Mifflin Company. All rights reserved.

answer the question posed in the title of this reading selection: Are there drugs that can make you smarter? _____

4. Skim the last two sections and then answer this question: Should we give up on the idea of taking drugs to make us smarter? _____

_____

College students are expected to read critically. Professors assign textbook chapters, journal articles, and other readings not just to have you memorize facts. They also want you to think about the texts so you can expand and refine your ideas. To discover how well you already read critically, complete the pre-test below.

PRE-TEST

A. Are the following statements facts or opinions? Write an **F** for fact and an **O** for opinion after each statement.

1. Mars is a planet. _____

2. Some people call Mars the red planet. _____

3. The *Washington Post* is a newspaper that is published every day. _____

4. The *Washington Post* is the best newspaper published today. _____

5. Some professional baseball teams now have Japanese players. _____

6. Some players on the Little League World Series team from New York are so big that they're probably older than the 12-year-old age limit. _____

7. The Jersey Shore beaches are the most beautiful in the world. _____

8. The Empire State Building was once the tallest building in the world. _____

9. The Statue of Liberty was given to America by the French. _____

10. Jackie Robinson was the first African American to play professional baseball. _____

Copyright © Houghton Mifflin Company. All rights reserved.

9

B. What is the tone of each of the following paragraphs? Read the paragraphs below and circle the correct answer.

11. The Friday-night routine never varied. I would hear my mother's heels clicking on the bathroom floor above me: clean, precise taps, in pairs. She would be getting a tissue to blot her lipstick, a brush to push through her thick, straight brown hair. Then she would cross the room to her dresser to pick up the bottle of perfume, upturning it again and again as she dabbed it on her wrists, neck, and behind her ears. I had watched her countless times.*

    a. Critical   c. Amused
    b. Neutral   d. Sad

12. I was hoping to open this magazine and be pleasantly surprised to find older, plus-size models, just as you promised on the cover. What did I find? Pencil-thin models, about twenty years my junior, in a magazine that touts its "all-inclusiveness," and attention to the older, plumper female. You guys have got to be kidding. Since when is a size 10 "plus-size"? Not in my world, sister.

    a. Sarcastic   c. Sad
    b. Neutral   d. Angry

C. Read the following "Letter to the Editor" from *USA Today* and answer the questions that follow. Circle the correct response.

    I am truly sick of people discrediting MTV because they have outgrown it.

    MTV has maintained the same target audience for the past 20 years by continuing to reinvent itself and remain in touch with its viewer base of teenagers and twentysomethings.

    If commentary writer Mark Goldblatt doesn't like MTV's programming, then most probably it's because he's too old. I don't hear anyone providing the same commentary on how childish or immature the programming is on Nickelodeon.

    Additionally, the social strides that MTV has made have been remarkable. Yes, maybe there is sophomoric (juvenile or immature) programming, but MTV has provided role models for people of color and homosexuals time and again.

    MTV also has made countless strides to get today's youth thinking "outside the box," and the network's recent yearlong initiative to stop hate crime in America is one example of what I consider to be very brave and powerful programming.

*From Amanda Hesser, "Message in a Bottle," *Allure*, September 2001, 170.

Copyright © Houghton Mifflin Company. All rights reserved.

If Goldblatt isn't concerned about what is on kids' minds, maybe he shouldn't watch MTV.*

13. The main point of this letter can be paraphrased:

   a. MTV has had some beneficial influence and does not deserve criticism.
   b. Today's teenagers have no taste when it comes to music.
   c. MTV is just not for older people.
   d. Music is an important cultural influence.

14. The author's tone is

   a. amused.   c. neutral.
   b. critical.   d. admiring.

15. In your opinion, does the author support his main point with sufficient

   and appropriate evidence? Why or why not? _____

   _____

Critical reading does not mean reading to criticize or find fault with a text. Instead, **critical reading** involves noticing certain techniques the writer is using to try to convince you of the validity and worth of his or her ideas or information. Once you learn to recognize these techniques, you are better able to evaluate a reading selection and decide what it means to you.

The ultimate goal of critical reading is critical thinking, an important skill in all areas of life, not just your academic courses. Critical thinkers don't just believe everything they hear or read. Instead, they approach new ideas and information with a healthy skepticism. They have learned how to analyze texts and ideas to not only understand them better, but also to decide whether they should accept those ideas, reject them, or think about them further.

This chapter will help you develop your own critical reading skills by showing you how to examine important features of a text as you evaluate it. First, you'll learn to distinguish facts from opinions. Then, you'll get some practice with asking two key questions to further guide your analysis.

Distinguishing Fact from Opinion

The first essential skill in critical reading is the ability to distinguish between facts and opinions. **Facts** are information that is verifiably true. They are based upon direct experience and observation, so they often include specific

9

Copyright © Houghton Mifflin Company. All rights reserved.

*From Jimmy Szczepanek, "Letter to the Editor," *USA Today,* August 3, 2001, 12A. Reprinted by permission of the author.

data such as numbers, dates, times, or other statistics. They also include information like names of people, places, or events. Therefore, facts can be proven. The following statements are all examples of facts:

> In 2000, 17.6 percent of the American population spoke a language other than English while at home.

> The last major eruption of Mount Etna, Europe's largest volcano, occurred in 2001.

> NASCAR champion Dale Earnhardt was killed on February 18, 2001, during the final lap of the Daytona 500.

You should be aware as you read that a statement presented as a fact can be incorrect. Writers are not always right, and, sometimes, they include inaccurate information by accident or even on purpose. If that's the case, how does a reader know what to believe? That question will be answered more fully in a later section of this chapter.

Opinions are statements that express beliefs, feelings, judgments, attitudes, and preferences. They cannot be verified because they are based on an individual's perceptions of the world. Thus, they are subject to change as a person modifies his or her views. They can also be argued or disputed. Here are some examples of each kind of opinion:

> BELIEF: Human cloning is morally wrong.

> FEELING: The lack of patriotism among young people is sad and disturbing.

> JUDGMENT: People who drive a sport utility vehicle obviously don't care about the environment.

> ATTITUDE: The majority of television shows are boring.

> PREFERENCE: Coffee is better than hot tea.

When you are trying to decide whether a statement is a fact or an opinion, you can look for some clue words that often appear in statements of opinion. One kind of clue is words that indicate the relative nature of something, words like *bigger, most important, strangest,* and *silliest.* These words relate and compare the subject to something else. For example, notice the boldfaced, italicized words in the following opinions:

> Alaska is one of the ***most beautiful*** states in America.

> Teenagers today are much ***lazier*** than they used to be.

> Tiger Woods is a ***better*** golfer than anyone else who's ever played the game.

Copyright © Houghton Mifflin Company. All rights reserved.

Another kind of clue is words that either qualify or limit statements or turn them into absolutes. Qualifying words and phrases include *some, several, many, quite a few, a lot, most, a majority, large numbers, usually, often, sometimes, frequently, seldom,* and *rarely.* Absolute words and phrases include *all, every, never, each, always, none,* and *no.* For example, notice the boldfaced, italicized words in the following opinions:

Allowing children to ride in the front seat of a vehicle will ***usually*** put them at higher risk in an accident.

All voters should be required to produce identification when they arrive at the polls to vote.

Space travel is ***always*** a waste of taxpayers' money.

One last type of clue is words or phrases that admit there are other possibilities. These terms include *may be, could be, seems, appears, probably, possibly, apparently,* and *seemingly.* This type of clue is boldfaced and italicized in the following examples:

There is a real ***possibility*** that life exists on another moon or planet.

Passing a law that outlaws a parent from leaving a child in the back seat of the car is ***probably*** a waste of time.

Apparently, fans are turned off by the commercialism of sports.

Just as they know that some "facts" may be inaccurate, critical readers are also aware that some opinions are more valid than others. Everyone has opinions, but they may not always be sound. First of all, some opinions can be unreasonable. For example, many opinions that include the absolute words mentioned earlier can be too all-inclusive to be valid. An author who claims, for example, that *everyone* feels a certain way or that *all* things of a certain type share some characteristic is probably not allowing for reasonable exceptions. Secondly, some opinions are based on shaky or inadequate evidence. Some people believe, for example, that the Holocaust never happened, and they manage to ignore all of the proof that it *did* happen. A later section in this chapter will further discuss how to evaluate the evidence offered in support of an opinion.

So, why do you need to recognize the difference between a fact and opinion? The distinction matters because you are going to see both used to explain and support ideas in reading selections. If you need to evaluate whether a text is valid, you'll have to sort out what is definitely true from what the writer *believes* to be true. Understanding the difference allows you, the reader, to make more sound interpretations. Thus, you can make more reliable judgments about the worth of information and ideas.

Copyright © Houghton Mifflin Company. All rights reserved.

9

Exercise 9.1

Read the following statements carefully and then label each of them **F** if it is a fact and **O** if it is an opinion.

_____ 1. Some day care centers are open 24 hours a day.

_____ 2. Phil Jackson, coach of the Los Angeles Lakers, is the greatest basketball coach of all time.

_____ 3. Phil Jackson has won many NBA championships as the coach of the Chicago Bulls and the Los Angeles Lakers.

_____ 4. The temperature is 90 degrees today.

_____ 5. Paris is the most beautiful city on the planet.

_____ 6. The Grand Canyon is one of the wonders of the world.

_____ 7. Writing a first draft is a lot harder than revising and editing that draft.

_____ 8. Raising children is the most difficult job on earth.

_____ 9. Some newspapers publish editions only during the week and not on weekends.

_____ 10. Space travel is very exciting.

Exercise 9.2

Read the passages and then label each of the sentences in the list **F** if it offers a fact and **O** if it offers an opinion.

1. (1) Despite the widespread emphasis on raising academic standards, the performance of high school seniors on a nationwide science test has declined since 1996, with 18 percent of those tested in 2000 proving proficient in the subject. (2) The scores of eighth graders who took the test, the National Assessment of Educational Progress, improved so slightly as to be statistically insignificant. (3) The scores of fourth graders remained flat. (4) These results underscore the urgent need for highly skilled science and mathematics teachers, as well as other improvements at the high school level.*

_____ Sentence 1

*Adapted from Abby Goodnough, "National Science Scores for 12th Graders Slip," The *New York Times*, November 21, 2001.

Copyright © Houghton Mifflin Company. All rights reserved.

_____ Sentence 2

_____ Sentence 3

_____ Sentence 4

2. (1) The most overrated chief executive is John Adams, the second president of the United States. (2) He is justly honored as a patriot and a diplomat. (3) John's biographers overplay their hand, however, when they defend his presidency. (4) Confronted by a menacing France, he lurched from war hawk to peacenik with an abruptness that finished his career and the Federalist party.*

_____ Sentence 1

_____ Sentence 2

_____ Sentence 3

_____ Sentence 4

3. (1) Today, several credit cards are designed specifically for high school and even middle school students: the Cobaltcard from American Express, Capital One's High School Student Card, and the Visa Buxx card. (2) With these programs, children as young as 12 or 13 can have their very own accounts, with lines of credit up to $1000. (3) According to many adults, this trend will create a generation of overspenders with no concept that just because you charge it doesn't mean it's free. (4) In my view, however, kids having credit cards is a good thing. (5) These young people will learn how to spend their money more wisely now and in the future. (6) They need more practice with managing their money, and credit cards can help teach them important financial lessons.†

_____ Sentence 1

_____ Sentence 2

_____ Sentence 3

_____ Sentence 4

_____ Sentence 5

_____ Sentence 6

Copyright © Houghton Mifflin Company. All rights reserved.

9

*Adapted from Richard Brookhiser, "Overrated, Underrated," _American Heritage,_ September 2001, 26.

†Adapted from Robin Marantz Henig, "Teen Credit Cards Actually Teach Responsibility," _USA Today,_ July 31, 2001, 15A.

4. (1) Nearly half of all grades at Harvard University last year were A or A-minus, says a university study that follows reports of grade inflation at the Ivy League school. (2) The report found that As and A-minuses grew from 33.2 percent of all grades in 1985 to 48.5 percent last year. (3) Failing grades, Ds, and Cs accounted for less than 6 percent. (4) The higher grades may be deserved, as students work harder and are better prepared. (5) But it's hard to believe that so many students are performing at that level.*

_____ Sentence 1

_____ Sentence 2

_____ Sentence 3

_____ Sentence 4

_____ Sentence 5

5. (1) Clinton's presidency got off to a slow and shaky start. (2) One of his first actions was to attempt to fulfill a campaign pledge to change the national health insurance system. (3) Chaired by his wife, the Task Force on National Health Care Reform in 1993 proposed providing universal insurance primarily by mandating that employers offer health insurance to their employees. (4) Much criticism greeted the task force's report. (5) Businesses objected to providing mandated health insurance. (6) The American Medical Association complained that adopting the recommendations would mean that government would decide how much health care an individual could receive and deny an individual's choice of doctors. (7) Such complaints found their mark in a public suspicious of big changes in medical care. (8) By mid-1994, it was apparent that health care reform was a dead issue.†

_____ Sentence 1

_____ Sentence 2

_____ Sentence 3

_____ Sentence 4

_____ Sentence 5

_____ Sentence 6

_____ Sentence 7

_____ Sentence 8

*Adapted from "Study Shows Harvard Has Boosted Its As," *USA Today,* November 26, 2001, 9D.
†Adapted from Berkin et al., *Making America.* Boston: Houghton Mifflin, 2001, 724.

Copyright © Houghton Mifflin Company. All rights reserved.

Two Critical Reading Questions

Now that you've practiced distinguishing between facts and opinions, you're ready to probe a text more deeply to understand *what* it says and *how* it says it. To do that, you can use two questions to guide your critical reading:

> Who is the author, and what is his or her purpose and approach?

> What is the main point and the evidence offered to support that claim?

When you actively search for the answers to these questions, you are examining the features of a text that will indicate its validity.

Question #1: Who Is the Author, and What Is His or Her Purpose and Approach?

As you preview a text before reading it, perhaps using the SQ3R method discussed earlier in this book, you should get in the habit of reading any biographical information provided about the author. Books will often include a paragraph or two about the author's background, and even articles will sometimes include a sentence or two of description. Pay attention to information about the writer's credentials, experience, interests, and goals. These details will help you decide, first of all, if the author is credible. Does he or she possess sufficient expertise (gained through either research or direct experience) to be considered a reliable authority on the subject? Such details will also help you determine the author's purpose. You read to know why an author believes the topic is important and what he or she hopes to accomplish by writing about that topic. Does the writer hope to merely increase your knowledge, or does he or she want to change your mind about something? Does the author want you to act on your new information or belief? Before you, the reader, can decide whether or not you agree that a text's ideas are significant, you need to know why the author thinks they are.

What if a text offers no information about the author? Even if a reading selection reveals nothing or little about the writer, you will still be able to gain a sense of who the writer is and what he or she hopes to achieve. How? Often, authors will tell you these things in the text itself. They may announce their purpose or summarize their credentials. They may offer you some details about their background that led them to write about the topic.

Even if they say nothing about themselves, however, you can usually detect something about authors' backgrounds and purposes from the way they wrote the text. The words authors choose, and even the way they put their sentences together, can reveal a great deal about their feelings, their attitudes, and their goals. A reader must learn how to recognize bias and how to determine the tone of a text.

Copyright © Houghton Mifflin Company. All rights reserved.

9

Recognizing Bias.   **Bias** is an inclination toward a particular opinion or viewpoint. The term describes our tendency to feel strongly that something is right or wrong, positive or negative. Even authors who try to present information neutrally, without revealing any of their own feelings about the topic, will often allow their own prejudices to creep into their writing. Conversely, authors can also make their bias perfectly clear. They often do so in hopes that they will influence the reader to agree.

Authors communicate their bias by using words that urge the reader to feel a certain way about a topic. Many of these words are emotional, and they provoke strong reactions in readers, encouraging them to feel either positive or negative. For example, the word *psychiatrist* is a respectful term, but the word *shrink* is negative and disrespectful. In the following pairs of sentences, the first sentence includes words that are relatively neutral. Notice how the substitution of a few more emotional words injects bias into the statement.

Neutral:	Our desire to own private property is the motivation that drives humans to want to achieve.
Emotional:	Our materialistic natures are the only thing preventing us all from becoming fat and lazy couch potatoes.
Neutral:	The recording industry should not sell records that contain objectionable lyrics to children.
Emotional:	The money-hungry recording industry is guilty of destroying children's morals with lewd and violent song lyrics.
Neutral:	The Egyptian pyramids are interesting for many reasons.
Emotional:	The awe-inspiring Egyptian pyramids will no doubt fascinate and astonish modern visitors.

In the second sentence of each pair, you can see that the choice of words makes the author's opinion more emotionally forceful.

Exercise 9.3

In each of the following statements, underline the words or phrases that reveal the author's bias. Then, on the blank, write POSITIVE if the words encourage you to feel positive about the subject and NEGATIVE if they urge you to feel negative.

1. Like a fox in a hen house, ruthless collectors are plundering Africa's cultural heritage by encouraging poor Africans to sell stolen treasures.

_____

Copyright © Houghton Mifflin Company. All rights reserved.

2. Ken Burns's spectacular outline of jazz history will surprise no one; in *Jazz,* his beautiful miniseries on the subject, Burns delights in the details. _____

3. Tyler Chicken turns your dinners into something to talk about—where ordinary meals become masterpieces. _____

4. Critics say that the McMahon family—the founders and gatekeepers of the World Wrestling Federation—are a menace to society. _____

5. The artificial heart may just be the most momentous invention of the late twentieth century because of its ability to prolong the lives of those who suffer from heart ailments. _____

6. Many people who engage in skydiving describe the event as exhilarating, heart pounding, and just plain fun. _____

7. A ferocious and vicious pit bull was responsible for the damage to my front tire. _____

8. Lovely bright purple and white flowers blanketed the peaceful landscape. _____

9. There's no better place to watch TV sports than leaning back in a nice, comfy recliner. _____

10. Many recliners are ugly—bulky and overstuffed—sort of like football linemen. _____

Determining Tone.   In addition to communicating either an overall positive or an overall negative view about a subject, an author can also reveal a more specific attitude, or **tone.** For example, the author may be angry, critical, or sarcastic about his subject. These attitudes express more particular types of negative bias. Or, an author might be excited, sympathetic, amused, or awed. These are some examples of positive bias. Of course, authors can present their ideas and information with a neutral, objective tone, too. The following series of passages illustrates how changing a few words here and there results in a very different tone:

This passage illustrates a **neutral tone:**

The Immigration and Naturalization Service ranks among the worst managed federal agencies rated by *Government Executive* magazine. It

Copyright © Houghton Mifflin Company. All rights reserved.

9

charges immigrants for doing basic paperwork and even for some informational phone calls. Additionally, its facilities aren't equipped to handle the volume of people it serves.*

This passage illustrates a **critical tone:**

The ***bureaucratic nightmare*** we call the Immigration and Naturalization Service ranks among the worst managed federal agencies rated by *Government Executive* magazine. It ***robs poor immigrants of their hard-earned money*** by charging them for basic paperwork, and it ***even has the nerve*** to require these people to pay for informational phone calls. Additionally, its ***embarrassingly substandard*** facilities aren't equipped to handle the volumes of people it serves.

This passage illustrates a **sympathetic tone:**

The ***overworked and struggling*** Immigration and Naturalization Service ranks among the ***worst*** managed federal agencies rated by *Government Executive* magazine. Its ***meager resources force it*** to charge immigrants for doing basic paperwork, and its ***pitiful lack of funding leaves it no choice*** but to charge people for informational phone calls. ***The agency has been ignored for so long that its cramped and outdated*** facilities just aren't equipped to handle the volumes of people it serves.

The first paragraph is relatively neutral. It includes one opinion and two facts, all of which are free of emotional words. Therefore, the reader is not encouraged toward any particular feeling or attitude. The second version, however, is clearly critical and angry. Words and phrases like *nightmare, robs,* and *embarrassingly substandard* leave no doubt in the reader's mind about the author's attitude, and they encourage the reader to blame the agency for its problems. Notice, though, how the tone changes to one of sympathy in the third version. In that paragraph, the boldfaced, italicized words and phrases suggest that we should feel sorry for the "ignored" agency, which is not to blame for its troubles.

Exercise 9.4

Read each of the paragraphs below and then use the boldfaced, italicized words to help you circle the correct tone in the list that follows.

*Adapted from "Amnesty Debate Only Skirts U.S. Immigration Troubles," *USA Today,* August 6, 2001, 12A.

Copyright © Houghton Mifflin Company. All rights reserved.

1. John Buell, a former high school history teacher who coauthored the book *The End of Homework: How Homework Disrupts Families, Overburdens Children and Limits Learning,* has finally proven once and for all that the benefits of homework assignments are **terribly overrated.** For one thing, homework is **useless** for the many students who don't go home to a quiet house with the required reference materials or support. For these kids, who are just like the fairy tale princess asked to spin straw into gold, homework is just another **misery.** It's **ridiculous,** too, to believe that homework teaches kids responsibility and discipline. Schools and teachers have no business taking over those lessons from parents, who can achieve the same results by assigning chores. Homework's **worst fault,** though, is its **shameful takeover** of limited family time. Families certainly have better things to do than supervise some teacher's agenda.*

    a. Critical   c. Neutral
    b. Amused

2. Your body has a way of telling you to chill out. When you're **overworked** and **overtired,** you can feel **tension** in **vulnerable areas** such as the neck, back, and shoulders. If you don't relax, your **stress zones** can become **chronically tight,** which can lead to strength imbalances and even more tension as other muscles work to compensate, says Greg Roskopf, a Denver-based exercise physiologist who works with the Utah Jazz and Denver Broncos. For fast relief in your most **stress-prone spots,** do some stretching activities.†

    a. Neutral   c. Sarcastic
    b. Amused

3. In the beginning, there was Lucy. Long before Marlo, Mary, Rhoda, Roseanne, Ellen, and other one-name TV women, Lucille Ball, the **queen of funny women, blazed a trail.** Whether packing chocolates or stomping grapes, she traveled a **wacky path** that has never been surpassed. Lucy, born 90 years ago this month in Jamestown, N.Y., died in 1989 after heart surgery. Her **escapades** on *I Love Lucy,* which debuted on CBS 50 years ago this fall, and later series still **delight** viewers. What do you know about this **zany redhead**?‡

    a. Admiring   c. Neutral
    b. Morbid

*Adapted from Greg Toppo, "How Much Is Too Much?" The *News Herald,* Morganton, NC, August 2, 2001, 5A.

†Adapted from Martica K. Heaner, "Delete Stress in 4 Minutes," *Glamour,* September 2001, 140.

‡Adapted from Kenneth C. Davis, "Don't Know Much About Lucille Ball," *USA Weekend,* August 26, 2001, 22.

Copyright © Houghton Mifflin Company. All rights reserved.

9

4. Ireland has no shortage of ***charming villages*** and ***spectacular scenery.*** Go almost anywhere, and you're bound to come upon ***wonderful vacation spots.*** My first stop is always Kenmare, a town of about 1,200 that sits at the head of the bay separating the 30-mile-long Beara from a peninsula to the north, more commonly known as the Ring of Kerry. If it seems to have been designed by a tourism board—***immaculate, colorful, timeless,*** situated on the sea and ringed by mountains—there's a reason for it: Kenmare is one of only two planned towns in Ireland. Last year it won the country's annual Tidy Town competition, and it really is hard to understand why it does not ***win by default*** every year.*

   a. Insulting   c. Admiring
   b. Neutral

5. Thank God the Democrats are no longer in the White House. We had eight years of scandal, impropriety, shady dealings, and general amorality. I used to be a Democrat, but now I am a Republican. You just can't trust Democrats. Remember the old joke, "A Republican is a Democrat who has been mugged"? Well, I think it should be "A Republican is a Democrat who has seen the light." Thank goodness I've come to my senses.

   a. Neutral   c. Admiring
   b. Critical

Question #2: What Is the Main Point and the Evidence Offered to Support It?

A second essential question for critical readers concerns the author's main point or position, and the evidence that supports it. A critical reader carefully scrutinizes both to make a determination about the text's validity.

In Chapters 2 and 3, you learned to recognize stated and unstated main ideas. A critical reader not only identifies this point but also examines it further to decide whether it is valid or not. In particular, you should evaluate these characteristics of a main idea:

- **Is it significant?** Does the main idea seem important? Does it impact a lot of people? Not every point has to have huge or far-reaching implications, of course, but some ideas are obviously more worthy of attention than others.

9

*Adapted from Thomas Kelly, "Island in the Stream," *Daily News/Travel,* August 26, 2001, 4.

Copyright © Houghton Mifflin Company. All rights reserved.

Copyright © Houghton Mifflin Company. All rights reserved.

- **Is it reasonable?** Does the idea seem logical, or does it seem weird or far-fetched? Even if an idea seems outlandish, you should not necessarily reject it. Some innovative thoughts probably seemed ridiculous at first, so you should reserve judgment until you've given the author an opportunity to explain. However, an idea that seems particularly dubious should put you on the alert, causing you to pay even more careful attention to the evidence offered as proof.

- **Is it appropriately qualified, or limited?** Beware of ideas that are expressed in absolute terms, as though they apply to everyone in every situation, with no exceptions. Authors are free to make generalizations, of course, but if they insist that the idea is universal, it may not be as valid as when they limit it with words like *most, many, several, a lot, quite a few,* and so forth.

- **Does it allow for other possibilities?** There are many different interpretations of the world around us, so reasonable authors often admit to that by using words such as *possibly, may be, could be, seems, appears, apparently,* and *seemingly,* that suggest that their idea offers *one* viewpoint, not the *only* viewpoint.

After you evaluate the main point of a reading selection, you're ready to examine the evidence offered in support of that idea. Evidence comes in many forms, including facts, statistics, examples, expert testimony, observation, experience, and opinions. A critical reader weighs all of the evidence presented to decide whether it provides a firm basis of support for accepting an idea. Weighing the evidence involves looking at two qualities:

- Is the evidence *adequate*? Does the author provide enough support, or is he or she trying to convince you on the basis of just one or two observations or examples? Some opinions or ideas are more informed than others, so you should add up the total amount of evidence and decide if it truly offers enough support. In addition, you should evaluate the kinds of evidence offered. Is it all derived from the author's personal experience, or is it based, at least in part, on verifiable facts and research? Be aware, too, that some paragraphs don't offer any real evidence at all; they merely repeat the main idea or offer irrelevant information that doesn't support the point.

- Does the evidence seem *accurate*? Where does the author get the information? If you are provided with any details about the sources of the evidence, you should examine those details to decide how trustworthy the information is. Even facts can be misrepresented or misinterpreted, so it's important to know who collected them and what methods they used.

9

The following passage offers an example of an idea that is sufficiently supported with sound evidence:

> Technology contributes to the erosion of parental authority. Video games are about letting kids manipulate reality, bend it to their will. That means when they get up at last from the console, the loss of power is hard to handle. You can't click your little brother out of existence. Plus, no generation has had access to this much information, along with the ability to share it and twist it. Teenagers can re-create themselves, invent a new identity online, escape the boundaries of the household into a very private online world with few guardrails. As Michael Lewis argues in his new book, *Next: The Future Just Happened,* a world in which 14-year-olds can threaten the whole music industry represents a huge shift in the balance of power.*

The first sentence of this paragraph offers the opinion that technology is allowing kids to gain more power over parents. Then, it explains how two kinds of technology—video games and the online world—contribute to an increase in kids' imagined and actual power. This paragraph blends both facts and opinions to support the main point. It includes one opinion from an author who is presumably an expert on the subject. Would you agree, then, that it gives adequate and accurate evidence to prove the main idea? Does it convince you to agree? Each reader must decide for him or herself, but most people would probably agree that the evidence presented here seems convincing.

Now, read a paragraph that offers less convincing evidence in support of the main idea:

> American university education is still the best in the world. Many talented foreign students come to this country to earn their college degrees. Also, most American students choose to attend college in their own country rather than studying abroad.

This passage begins with an opinion that American universities are superior to those in the rest of the world. However, it offers very little evidence in support of that opinion. The two reasons given are not nearly enough to prove that American education is the "best." To do that, you'd have to add more evidence about its resources and its "products," such as its graduates' and faculties' contributions to society. Also, you'd want to add the specific data—the numbers and other statistics—that would back up those points. As it stands now, though, the evidence in this paragraph is inadequate, so the reader has no reason to accept the author's opinion as true.

*Adapted from Nancy Gibbs, "Who's in Charge Here?" *Time,* August 6, 2001, 44–45.

Copyright © Houghton Mifflin Company. All rights reserved.

Exercise 9.5

Read each of the following passages and then answer the questions that follow by circling the letter of the correct response or by writing your answer on the blank provided.

A. The bull shark usually grows no longer than ten feet and weighs up to 500 pounds, but what it lacks in size it makes up for in aggressiveness. Experts regard it as the most pugnacious of sharks. It has, according to Robert Heuter, director of the Center of Shark Research at the Mote Marine Laboratory in Sarasota, Florida, the highest level of testosterone in any animal, including lions and elephants. Its jaws are a steel trap: lower spiked teeth are designed to hold prey while the upper triangular serrated teeth gouge out flesh. "The bull is an ambush type of predator. It makes this big mortal wound," says Heuter. It is fearless, taking on prey as large as it is.*

1. The main point of this passage can be paraphrased:
   a. The bull shark has spiked teeth.
   b. The bull shark shares some similarities with elephants and lions.
   c. The bull shark is an aggressive animal.

2. How many pieces of evidence support the main idea?
   a. Two   c. Eight
   b. Four

3. Is the evidence mostly facts or mostly opinions?
   a. Facts   b. Opinions

4. Would you say this evidence is accurate or inaccurate? Why or why not?

   _____

   _____

B. I hope we've finally stopped glorifying the supposedly godlike Middle Eastern soldier. During the Gulf War, everyone was worried about Saddam Hussein's "elite" Republican Guard in Iraq. These soldiers were supposed to be fierce fighters who would ruthlessly snuff out large numbers of American lives. But they were really just cowards who threw up their hands in surrender as soon as they saw us coming. It is time to recognize that the American soldier is the best-trained, best-equipped, and best-motivated warrior this world has to offer. The American military is by far more powerful than any

Copyright © Houghton Mifflin Company. All rights reserved.

9

*Adapted from Terry McCarthy, "Why Can't We Be Friends?" *Time,* July 30, 2001, 39.

other country's military, and we don't need to romanticize the power of the enemy.

1. The main point of this passage can be paraphrased:
   a. American soldiers are better than Middle Eastern soldiers.
   b. Middle Eastern soldiers are fierce fighters.
   c. The Gulf War was a severe test of American bravery.
   d. The military is no place for cowards.

2. How many pieces of evidence support the main idea?
   a. One   c. Six
   b. Four   d. Eight

3. Is the evidence mostly facts or mostly opinions?
   a. Facts   b. Opinions

4. Does the evidence presented adequately support the main point of this selection? Why or why not?

_____

_____

_____

C. American Indians on and off reservations in the 1960s called for changes in federal and state policies. Increasingly militant Indian leaders demanded the protection and restoration of their ancient burial grounds, along with fishing and timber rights. They asked museums to return the remains of dead Indians on display. The National Indian Youth Council called for Indians to resist further loss of Indian lands. Vine DeLoria's* popular *Custer Died for Your Sins* (1969) informed readers that Indians asked "only to be freed of cultural oppression." "The white does not understand the Indian," he wrote, "and the Indian does not wish to understand the white." The central issue was not equality and assimilation, DeLoria explained, but Indian self-determination. Indians wanted economic prosperity and opportunity, but on terms that would ensure their continued tribal existence.†

1. The main point of this passage can be paraphrased:
   a. Vine DeLoria was the voice of the American Indian in the 1960s.
   b. "Indian self-determination" was a catch phrase in the 1960s.

*Deloria is a Lakota Sioux Indian and a well-known spokesperson on Native American rights.
†From Berkin et al., *Making America*. Boston: Houghton Mifflin, 2001, 674–675.

Copyright © Houghton Mifflin Company. All rights reserved.

    c. The government resisted change when it came to the American Indians in the 1960s.

    d. In the 1960s, American Indians fought for changes in government policy with the hope of keeping their tribal existence intact.

2. How many pieces of evidence support the main idea?

    a. One   c. Four

    b. Two   d. Six

3. Is the evidence mostly facts or mostly opinions?

    a. Facts   b. Opinions

4. Would you say this evidence is accurate or inaccurate? Why? _____

_____

_____

_____

D. Where I live, although the speed limit is 55 miles per hour, people who drive large cars, vans, and SUV's go in excess of 75 miles an hour. I am always very careful not to exceed the speed limit and it really burns me up that so many people are careless with their lives and the lives of fellow drivers. Speeding is one thing, but the same crazy drivers also tailgate, pulling right up to and sometimes bumping my bumper as I drive in the left lane. They flash their lights and zoom up next to me to show their displeasure with the fact that I am driving in the "fast" lane and not going fast enough for their liking. What is the point of posting speed limits if nobody is going to drive the limit posted?

1. The main point of this passage can be paraphrased:

    a. People do not pay attention to speed limits.

    b. People who drive SUVs and other "fancy" vehicles have bad manners.

    c. Tailgating should be illegal.

    d. There are many cars on the road today.

2. Is the evidence mostly facts or opinions?

    a. Facts   b. Opinions

3. Would you say this evidence is accurate and adequate? Why? _____

_____

_____

_____

Copyright © Houghton Mifflin Company. All rights reserved.

9

Deciding for Yourself

Once you are able to separate fact from opinion, detect bias and different types of tone, and evaluate the main point and the evidence, you should be able to better evaluate whether a text is valid or worthy. Then, you can determine what you should do about the new ideas or information. Should you accept them as true? Should you change your own opinions in response? Should you reject the text outright? Or should you resolve to gather more information before you respond? Critical readers know how to scrutinize a text so they can decide for themselves.

CHAPTER 9 REVIEW

Fill in the blanks in the following statements.

1. _____ reading means noticing certain techniques the writer is using to convince you of the validity and worth of his or her ideas or information.

2. _____ are information that is verifiably true.

3. _____ are statements that express beliefs, feelings, judgments, attitudes, and preferences.

4. Certain _____ words—such as relative terms, qualifying terms, absolute terms, or terms that admit other possibilities—often appear in statements of opinion.

5. You can use two critical reading _____ to guide your interpretation of a text. These questions focus on the author's background and goals and the main point and evidence.

6. Information about the author's background and purpose can help you evaluate his or her _____

7. _____ is an inclination toward a particular opinion or viewpoint.

8. _____ is the author's specific attitude about his or her subject.

9. A sound main point is usually _____, reasonable, _____, and mindful of other _____.

10. _____ includes facts, statistics, examples, expert testimony, observations, experiences, and opinions.

11. Sound evidence is both _____ and _____.

Copyright © Houghton Mifflin Company. All rights reserved.

9

Reading Selection

My 60-Second Protest from the Hallway
By Emily Lesk

1   It's 8:32 A.M. School began two minutes ago. My bulging book bag is inside my first-period classroom saving my favorite seat. I am standing in the near-empty hallway, leaning against a locker right outside the classroom. I should be in class, yet my teacher has never objected to my minute-long absence, which has become a daily routine. I trace around the edges of the floor tiles with the toe of my running shoe, pausing several times to glance up at the second hand of the standard-issue clock mounted across the hall.

2   Although I have casually checked this clock countless times during my high school career, this year looking at it has made me think about how significant 60 seconds can be. Last spring, the Common-wealth of Virginia passed a law that requires every public school in the state to set aside one minute at the beginning of each day during which students must remain seated while they "meditate, pray, or engage in any other silent activity." Every morning, at around 8:31, a resonant voice echoes over the school intercom, "Please rise for the Pledge of Allegiance." I stand up straight and salute the flag. After the pledge the voice commands me to "pause for a minute of silence." I push my chair under my desk and stride out of the classroom.

3   My objection to Virginia's Minute of Silence law is very simple. I see the policy as an attempt to bring organized prayer into the public schools, thus violating the United States Constitution. Last June at a statewide student-government convention, I spoke with state lawmakers, who confirmed my suspicion that the minute of silence is religiously motivated. One delegate proudly told me that she supported the law because reciting the Lord's Prayer had been a part of her own public school education.

4   I agree with the law's strongest critics, who argue that it promotes religious discrimination because many faiths do not pray in the seated position mandated by the legislation. How would a Muslim third grader react to those students (and maybe a teacher) who might fold their hands and bow their heads to pray? Would she feel pressured to join in just to avoid criticism?

5   My opposition to this law is ironic because I consider myself religious and patriotic. I recite the Pledge of Allegiance daily (including the "one nation under God" part, which to me has historical, not religious, implications). As a Reform Jew, I get peace and self-assurance from religious worship and meditation, both at my synagogue and in my home. But my religious education also taught me the importance of standing up against discrimination and persecution. In a school of 1,600 students, fewer than two dozen have joined me in protest. I usually walk out of class with one or two kids, sometimes none. Most days, when I glance back into the classroom, I see several students praying, heads bowed or eyes closed, while others do homework or daydream. Although I have not encountered any outright opposition, I often overhear classmates making

Copyright © Houghton Mifflin Company. All rights reserved.

sarcastic comments or dismissing the protest as futile. When I see that so many of my peers and teachers find no reason to question something I feel so strongly about, I wonder if my objection is justified. What do my 30 extra daily paces accomplish?

6   In contemplating that question, I've come to realize that taking a stand is about knowing why I believe what I do and refusing to give in despite the lack of support. My decision to protest was largely personal. Though I stayed in class the first morning the law was implemented—because I was caught off guard and because I was curious to see how others would respond—sitting there felt like a betrayal of my values. I also felt an obligation to act on behalf of the students all over Virginia who found their own beliefs violated but don't attend schools that allow them to express their opinions.

7   Deep down, I know this issue will be decided in a courtroom, not in my corridor. On May 8, the Fourth U.S. Circuit Court of Appeals heard oral arguments from ACLU lawyers representing seven families who are challenging the law, and will probably reach a decision over the summer. But for now I'll walk out of class each day to show my school community that an easy alternative to complacency does exist. This year I will have spent approximately three hours standing in the hallway in protest, watching the second hand make its 360-degree journey. As a senior about to graduate, I've thought about the impact I've had on my school. I hope that my protest inspired other kids to use the time to think, not about a beckoning test, but about their views—even if those views differ from my own.

(From *Newsweek*, June 11, 2001, 13. All rights reserved. Reprinted by permission.)

VOCABULARY

Read the following questions about some of the vocabulary words that appear in the previous selection. Circle the correct responses.

1. In paragraph 2, the author uses the term *resonant* to describe someone's voice. What does *resonant* mean in this context?

   a. Soft
   b. Loud

   c. Shaky
   d. Heavily accented

2. What does the word *delegate* mean in paragraph 3? Reread the paragraph to see the context in which the word is used.

   a. Member of the state government
   b. Member of the student body

   c. Classmate
   d. Friend

3. What does it mean to *mandate* something? In paragraph 4, the author writes "I agree with the law's strongest critics, who argue that it promotes

Copyright © Houghton Mifflin Company. All rights reserved.

9

religious discrimination because many faiths do not pray in the seated position *mandated* by the legislation."

a. To require
c. To make accessible
b. To deny
d. To incline

4. In paragraph 5, Lesk writes, ". . . I often overhear classmates making sarcastic comments or dismissing the protest as *futile*." What does *futile* mean?

a. Energetic
c. Worthless
b. Lively
d. Expensive

5. In paragraph 7, the author writes, "But for now I'll walk out of class each day to show my school community that an easy alternative to *complacency* does exist." What does *complacency* mean?

a. Indifference
c. Exercise
b. Activity
d. Argument

6. The author uses the word *beckoning* to describe a test in paragraph 7. What does *beckoning* mean in this context?

a. Gesturing
c. Pointing
b. Waving
d. Forthcoming

CRITICAL READING

Are the following sentences (1–6) from the reading selection facts (F) or opinions (O)? Write your answer next to each sentence. In sentences 7–9, circle the correct response.

1. Last spring, the Commonwealth of Virginia passed a law that requires every public school in the state to set aside one minute at the beginning of each day during which students must remain seated while they "meditate, pray, or engage in any other silent activity." _____

2. My objection to Virginia's Minute of Silence law is very simple. _____

3. Last June at a statewide student-government convention, I spoke with state lawmakers, who confirmed my suspicion that the minute of silence is religiously motivated. _____

4. My opposition to this law is ironic because I consider myself religious and patriotic. _____

5. In a school of 1,600 students, fewer than two dozen have joined me in protest. _____

9

Copyright © Houghton Mifflin Company. All rights reserved.

6. Deep down, I know this issue will be decided in a courtroom, not in my corridor. _____

7. What is Emily Lesk's tone in this selection?
   a. Amused   c. Serious
   b. Outraged   d. Lighthearted

8. The main point of this selection can be paraphrased:
   a. Emily Lesk likes to pray.
   b. Most high school students do not understand serious national issues.
   c. Emily Lesk is opposed to the Virginia Minute of Silence law and protests it daily.
   d. Emily Lesk should run for Congress.

9. Is the evidence mostly facts, opinions, or a combination of both?
   a. Facts
   b. Opinions
   c. Combination of both

10. Would you say this evidence is adequate and accurate? Why?

   _____

   _____

QUESTIONS FOR DISCUSSION AND WRITING

Answer the following questions based on your reading of the selection.

1. Do you agree or disagree with Emily Lesk's statement that she sees "the policy as an attempt to bring organized prayer into the public schools, thus violating the United States Constitution"? Why? _____

   _____

2. Have you ever protested something that you considered an injustice? If so, what was it and what were the consequences of your actions?

   _____

   _____

3. Do you think Emily Lesk makes a good argument against prayer in public schools? Why or why not? If not, what do you think she could have done to make her argument more convincing? _____

   _____

Copyright © Houghton Mifflin Company. All rights reserved.

9

◗ Vocabulary: Figures of Speech

Figures of speech are creative comparisons between things that have something in common. An author uses figures of speech because they are clever, interesting, vivid, and imagistic. In other words, they tend to create pictures, or images, in the reader's mind. An author also includes figures of speech because they help readers understand something new and unfamiliar by comparing to something already known or understood. Four types of figures of speech are analogies, metaphors, similes, and personification.

An **analogy** is an extended comparison between two things or ideas. Analogies can aid readers in grasping new concepts. For example, look at the following analogy:

> There are much better ways to get the acceptance we crave from other people. One of the easiest is what I call "tossing fish." If you've ever been to Sea World, you've probably seen trainers reward the dolphins and seals by feeding them fish. Sea mammals will do anything for anyone who's carrying a bucket of what they love most. They're a lot like people, that way—and you just happen to have a bottomless bucket of what humans love most: approval.*

In this passage, humans who seek approval are compared to dolphins and seals who perform for fish. This analogy helps the reader better understand the author's point about the nature of seeking approval from others.

A **simile** is much like an analogy, but briefer. Rather than being developed over several sentences, a simile is usually just a phrase inserted into a sentence. It compares one thing or idea to another by using the words *like* or *as*. For example, look at this example from this chapter:

> *Like a fox in a hen house*, ruthless collectors are plundering Africa's cultural heritage by encouraging poor Africans to sell stolen treasures.

This simile compares collectors to a fox to express the idea that they are stealing and causing havoc just like a hungry predator does.

A **metaphor** makes a more direct comparison by stating that something actually *is* something else rather than just *like* it. For example, read this next sentence:

> Its jaws *are a steel trap*: lower spiked teeth are designed to hold prey while the upper triangular serrated teeth gouge out flesh.

A shark's jaws are not actually a steel trap, but this metaphor says they are to create an interesting and informative comparison.

*Adapted from Martha Beck, "Equal Encounters of the Human Kind," *O* Magazine, September 2001, 118.

9

Copyright © Houghton Mifflin Company. All rights reserved.

One last type of figure of speech is **personification,** which compares nonhuman objects or animals to humans by giving them human abilities or characteristics. When we say the wind is *whistling* through the trees or the fire engine's siren *screams* in the night, we are giving the wind and the siren human abilities. Here's another example, which comes from Chapter 8:

> It was an unusual ceremony because all the graduates were convicted felons, and it took place in a gym *embraced* by locked metal gates and razor wire at the Bedford Hills Correctional Facility, a maximum security prison.

In this sentence, the gates and razor wire are given the human ability to embrace.

Vocabulary Exercise

The following sentences all come from this chapter and previous chapters. In each one, underline the figure of speech. Then, on the blank provided, write the two things or ideas that are being compared.

1. For these kids, who are just like the fairy tale princess asked to spin straw into gold, homework is just another misery.

   _____

   _____

2. On the bank of the Ottawa River, at 6 A.M., Colorado Avalanche hockey coach Bob Hartley removed the championship Stanley Cup trophy from its case like a father cradling a baby out of a crib, joking that he thought it was still sleeping.

   _____

3. About 60 showed up at the docks starting at 5:30 A.M. to fish with Hartley and the Cup, or at least to help launch his official day with what is arguably professional sports' most storied trophy and the Holy Grail of hockey.

   _____

4. Wife Sharon Stone has been calling him a hero ever since their private tour of the Los Angeles Zoo ended when a Komodo dragon, a small Godzilla, bit him in the foot.

   _____

9

Copyright © Houghton Mifflin Company. All rights reserved.

5. I love feeling empty, like a hollow gourd.

_____

6. Using the Internet, anyone willing to break a few laws can be a mass producer of fake IDs, the gateway to underage drinking. . .

_____

7. Mother England made the mistake of withholding liberty too long from her "children" in the American colonies. They grew to be rebellious "teenagers" who demanded their freedom. In response, their "mother" refused to release them. As a result, a war had to be fought.

_____

_____

8. When attention dropped, Escalante would begin the "wave," a cheer in which row after row of students, in succession, stood, raising their hands, then sat quickly, creating a ripple across the room like a pennant bellowing in victory.

_____

9. Anne then proceeded to Step Two, which—as you have probably already guessed—was to slip and fall face-first into the glue coat she created in Step One, thus bonding herself to the floor like a gum wad on a hot sidewalk.

_____

Copyright © Houghton Mifflin Company. All rights reserved.

9

Name _____ Date _____

POST-TEST 1

A. Read the following questions carefully and then answer them by circling the correct response.

1. Which of the following is a fact?

    a. Most computers use Microsoft Windows.
    b. Microsoft has too much power over computers.
    c. Microsoft is the computer user's best friend.
    d. Everybody uses Microsoft Windows.

2. Which of the following is an opinion?

    a. Tiger Woods is one of today's best golfers.
    b. Tiger Woods worked hard to develop his championship skills.
    c. Tiger Woods is the best golfer who ever lived.
    d. Tiger Woods has a lot of commercial endorsements.

3. Which of the following is a fact?

    a. Ashley's abnormal liking for seafood is disgusting.
    b. Nobody eats seafood more often than Ashley.
    c. Ashley must get her seafood for free.
    d. Ashley usually eats seafood twice a week.

4. Which of the following is an opinion?

    a. Cell phones are dangerous.
    b. One study has shown that the normal radiation emitted by cell phones has been harmful to rats.
    c. Other studies in humans have shown no difference in cancer rates between those who use cell phones and those who don't.
    d. Many people regularly use cell phones these days.

5. Which of the following is a fact?

    a. I just hate it when it's really hot outside.
    b. It was 95 degrees in the shade yesterday.
    c. I prefer to stay inside when it's super-hot outside.
    d. Air conditioning was mankind's greatest invention.

For additional tests, see the Test Bank.

Copyright © Houghton Mifflin Company. All rights reserved.

9

B. Read the following passages, then answer the questions that follow by circling the correct choice.

I. (1) Patty Murray was a young mother of two when she first visited the Washington State Senate in the early '80s. (2) Then a homemaker, she had come to fight against budget cuts for an educational program that had helped her improve her parenting skills. (3) "I was trying to figure out why these people couldn't understand what was happening with kids and families," she says. (4) "And I realized that I was looking down on all these old bald heads." (5) She lost the battle, at least temporarily. (6) But the encounter helped spur Murray, 51, to enter local politics a few years later, starting down a path that would lead her to the U.S. Senate. (7) There she has made a name for herself as a one-time soccer mom who represents the interest of ordinary folks. (8) "She didn't create this image to win a political race," says Sid Snyder, majority leader of the state senate. (9) "That's who she is."*

6. Sentence 1 is a/an

   a. fact.   b. opinion.

7. Sentence 2 is a/an

   a. fact.   b. opinion.

8. Sentence 8 is a/an

   a. fact.   b. opinion.

II. (1) The role of deer predator is an apt one for humans. (2) We are biologically specialized for hunting game and can do it accurately and well. (3) When it comes to the predation of small animals, we are not so well equipped. (4) Our ears aren't attuned to grubs chewing on a root. (5) Our noses are too dull to sniff mice hiding in a hole. (6) I really hate those bug zappers that buzz and blink near swimming pools and patios, creating unnecessary holes in the nocturnal community of insects. (7) They kill insects that navigate by celestial light or orient toward brightness, such as moths that guide their course by moonlight or search for pale blossoms blooming in the night. (8) Mosquitoes out for blood are guided by the exhalations of their victims. (9) They don't fly to light, so they aren't electrocuted by zappers.†

9. Sentence 1 is a/an

   a. fact.   b. opinion.

10. Sentence 8 is a/an

   a. fact.   b. opinion.

*From Thomas Fields-Meyer, Elizabeth Velez, and Mary Boone, "Welfare to Washington," *People Weekly*, December 3, 2001, 105.

†From Sara Stein, *Noah's Garden*. Boston: Houghton Mifflin, 1993, 83.

Copyright © Houghton Mifflin Company. All rights reserved.

9

III. (1) Our city block has become a much more pleasant place in the last few years. (2) I think it's because some of us in the block association made a big push to plant trees on the block. (3) I'm also pleased that the trees we planted are steadily growing and seem to be very healthy. (4) We deliberately selected the types of trees that have proven to withstand and even flourish in an urban environment. (5) In fact, now that we know this has been a success, I think we should plant even more trees on the block to fill in the gaps.

11. Sentence 1 is a/an

   a. fact.   b. opinion.

12. Sentence 2 is a/an

   a. fact.   b. opinion.

13. Sentence 5 is a/an

   a. fact.   b. opinion.

IV. (1) The on-off switch on our old coffeemaker suddenly stopped working, and neither turned the machine on nor off. (2) We needed a new coffeemaker. (3) The choice was between a coffeemaker that is programmable and one that is not. (4) A programmable coffeemaker would allow us to prepare the water and proper amount of coffee in it before we go to sleep and have it come on in the morning just before we wake up so that there'll be a fresh cup of coffee waiting for us. (5) But a programmable coffeemaker costs more than one that isn't programmable. (6) And besides, our lives are already too programmed. (7) We decided on a coffeemaker that is not programmable.

14. Sentence 1 is a/an

   a. fact.   b. opinion.

15. Sentence 6 is a/an

   a. fact.   b. opinion.

POST-TEST 2

A. Read each of the following statements and answer the questions that follow. Circle the correct choice.

Many schools in our district are unruly and even dangerous.

  1. Which of the following words indicates the author's bias?

    a. Schools   c. Dangerous

    b. District   d. Even

9

Copyright © Houghton Mifflin Company. All rights reserved.

2. Does the author's choice of words make you feel positive or negative about the subject?

   a. Positive   b. Negative

The dancers in our local ballet company are highly trained and beautiful to watch when they perform.

3. Which of the following words indicates the author's bias?

   a. Dancer   c. Beautiful
   b. Local   d. Perform

4. Does the author's choice of words make you feel positive or negative about the subject?

   a. Positive   b. Negative

Rebuilding a 100-story building on the World Trade Center site would lead to economic destruction to the downtown New York City area because nobody will want to rent out the higher, and more vulnerable, floors of the building.

5. Which of the following word or words indicate(s) the author's bias?

   a. Destruction   c. Rebuilding
   b. Downtown   d. Would lead to

6. Does the author's choice of words make you feel positive or negative about the subject?

   a. Positive   b. Negative

B. Select the statement that reveals the author's bias. Circle your choice.

7. a. Our country is dependent on fossil fuels for energy.
   b. Our country relies much too heavily on fossil fuels for energy.
   c. Our country must import a substantial portion of the oil it uses.
   d. Our country used to produce all the fossil fuels it needed.

8. a. The property taxes in our town primarily go toward paying for our local schools' expenses and educators' salaries.
   b. The property taxes in our town have gone up every year for the past eight years.
   c. The property taxes in our town are determined by our town council.
   d. The property taxes in our town are ridiculously high and keep going up with no end in sight.

9. a. Many people do not like to receive telemarketing calls.
   b. Donna is normally very polite and friendly to telemarketers when they call.

Copyright © Houghton Mifflin Company. All rights reserved.

9

    c. Joan gets justifiably angry when a rude telemarketer calls during dinner.

    d. People have different ways of saying "no" to a telemarketer.

10. a. If you want to make this city safer, then vote for Councilman Moran, a man who cares.

    b. Councilman Moran has repeatedly stated that, if elected, he would make this city safer.

    c. It could be useful to review Councilman Moran's past voting record on law and order issues.

    d. Mr. Moran is currently our longest-serving councilperson.

11. a. Some people believe that our town's new, extra-large street signs have cut down on traffic accidents.

    b. We don't yet know if the extra-large street signs have reduced traffic accidents.

    c. Several town council members voted against installing the extra-large street signs.

    d. The new large street signs make our town much safer, friendlier, and more accessible for newcomers.

C. Read the following passages, then answer the questions that follow. Circle the correct response.

12. Few doubt that pesticides as presently used are damaging the environment. American agriculture now uses annually an alarming 700 million pounds of pesticides to control crop damage at a cost of $4.1 billion; an additional $1 billion is wasted to counteract the adverse effects of pesticides on human and environmental health. Less appreciated is the fact that synthetic pesticides have not worked.

What is the tone of the passage?

    a. Critical   c. Insulting

    b. Neutral   d. Amused

13. The great Hollywood film mogul Samuel Goldwyn was the owner of the Goldwyn Picture Company. But the company was not in fact named for Goldwyn, but rather he for it. His real name was Schmuel Gelbfisz, though for his first thirty years in America he had called himself—perhaps a little unwisely—Samuel Goldfish. "Goldwyn" was a combination of the names of the studio's two founders: Samuel Goldfish and Edgar Selwyn. It wasn't until 1918, tired of being the butt of endless fishbowl jokes, that he named himself after his corporation.*

*Adapted from Bill Bryson, *Made in America*. New York: Avon Books, Inc., 1994, 255.

Copyright © Houghton Mifflin Company. All rights reserved.

What is the tone of the passage?

a. Critical   c. Insulting
b. Sarcastic   d. Amused

14. Boot camp was actually one of the most enjoyable experiences of my life. I think I liked it so much because it was so well organized. The first week we were there, we ran everywhere, even to and from the bathroom and the shower. At the cafeteria, we'd wait in the chow line for several minutes until we finally were able to get some food on our plates, then one minute after we sat down to eat, our company commander would say we had to get started running to our next class. Even sleeping was highly organized. Our beds were closely inspected every day for wrinkles and improper folds. The problem was, we didn't have time to fold everything properly, and who knew how to fold it anyway? So we all slept on the floor under our beds. Ever since, I have valued highly the importance of a properly folded bed.

What is the tone of this passage?

a. Critical   c. Insulting
b. Sarcastic   d. Neutral

15. While famous among tourists for its ancient ruins, medieval walled cities, and enchanting Mediterranean beaches, the island nation of Malta is notorious among conservationists for its killing fields. Each year, up to one million birds, from finches to herons, are shot or trapped in this tiny country, which is less than twice the size of Washington, D.C. Although hunting and trapping laws exist, they are generous, and restrictions are poorly enforced. The greenfinch and six other finch species are prized by trappers, who locally sell or trade them as pets. Meanwhile, hunters take aim at a variety of migrating birds just for target practice or for trophies, rarely eating their quarry.*

What is the tone of this passage?

a. Critical   c. Insulting
b. Sarcastic   d. Neutral

Copyright © Houghton Mifflin Company. All rights reserved.

*From Howard Youth, "The Killing Fields," *Wildlife Conservation,* July/August, 1999, 16.

Copyright © Houghton Mifflin Company. All rights reserved.

CHAPTER **10**

Reading Longer Selections

GOALS FOR CHAPTER 10

▶ Explain the difference between skimming and scanning, and scan a text for information.

▶ Define the term *thesis statement*.

▶ Recognize the topic and thesis statement of longer reading selections.

▶ Define the term *headings* and explain the purpose of headings.

▶ Identify major and minor supporting details in longer reading selections.

▶ Determine implied main ideas in longer reading selections.

▶ Recognize patterns of organization in longer reading selections.

▶ Identify transitions in longer reading selections.

READING STRATEGY: Scanning

The last time you went to a restaurant hungry for a particular dish, like fried chicken, did you read every word of the menu before placing your order? You probably didn't. Instead, you glanced over the lists and descriptions of the items available until you found the ones that included fried chicken, and you probably ignored most of the other sections of the menu. This is called **scanning,** and it is a useful strategy to use when you are searching for a particular piece of information. You also scan when you look for a certain topic in a book's table of contents or index, or when you read a visual aid like a table. You are scanning when you look at classified ads, telephone books, dictionaries, or a list of Web sites generated by an Internet search engine.

When you scan a text, you don't read the whole thing; rather, you run your eyes over the page, reading words or phrases here and there until you discover what you are looking for. Though this seems like

Continued

10

skimming, the strategy explained in Chapter 9, it is different because when you scan, you know what you are looking for. When you skim, you don't; you are just trying to gain a general understanding of a text and/or its main features.

When might scanning be appropriate for longer texts such as chapters or articles? If you are looking for an answer to a particular question, or if you are searching for a specific fact, name, or other type of detail, scan the text to find what you need. Scanning is often useful, then, for completing assignments or for refreshing your memory about some piece of information you remember reading about. If you need to form a complete understanding of the ideas in a text, however, you'll have to read it more thoroughly.

On page 413 is a page from a textbook's index. Scan it to answer the questions that follow.

1. On what page can you find information about the assassination of John F. Kennedy? _____

2. On how many different pages is Little Rock Central High School mentioned? _____

3. If you want to find information about Latinos, to what topic in the index must you turn? _____

4. What are the two types of lawsuits addressed in this textbook? _____

5. If you want to learn about Lincoln's Gettysburg Address, to which page should you turn? _____

Copyright © Houghton Mifflin Company. All rights reserved.

Copyright © Houghton Mifflin Company. All rights reserved.

112   *Index*

Source: From James Q. Wilson and John J. Dilulio, *American Government*, 8th ed. Boston: Houghton Mifflin, 2001, 112. Copyright © 2001 by Houghton Mifflin Company. Reprinted with permission.

Now that you've practiced improving your comprehension of paragraphs, you are ready to move on to reading longer passages. To see how well you already comprehend longer selections, complete the following pre-test.

PRE-TEST

Read the following selection from a college history textbook. As you continue in your academic career, you will be asked to read longer and more challenging selections, most of which will come from textbooks. Take some time to do this pre-test and warm up for the longer, more challenging readings you will encounter in the rest of this chapter. If you come across any difficult or unfamiliar words, consult your dictionary.

MAKING A NEW WORLD, TO 1558: AMERICAN ORIGINS

1 The settlement of the Western Hemisphere (the half of the earth that includes North America, Mexico, Central America, and South America) took place fairly recently in human history. Although human culture began about four million years ago in what is now northern Tanzania, anthropologists believe that the peopling of the Americas did not begin until at least 70,000 years ago. Some theorize that this process did not begin until about 20,000 years ago.

2 The movement of people from Asia to North America is intimately connected to the advance and retreat of glaciers during the Great Ice Age, which began about 2.5 million years ago and ended only about 10,000 years ago. During the Wisconsin glaciation, the last major advance of glaciers, a sheet of ice over 8,000 feet thick covered the northern half of both Europe and North America. So much water was frozen into this massive glacier that sea levels dropped as much as 450 feet.

3 Consequently, this drop in sea levels created a land bridge called Beringia between Siberia and Alaska. During the Ice Age, Beringia was a dry, frigid grassland that was free of glaciers. It was a perfect grazing ground for animals such as giant bison and huge-tusked woolly mammoths. Hunters of these animals, including large wolves, saber-toothed cats, and humans, followed them across Beringia into North America. Geologists believe that sea levels were low enough to expose Beringia between 70,000 and 10,000 years ago. Archaeological evidence yields a wide variety of dates for when people first moved southward into North America, ranging from about 40,000 to about 12,000 years ago.

4 Other evidence, from blood DNA, tooth shapes, and languages, suggests that the majority of North America's original inhabitants descended from three separate migrating groups. The first of these, the Paleo-Indians, proba-

Copyright © Houghton Mifflin Company. All rights reserved.

10

bly arrived 30,000 to 40,000 years ago. Their descendants ultimately occupied the entire Western Hemisphere. The second group, the Na-Dene people, arrived near the end of the Wisconsin era, between 10,000 and 11,000 years ago. Their descendants are concentrated in subarctic regions of Canada and in the southwestern United States. The final group, the Arctic-dwelling Inuits, or Eskimos, probably arrived after the land bridge between North America and Asia disappeared.

5   About 9,000 years ago, a warming trend began that ended the Ice Age and brought temperatures to what we now consider normal. As temperatures warmed and grasslands disappeared, the gigantic Ice Age creatures that had supplied early hunters with their primary source of meat, clothing, and tools began to die out. The hunters faced the unpleasant prospect of following the large animals into extinction if they kept trying to survive by hunting big game.*

1. What is the topic of this selection? (Circle the correct response.)

   a. The Ice Age   c. Prehistoric man
   b. American origins   d. Beringia

2. Which of the following is a *major* supporting detail from the selection?

   a. The settlement of the Western Hemisphere took place fairly recently in human history. (paragraph 1)
   b. The movement of people from Asia to North America is intimately connected to the advance and retreat of glaciers during the Great Ice Age, which began about 2.5 million years ago and ended only about 10,000 years ago. (paragraph 2)
   c. The first of these, the Paleo-Indians, probably arrived 30,000 to 40,000 years ago. (paragraph 4)
   d. This drop in sea levels created a land bridge called Beringia between Siberia and Alaska. (paragraph 3)

3. Which of the following is a *minor* supporting detail from the selection?

   a. The settlement of the Western Hemisphere took place fairly recently in human history. (paragraph 1)
   b. This drop in sea levels created a land bridge called Beringia between Siberia and Alaska. (paragraph 3)
   c. The movement of people from Asia to North America is intimately connected to the advance and retreat of glaciers during the Great Ice Age, which began about 2.5 million years ago and ended only about 10,000 years ago. (paragraph 2)
   d. The second group, the Na-Dene people, arrived near the end of the Wisconsin era, between 10,000 and 11,000 years ago. (paragraph 4)

*Adapted from Berkin et al., *Making America*. Boston: Houghton Mifflin, 2001, 5–6.

Copyright © Houghton Mifflin Company. All rights reserved.

10

4. What pattern organizes the *major* supporting details in this selection?

   a. Cause/effect
   b. Comparison/contrast
   c. Series
   d. Definition

5. Which two paragraphs begin with transition words or phrases?

   a. 1 and 3
   b. 2 and 5
   c. 3 and 5
   d. 1 and 5

6. What is the tone of this selection?

   a. Annoyed
   b. Scholarly
   c. Silly
   d. Sarcastic

7. Which of the following is NOT given as evidence that suggests that the majority of North America's original inhabitants descended from three separate migrating groups? (paragraph 4)

   a. Tooth shapes
   b. Languages
   c. Cave paintings
   d. Blood DNA

So far, this book has focused mainly on helping you improve your reading comprehension by awareness and understanding of important features in *paragraphs*. But what about longer selections, those that are composed of multiple paragraphs? You may be wondering if you'll have to learn a whole new set of concepts in order to understand long selections such as chapters or articles. Fortunately, the answer is no. Many of the same principles apply to reading longer passages. This chapter, therefore, will focus on applying the information you've already learned in previous chapters to help you get more out of a reading composed of more than one paragraph.

Topic, Main Idea, and Thesis

In Chapter 2 of this book, you learned about topics, main ideas, and topic sentences. Like paragraphs, longer reading selections contain all three of these elements. A longer selection such as an essay or an article will be about a topic, and it will make a point about that topic just as a paragraph's topic sentence states the main idea.

However, in a longer reading selection, the main point is usually referred to as a thesis. The **thesis** is the one idea or opinion the author wants readers to know or to believe after they have read the piece. Just like the paragraph's topic sentence, the thesis includes the subject plus what is being said about

Copyright © Houghton Mifflin Company. All rights reserved.

10

that subject. You'll notice when you read the following thesis statements that they sound a lot like topic sentences:

> Although memory lapses are normal, following certain strategies will help improve your ability to recall information.

> Modern archeologists are making discoveries that affirm the historical truth of Biblical stories in both the Old and New Testaments.

> People in drug or alcohol detoxification programs, chemotherapy patients, and patients suffering from chronic pain can all benefit from acupuncture.

Rather than being developed in one paragraph, however, a thesis statement generally presents an idea that needs several paragraphs of explanation. It is often a point that is broader than one you would see in a topic sentence. That is why it takes longer to explain.

The thesis statement almost always appears near the beginning of the selection, most often in the opening paragraph. It is the main idea that will be developed throughout the rest of the piece. It may be useful here to recall what you learned about the terms *general* and *specific*. These concepts apply to longer readings, too. Just as paragraphs include a general topic and a specific point about that topic, longer selections also focus on one particular idea about a broader subject.

To find the thesis statement, determine first what the subject is. What does the opening paragraph seem to be about? Then look for a sentence that includes both this topic and a particular point about that topic.

A longer selection will still include topic sentences, too. Each paragraph will present a particular idea, just like those you studied in Chapter 2, and many of these paragraphs will state the point in a topic sentence that appears at the beginning, in the middle, or at the end of the paragraph. The major difference, however, is that these paragraphs do not stand alone; instead, they are smaller units within a larger whole.

For an illustration of how a longer selection includes a topic, a thesis statement, and topic sentences, read the following passage:

Will Your Hotel Be Super-safe?

If your summer vacation plans include a hotel stay, you have a lot of company. Americans spent over $300 billion on hotels last year. And, of course,

you want to stay in the safest hotel. Well, you can make sure you do by

TOPIC

Copyright © Houghton Mifflin Company. All rights reserved.

10

THESIS

asking some simple questions when you call for reservations. The safest hotels (those where crime rarely happens) have five features.

TOPIC SENTENCE

Magnetic cards or cards with punch holes are much safer than room keys, say experts. Management changes these cards every time someone checks out, and with them, the hotel can track who goes in and out. Plus, they don't show your room number like most keys do, so potential thieves won't see where you're staying.

TOPIC SENTENCE

The second floor is definitely the safest, so try to get a room on that level. The first floor makes your room accessible from the windows, while higher floors can present problems if there's a fire. And avoid rooms around corners and at the end of dead-end hallways. You want a room with lots of traffic, lots of light, and more than one direction to go in case you need to get out fast.

TOPIC SENTENCE

Safe hotels include some type of deadbolt lock on the inside of room doors. Just like in your home, they add extra protection at night while you're asleep.

TOPIC SENTENCE

The safest hotels staff their premises with more than just one employee during the night shift. You want a security guard working there at all times, not just a manager doubling as security.

TOPIC SENTENCE

In a safe hotel, you can get to your room only through the lobby. Staying in a hotel with only one entrance cuts your risk of robbery by half because intruders can't slip in unnoticed.*

In longer selections, sections of the text will often be labeled with headings. **Headings** are like mini-titles that identify the topic of one part of a longer work like a chapter or an article. They help the reader understand the focus of a particular section of text, and they also reveal how various sections are related to each other. For example, look at the following passage:

Flexible Work Schedule Opportunities

To recruit and retain the top talent in the labor market, many organizations offer a variety of flexible work schedules. Demand for greater flexibility has increased in recent years, and some predict that more than 80 percent of large companies will offer some form of flexible work schedules by the year 2000.

Flextime. Flextime typically includes a core time when all employees work, often 10 A.M. to 3 P.M. Employees can choose their own

*Adapted from Rosemarie Lenner, "Will Your Hotel Room Be Super-safe?" *Woman's Day,* June 19, 2001, 17. Reprinted by permission of *Women's Day.*

Copyright © Houghton Mifflin Company. All rights reserved.

10

schedule during the flexible time, which may mean arriving at 7 A.M. or leaving at 7 P.M.

Compressed Workweek. Typically, a **compressed workweek** consists of four ten-hour days—for example, Tuesday through Friday, or Thursday through Sunday. Employees may be given the opportunity to adjust their work schedules to fit their lifestyle. One of the newest compressed workweek schedules, often called the 9/80, is growing in popularity. Employees work one extra hour each day for nine days, a total of eighty hours, and receive a three-day weekend every other week.

Job Sharing. With **job sharing,** two employees share the responsibilities of one job. For example, one employee might work the mornings and the other work the afternoons. At Schreiber Foods, Inc., in Green Bay, Wisconsin, job sharing has worked so well that the company has produced a video outlining the options. The firm encourages all of its 2,600 employees to work out the details with a coworker.

Telecommuting. The availability of powerful home-office computer and communication technologies, large-scale use of temporary workers due to massive downsizing, and the demands of workers who want to blend work and family have fueled a major increase in **telecommuting**—employees working at home at a personal computer linked to their employer's computer. In the year 2000, the number of telecommuters is expected to reach 15 million, up from 2.4 million in 1990. When done correctly, telecommuting can increase employee productivity 15 to 20 percent and increase employee retention and morale.

Phased Retirement. Older workers may choose **phased retirement** to reduce the number of hours they work over a period of time prior to their retirement. This option gives workers an opportunity to adjust more easily into a new phase of their lives, and companies benefit when older workers train those who will replace them.*

The passage above is just one section of a longer textbook chapter called "The Changing Roles of Men and Women." The topic of this one particular section is identified in the heading "Flexible Work Schedule Opportunities." Then, this section is subdivided into five smaller sections with subheadings that reveal the topic of each one.

*Adapted from Barry L. Reece and Rhonda Brandt, *Effective Human Relations in Organizations.* Boston: Houghton Mifflin, 1999, 436.

Copyright © Houghton Mifflin Company. All rights reserved.

10

Exercise 10.1

Read the selection below, and then answer the questions that follow by circling the correct response.

Ford's Road Map for a Healthier Environment

1   Henry Ford knew that environmental protection is a journey, not a destination. A nature lover as well as an industrialist, the founder of Ford Motor Company was a firm believer in conserving the planet's resources. As early as the 1920s, he was showing concern for the environment by recycling wood scraps and sawdust for fuel and selectively harvesting trees to prevent deforestation. Today's environmental challenges are even more complex; yet all over the world Ford is finding ways to control pollution and recycle materials.

2   One challenge is to meet government mandates for reducing harmful fuel emissions by developing alternative-fuel vehicles and electric vehicles. In response, Ford has created the Flexible Fuel Taurus car, the Ecostar electric van, the Ranger EV electric vehicle, and other experimental vehicles. Long-term tests are underway to determine whether these fuel-efficient vehicles can live up to real-world driving conditions.

3   A second challenge is to put recycling to work throughout the entire life cycle of a vehicle. In the manufacturing phase, Ford is incorporating more and more parts made from recycled materials. The company has also established a recycling research center in Cologne, Germany, where experts study ways of building cars that can be easily dismantled for recycling. Because each model line must meet increasingly stricter internal standards for recoverability of parts, recycling has become an integral part of the design and manufacturing process of every Ford vehicle.

4   In Europe, recycling is a major cornerstone of Ford's corporate citizenship program. The company's "Clean and Safe" campaign was the first to offer German customers cash in exchange for older cars without catalysts; the vehicles go to a network of dismantlers who have been trained to remove fluids and recyclable parts without damaging the environment. A similar program in Belgium offers financial incentives to customers who turn in old cars and buy new Ford cars.

5   A third challenge is to reduce or recycle wastes in factories around the world. Ford plants in North America have found innovative ways of recycling wastes. For example, plants in Cleveland, Ohio, and Windsor, Ontario, use sand for casting molds to make engine blocks and other car components. In the past, the factories sent the sand to landfills once the casting process was complete; these days, the factories recycle the sand for use in paving and building materials.

Copyright © Houghton Mifflin Company. All rights reserved.

10

6   Given Ford's long and active role in safeguarding the environment, the company is not about to put on the brakes. Indeed, its socially responsible environmental programs are only going to pick up speed as Ford drives into the new millennium.*

   1. What is the topic of this selection?

      a. Henry Ford
      b. Environmental challenges
      c. Environmental programs at Ford Motor Company
      d. Electric cars

   2. Which of the following sentences states the thesis of this selection?

      a. "Henry Ford knew that environmental protection is a journey, not a destination." (paragraph 1)
      b. "Today's environmental challenges are even more complex; yet all over the world Ford is finding ways to control pollution and recycle materials." (paragraph 1)
      c. "A second challenge is to put recycling to work throughout the entire life cycle of a vehicle." (paragraph 3)
      d. "Given Ford's long and active role in safeguarding the environment, the company is not about to put on the brakes." (paragraph 6)

   3. Which of the following functions as a topic sentence in this selection?

      a. "Henry Ford knew that environmental protection is a journey; not a destination." (paragraph 1)
      b. "Long-term tests are underway to determine whether these fuel-efficient vehicles can live up to real-world driving conditions." (paragraph 2)
      c. "Today's environmental challenges are even more complex; yet all over the world Ford is finding ways to control pollution and recycle materials." (paragraph 1)
      d. "A third challenge is to reduce or recycle wastes in factories around the world." (paragraph 5)

Supporting Details

Longer reading selections also contain both major and minor supporting details, just as paragraphs do. The diagram below summarizes how the parts of a paragraph correspond to those of many longer selections. Each box represents a different paragraph.

Copyright © Houghton Mifflin Company. All rights reserved.

*From Pride/Hughes/Kapoor, *Business*, 6th ed. Boston: Houghton Mifflin, 1999, 30.

10

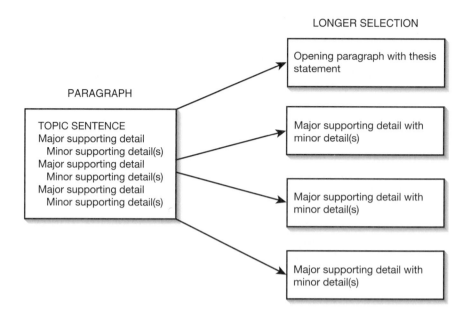

In other words, a longer selection spreads the major supporting details over several paragraphs. Each of these major details is the topic of a separate paragraph, and each is developed with the examples, anecdotes, explanations, or other information that functions as minor details. Here is an example of a longer selection that labels the major and minor details:

Add 10 Years to Your Life Just by Loving a Pet

Almost 60 percent of us house, feed, and care for a furry, finned, or feathered friend—and in return they give us unconditional love. But pet ownership brings more than just warm fuzzies: studies have documented that caring for a pet relieves stress, depression, and even pain.

THESIS

"Now the latest research suggests that the health benefits go even deeper than that," says animal ecologist Alan Beck, Sc.D., at Purdue University. In fact, experts now say just having a pet in the house can improve your health in several more significant ways.

MAJOR DETAIL

First of all, pet ownership can lower your blood pressure and cholesterol. In one National Institutes of Health (NIH) study, just interacting with animals caused an eight-point drop in blood pressure—enough to reduce the risk of stroke 15 percent. And another NIH study showed that animal owners have 13 percent lower cholesterol than those without pets! "We believe these benefits are due to the fact that

Minor Details

pets help lower our production of damaging stress hormones," says Beck, author of *Between Pets and People*.

Copyright © Houghton Mifflin Company. All rights reserved.

The health payoff can be dramatic: in one study, pet owners were four times less likely to have a heart attack—and 78 percent less likely to have a second one if they'd already had one.

Owning a pet can also get you in better shape—effortlessly. Only one in four Americans gets enough exercise, but research shows pet owners—especially dog owners—are twice as likely to exercise regularly. "Walking a dog on a leash actually burns 75 more calories per hour than walking alone, because dogs keep people moving at a more energetic pace," says Beck.

MAJOR DETAIL

Minor Details

Finally, pets can strengthen your immune system—and lengthen your life. Studies show that 74 percent of people feel healthier if they have a pet, and need to see their doctor 21 percent less often. Doctors believe that's because by reducing depression and anxiety and lowering stress hormones like cortisol, pets help strengthen our immune defenses against colds, flu, infections—even major diseases.

MAJOR DETAIL

Minor Details

Research suggests even gazing at goldfish helps reduce stress-related headaches, cold sores, and other chronic infections. Toss in the benefits of pet-lowered blood pressure and cholesterol, and doctors say that could add up to ten years to your life!*

Minor Details

In this selection, three of the topic sentences announce major supporting details, the three health benefits mentioned in the thesis statement. Then, each major detail is developed with one or two paragraphs of minor details.

Exercise 10.2

Read the selection below and answer the questions that follow by circling the correct response.

McGregor's Theory X and Theory Y

1   In most organizations, day-to-day operations are significantly influenced by the relationship between workers and managers. One management consultant, Douglas McGregor, believes that many managers do not understand or accept the idea that workers are motivated by different kinds of needs. McGregor's influential book *The Human Side of Enterprise* outlines a set of assumptions that he says influence the thinking of most managers. He divides these assumptions into two categories: Theory X and Theory Y.

*Adapted from Caitlin Castro, "Add 10 Years to Your Life by Loving a Pet!" *Woman's Day*, June 26, 2001, 16. Reprinted by permission of *Women's Day*.

Copyright © Houghton Mifflin Company. All rights reserved.

10

2   Theory X represents a pessimistic view of human nature. According to this theory, people do not really want to work. They have to be pushed, closely supervised, and prodded into doing things, either with incentives such as pay or with punishments for not working. Because they have little or no ambition, workers prefer to avoid responsibility and do only as much work as they have to. The general belief of management under this theory is that workers are paid to do a good job and management's function is to supervise the work and correct employees if they go off course.

3   Theory Y reflects an optimistic view of human behavior. According to this theory, work is as natural to people as play or rest. People are capable of self-direction and can learn to both accept and seek responsibility if they are committed to the objectives of the organization. Another Theory Y assumption is that people will become committed to organizational objectives if they are rewarded for doing so.

4   A healthy, mutually supportive relationship based on trust, openness, and respect can create a work climate in which employees want to give more of themselves. Goethe, the German poet and philosopher, may have said it best: "Trust people as if they were what they ought to be and you help them become what they are capable of being."*

1. What is the topic of this selection?

   a. Douglas McGregor
   b. Theory X and Theory Y
   c. Management
   d. Optimism and pessimism

2. Which of the following sentences states the thesis of this selection?

   a. "He divides these assumptions into two categories: Theory X and Theory Y." (paragraph 1)
   b. "Theory X represents a pessimistic view of human nature." (paragraph 2)
   c. "Goethe, the German poet and philosopher, may have said it best: 'Trust people as if they were what they ought to be and you help them become what they are capable of being.'" (paragraph 4)
   d. "Because they have little or no ambition, workers prefer to avoid responsibility and do only as much work as they have to." (paragraph 2)

3. Which of the following functions as a topic sentence in this selection?

   a. "He divides these assumptions into two categories: Theory X and Theory Y." (paragraph 1)
   b. "Theory X represents a pessimistic view of human nature." (paragraph 2)

*Adapted from Barry L. Reece and Rhonda Brandt, *Effective Human Relations in Organizations,* 7th ed. Boston: Houghton Mifflin, 1999, 183.

10

Copyright © Houghton Mifflin Company. All rights reserved.

    c. "Goethe, the German poet and philosopher, may have said it best: 'Trust people as if they were what they ought to be and you help them become what they are capable of being.'" (paragraph 4)

    d. "Because they have little or no ambition, workers prefer to avoid responsibility and do only as much work as they have to." (paragraph 2)

4. Which of the following sentences offers a *major* supporting detail?

    a. "He divides these assumptions into two categories: Theory X and Theory Y." (paragraph 1)

    b. "Theory Y reflects an optimistic view of human behavior." (paragraph 3)

    c. "Another Theory Y assumption is that people will become committed to organizational objectives if they are rewarded for doing so." (paragraph 3)

    d. "People are capable of self-direction and can learn to both accept and seek responsibility if they are committed to the objectives of the organization." (paragraph 3)

5. Which of the following is a *minor* supporting detail?

    a. "He divides these assumptions into two categories: Theory X and Theory Y." (paragraph 1)

    b. "Theory X represents a pessimistic view of human nature." (paragraph 2)

    c. "The general belief of management under this theory is that workers are paid to do a good job and management's function is to supervise the work and correct employees if they go off course." (paragraph 2)

    d. "Theory Y reflects an optimistic view of human behavior." (paragraph 3)

Implied Main Ideas

In Chapter 4 of this book, you learned to determine the main idea of a paragraph when it is not actually stated. Longer selections, too, will occasionally ask you to infer the author's overall point. You do this using the same procedure you used for paragraphs; however, you make adjustments for the multiple paragraphs. Instead of examining the topic of each sentence, for instance, you study the topic and point of each *topic sentence* and then add up those details to draw your conclusion. For example, read the following passage:

The Awesome Power of Volcanoes

A volcanic explosion can spew rocks into the air up to 800 m.p.h., and toss large boulders like pebbles—for miles. When Indonesia's Tambora volcano exploded in 1815, for example, it killed over 10,000

Copyright © Houghton Mifflin Company. All rights reserved.

10

people. Then the ash falling from the sky piled so thick that it ruined crops, and more than 80,000 people perished from famine and disease. The gases and dust emitted into the atmosphere brought the "year without a summer" in New England and may have inspired the red skies painted by J. M. W. Turner.

Seven decades later, Krakatau, another Indonesian volcano, erupted and much of the island collapsed. The explosion produced a 100-foot-high tsunami that wiped out some 36,000 people on nearby shores. As recently as 1985, the relatively small eruption of Nevado del Ruiz in Colombia dropped some 20 million cubic meters of hot ash and rocks on its ice cap. This melting ice created massive mudflows that buried the nearby town of Armero, killing more than 23,000 people.

It can take 10,000 years for molten rock to inch its way to the earth's surface, but once it does, volcano building can be surprisingly rapid. One day in 1943, volcanic steam began rising from a cornfield in Mexico. Within 24 hours, a 150-foot volcano punctuated the field. A year later it had grown to more than 1,000 feet. Closer to home, the blast of Mount St. Helens, Washington, in 1980 killed 57 people—a comparatively low number of deaths—but it made up in property damage what it spared in lives. The eruption cost nearby residents, businesses, and industries an estimated $1 billion.*

This selection never actually states a thesis, but you can infer that it means to suggest that volcanic eruptions can cause devastating losses in property and human lives. You arrive at that conclusion by looking first at the topic of each paragraph. Each topic is a different volcano. Next, what is being said about each one? The details presented all relate to the specific kinds of damage these volcanoes caused when they erupted. Therefore, you can conclude that the whole passage says that volcanic eruptions can be very destructive.

Exercise 10.3

Read the passage on page 427 and answer the questions that follow by circling the correct response.

*From William Garvey, "The Awesome Power of Volcanoes," *Reader's Digest*, May 2001, 212–213. Reprinted with permission from the May 2001 *Reader's Digest*. Copyright © 2001 by the Reader's Digest Assn., Inc.

Copyright © Houghton Mifflin Company. All rights reserved.

10

A Very Lucky Daughter

1   I should have been just another face in the hotel lobby in Zhangjiajie, a city in central China. But my words singled me out.

2   "*Yun dou*," I repeated to the clerk. Maybe he understood English: "Do you have a gym here?"

3   The clerk blinked, and then reached behind the counter and pulled out an iron.

4   I smiled blankly. My brain rooted through my limited Chinese vocabulary. Just then my dad strolled up, his eyebrows arched in amused triangles.

5   "She wants to know where the gym is," he supplied in rapid Mandarin Chinese, his native language. He turned to me and explained gently, "*Yun dong* is exercise, Sharon. *Yun dou* means iron.*"

6   I mumbled a sheepish apology to the laughing clerk and glanced at my dad. A look of recognition flashed through his eyes. We'd gone through this before. Only this time, the tables were turned.

7   When I was younger, I would try to imagine my parents growing up in China and Taiwan. But I could only envision them in the grainy black-and-white of their faded childhood pictures. Their childhood stories didn't match the people I knew. I couldn't picture my domestic mom, unsure of her halting English, studying international economics at a Taiwanese university. I laughed at the image of my stern father, an electrical engineer, chasing after chickens in his Chinese village.

8   I related to my parents' pre-American lives as only a series of events, like facts for some history exam. My dad fled to Taiwan in 1949 as a 14-year-old, after the Communists won the civil war. His father fought for the losing side, the Nationalists. My mom's father, a Nationalist navy captain, also retreated to Taiwan. My mom, who was born in Taiwan, grew up thinking that her family would eventually return to China, after the Nationalists reclaimed their homeland.

9   But that didn't happen. As young adults, my parents moved to the United States to lead better lives. They did not step onto Chinese soil for more than 50 years. Then their friends arranged a trip to China. And they asked me to join them on the six-city tour.

10   My list of why-nots was jam-packed. And yet something inside—I could not explain what—urged me to go.

11   When the plane jerked to a stop in Shanghai, our first destination, all of those reasons I decided to go materialized in the expression on my parents' faces. My mom folded and unfolded her hands impatiently in her lap. I was surprised and slightly scared to see my stoic dad's eyes glimmering with emotion. He slipped his hand, soft and spotted with age, in mine.

12   "Last time I was here," he said, "my parents going from north to south,

Copyright © Houghton Mifflin Company. All rights reserved.

10

away from the Communists. So much bombing. A lot of people starving." He leaned close. "You very lucky, Sharon."

13   That was my dad's line. When I would whine as a child, my dad's response was inevitable: "Some people not as lucky as you."

14   But I never cared about being lucky. I just wanted to be like the other American kids.

15   My parents, however, intended me to become a model Chinese American. Starting when I was six, they would drag me away from Saturday cartoons to a Chinese church. I would squirm like a worm in my seat while a teacher recited Chinese vocabulary. I dutifully recited my *bo po mo fos*—the ABCs of speaking Mandarin. But in my head, I rearranged the chalk marks that made up the characters into pictures of houses and trees.

16   When I turned nine, I declared I wasn't going to Chinese school anymore. "This stinks," I yelled. "None of my friends have to go to extra school. Why do I have to go?"

17   "Because you Chinese," my mom replied coolly.

18   "Then I don't want to be Chinese," I shouted back. "It's not fair. I just want to be normal. Why can't you and Dad be like everybody else's parents? I wish I were somebody else's kid."

19   I waited for my mom to shout, but she just stared at me with tired eyes. "If you don't want to go, don't have to," she said.

20   Though my parents had lived in the United States for decades, they still led a Chinese life at home. They spoke to each other in Chinese and read a Taiwanese paper. Chinese food covered our dinner table. Breakfast consisted of watery rice with pickled vegetables and meat, or fried eggs with soy sauce. At dinner I would douse my rice with ketchup and remind my parents that Sara's family ate hamburgers.

21   I envied my friends' relationships with their parents. My friends didn't have to worry that their parents would embarrass them with questions like "Is this good price?" and "What's this meaning?"

22   My friends' parents chatted easily with each other and our teachers. Their parents understood dating, and what it was like to grow up with the pressures of drinking, drugs, and sex. My parents discussed only my grades, career, and prospective salary.

23   My mom speaks English like I speak Chinese: slowly and punctuated by ums and ahs. When someone speaks English too rapidly, my mom's eyes cloud with confusion. I instantly recognize her I-don't-get-it look, and I know it's time to explain something.

24   About a month before we left for China, I helped my mom return a purchase to Wal-Mart.

25   The clerk rudely ignored my mom's slow English, speaking to me instead.

26   Later my mom thanked me for my help. "*Xie xie*, Sharon," she said, patting my shoulder. "I have good American daughter."

Copyright © Houghton Mifflin Company. All rights reserved.

10

27   "It's nothing, Mom," I said.

28   In the airport before we departed for China, my parents' friends herded around me. "Your parents so proud of you," said one man. "Always talking about you."

29   His words surprised me. I felt like I barely spoke with my parents. Did they really know who I was? Then another question, the one I always managed to skirt, surfaced in my conscience: did I even come close to understanding *them*?

30   The tour was a 17-day whirlwind. We visited lakes laden with lotus flowers, snapped pictures of jagged mountains rising out of the Yellow River, and hiked up stone stairs to intricately painted temples.

31   I saw rice paddies cut like square emeralds into the mountainside. I toured a factory where the employees spun silk into sheets of gloss.

32   But the best part of the trip was watching my parents. They carried themselves with an ease unfamiliar to me. They blended into the throngs of Chinese people instead of sticking out in the crowd. Their voices swelled with authority. My mom translated the tour guide's Chinese in her unwavering voice, whispering historical anecdotes she'd learned in school.

33   Often during the tour, my own face resembled my mom's I-don't-get-it look. At meals, my parents answered my constant questions about each colorful bowl that would rotate by on the Lazy Susan.*

34   My parents chuckled at my response when a waiter put a bowl of soup on our table. While the other diners shouted with excitement, I was horrified to see the remnants of a turtle floating in the clear yellow broth.

35   My table cried in dismay when I let the soup circle past me. "Strange," said one man, shaking his head. "Such good soup."

36   A few days after "the iron incident," as my run-in with the hotel clerk became known in our tour group, my parents and I sat on a bench overlooking stone monoliths. "Too bad I don't speak fluent Chinese," I said. "I should have listened when you tried to teach me."

37   My dad looked at me with understanding. "It's okay," he said. "You learning it now."

38   My mom smiled supportively. "Never too late," she said.†

1. What is the implied main idea of this entire longer selection?

    a. A trip to China helped the author understand her parents and her heritage.
    b. The author wanted to be American, not Chinese.
    c. The author's parents never liked America because they were treated badly there.
    d. Everyone should visit China as soon as he or she gets a chance.

*Lazy Susan: A revolving tray for food.

†From Sharon Liao, "A Very Lucky Daughter," *Reader's Digest*, June 2001, 81–87, originally appeared as "A Daughters Journey" in *Washingtonian*, January 2001. Reprinted with permission from the June 2001 *Reader's Digest* and the January 2001 *Washingtonian*.

Copyright © Houghton Mifflin Company. All rights reserved.

10

2. Which of the following supporting details helps the reader figure out the implied main idea?

   a. "Breakfast consisted of watery rice with pickled vegetables and meat, or fried eggs with soy sauce." (paragraph 20)
   b. "The tour was a 17-day whirlwind." (paragraph 30)
   c. "My dad fled to Taiwan in 1949 as a 14-year-old, after the Communists won the civil war." (paragraph 8)
   d. "Often during the tour, my own face resembled my mom's I-don't-get-it look." (paragraph 33)

3. Many of the supporting details are in the form of:

   a. steps and reasons.
   b. events and points of comparison and contrast.
   c. causes and effects.
   d. reasons and examples.

Patterns of Organization

Chapter 6 of this book explained five common patterns of organization (series, time order, cause/effect, comparison/contrast, and definition) used to arrange supporting details within paragraphs. Conveniently, longer selections are organized according to the very same patterns. Here is an example of a passage that's organized with a series of types:

THESIS

The fossil record is vital to the understanding of geologic time. A **fossil** is any remnant or indication of prehistoric life preserved in rock. The study of fossils is called **paleontology,** an area of interest to both biologists and geologists. Evidence of ancient plants and animals can be preserved in several ways.

Type #1

Some fossils are in the form of original remains. Ancient insects have been preserved by the sticky tree resin, in which they were trapped. The hardened resin, called *amber* and often used for jewelry, is found in Eastern Europe and the Dominican Republic. The entire bodies of woolly mammoths have been found frozen in the permafrost of Alaska and Siberia. More often, only the hardest parts of organisms are preserved, such as bones. Shark teeth and the shells of shallow-water marine organisms endure well, are easily buried in sediment, and are thus common types of fossils.

Type #2

Other fossils are in the form of replaced remains. The hard parts (bone, shell, etc.) of a buried organism can be slowly replaced by minerals such as silica (SiO_2), calcite ($CaCO_3$), and pyrite (FeS_2) in circulating

Copyright © Houghton Mifflin Company. All rights reserved.

10

groundwater. A copy of the original plant or animal material results. Petrified wood, such as the beautiful samples from Arizona's Petrified National Forest, is a common type of replacement fossil. *Carbonization* occurs when plant remains are decomposed by bacteria under anaerobic (airless) conditions. The hydrogen, nitrogen, and oxygen are driven off, leaving a carbon residue that may retain many of the features of the original plant. In this way, coal was formed.

Still other fossils are molds and casts of remains. When an embedded shell or bone is dissolved completely out of a rock, it leaves a hollow depression called a *mold*. If new mineral material fills the mold, it forms a *cast* of the original shell or bone. Molds and casts can only show the original shape of the remains.

Type #3

One final type of fossil is the trace fossil, a fossil imprint made by the movement of an animal. Examples are tracks, borings, and burrows.*

Type #4

The preceding selection offers a series of four types of fossils in support of the thesis. Each type of fossil is stated and explained in a separate paragraph. This next passage is organized with the time order pattern.

The first wiring of the world began in 1850, only six years after Samuel Morse demonstrated the reality of telegraphy. British engineers made a copper-wire cable, insulated it with gutta-percha (a rubberlike Malayan tree sap), and laid it across the English Channel.

Soon came a cable across the Atlantic. On August 16, 1858, Queen Victoria sent a hundred-word message to President James Buchanan. Some of the royal words reached Washington that day; the rest came through on the 17th. Agonizingly slow and chronically unreliable, the cable went dead after three weeks.

The problem was the behavior of electricity in cables. Convinced that they had found the solution, engineers tried again, this time with the world's largest ship, the *Great Eastern*. In July 1865 she set out from England with a crew of 500, a dozen oxen for hauling, a cow for fresh milk, a herd of pigs for bacon—and a thickly insulated 2,800-mile cable that weighed 5,000 tons. They had almost finished laying it when the cable snapped. The next year they succeeded.

Cable laying continued through the 19th century and into the 20th. Words were humming along at more than 200 a minute, compared with twelve a minute in 1866. But cable met competition when wireless telegraphs, in 1901, and commercial telephone calls, in 1927,

*Adapted from James T. Shipman et al., *An Introduction to Physical Science*, 9th ed. Boston: Houghton Mifflin, 2000, 634.

Copyright © Houghton Mifflin Company. All rights reserved.

10

began crackling across the Atlantic on radio waves. Not until 1956 did a telephone cable span the Atlantic. Then in 1965 the first Early Bird Satellite went into orbit, and again cable became a has-been.

But by the mid-1990s, thank to fiber optics, cable was making a comeback, carrying most telephone calls between the United States and Europe, Japan, and Australia. Pulsing with Internet data packets, cables connect more than 80 nations, carrying far more telephone calls than satellites or mobile phones. But those mobile phones and satellites are bridging the digital divide, using wireless networks as a way to connect the unconnected.*

Longer passages are more likely to use a combination of patterns to organize details. This next selection from a textbook, for example, combines time order and cause/effect to explain the events and results of the California Gold Rush.

The market economy provided a great impetus for expansion. Early on, the fur trapper system brought the Far West—way beyond settlement—into a market system that extended through St. Louis, Montreal, and New York to the hat merchants of Europe. Then, in the late 1840s, settlement jumped over the trapping areas to the West Coast of the American continent, when the promise of instant wealth in the form of gold sparked a gold rush.

Gold stimulated a mass migration to the West Coast. The United States had acquired Alta California in the Treaty of Guadalupe Hidalgo from Mexico, and the province was inhabited mostly by native peoples, some Mexicans living on large estates, and a chain of small settlements around military forts (presidios) and missions. That changed almost overnight after James Marshall, a carpenter, spotted gold particles in the millrace† at Sutter's Mill (now Coloma, California, northwest of Sacramento) in January. Word of the discovery spread, and other Californians rushed in like ants to a picnic to scrabble for instant fortunes. When John C. Fremont reached San Francisco five months later, he found that "all or nearly all its male inhabitants had gone to the mines." The town, "which a few months before was so busy and thriving, was then almost deserted."

By 1849, the news had spread around the world, and hundreds of thousands of fortune seekers, mostly young men, streamed in from Mexico, England, Germany, France, Ireland, and all over the United

*Excerpt adapted from Thomas B. Allen, "The Future Is Calling," *National Geographic*, December, 2001, 82–83. Reprinted by permission of the National Geographic Society.

†Millrace: Fast-moving stream of water.

Copyright © Houghton Mifflin Company. All rights reserved.

10

States. The newcomers came for one reason: instant wealth. In search of gold and silver, they mined the lodes and washed away the surface soil with hydraulic mining, leaving the land unsuitable for anything after they abandoned it.

Success in the market economy required capital, hard labor, and time; by contrast, gold mining seemed to promise instant riches. Most "forty-niners," however, never found enough gold to pay their expenses. "The stories you hear frequently in the States," one gold seeker wrote home, "are the most extravagant lies imaginable—the mines are a humbug. . . . The almost universal feeling is to get home." But many stayed, either unable to afford the passage home or tempted by the growing labor shortage in California's cities and agricultural districts.

San Francisco, the former presidio and mission of Yerba Buena, the gateway from the West Coast to the interior, became an instant city, ballooning to 35,000 people in 1850. In 1848 it had been a small settlement of about a thousand Mexicans, Anglos, soldiers, friars, and Indians. Ships bringing people and supplies continuously jammed the harbor, a scene that artist Frank Marryat captured in an 1849 painting. A French visitor in that year wrote, "At San Francisco, where fifteen months ago one found only a half dozen large cabins, one finds today a stock exchange, a theater, churches of all Christian cults, and a large number of quite beautiful homes."*

This passage covers the events of 1848–1850 related to the Gold Rush, and it presents some of the results of those events, too.

Exercise 10.4

Read the passage below and answer the questions that follow by circling the correct response.

The Moral Lessons of Harry Potter

1 For adults who haven't read them, the frenzy over the Harry Potter books—and now the movie version of *Harry Potter and the Sorcerer's Stone*—can seem perplexing. What, after all, could be so special about a boy wizard and his friends? Some parents have expressed concern about author J. K. Rowling's

*Adapted from Norton et al., *A People and a Nation,* Vol. I, 5th ed. Boston: Houghton Mifflin, 1998, 279–280.

Copyright © Houghton Mifflin Company. All rights reserved.

10

use of magic and what they believe to be elements of witchcraft in the books. But a variety of academic experts believe that Harry's life and adventures offer valuable lessons to his young fans.

2   **Adversity can be overcome through perseverance and hard work.** Despite the circumstances surrounding his early life, Harry is hopeful and able to thrive. "He isn't bitter," says Leah J. Dickstein, M.D., professor of psychiatry at the University of Louisville in Kentucky and a former sixth-grade teacher. "He gets the opportunity to go to the Hogwarts School, and while it's risky to try something new, he does it." Life improves at Hogwarts, but he still faces plenty of frightening obstacles, such as battling the evil and powerful Professor Quirrell and Voldemort, the terrible wizard who killed his parents. But even though he and his friends are only first-year students of magic, they never consider giving up.

3   "Harry is always having to confront his fears," says Kylene Beers, assistant professor of reading at the University of Houston and author of Scholastic's online Harry Potter discussion guide. It is his wise teacher, the wizard Dumbledore, who advises Harry to name those fears. "Fear of the name increases fear of the thing itself," Dumbledore tells him. Part of the genius of Rowling's story is that it allows children to confront their own fears in a manageable way.

4   **It's important to be accepting of differences in others and to treat everyone equally.** Having been rejected by his own relatives, Harry is particularly sensitive to others' suffering, whether it's Ron's embarrassment that his family doesn't have much money or Hagrid's large size, which makes him something of an outcast. "J. K. Rowling appears to be creating a caste system so readers can explore the notion of what it means to be different and how much surface differences matter in our lives," says Beers. A good example is Harry's nemesis, Draco Malfoy, who hails from a family with elite bloodlines. Rather than befriending Malfoy, which could have assured Harry's popularity, he distances himself from the mean snob. From then on, Malfoy taunts Harry about being an orphan and makes cracks about Ron's financial hardships. Racism, classism, and other biases also emerge, such as a prejudice against Muggles (non-wizards), something Harry won't stand for since his friend Hermione is Muggle-born.

5   **You don't have to be perfect.** Harry's not your standard hero. In fact, he's rather gawky, and his hair won't even stay in place. "He has a scar on his forehead. He's not perfect," says Dr. Dickstein. Nonetheless, he prevails, using logic, kindness, patience, and bravery when strength or special powers fail him. "There are so many negative messages out in society—that you're too fat or you're not smart enough—and children are very aware of that," Dr. Dickstein says. "These characters gain self-acceptance, which is something parents can discuss with their children."

Copyright © Houghton Mifflin Company. All rights reserved.

10

6   **Education and knowledge are essential.** School plays a prominent role in all the Harry Potter books. "There is nothing wrong with being smart in the book," says Dr. Elizabeth Schafer, a specialist in children's literature and author of *Exploring Harry Potter*. Harry admires his friend Hermione for her intelligence and hard work. Often, it is her knowledge that helps them get out of a predicament, whether it's using logic to determine which liquid is poisonous or casting a spell on an evil wizard who has put a curse on Harry. The friends spend a great deal of time in the immense Hogwarts library researching questions such as the contents of a mysterious package hidden in the school. Dr. Dickstein also points to the fabulous use of language throughout the story. Rowling employs rich vocabulary words, such as *flouted, prudent*, and *abashed*, and also incorporates other languages. For example, the murderous Voldemort's name borrows from the French word for *death*, and the name of Harry's nemesis, Draco, means "serpent" or "dragon" in Latin. So consider the story something of an early SAT prep class!

7   **Loyalty to friends is important.** From the moment Harry and Ron meet on the train to Hogwarts, they're inseparable. And after a few rocky encounters, they forge a strong friendship with Hermione as well. "Even though the characters are strong as individuals, it's as a team that they solve all their problems," such as when they band together to support their awkward friend Neville, says Dr. Schafer. She suggests using the characters' friendship as a starting point to talk with kids about whom they want to emulate in life and why. "It might also help children identify negative behaviors [like Draco's] that they don't want to continue," she adds.

8   Though parents may be concerned that parts of the story are too scary, the key—after gauging your child's maturity—is to share the books and movie as a family. "The lessons offered by the Harry Potter books are ones that readers can use throughout their lives and build upon as they gain life experiences and acquire new insights about familial, social, cultural, intellectual, and professional situations," Dr. Schafer says.*

1. Which of the following sentences states the thesis of this selection?

   a. "Some parents have expressed concern about author J. K. Rowling's use of magic and what they believe to be elements of witchcraft in the books." (paragraph 1)
   b. "But a variety of academic experts believe that Harry's life and adventures offer valuable lessons to his young fans." (paragraph 1)
   c. "Adversity can be overcome through perseverance and hard work." (paragraph 2)
   d. "Despite the circumstances surrounding his early life, Harry is hopeful and able to thrive." (paragraph 2)

*Adapted from Michelle Holcenberg, *Child*, November 2001. Copyright © 2002. Originally published by Gruner + Jahr USA Publishing in the Dec./Jan. 2002 issue of *Child* Magazine. Used with permission. For subscription information, please call 1-800-777-0222.

Copyright © Houghton Mifflin Company. All rights reserved.

10

2. What pattern of organization organizes the *major* supporting details?

    a. time order   c. cause/effect
    b. definition   d. series

3. How many supporting points develop the thesis statement?

    a. two   c. four
    b. three   d. five

Transitions

As you learned in Chapter 5 of this book, paragraphs include transitions, words that signal relationships between sentences. Longer reading selections employ transitions for the very same purpose, but they also show how whole *paragraphs* are related to one another. As you read the following example of a time order (process) paragraph, notice how the boldfaced, italicized transitions help you understand the relationships between major details.

Time Out the Right Way

Time Out is probably the most widely researched technique for dealing with unwanted behavior in young children. Unfortunately, it is often used incorrectly. It is therefore worth knowing that Time Out means removing the child from all rewarding activities for a short period. The common practice of sending a child to his room, where he can play computer games, watch TV, or talk with friends on the telephone, is not Time Out behavior. Time Out means exposing the child to a very boring, unrewarding environment. For the sake of illustration, let's assume that your child has bitten someone. Here is a simple, highly effective way of discouraging this behavior.

THESIS STATEMENT

    First, say to her: "We do not bite." Say nothing more than this—give no further description of the behavior, no explanation of what you are doing. Say nothing except, "We do not bite."

    Second, take her by the hand and seat her in a small chair facing a blank wall. Stand close enough so that if she attempts to leave the chair you can immediately return her to it.

    Next, keep her in the chair for three minutes. (Do not tell her how long she will be in the chair. Say nothing.) If she screams, kicks the wall, asks questions, or says she has to go to the bathroom, ignore her. It is absolutely essential that you say nothing.

    Then, at the end of three minutes, keep her in the chair until she has been quiet and well behaved for five more seconds. When she does

Copyright © Houghton Mifflin Company. All rights reserved.

10

so, tell her she has been good and may now leave the chair. Never let her leave until she has been well behaved for at least a few seconds.

Finally, following Time Out, say nothing about it. Do not discuss the punished behavior or the fairness of the punishment. Say nothing except, "We do not bite."

Once the child realizes that you mean business, that she cannot manipulate you into providing attention for bad behavior, Time Out will proceed more smoothly and quickly and there will be far fewer times when you need to use it.*

Exercise 10.5

Read the passage below and answer the questions that follow by circling the correct response.

Looking Backward: 1964–1991

1   For two years, from 1988 to 1990, I visited schools and spoke with children in approximately thirty neighborhoods from Illinois to Washington, D.C., and from New York to San Antonio. Wherever possible, I also met with children in their homes. There was no special logic in the choice of cities that I visited. I went where I was welcomed or knew teachers or school principals or ministers of churches. As a result, I was startled by the remarkable degree of racial segregation that persisted almost everywhere.

2   Like most Americans, I knew that segregation was still common in the public schools, but I did not know how much it had intensified. The Supreme Court decision in *Brown v. Board of Education* thirty-seven years ago, in which the court had found that segregated education was unconstitutional because it was "inherently unequal," did not seem to have changed very much for children in the schools I saw, not, at least, outside of the Deep South. Most of the urban schools I visited were 95 to 99 percent nonwhite. In no school that I saw anywhere in the United States were nonwhite children in large numbers truly intermingled with white children.

3   For anyone who came of age during the years from 1954 to 1968, these revelations could not fail to be disheartening. What seems unmistakable, but, oddly enough, is rarely said in public settings nowadays, is that the nation, for all practice and intent, has turned its back upon the moral implications, if

*Adapted from Jacob Azerrad, Ph.D., "Why Our Kids Are Out of Control," *Psychology Today,* Sept./Oct. 2001, 46. Reprinted with permission from *Psychology Today Magazine.* Copyright © 2001 Sussex Publishers, Inc.

Copyright © Houghton Mifflin Company. All rights reserved.

10

not yet the legal ramifications, of the *Brown* decision. The struggle being waged today, where there is any struggle being waged at all, is closer to the one that was addressed in 1896 in *Plessy v. Ferguson,* in which the court accepted segregated institutions for black people, stipulating only that they must be equal to those open to white people. The dual society, at least in public education, seems in general to be unquestioned.

4   These, then, are a few of the impressions that remained with me after revisiting the public schools from which I had been absent for a quarter-century. However, my deepest impression was less theoretical and more immediate. It was simply the impression that these urban schools were, by and large, extraordinarily unhappy places. With few exceptions, they reminded me of "garrisons" or "outposts" in a foreign nation. Housing projects, bleak and tall, surrounded by perimeter walls lined with barbed wire, often stood adjacent to the schools I visited. The schools were surrounded frequently by signs that indicated a drug-free zone. Their doors were guarded. Police sometimes patrolled the halls. The windows of the schools were often covered with steel grates. Taxi drivers flatly refused to take me to some of these schools and would deposit me a dozen blocks away, in border areas beyond which they refused to go. I'd walk the last half-mile on my own. Once, in the Bronx, a woman stopped her car, told me I should not be walking there, insisted I get in, and drove me to the school. I was dismayed to walk or ride for blocks and blocks through neighborhoods where every face was black, where there were simply *no white people anywhere.*

5   It occurred to me that we had not been listening much to children in these recent years of "summit conferences" on education, of severe reports and ominous prescriptions. The voices of children, frankly, had been missing from the whole discussion.

6   This seems especially unfortunate because the children often are more interesting and perceptive than the grown-ups are about the day-to-day realities of life in school. For this reason, I decided early in my journey to attempt to listen very carefully to children and, whenever possible, to let their voices and their judgments and their longings find a place within my book—and maybe, too, within the nation's dialogue about their destinies. I hope that, in this effort, I have done them justice.*

1. What pattern of organization is used to arrange the *major* supporting details?

    a. cause/effect   c. series
    b. time order   d. definition

*Adapted from Jonathan Kozol, *Savage Inequalities: Looking Backward: 1964–1991.* New York: Crown, 1991, 1–6. Copyright © 1991 by Jonathan Kozol. Used by permission of Crown Publishers, a division of Random House, Inc.

Copyright © Houghton Mifflin Company. All rights reserved.

10

2. Which of the following sentences begins with a cause/effect transition?

   a. "Most of the urban schools I visited were 95 to 99 percent nonwhite." (paragraph 2)

   b. "As a result, I was startled by the remarkable degree of racial segregation that persisted almost everywhere." (paragraph 1)

   c. "Once, in the Bronx, a woman stopped her car, told me I should not be walking there, insisted I get in, and drove me to the school." (paragraph 4)

   d. "However, my deepest impression was less theoretical and more immediate." (paragraph 4)

3. Which of the following transitions from the selection is a cause/effect transition?

   a. For two years (paragraph 1)

   b. Then (paragraph 4)

   c. Frankly (paragraph 5)

   d. For this reason (paragraph 6)

CHAPTER 10 REVIEW

Fill in the blanks in the following statements.

1. Like paragraphs, longer reading selections include a _____ and a

   _____.

2. The main idea of a longer passage is usually called a _____.

3. A thesis statement includes the _____ along with what is being said about that subject.

4. _____ are mini-titles that identify the topic of one section of a longer work like a chapter or an article.

5. Like paragraphs, longer reading selections include _____ and

   _____ supporting details.

6. Though not as common, a longer reading selection can offer an

   _____ main idea.

7. Longer reading selections, like paragraphs, organize supporting details

   according to common _____, and they include _____ to show how paragraphs are related to one another.

Copyright © Houghton Mifflin Company. All rights reserved.

10

▶ **Vocabulary: Review**

You've covered many important vocabulary concepts in Chapters 1–9 of this book. The following exercise, which draws sentences from examples in Chapter 10, will give you practice reviewing several of these concepts.

Vocabulary Exercise

A. On the blanks following each paragraph, write in the synonyms that the sentence or passage includes for the boldfaced, italicized word or phrase.

  1. A volcanic explosion can spew ***rocks*** into the air up to 800 m.p.h., and toss large boulders like pebbles—for miles.

    Two synonyms for italicized word: _____

  2. My dad ***fled*** to Taiwan in 1949 as a 14-year-old, after the Communists won the civil war. His father fought for the losing side, the Nationalists. My mom's father, a Nationalist navy captain, also retreated to Taiwan.

    One synonym for italicized word: _____

B. In the sentences that follow, look up the boldfaced, italicized words in a dictionary and determine which definition best describes how each word is being used. Write that definition on the blank provided.

  3. I couldn't picture my ***domestic*** mom, unsure of her halting English, studying international economics at a Taiwanese university.

    _____

  4. Their descendants are ***concentrated*** in subarctic regions of Canada and in the southwestern United States. _____

  5. Success in the market economy required ***capital,*** hard labor, and time; by contrast, gold mining seemed to promise instant riches.

    _____

  6. Second, take her by the hand and seat her in a small chair facing a ***blank*** wall. _____

C. In each of the following sentences, underline the context clue that helps you understand the meaning of the boldfaced, italicized word, and write what kind of context clue (definition/restatement, example, explanation, or contrast) it is on the blank provided.

Copyright © Houghton Mifflin Company. All rights reserved.

10

7. The availability of powerful home-office computer and communication technologies, large-scale use of temporary workers due to massive downsizing, and the demands of workers who want to blend work and family have fueled a major increase in ***telecommuting***—employees working at home at a personal computer linked to their employer's computer.

_____

8. Theory X represents a ***pessimistic*** view of human nature. According to this theory, people do not really want to work. They have to be pushed, closely supervised, and prodded into doing things, either with incentives such as pay or with punishments for not working.

_____

9. Racism, classism, and other ***biases*** also emerge, such as a prejudice against Muggles (non-wizards), something Harry won't stand for since his friend Hermione is Muggle-born.

_____

10. She suggests using the characters' friendship as a starting point to talk with kids about whom they want to ***emulate*** in life and why. "It might also help children identify negative behaviors [like Draco's] that they don't want to continue," she adds.

_____

11. The explosion produced a 100-foot-high ***tsunami*** that wiped out some 36,000 people on nearby shores.

_____

D. In each of the following sentences, underline the figure of speech (analogy, metaphor, simile, or personification).

12. I would squirm like a worm in my seat while a teacher recited Chinese vocabulary.

13. I saw rice paddies cut like square emeralds into the mountainside.

14. Word of the discovery spread, and other Californians rushed in like ants to a picnic to scrabble for instant fortunes.

15. Given Ford's long and active role in safeguarding the environment, the company is not about to put on the brakes.

Copyright © Houghton Mifflin Company. All rights reserved.

10

Name _____ Date _____

COMBINED SKILLS TEST 1

Read the essay below and answer the questions that follow by circling the correct response.

The Ones Who Turn Up Along the Way

1 Not long ago my building super, Walter, stopped by my apartment. He rang the bell saying, "Super," in a way to which I had grown accustomed, dragging out the "u" and adding a slight roll to the "r." I imagined that he was coming to fix something or maybe to bring me a package. But when I opened the door, he was holding the spare set of keys that he kept to my place.

2 Walter told me he had come to return the keys because he would no longer be working in my building. His family had gotten too big for the basement apartment that came with the job, he explained. Walter had been there for 11 years, even since coming to the United States from Colombia. He had been available at all hours for the occasional maintenance crisis, but, more important, he always gave me the sense that he looked out for me—which is a great comfort when you're living alone in Manhattan. It was hard to imagine the building without him.

3 Just before Walter came by, I had been unpacking groceries and reflecting on a conversation I had just had with Ali, the manager of my neighborhood grocery store. Ali is a devout Muslim from Bangladesh. He has a wife and three children and a Ph.D. in geography. On visits to his native country, he often gives lectures on Islam. He hopes to publish a book encouraging Bangladeshi people to see Jews as friends. It's a project he has been working on for some time, and to which he feels even more committed since September 11th. "This is what Allah tells me I must do," he says. "I must love all people. I cannot hate people and love Allah."

4 I have been shopping in this grocery store for years now, and Ali and I have always waved and said hello. But several months ago the hellos turned into conversation. When I told him that I am a rabbi, we began discussing the connections between Judaism and Islam, the purpose of religion, the sorrow and anger we feel when people use religion as a justification for violence. Every time we talk I feel as if I have learned Torah—the wisdom of my own faith tradition—from a man who quotes the Quran.

Copyright © Houghton Mifflin Company. All rights reserved.

5   I share these stories because they are a part of the puzzle of community. I am well aware that Walter and Ali do not fall into the simple categories of family member, coworker, or friend. We are from different backgrounds, different countries, and we occupy different socioeconomic spheres. We don't go to each other's home for dinner or make plans to meet for coffee, and we probably won't. Our connections are site-specific and episodic. And yet they make real claims on my heart and mind.

6   In the Book of Exodus, even as God continued to harden Pharaoh's heart, the Israelites began their journey out of Egypt. More than 600,000 packed up and headed out on foot, but they were not alone. An *erev rav*—a mixed multitude—went with them. The ancient rabbis' reviews are mixed when it comes to characterizing this anonymous crew. Some see them as a group of hangers-on ultimately responsible for the building of the golden calf. Others suggest that they were Egyptians who simply shared the basic human longing to be free. Either way, I imagine that by the time the travelers made it to shore and fanned out into the desert, called to different purposes and directions, they were bound to one another forever.

7   About a year ago, a guy came to replace the intercom system in my apartment. While he worked, he told me that he had been born in Ukraine, immigrated to Israel with his family and fought in the country's 1948 independence war. He explained that he was an atheist and knew he could never believe in God. Nevertheless, as he was leaving he asked in Hebrew, "What blessing may I give you?" Before I could answer, he prayed that I would find my *bashert* (soulmate), kindly even suggesting one of his sons.

8   When he was gone I noticed that he had forgotten a bunch of different-colored wires. I saved them. I keep them in a tin with the quarters I use for doing laundry. They remind me that we are traveling not only with the people we have chosen but with the ones who turn up along the way. The repairman, Walter, and Ali are part of my *erev rav,* and I am a part of theirs.

9   It's been months now since Walter and his family moved across the river to New Jersey. Soon Ali will take another trip to Bangladesh. I don't know what's next for me, but I know I won't be going alone.*

1. Which of the following sentences from the selection best expresses the main idea of the entire selection?

   a. "Not long ago my building super, Walter, stopped by my apartment." (paragraph 1)
   b. "It was hard to imagine the building without him." (paragraph 2)
   c. "In the Book of Exodus, even as God continued to harden Pharaoh's heart, the Israelites began their journey out of Egypt." (paragraph 6)

*Rabbi Jennifer Krause, "My Turn," *Newsweek,* November 26, 2001, 14–15. All rights reserved. Reprinted by permission.

Copyright © Houghton Mifflin Company. All rights reserved.

d. "The repairman, Walter, and Ali are part of my *erev rav,* and I am a part of theirs." (paragraph 8)

2. Which of the following is the topic sentence of paragraph 6?

 a. "An *erev rav*—a mixed multitude—went with them."
 b. "The ancient rabbis' reviews are mixed when it comes to characterizing this anonymous crew."
 c. "Some see them as a group of hangers-on ultimately responsible for the building of the golden calf."
 d. "Others suggest that they were Egyptians who simply shared the basic human longing to be free."

3. Which of the following is a *major* supporting detail in paragraph 6?

 a. "More than 600,000 packed up and headed out on foot, but they were not alone."
 b. "An *erev rav*—a mixed multitude—went with them."
 c. "The ancient rabbis' reviews are mixed when it comes to characterizing this anonymous crew."
 d. "Some see them as a group of hangers-on ultimately responsible for the building of the golden calf."

4. What is the implied main idea of paragraph 3?

 a. Both Rabbi Krause and Ali are fascinated by geography.
 b. Ali's faith has made an impression on Rabbi Krause.
 c. Jews and Muslims have more in common than they realize.
 d. Rabbi Krause researches faiths other than her own.

5. Which of the following sentences does NOT begin with a transition?

 a. "But when I opened the door, he was holding the spare set of keys that he kept to my place." (paragraph 1)
 b. "Soon Ali will take another trip to Bangladesh." (paragraph 9)
 c. "In the Book of Exodus, even as God continued to harden Pharaoh's heart, the Israelites began their journey out of Egypt." (paragraph 6)
 d. "About a year ago, a guy came to replace the intercom system in my apartment." (paragraph 7)

6. Which pattern of organization arranges the details in paragraphs 7–9?

 a. Cause/effect   c. Series
 b. Time order   d. Definition

7. What can you infer about the author from paragraph 2?

 a. She is a Catholic.   c. She likes to read the Bible.
 b. She is not married.   d. She can't afford a house.

Copyright © Houghton Mifflin Company. All rights reserved.

8. Which of the following sentences is a fact?

    a. "Not long ago my building super, Walter, stopped by my apartment." (paragraph 1)

    b. "It was hard to imagine the building without him." (paragraph 2)

    c. "And yet they make real claims on my heart and mind." (paragraph 5)

    d. "I don't know what's next for me, but I know I won't be going alone." (paragraph 9)

9. The author's tone in this selection is

    a. Silly   c. Serious

    b. Sorrowful   d. Angry

COMBINED SKILLS TEST 2

Read the article below and answer the questions that follow by circling the correct response.

Lessons I Learned Staying Up All Night

1 Tiptoe through the stacks of any college library—especially around final exams—and you'll find them: college students so tired they've fallen asleep. "No matter what time of day," students are slumped over their textbooks, says Faye Backie, assistant director for public services at Michigan State University. The library at the East Lansing, Michigan, school is open 24 hours every day but Saturday. "When I taught, I found them falling asleep in class too," adds Backie, a former professor.

2 Students, even the most prepared, sometimes have to cut back drastically on sleep to finish a term paper or cram for a final exam. "So many things are happening at once, in a really condensed period of time, once or twice I'll have to stay up all night," explains Scott Kaplan, a senior political science major at the University of Pennsylvania.

3 Brian Babcock, a senior international relations and strategic history major at the U.S. Military Academy at West Point, N.Y., tries to avoid the full all-nighters, but he's still not getting his beauty sleep. "I usually call it quits around 4:30 or 5 [A.M.]*" But being at a military academy means Babcock is at mandatory formation at 6:55 A.M., and there is no wiggle room when it comes to sleeping or skipping classes. "When you feel tired, instead of falling asleep at your desk, you stand up for 10–15 minutes," he says; otherwise, you could end up in five-hour marching duty.

*Brackets indicate author's addition.

Copyright © Houghton Mifflin Company. All rights reserved.

4   Dalia Alcazar, a sophomore at University of California at Berkeley, recalls staying up all night to write a paper for an 8 A.M. class. Around 6 A.M. she took a break to eat breakfast and decided to take some caffeine pills to boost her energy. It was a mistake, she says, leaving her nauseous and feeling sick.

5   Kelly Tanabe, founder of Supercollege.com, a Web site that helps students adjust to college life, says students will try anything to stay awake when it seems there just aren't enough hours in the day. Tanabe, a Harvard graduate who pulled her fair share of all-nighters, says a "coffee bomb" was very popular with her classmates. "Fill a cup halfway with (powdered) instant coffee. Fill the remainder with hot water. Drink. It's not pleasant, but the caffeine will power you through the night." Tanabe urges students to be realistic and accept that they're not going to learn everything they neglected the whole semester. Unfortunately, most don't grasp this until it's creeping toward 3 A.M.

6   "Sometimes students who pull all-nighters sleep through the very exam they stayed up all night for," says Amy Wolfson, associate professor of psychology at College of the Holy Cross, in Worcester, Massachusetts. Wolfson says there are factors working against students that won't go away. "As we get further from where we last slept, we're likely to begin to feel more tired." According to Wolfson, it's generally recommended that college students get between 8.4 and 9.2 hours of sleep per night. "Every semester I have someone that falls asleep through a final exam," she adds. "Cramming has never been a recommended study habit. In fact, you're probably better off going to sleep, assuming you're someone who's attended class."

7   The author of *How to Ace Any Test* agrees. "It's absolutely, totally impossible to cram a whole semester's study in one night," says Ron Fry, who also wrote *How to Study* and *How to Improve Your Memory* (Career Press). Ideally, Fry says, students should be reviewing their notes on a weekly basis, but if that hasn't been the case and the semester is winding down, they should be choosy about what to study. "Selectivity is very important. Smart kids always figure this out; smart kids never study everything," he says. Fry suggests students go through their notes and see how much time a teacher dedicated to a particular subject. "If a teacher spent two weeks on one general topic and three days on another, chances are the two-week topic is going to be on [the exam]."

8   To recall facts, Fry notes there are several memorization techniques. If someone has a great musical memory, put a definition or fact to the rhythm of a song. Others have strong kinetic memories and can easily associate some sort of body movement to it.

9   Another helpful shortcut at students' fingertips—one that previous generations didn't have—is online research. Many campus libraries offer free Internet access or a service such as Questia.com, which charges a small monthly fee and offers full-text reference materials in a user-friendly format.

Copyright © Houghton Mifflin Company. All rights reserved.

"When you cut and paste, we automatically create a footnote for you in the correct format. We even hyperlink it back to the right page on the service," says Troy Williams, founder and CEO.

10   But, adds Tanabe, hopefully one of the most important lessons learned while cramming for an exam is to space out assignments and study in the future. It will probably benefit students' grades as well as their sleeping habits. "What seems brilliant at 4 A.M. is oftentimes not truly brilliant."*

1. What is the topic of this selection?

    a. School   c. Cramming
    b. Bad planning   d. Falling asleep

2. Which of the following is a *minor* supporting detail in paragraph 9?

    a. "Another helpful shortcut at students' fingertips—one that previous generations didn't have—is online research."
    b. "Many campus libraries offer free Internet access or a service such as Questia.com, which charges a small monthly fee and offers full-text reference materials in a user-friendly format."
    c. "'When you cut and paste, we automatically create a footnote for you in the correct format. We even hyperlink it back to the right page on the service,' says Troy Williams, founder and CEO."

3. What is the implied main idea of paragraph 1?

    a. College students do not get enough sleep.
    b. College students don't spend enough time in the library.
    c. College students don't read their textbooks thoroughly.
    d. The library is a boring place to be.

4. Which of the following sentences begins with a transition?

    a. "'So many things are happening at once, in a really condensed period of time, once or twice I'll have to stay up all night,' explains Scott Kaplan, a senior political science major at the University of Pennsylvania." (paragraph 2)
    b. "Ideally, Fry says, students should be reviewing their notes on a weekly basis, but if that hasn't been the case and the semester is winding down, they should be choosy about what to study." (paragraph 7)
    c. "But being at a military academy means Babcock is at mandatory formation at 6:55 A.M., and there is no wiggle room when it comes to sleeping or skipping classes." (paragraph 3)
    d. "To recall facts, Fry notes there are several memorization techniques." (paragraph 8)

*From Maria Coder, "Lessons I Learned Staying Up All Night," Morganton, NC, *News Herald*, December 2, 2001, 7C. Reprinted with permission of the Associated Press.

Copyright © Houghton Mifflin Company. All rights reserved.

5. Which of the following patterns organizes many of the details in paragraph 5?

   a. Comparison/contrast   c. Process
   b. Cause/effect   d. Series

6. What can you infer about the West Point Military Academy from paragraph 3?

   a. The Academy has strict rules that students must follow or face punishment.
   b. Only men attend that school.
   c. It is located in a beautiful section of New York State.
   d. The students march a lot.

7. Which of the following sentences is an opinion?

   a. "Students, even the most prepared, sometimes have to cut back drastically on sleep to finish a term paper or cram for a final exam." (paragraph 2)
   b. "Ideally, Fry says, students should be reviewing their notes on a weekly basis, but if that hasn't been the case and the semester is winding down, they should be choosy about what to study." (paragraph 7)
   c. "The library at the East Lansing, Michigan, school is open 24 hours every day but Saturday." (paragraph 1)
   d. "But being at a military academy means Babcock is at mandatory formation at 6:55 A.M., and there is no wiggle room when it comes to sleeping or skipping class." (paragraph 3)

8. The author's tone in this selection is

   a. Outraged   c. Serious
   b. Depressed   d. Silly

COMBINED SKILLS TEST 3

Read the textbook passage below and answer the questions that follow by circling the correct response.

Lil' Orbits Makes Dough through Global Franchising

1 "Donuts to Dollars" has long been the slogan of Ed Anderson's fast-growing Lil' Orbits donut business. But now that his miniature donuts are available through 20,000 vendors in 78 countries, he may also want to export new

Copyright © Houghton Mifflin Company. All rights reserved.

slogans, such as "Donuts to Deutsche Marks" for Germany or "Donuts to Drachmas" for Greece.

2   Anderson founded the Minneapolis-based company in 1974 as a chain of donut shops in Minnesota and Tampa, Florida. He soon branched out to sell donut-making equipment and special mix to individual operators throughout the United States. Global sales of equipment and mix, however, have been a critical ingredient in Lil' Orbits' long-term success.

3   In 1987, Anderson approached a U.S. export assistance office for help in expanding globally. He learned about a magazine that showcases U.S. products and services available for export, placed an advertisement in it, and received 400 responses from all over the world. Encouraged, he put together an international network of distributors to license the brand name and know-how through global franchising.

4   These days, franchisees all over the world, from Europe to Asia, are learning how to turn $1\frac{1}{2}$-inch donuts into "dough." The franchisees buy equipment and sacks of concentrated donut mix from the company's international distributors. In addition, they pay franchise fees and royalties for the right to use the Lil' Orbits brand name, donut-making methods, and promotional materials to sell Lil' Orbits donuts by the bagful and at considerable profit.

5   Working with knowledgeable international distributors helps the company learn more about each market and give local franchisees the support they need to succeed. For example, franchisees are encouraged to use donut toppings that satisfy local tastes. A cinnamon sugar topping is popular in the United States but is not offered in China, where cinnamon is considered a medicine; donuts are dipped in honey in Greece, while chocolate sauce is a favorite in Spain. Even the name is different in some areas. "We found people couldn't pronounce 'Lil' Orbits' in France and Belgium, so 'Orbie' is used in those countries," explains Anderson.

6   Over the years, global franchising has helped Lil' Orbits sell $10 billion worth of mini-donuts while smoothing out the peaks and valleys of customer demand. "Since the vast majority of our vendors operate outdoors, our business is dependent on good weather," says Anderson. "The beautiful thing about exporting is it's not seasonal; when it's winter in Minneapolis, it's summer in Sydney. Without exports, our sales would be low in the fourth quarter because of the weather."*

1. What is the main idea of this selection?

   a. Ed Anderson is a smart businessman.

   b. Ed Anderson has taken his company international, with great success.

*From Pride/Hughes/Kapoor, *Business*, 6th ed. Boston: Houghton Mifflin, 1999, 58.

Copyright © Houghton Mifflin Company. All rights reserved.

    c. Ed Anderson wanted to expand globally but couldn't due to climate.

    d. Franchisees all over the world have learned to make donuts.

2. Which of the following sentences from the selection is a *major* supporting detail?

    a. "'Donuts to Dollars' has long been the slogan of Ed Anderson's fast-growing Lil' Orbits donut business." (paragraph 1)

    b. "Global sales of equipment and mix, however, have been a critical ingredient in Lil' Orbits' long-term success." (paragraph 2)

    c. "Working with knowledgeable international distributors helps the company learn more about each market and give local franchisees the support they need to succeed." (paragraph 5)

    d. "A cinnamon sugar topping is popular in the United States but is not offered in China, where cinnamon is considered a medicine; donuts are dipped in honey in Greece, while chocolate sauce is a favorite in Spain." (paragraph 5)

3. What is the implied main idea of paragraph 1?

    a. Ed Anderson expanded his business globally.

    b. Ed Anderson needs more slogans.

    c. Ed Anderson is the "slogan king."

    d. Ed Anderson makes really greasy donuts.

4. Which of the following paragraphs begins with a transition?

    a. Paragraph 1   c. Paragraph 5

    b. Paragraph 2   d. Paragraph 6

5. What pattern organizes the supporting details in paragraph 6?

    a. Cause/effect   c. Time order

    b. Definition   d. Series

6. What can you infer about Ed Anderson from reading this selection?

    a. He does not eat donuts.

    b. He is overweight.

    c. He is a very smart and forward-thinking businessman.

    d. He can speak Greek.

7. Would you say that the selection is made up of mostly facts or mostly opinions?

    a. Facts   b. Opinions

8. What is the purpose of this selection?

    a. To inform   c. To entertain

    b. To persuade

Copyright © Houghton Mifflin Company. All rights reserved.

COMBINED SKILLS TEST 4

Read the passage below and answer the questions that follow by circling the correct response.

The Classroom

1   The sun beamed in through the dining room window, lighting up the hardwood floor. We had been talking there for nearly two hours. The phone rang yet again and Morrie asked his helper, Connie, to get it. She had been jotting the callers' names in Morrie's small black appointment book. Friends. Meditation teachers. A discussion group. Someone who wanted to photograph him for a magazine. It was clear I was not the only one interested in visiting my old professor—the *Nightline* appearance (on which Morrie discussed his illness and his philosophy on life and death) had made him something of a celebrity—but I was impressed with, perhaps even a bit envious of, all the friends that Morrie seemed to have. I thought about the "buddies" that circled my orbit back in college. Where had they gone?

2   "You know, Mitch, now that I'm dying, I've become much more interesting to people."

3   You were always interesting.

4   "Ho." Morrie smiled. "You're kind."

5   No, I'm not, I thought.

6   "Here's the thing," he said. "People see me as a bridge. I'm not as alive as I used to be, but I'm not yet dead. I'm sort of . . . in-between."

7   He coughed, then regained his smile. "I'm on the last great journey here—and people want me to tell them what to pack."

8   The phone rang again.

9   "Morrie, can you talk?" Connie asked.

10   "I'm visiting with my old pal now," he announced. "Let them call back."

11   I cannot tell you why he received me so warmly. I was hardly the promising student who had left him sixteen years earlier. Had it not been for *Nightline*, Morrie might have died without ever seeing me again. I had no good excuse for this, except the one that everyone these days seems to have. I had become too wrapped up in the siren song of my own life. I was busy.

12   *What happened to me?* I asked myself. Morrie's high, smoky voice took me back to my university years, when I thought rich people were evil, a shirt and tie were prison clothes, and life without freedom to get up and go—motorcycle beneath you, breeze in your face, down the streets of Paris, into the mountains of Tibet—was not a good life at all. *What happened to me?*

Copyright © Houghton Mifflin Company. All rights reserved.

13   The eighties happened. The nineties happened. Death and sickness and getting fat and going bald happened. I traded a lot of dreams for a bigger paycheck, and I never even realized I was doing it.*

1. What can you infer about Morrie's illness from paragraphs 6 and 7?
   a. His illness is incurable.
   b. He developed his illness while traveling.
   c. He is dying of tuberculosis.
   d. His lifestyle contributed to his illness.

2. What of the following statements best states the implied main idea in paragraph 12?
   a. The author regrets not graduating from college.
   b. The author is startled by how much he has changed since his college days.
   c. The author's ideas about good and evil were just beginning to form during college.
   d. The author now regrets the judgmental attitudes he had while in college.

3. Which of the following is the topic sentence of paragraph 13?
   a. "The eighties happened."
   b. "The nineties happened."
   c. "Death and sickness and getting fat and going bald happened."
   d. "I traded a lot of dreams for a bigger paycheck, and I never even realized I was doing it."

4. What can you infer about the relationship between the author and Morrie from paragraphs 10 and 11?
   a. They were best friends in college.
   b. Morrie was a college professor and the author was one of his students.
   c. They parted ways after a terrible argument.
   d. Morrie is the author's father.

5. Which of the following sentences states a fact?
   a. "We had been talking there for nearly two hours." (paragraph 1)
   b. "'You know, Mitch, now that I'm dying, I've become much more interesting to people.'" (paragraph 2)
   c. "You were always interesting." (paragraph 3)
   d. "I was hardly the promising student who had left him sixteen years earlier." (paragraph 11)

*From Mitch Albom, *Tuesdays with Morrie*. New York: Bantam Doubleday Dell, 1997, 32–33. Copyright © 1997 by Mitch Albom. Used by permission of Doubleday, a division of Random House, Inc.

Copyright © Houghton Mifflin Company. All rights reserved.

6. What can you infer about the author's feelings from paragraphs 12 and 13?

    a. He is devastated by the possibility of losing Morrie.
    b. He is furious at himself for not contacting Morrie sooner.
    c. He regrets changing his values in order to make more money.
    d. He feels confused and alone.

COMBINED SKILLS TEST 5

Read the textbook passage below and answer the questions that follow by circling the correct response.

The "Fourth Law of Motion": The Automobile Air Bag

1 A major automobile safety feature is the air bag. Seat belts restrain you so you don't follow along with Newton's first law of motion ("An object will remain at rest or in uniform motion in a straight line unless acted on by an external, unbalanced force") when the car comes to a sudden stop. But where does the air bag come in, and what is its principle?

2   When a car has a head-on collision with another vehicle or hits an immovable object such as a tree, it stops almost instantaneously. Even with seat belts, the impact of a head-on collision could be such that seat belts might not restrain you completely, and injuries could occur.

3   Enter the air bag. This balloon-like bag inflates automatically on hard impact and cushions the driver. Passenger-side air bags are becoming more common, and back-seat air bags are available.

4   The air bag tends to "cushion" or increase the contact time in stopping a person, thereby reducing the impact force (as compared to hitting the dashboard or steering column). Also, the impact force is spread over a large general area and not applied to certain parts of the body as in the case of seat belts.

5   Being inquisitive, you might wonder what causes an air bag to inflate and what inflates it. Keep in mind that this must occur in a fraction of a second to do any good. (How much time would there be between the initial collision contact and a driver hitting the steering wheel column?) The air bag's inflation is initiated by an electronic sensing unit. This unit contains sensors that detect rapid decelerations, such as those in a high-impact collision. The sensors have threshold settings so that normal hard braking does not activate them, and they are equipped with their own electrical power source because, in a front-end collision, a car's battery and alternator are among the first things to go.

Copyright © Houghton Mifflin Company. All rights reserved.

6   Sensing an impact, a control unit sends an electric current to an igniter in the air bag system that sets off a chemical explosion. The gases (mostly nitrogen) rapidly inflate the thin nylon bag. The total process of sensing to complete inflation takes about 25 thousandths of a second (0.025/s). Pretty fast, and a good thing, too!

7   However, a recent concern about air bags is the injuries and deaths resulting from their deployment. An air bag is not a soft, fluffy pillow. When activated, it comes out of the dashboard at speeds of up to 200 miles per hour and could hit a person close by with enough force to cause severe injury and even death. Therefore, adults are advised to sit at least ten inches from the air bag cover. This allows a margin of safety from the two- to three-inch "risk zone." Seats should be adjusted to allow for the proper safety distance.

8   Probably a more serious concern is associated with children. Children may get close to the dashboard if they are not buckled in or not buckled in securely so that they can see. Another bad situation is using a rear-facing child seat in the front passenger seat. An inflating air bag could have serious effects.

9   Sometimes it may be impossible to follow these safety rules. So, air bag deactivation may be authorized for one of four reasons. A rear-facing child restraint might need to be placed in the front seat because the car either has no back seat or has one that is too small. A child 12 years old or younger might need to ride in the front seat because of a medical condition that requires frequent monitoring. An individual who drives (or rides in the front seat) might have a medical condition that would make it safer to have the air bags turned off. A driver might need to sit within a few inches of the air bag (typically because of extremely short stature, 4 feet 6 inches or less).

10   Specific problems may exist, but air bags save many lives. All new passenger cars must have dual air bags, and manufacturers are beginning to install air bags that inflate with less force, so as to reduce the possibility of injuries. Even if your car is equipped with air bags, however, always remember to buckle up. (Maybe we should make that Newton's "fourth law of motion.")*

1. Which of the following sentences best states the thesis of the whole selection?

   a. "However, a recent concern about air bags is the injuries and deaths resulting from their deployment." (paragraph 7)
   b. "Specific problems may exist, but air bags save many lives." (paragraph 10)
   c. "A major automobile safety feature is the air bag." (paragraph 1)
   d. "So, air bag deactivation may be authorized for one of four reasons." (paragraph 9)

*Adapted from James T. Shipman et al., *An Introduction to Physical Science,* 9th ed. Boston: Houghton Mifflin, 2000, 54–55.

Copyright © Houghton Mifflin Company. All rights reserved.

2. What pattern organizes most of the supporting details in paragraphs 5 and 6?

   a. Comparison/contrast   c. Time order

   b. Series   d. Definition

3. What pattern organizes the supporting details in paragraph 2?

   a. Comparison/contrast   c. Time order

   b. Cause/effect   d. Series

4. Which sentence expresses the main idea in paragraph 8?

   a. "Probably a more serious concern is associated with children."

   b. "Children may get close to the dashboard if they are not buckled in or not buckled in securely so that they can see."

   c. "Another bad situation is using a rear-facing child seat in the front passenger seat."

   d. "An inflating air bag could have serious effects."

5. Is the opinion stated in paragraph 8 informed or uninformed?

   a. informed   b. uninformed

6. What is the implied main idea of paragraph 4?

   a. Seat belts aren't as effective as air bags.

   b. People should drive more carefully.

   c. Automobile manufacturers could make cars safer from impacts.

   d. Air bags protect people from injuries.

7. Which of the following sentences is NOT a *major* supporting detail in paragraph 9?

   a. "So, air bag deactivation may be authorized for one of four reasons."

   b. "A rear-facing child restraint might need to be placed in the front seat because the car either has no back seat or has one that is too small."

   c. "A child 12 years old or younger might need to ride in the front seat because of a medical condition that requires frequent monitoring."

   d. "An individual who drives (or rides in the front seat) might have a medical condition that would make it safer to have the air bags turned off."

8. Which of the following inferences can you make based on the information in paragraph 3?

   a. New cars have too many airbags.

   b. Air bags are not easy to pop.

   c. Air bags installed in the front seat have proven to be effective.

   d. Auto manufacturers think drivers are more important than passengers.

Copyright © Houghton Mifflin Company. All rights reserved.

Index

Copyright © Houghton Mifflin Company. All rights reserved.

Copyright © Houghton Mifflin Company. All rights reserved.

Copyright © Houghton Mifflin Company. All rights reserved.

Copyright © Houghton Mifflin Company. All rights reserved.